The Language of War

The Language of War

∽ LITERATURE AND CULTURE IN THE U.S.
FROM THE CIVIL WAR THROUGH
WORLD WAR II

JAMES DAWES

HARVARD UNIVERSITY PRESS

Cambridge, Massachusetts, and London, England   2002

Library of Congress Cataloging-in-Publication Data

Dawes, James, 1969–
    The language of war : literature and culture in the U.S. from the Civil War
through World War II / James Dawes.
        p. cm.
    Includes bibliographical references (p.) and index.
    ISBN 0-674-00648-8
    1. American literature—20th century—History and criticism.   2. War in literature.
3. United States—History—Civil War, 1861–1865—Literature and the war.
4. American literature—19th century—History and criticism.   5. United States —
History, Military—Historiography.   6. English language—Social aspects—United
States.   7. Language and culture—United States—History.   8. World War, 1914–
1918—Literature and the war.   9. World War, 1939–1945—Literature and the war.
10. Violence—United States—Historiography.   11. Violence in literature.   I. Title.

PS228.W37 D38 2002
810.9'358—dc21   2001043085

Contents

Acknowledgments

Many thanks are owed to Harvard University's English Department, the Program in Ethics and the Professions, and the Society of Fellows. I am grateful to all those who have, in ways small and large, given help to me along the way: Daniel Aaron, Arthur Applbaum, Sacvan Bercovitch, Philip Fisher, Danny Fox, Geoffrey Harpham, Yunte Huang, Erin Kelly, Martha Minow, Diana Morse, Patrick O'Malley, Barbara Rodriguez, Miryam Sas, Tamar Schapiro, Werner Sollors, Richard Weisberg, James Willis, the faculty and staff of Quincy House, and the outstanding reference librarians at Widener Library. Thanks also to Dan Constanda, Merrick Hoben, Trish Hofmann, Juliet Osborne, and my little father and little mother, Ismail Bey and Esin Hanim. Portions of this book were cobbled together from audiotapes—to my transcribers, my deep appreciation. An early version of Chapter 6 appeared as "Language, Violence, and Human Rights Law" in the *Yale Journal of Law and the Humanities* 11 (Summer 1999): 215–250. I am grateful for permission to republish. "Requiem" and "Instead of a Preface" by Anna Akhmatova are reprinted from *Poems of Akhmatova,* trans. Stanley Kunitz with Max Hayward (Boston: Houghton Mifflin, 1998).

Wai Chee Dimock, Charles Perrow, and Priscilla Wald have been encouraging, trenchant, thoughtful, and utterly brilliant. Paul Korshin, Derek Pearsall, and Lindsay Waters have been supportive beyond anything I deserve. Lisa New and Helen Vendler have been wise advisers, beloved teachers, and continual sources of poetry and revelation. I especially want to thank Lawrence Buell and Elaine Scarry. I have benefited vastly from Lawrence Buell's seemingly unlimited knowledge and his unparalleled sense of the concealed connectors between disciplines and discourses—to say nothing of his inexhaustible good will, which continues to be an example for me. The debt of gratitude I owe to Elaine Scarry, both intellectually and personally, is tremendous. She has cultivated a garden of iridescent ideas that has revealed a mind of apparently limitless capacity and a spirit equally generous.

More than gratitude is owed to my family: Suzanne, David, Don, and Bill. Time-marking occasions like this offer the opportunity to thank them for the love and support that has been, throughout my life, the ground upon which I stand.

And finally, Baris, my dearest and most generous friend, and my most trusted counselor. Let the cadence of each day that follows be our declaration.

In the terrible years of the Yezhov terror I spent seventeen months waiting in line outside the prison in Leningrad. One day somebody in the crowd identified me. Standing behind me was a woman, with lips blue from the cold, who had, of course, never heard me called by name before. Now she started out of the torpor common to us all and asked me in a whisper (everyone whispered there):

"Can you describe this?"

And I said: "I can."

Then something like a smile passed fleetingly over what had once been her face.

—ANNA AKHMATOVA, LENINGRAD, 1 APRIL 1957

Language and Violence: The Civil War and Literary and Cultural Theory

This book examines the reimagination of language and culture in the United States in the wake of the Civil War, World War I, and World War II. How does the strategic violence of war affect literary, legal, and philosophical representations? And, in turn, how do such representations affect the reception and initiation of violence itself? In this introduction I begin to sketch out an answer to these questions by establishing and analyzing two of the primary models available for understanding the relationship between language and violence: what I call the emancipatory model, which presents force and discourse as mutually exclusive, and the disciplinary model, which presents the two as mutually constitutive. The emancipatory model is derived from the work of theorists of political discourse and deliberative democracy: it is predicated on the idea that social structures built around democratic language practices emancipate us from the reign of force. Against this stands the disciplinary model, derived primarily from poststructuralism and its avatars: it treats language both as a disciplinary regime premised on the use of force and as a method of disciplining and controlling violence in order to concentrate its effects.

War is the limit case for understanding violence.[1] War is violence maximized and universalized. In its "ideal" or theoretical form, Carl von Clausewitz famously argued, war achieves unlimited violence: the logic of combat is mutual escalation, as cultures sacrifice blood and treasure in ever increasing volume in their efforts to match and overmaster one another. During war, the effect of violence upon language is amplified and clarified: language is censored, encrypted, and euphemized; imperatives replace dialogue, and nations communicate their intentions most dramatically through the use of injury rather than symbol; talks are broken off, ambassadors are withdrawn, and threats and lies are elevated to the status of communicative paradigms. As war reveals, violence harms language; it imposes silence upon groups and, through trauma and injury, disables the capacity of the individual to speak effectively.[2] Writing after World War II about the Revolutionary War in America, Hannah Arendt theorizes the relationship between language and violence as a physical architecture. Outside the city-state, violence reigns; inside, people live free of violence. The wall separating the two, granite and impermeable, is the wall of language. She writes later: "Where violence rules absolutely, as for instance in the concentration camps of totalitarian regimes, not only the laws . . . but everything and everybody must fall silent . . . the point here is that violence itself is incapable of speech, and not merely that speech is helpless when confronted with violence."[3] Simone Weil, writing after the fall of France, describes in lyrical detail how in the world of the *Iliad* both those who endure violence and those who use it become impervious to language: the kingdom of force renders mute all its subjects. "The conquering soldier is like a scourge of nature," she writes. "Possessed by war, he, like the slave, becomes a thing . . . over him too, words are as powerless as over matter itself. And both, at the touch of force, experience its inevitable effects: they become deaf and dumb."[4] The thesis that violence annuls verbal intercourse has implications so pervasive for our culture that its inverse is often also asserted to be true: the expansion of discourse through witnessing and storytelling, by this argument, directly corresponds to the cessation and prevention of violence. Insofar as violence-as-coercion is an assault upon free agency, and the act of speaking is conceived of as the fundamental sign and application of our free agency, then the volitional use of language is miraculously an assault upon violence, a contradiction of its felt coercion through assertion of the will. In prison camps and torture blocks, the achievement of communication and recognition through an undetected note or an answered whisper is the first step in rebuilding the world.[5]

This account of the mutual exclusivity of language and violence, while contested in the discipline of literary studies, has become an increasingly important premise in contemporary political philosophy. Recent theorists of democracy have figured language and violence as existing on a spectrum: on one end unconstrained violence, on the other unconstrained language, and in between an ambient blending. As one approaches pure violence, as Elaine Scarry would argue, language is twisted, distorted, and diminished, until with physical pain it is shattered altogether into the prelanguage of cries and groans. As one approaches the pole of pure language—or ideal speech conditions, as Jürgen Habermas puts it—violence shrinks and retreats, moving from overt physical injury to threats to cloaked domination through exclusion and deceit until finally, with the achievement of unrestricted access to speech for all, it disappears altogether.[6] For these thinkers human language minimally conceived, as a built-in system of communication with particular features, is not fully separable from language broadly construed as a set of normative social practices. In other words, language as a property of human behavior (within a historical horizon) helps to construct and is constructed by the larger rule system of intersubjective discourse that, according to Habermas, reveals the regulative ideals of sincerity, consensus, and equal access to speech. Such liberal theorists thus provide not only practical guidelines for the structuration of discourse in political life, but also a foundational account of the nature of language.

This emancipatory model of language recurs throughout the literature of war: from Ivo Andric's *Bridge on the Drina,* which depicts interethnic conversation as a fragile stay against Bosnia's culturally inherited conflict, to Norman Mailer's *Armies of the Night,* which connects state violence against Vietnam War protesters to an order forbidding troops from responding to any appeals for communication;[7] from Bao Ninh's *Sorrow of War,* which presents writing as a release from trauma, a method of undoing the continuing work of violence,[8] to the memoirs of Albert Speer, which insistently juxtapose accounts of escalating destruction with Hitler's tendency to truncate speech and close off dialogue among his counselors.[9] In U.S. war literature such a deliberative model receives especially prominent expression, and in the discourse surrounding the Civil War it appears with greatest frequency. In wartime articulation, the United States is repeatedly depicted as an experiment to determine whether or not a liberal democratic state can maintain order and prevent violence simply through the consent of a written contract. Many were doubtful. "What is your safeguard?" asked Thomas Wentworth Higginson in a polemical sermon in 1854. "Nothing but a parchment Constitution, which has been riddled through and through whenever it pleased the Slave Power."[10] Others, however, believed. As James McPherson reveals, Union soldiers of all ranks, ethnicities, and levels of education were motivated to fight because they perceived secession as an unacceptable subversion of the hallowed idea that a generalized communicative consensus buttressed by a verbal artifact could achieve a force equivalent to the physical coercion that underwrites monarchy.[11] In an early speech deploring mob violence, Abraham Lincoln sought to unite words with binding motivation, to link textuality, broadly construed, with pacification: "Let reverence for the laws, be breathed by every American mother, to the lisping babe, that prattles on her lap . . . let it be written in Primmers, spelling books, and in Almanacs;— let it be preached from the pulpit, proclaimed in legislative halls, and enforced in courts of justice. And, in short, let it become the *political religion* of the nation." Whenever such practices should prevail, he concluded, vain will be any attempt to subvert national order.[12] After the outbreak of the Civil War, however, Lincoln evaluated the situation with grim pessimism. "Would *my word* free the slaves," he argued early on against an emancipation proclamation, "when I cannot even enforce the Constitution in the rebel States?"[13] For Lincoln, the violence of secession overturned the power of the word and consequently the power of law. To achieve victory for the law Lincoln in turn needed violence, and violence depended upon the suppression of discourse. Lincoln's restrictions on civil and political rights, and in particular on free speech, were pervasive and unflinching. His description of a projected victory demonstrates his reluctant conviction that the prosecution of war works best with a silent population: "There will be some black men who can remember that, with silent tongue, and clenched teeth, and steady eye, and well-poised bayonet, they have helped mankind on to this great consummation; while, I fear, there will be some white ones, unable to forget that, with malignant heart, and deceitful speech, they have strove to hinder it."[14]

The increasingly violent conflicts that immediately preceded the war, no less than the war itself, challenged the communicative and deliberative procedures of the republic. Believing Charles Sumner's May 1856 senatorial oration, "The Crime against Kansas," constituted an act of libel against his uncle and other colleagues, the formerly unremarkable Preston Brooks approached the senator and, in accordance with what he believed the code of a gentleman required, beat him nearly to death with a gold-tipped cane. In the records of the congressional debates over the next four weeks, the battery was continually depicted by Yankee congressmen in a series of tightly coupled binaries: "words . . . violence," "speech . . . blows," "ruthless attack . . . liberty of speech."[15] Sumner himself, who in his response to the Southern rebuttal to his oration had contrasted "the proper elements of senatorial debate" with "the bowie-knife and bludgeon,"[16] ultimately came to stand for the intact referentiality of clear language as against the reckless and aggressive "looseness" of speech typified in his Southern colleagues; and the opposition of these rhetorical qualities themselves, in Senator Wilson's characterization, came to stand for the opposition between nonviolence and aggression.[17] In a reelection speech for the Massachusetts senatorial seat, one campaigner declared that a vote for Sumner was a vote for "liberty of speech," and in a rally at Faneuil Hall days after the attack, Brooks's battery was described as "a crime against the right of free speech."[18] In response to such characterizations, a group of Southern senators protested that it was a distortion to allegorize the conflict between the two men as a collision between the opposed forces of Violence and Free Speech; the violence was justified and, indeed, already present in the "gross personal affronts" and "personal injuries" of Sumner's speech. As the session progressed, however, Northern senators continued to deploy the same exclusionary conceptual paradigm. In the debate over whether or not Congress had the authority to punish Brooks, for instance, Senator Seward repeatedly put it as a matter of determining whether or not the text of the Constitution could "protect" Sumner and, if so, how far its sheltering reach extended beyond the halls of Congress.[19]

In floor debates nearly five years later, however, it was the Constitution that required protection from violent assault. Senator Wigfall declared that "the Constitution has been trampled under foot," and Senator Hale argued that the text which had secured American freedom was now seriously imperiled by "every blow that is aimed at [it]."[20] Violence was depicted as both cause and result of the breakdown of the linguistic structures of governance. Senator Mason warned of the "civil war that must ensue . . . when negotiation and deliberation are ended" and ultimately proclaimed that, for Unionists like Seward and indeed for the North more generally, the *"ultima ratio regum"* of "force, compulsion, power" had displaced the communicative procedures of deliberation and consent.[21]

The war's disruption of language was figured aesthetically as well as politically. Southern novelist William Gilmore Simms declares of the war years: "Literature, poetry especially, is effectually overwhelmed by the drums, & the cavalry, and the shouting. War is here the only idea."[22] Northern novelist Harold Frederic writes similarly: "It seems as if the actual sight of a battle has some dynamic quality in it which overwhelms and crushes the literary faculty of the observer."[23] War attacks language not only through confusion and astonishment but also through impotence, and through the aversion to recall that manifests itself as apathy. What can we possibly say that has not been said before, or that will make a difference? "Let us change the disgusting topic," Mark Twain writes in an emblematic moment of correspondence.[24] With the ascendance of violence, speech is made irrelevant. Walt Whitman recounts how the advent of war transformed the public forum from a space of activity into a space of resignation:

> I bought an extra and cross'd to the Metropolitan hotel (Niblo's) where the great lamps were still brightly blazing, and, with a crowd of others, who gather'd impromptu, read the news, which was evidently authentic. For the benefit of some who had no papers, one of us read the telegram aloud, while all listen'd silently and attentively. No remark was made by any of the crowd, which had increas'd to thirty or forty, but all stood a minute or two, I remember, before they dispers'd. I can almost see them there now, under the lamps at midnight again.[25]

In his "Beat! Beat! Drums!" war is an apocalyptic noise that threatens the possible end to language. Meaning is swept away in a relentless list of negations—"not," "no," "nor,"—and the whole of the body politic, from the businessman to the lawyer to the mother and child, is rendered mute:

> No bargainers' bargains by day—no brokers or speculators—
> would they continue?
> Would the talkers be talking? would the singer attempt to sing?
> Would the lawyer rise in the court to state his case before the
> judge?

Then rattle quicker, heavier drums—you bugles wilder blow.
Beat! beat! drums!—blow! bugles! blow!
Make no parley—stop for no expostulation,
Mind not the timid—mind not the weeper or prayer,
Mind not the old man beseeching the young man,
Let not the child's voice be heard, nor the mother's entreaties,
Make even the trestles to shake the dead where they lie awaiting
the hearses,
So strong you thump O terrible drums—so loud you bugles
blow.[26]

War, Whitman seems to suggest, not only produces but also is produced by the suppression of voice.

The summary image of Civil War representation in this emancipatory conceptual framework is Ambrose Bierce's "Chickamauga," a short story that details battle's aftermath from the perspective of a small child. Here, accumulated survivors seemingly bereft of the power to walk upright and to speak appear as parodies of the human, like painted clowns, or as inhuman: with bodies grotesquely opened and disfigured, they emerge like beetles, like pigs, like undulations in the soil itself. The story's only face-to-face encounter occurs between the mysteriously silent child and a soldier who has had his jaw shot off, leaving a red gap between his upper teeth and throat. The two can articulate only a series of grunts and hisses, and the story culminates in a nightmare vision of violence overseeing the end of all human speech: "The child moved his little hands, making wild, uncertain gestures. He uttered a series of inarticulate and indescribable cries—something between the chattering of an ape and the gobbling of a turkey—a startling, soulless, unholy sound, the language of a devil. The child was a deaf mute."[27]

When Whitman asserted that the real war would never get into the books, he was arguing not only that the scale of the war defied comprehensive encapsulation, but also that the attempt to depict war's violence through language afterward is impossible, necessarily, because the essential nature of violence is always in excess of language. All that is ever produced amounts to "scraps and distortions."[28] Violence and language exist on different planes and therefore the best we can do as artists is to mime violence through language, to approach it analogically like a painter attempting to simulate the physical sensation of cold by using the color blue. How else can the literary mind wrap itself around the fact of violence, attempting to put it into language? Whitman remained unconvinced that it had an absolute right to do so: the intimate vulnerability of combat and injury demanded the chaste silence of respect. Future generations will never know the "interiors" of the war, he argued, "and it is best they should not."[29]

Whitman's uncharacteristic moment of doubt over the right to represent offers a useful starting point for consideration of the primary alternative in the modern Western intellectual tradition to the emancipatory model of language and violence. Herman Melville and Mary Chesnut, two of the Civil War's most penetrating recorders, struggled like Whitman with what Sidra DeKoven Ezrahi calls the "basic tension" between the "instinctive revulsion against allowing the monstrous to be heard" and the equally powerful "instinct against repressing reality, against the amnesia that comes with concealment."[30] Their particular methods of articulating violence seem at first glance to oppose one another, to define the extreme range of literary possibility: one begins by turning away from the scene of injury, the other gazes insistently at the wounded. It is the basic convergence of these two standpoints, however, that I shall finally want to emphasize.

Mary Chesnut wrote fiction, but her great achievement was her diary of the war years, revised for publication between 1881 and 1884. Daniel Aaron argues that the diary "is more genuinely literary than most Civil War fiction," Edmund Wilson justly calls it a "masterpiece," and C. Vann Woodward describes it as "a preeminent classic of Civil War literature."[31] Such late recognition would have gratified Chesnut, who had high literary ambitions and an ardent attachment to literature. With Sherman "barely a day's journey from Columbia" she fled the city, forsaking valuable possessions and even, with her husband's reassurance, flour, sugar, rice, coffee, and other important food supplies. She did not fail, however, to bring along a library that included the works of Shakespeare, Molière, Sir Thomas Browne, *The Arabian Nights* in French, and the letters of Pascal.[32] Chesnut's diaries are not only a startling record of civilian life during the war but also a thoughtful and devoted account of the act of recording itself. As we shall see, Chesnut makes a virtue of violence's inability to be inserted into language, showing that the nature of force can be revealed through the very strategy of thematizing its inability to achieve verbal expression.

In one strange passage of her diaries, a compressed entry no more than two pages in length, Chesnut becomes obsessed with hands. Her fixation with hands as a synecdoche for human sentience (the hand that writes, identifies, expresses) and as a symbol of human agency ("my hands are tied," "it is out of my hands") is in many ways emblematic. Her diaries commemorate her efforts to control an environment that was spinning out of control, and to bridge her isolation by making *contact*. But in this particular entry, the continual return to hands has a physical urgency that short-circuits the indirection of metaphorical interpretation, or rather points to an indirection of an altogether different kind:

> Mrs. Bartow's adopted son has had the ball extracted from his arm. She is nursing him faithfully. The doctors fear a sinew has been cut, which may disable him—that is, that he may never regain the use of his hand . . . He began with "Break, Break, O Sea." And I thought of poor Frank in the next room. "Oh, for the touch of a vanished hand and the sound of a voice that is still." . . . "Now," says Mrs. Browne, "I call that a Yankee spy." "If he were a spy, he would not dare show his hand so plainly." . . . The Prince conformed at once to whatever he saw was the way of those in whose house he was and closely imitated President Buchanan's way of doing things. He took off his gloves at once when he saw that the president wore none. By the by, I remember what a beautiful hand Mr. Buchanan has. The Prince of Wales began by bowing to the people who were presented to him, but when he saw Mr. Buchanan shaking hands, he shook, too . . . As I walked up to the Prestons', along a beautifully shaded back street, a carriage passed, with Governor Means in it. As soon as he saw me, he threw himself half out of it. And kissed both hands to me—again and again. It was a *whole-souled* greeting, as the saying is. And I returned it with my whole heart, too. "Goodbye," he cried—and I answered, "Goodbye." I may never see him again. I am not sure that I did not shed a few tears. [*Rest of page and top of next page cut off.*][33]

There are at least eight ways to interpret this passage: four primary ways each of which contains the dual alternatives of design for readerly effect versus manifestation of authorial affect. Perhaps this passage is the conscious literary representation (or unconscious reflex) of trauma. By this argument, Chesnut's act of repeatedly looking at hands is the verbal equivalent of a wince. In her visual field she can no longer take hands for granted; her eyes continually flick back to the hands of those around her, as if to discover the gory wound she fears so that it cannot surprise her. One might argue, alternatively, that she lingers over hands now in an effort to *banish* from her mind (or the reader's) the image of the wound. She looks at the hands around her—hands that move nimbly, hands that can be kissed, hands that are *intact*—with the deep craving of Andromache looking upon Astyanax, dreaming of the rebirth of an unmutilated Hector. Just as she here re-peoples her imagination with unwounded bodies, she will later imaginatively reconstruct the lost, prewar South with her detailed accounts of the traditional meals she ever more rarely is able to enjoy. The representation of sensuous largesse is not only a form of self-gratification, however; it is also a way of forcing the contemplation of cost: Chesnut presents the wound and then provides a litany of the simple, tender domestic acts that now have been rendered poignantly impossible. Finally, it could be argued that Chesnut imaginatively fills the household with the wounds of the battlefield in order to challenge the assumed separation between domestic space and war space, and moreover to disrupt the larger epistemological distinction between war and peace. Damage is everywhere implicit: the bodies of those surrounding us are fragile, continually vulnerable to breach and to harm. Her subversion of assumptions about safety are a comment not only upon the potential universality of violence, but also upon the specific policies of Northern generals like Sherman and Grant, who abrogated soldier-civilian distinctions and thereby transformed all Southern bodies (the dignitary shaking hands, the woman kissing hands to a friend in the street) into targets. Chesnut never lets us forget that she also once read books and made careless plans for the future, and that she never once questioned the durability of the social structures that cradled her, as if in the palm of a loving, mortal hand.

Chesnut speaks most copiously and elegantly about violence and damage when she is pointedly *not* speaking about it or, rather, when she is speaking about it only indirectly. If her aesthetics of indirection attest to the fundamental opposition of language and violence, so too, implicitly, does her act of writing itself. With the ascendance of violence during Sherman's invasion, speech and discourse continue to diminish, such that her act of writing becomes an act of resistance, a step toward preserving through written record the civilization that is being systematically destroyed. She knew she was watching "our world, the only world we care for, literally kicked to pieces," and she told her story "with horror and amazement."[34] Her memoirs are an encyclopedic record of the process through which violence destroys both civilization and the language that constitutes it. Frequently Chesnut records her inability to write and her inability to express adequately what she sees or feels; she lingers over stories of how conversations are forced into code or even to an end by the suspected presence of spies, and on multiple occasions she recounts instances when she is forced to burn her papers. In her text, communication is damaged, like bodies and homes: damaged through misinformation, rumor, insult, and commands to be silent. But her memoirs are also, at the same time, a catalog of productive and successful linguistic forms, a celebration of speech and writing at all levels. She describes the books she has read, the songs she has heard, the dialects and unusual instances of spelling she encounters, and she focuses with luxurious detail upon the various sorts of paper she uses. By cherishing and preserving language her diaries defy force—for language interferes with the release of violence, she notes when observing prewar debate; the tendency of deliberation to proliferate impedes the progress toward war. Chesnut's diaries are thus an act of contestation. The struggle to talk during and after violence is language's struggle to regain mastery over violence, whether manifest in the individual's attempt to speak her trauma or a culture's attempt to produce a literary record. The language that has been destroyed by war reasserts its primacy by wrapping words around the past experience of violence, by attempting to subdue violence with language, much in the same way that traumatic recall, according to Freud, reestablishes agency by *choosing* to replay and direct an original scene of helplessness. "Repetitions," writes one scholar, "serve to bind and structure the original raw overload of excitation."[35]

To perceive Chesnut's diary-writing as a repudiation of violence is, however, to ignore her participation in and desire for the maintenance of a society built upon the elaborate brutality and coercion of slavery. I will return to the question of the slave system's relationship to language shortly; for now I want to take this unsettling of the emancipatory thesis as a starting point for reading Herman Melville. Melville's poem "Shiloh" begins with a vantage point very different from Chesnut's; it begins by focusing directly upon the battlefield littered with bodies. "Shiloh" is a requiem for the dead of the Civil War's first large-scale slaughter. More than twenty thousand men were killed or wounded at Shiloh—nearly seven times the battle casualties at First Manassas. Melville's poem struggles to give form to an event that was in its time nearly intractable to imaginative reshaping. "Shiloh" in its very structure pits control against the disruption of trauma: its rhythmical progression of line units (4–5, 4–5) is shot through at the end by a line that punctures the poem like a bullet punctures flesh. Significantly, it is the only line of the poem that directly mentions the materials of war.

> Skimming lightly, wheeling still,
>   The swallows fly low
> Over the field in clouded days,
>   The forest-field of Shiloh—
> Over the field where April rain
> Solaced the parched ones stretched in pain
> Through the pause of night
> That followed the Sunday fight
>   Around the church of Shiloh—
> The church so lone, the log-built one,
> That echoed to many a parting groan
>   And natural prayer
>   Of dying foemen mingled there—
> Foemen at morn, but friends at eve—
>   Fame or country least their care:
> (What like a bullet can undeceive!)
>   But now they lie low,
> While over them the swallows skim,
>   And all is hushed at Shiloh.[36]

"Shiloh" is a poem about transformations, distortions of vision, and attempts to avert the gaze. It opens, in fact, by *not* looking at the dead. Instead it focuses upon the swallows that skim and wheel above like souls released from the prison of the body and climbing to heaven. The reader sees the killing fields through the distorting lens of pastoral convention, as if through the mist of "clouds": the free movement of the swallows banishes the thought of the wounded's aversive immobility, just as the image of a gentle rainfall quenching thirst banishes the image of dying men lying through the night in cold mud. Even when the wounded are directly mentioned they are only tangentially apprehended: they are more like dry leaves of grass arching toward the wet clouds in painful thirst than like dying men. Indeed, in the second stanza, they are reimagined as penitent parishioners whose groans of remorse echo through the church like prayers. We are twice removed: the echo, after all, is a sound of the past. Romantic and sentimentalized diction ("foemen," "mingled," "friends") combine to transform the battle into the story of a conflict leading toward amity and universal understanding. The bullet that here interrupts the poem's gentle cadences with the startling speed of an exclamation point curtails enchantment—it brutally undeceives the ghostly wounded (did it all matter? was it worth it?) and with them the reader: it forces us to step backward from the poem and to look at its diction and conventions, along with our own original responses to these, in a new, more critical manner. Only now do we realize that this poem about the war dead has never directly looked upon them. How different would a poem look that traced the path of the penetrating weapon? But quickly the poem moves on, closing parentheses over the bullet like scars over a wound and stifling questions with the respectful bow of silence. "And all is hushed at Shiloh." Melville's startling, self-consuming poetics have alienated critics since the publication of *Battle-Pieces*. In the *Atlantic Monthly,* William Dean Howells commented that Melville's poems were filled with the "phantasms" of "inner consciousness" rather than real events, showing "tortured humanity shedding, not words and blood, but words alone,"[37] and one contemporary critic has asserted that the "failure" of Melville's poetry is an inability "to particularize, *to see.*" The poetry is lacking in immediacy and feeling, he explains; Melville writes "as a distant spectator, observing men and events through a telescope."[38] In focusing so intently upon the noncorporeality of Melville's work, such criticisms lose sight of the poetry's internal logic, which calls upon the reader to participate in and be alienated by its peculiar detachment from the actual.

Throughout *Battle-Pieces* Melville remains preoccupied with the new requirements that war demands of poetry. He experiments with a variety of forms and devices, as if searching unsatisfied for the word that will suffice. As Helen Vendler notes, he makes "a hybrid of the paean, the narrative, and the elegy," and inverts the normative structure of lyric poems by offering first "an impersonal philosophical conclusion, next the narrative that has produced it, and last the lyric feelings accompanying it." Is the war poem best served by an attention to detail, or the broad, generalizing view? High diction, classical allusion, or the language of democracy (daily newspaper bulletins, regional dialects)? Should the poem body forth from the lyric "I" or the omniscient narrator? Indeed, is rhyme itself appropriate?[39] Melville asks these questions again and again throughout his poems, but he asserts in the end that none of the possible answers can capture war's essence.

> None can narrate that strife in the pines,
> A seal is on it—Sabaean lore!
> Obscure as the wood, the entangled rhyme
> But hints at the maze of war—
> Vivid glimpses or livid through peopled gloom,
> And fires which creep and char—
> A riddle of death, of which the slain
> Sole solvers are.[40]

The real war will never get into the books. But if inaccessibility is inevitable, what should we make of our continual efforts to represent? "Shiloh" ends with the repetition of the verb "to skim," a word important for Melville because of its density of associations. As plowing, "to skim" evokes the regenerative images of the Georgic; signifying to lift away or to scoop up, it recapitulates the image of ascending souls. By Melville's time "skimming" also had become associated with notions of surfaces and thinning out: superficial attention, slight contact, and covering over. The poem contains within itself a critique of its own diction and conventions. The way we talk about war, the poem seems to assert, is a way of obscuring the brute facts of suffering and death; it is a form of erasure, and therefore, a means of killing the war dead all over again. "To skim," after all, had also by Melville's time acquired the meaning of reaping with a scythe. If the Chesnut passages suggest that being silent is sometimes the most appropriate way of talking about the war, Melville's poem suggests that talking about the war is sometimes only a means of being silent about it—or, rather, that talking about war is sometimes an act of complicity with it. As Kerry Larson writes, in *Battle-Pieces* "words and weapons share an intimacy that demonstrates how readily the poet may exchange the role of mourner for that of executioner."[41]

While accounts of war trauma like Chesnut's point to the mutual exclusivity of language and violence, accounts of the cultural and material organization of war like Melville's point to their interdependence. War initiated, executed, and remembered, Melville reminds us, is an example of massive, organized violence that is precisely dependent upon speech, that is decidedly full with rich and supple uses of language, with negotiation, appeal, argument, propaganda, and justification. Wars are born and sustained in rivers of language about what it means to serve the cause, to kill the enemy, and to die with dignity; and they are reintegrated into a collective historical self-understanding through a ritualistic overplus of the language of commemoration. Indeed, asks Clausewitz, is not war just another mode of political discourse, "another form of speech or writing?"[42] Mere accumulation of words bears no fixed relationship to the processes of liberation and peace: the expansion of discourse is itself sometimes a form of violence, as thinkers from Antonio Gramsci to Michel Foucault have observed, and very specific conditions must obtain for language and force to exclude each other. Sidney Lanier recalls that in 1861 war was like a collective exhalation: "the earnest words of preachers," "the impassioned appeals of orators," "the half-breathed words of sweet-hearts," and "the lectures in college halls," all together blew men toward war as wind shakes out a flag.[43] As the rich tradition of Civil War songs reveal, verse was part of war's arsenal as surely as uniforms and training camps. In songs and poems ranging from "The Battle Cry of Freedom" and "Carolina" to "My Maryland" and "A Cry to Arms,"[44] the invocation of the word, or the "call," is always a call to violence. Collectively chanted verse helps to unite soldiers, through the rhythms of thought, step, and breath, into a single fighting body. "John Brown's Body," the basis of the "Battle Hymn of the Republic," was sung in the spring of 1861 as federal troops marched into Washington.

> John Brown's body lies a-mould'ring in the grave,
> John Brown's body lies a-mould'ring in the grave,
> John Brown's body lies a-mould'ring in the grave,
> His soul goes marching on!
>
> *Chorus:*
> Glory, glory! Hallelujah!
> Glory, glory! Hallelujah!
> Glory, glory! Hallelujah!
> His soul is marching on![45]

The function of the song or chant, which represents both a surplus of language and a constraint upon it, is perhaps nowhere in nineteenth-century literary history more tellingly illuminated than in the work of Sir Walter Scott, the prolific romancer whose writings Mark Twain

characterized as constitutive of the Southern identity and consequently as a primary cause of the war. In his *Old Mortality* Scott
depicts the overflow of discourse as the precursor to violence. Here
leaders of the Covenanting Whigs instigate rebellion and sustain
their troops through continual acts of hortatory speech-making. The
speech of the rebels is portrayed as frighteningly excessive. This excess is enabled, paradoxically, by the severe internal constraints
placed upon its lexicon. Reliance upon traditional religious forms and
rhetorical devices in this case allows an almost automatic production
of speech. Language functions to prevent thought; speech distorts
through its overabundance. The novel replaces the model of discourse
as exchange and questioning with a model of discourse as declaration
and repetition. Preacher Macbriar's postbattle exhortation is exemplary:

> "Your garments are dyed—but not with the juice of the winepress; your
> swords are filled with blood," he exclaimed, "but not with the blood of
> goats or lambs; the dust of the desert on which ye stand is made fat with
> gore, but not with the blood of bullocks, for the Lord hath a sacrifice in
> Bozrah, and a great slaughter in the land of Idumea. These were not the
> firstlings of the flock, the small cattle of burnt-offerings, whose bodies
> lie like dung on the ploughed field of the husbandman; this is not the sa-
> vour of myrrh, of frankincense, or of sweet herbs, that is steaming in
> your nostrils; but these bloody trunks are the carcasses of those who
> held the bow and the lance, who were cruel and would show no mercy,
> whose voice roared like the sea, who rode upon horses, every man in ar-
> ray as if to battle—they are the carcasses even of the mighty men of war
> that came against Jacob in the day of his deliverance, and the smoke is
> that of the devouring fires that have consumed them."[46]

The wounded rebels, rededicated to the cause of violence, respond
with a "deep hum"[47]—this unified vocalization, offered up as if from
one mouth, signifies both the blending of the many into one violent
corporate identity, as well as the breakdown of coherent talk into
generalized noise. Years later Leo Tolstoy would present the conta-
gious enthusiasm of the patriotic crowd as a form of "psychopathic
epidemic."[48] The stupidity of the crowds that celebrated the Franco-
Russian *accorde* of 1891—a "peace" treaty designed to preface a war
with Germany—is a stupidity premised upon the crowd's simultaneous fragmentation and shrinkage of linguistic forms. The capa-

ciousness of discussion is replaced by the self-enclosed "refrain," by "speeches," "announcements," "greetings," "hymns," "rites," "public prayers," and "telegrams."[49] The massive accumulation of such fragmented, repetitive, and unidirectional talk is complicit in the progress toward violence.

If, as Habermas theorizes, reciprocally sincere, mutual understanding is the telos that determines the interior structure of discourse,[50] then propaganda and other commands disguised as arguments are a form of *false discourse* in the same way that forced dancing on slave ships was a form of false mobility. Dialogue unsutured represents not the violence of language but rather the victory of violence over language. For many, however, such instrumental and coercive communication is not a marginal, conceptually separable, or deformed manifestation of language use but rather a definitive one. Against Arendt and contemporary deliberative democrats like Habermas and Seyla Benhabib stand a group of theorists, representing variations of French surrealism, poststructuralism, and postmodernism, who orient intellectual action around a notion of the mutually constitutive nature of language and violence. By modeling language on the thought-destroying structure of propaganda these thinkers, including Foucault, Pierre Bourdieu, Chantal Mouffe, Georges Bataille, Judith Butler, and Maurice Blanchot, have attempted to break down liberal assumptions about the legitimacy of certain types of institutionalized power.[51] According to the disciplinary model, the most basic and simple act of language, naming, is also the most basic and simple act of coercion. I will return to the topic of naming later in the book and will then attempt to do justice to the remarkable depth and diversity presented by this constellation of thinkers. For now I want quickly to juxtapose three very different figures to illustrate in a broad and basic way the borders of the disciplinary theory of language's relationship to violence.

Catherine McKinnon, most notably in *Only Words,* argues that in societies structured by asymmetries of power speech functions to perpetuate violence against the disenfranchised.

In the cases both of pornography and of the Nazi march in Skokie, it is striking how the so-called speech reenacts the original experience of the abuse, and how its defense as speech does as well. It is not only that both

groups, through the so-called speech, are forcibly subjected to the spectacle of their abuse, legally legitimized. Both have their response to it
trivialized as "being offended," that response then used to support its
speech value, hence its legal protection.

The free speech position, she concludes, thus supports patterns of social domination.[52] Jonathan Culler, writing against Habermas's assertion that communicative action foundationally presupposes an orientation toward symmetries of understanding productive of rational
social consensus, contends that communicative *asymmetry*—that is,
consensus-disrupting interpretative mismatches and differential
claims to authoritative "knowledge" (arguably generative of the social asymmetry illuminated by McKinnon)—is integral rather than accidental to the structure of human interaction. "Communication, one
might say," he writes, "is structurally asymmetrical, and symmetry is
an accident and a myth of moralists, not a norm."[53] And Judith Butler,
to complete this thumbnail sketch, critically evaluates in *Excitable
Speech* the argument that language can be a form of physical violence,
not simply analogous to physical injury but rather an actual though
distinctive form of injury itself. She points to scholars who have
drawn upon J. L. Austin's seminal *How to Do Things with Words* in
order to argue that certain assaultive representations are illocutionary
rather than perlocutionary: that is, they "do not state a point of view
or report on a reality, but constitute a certain kind of conduct."[54] Hate
speech does not symbolize domination but rather reconstitutes it; it
performs that which it declares, much like a judge announcing: "I find
you guilty." The injurious power of a derogatory epithet springs from
this capacity to enact rather than simply reflect the subject's social
subordination and from its capacity to intervene coercively in the actions of the body, to function as a corporeal disciplinary mechanism
regulating the motor dispositions (posture, manner of walking, and so
on) that constitute the (norm-reinforcing) bodily hexis, as Bourdieu
puts it.[55]

In the numerous and compelling works derived from the principles
of such theorists, insult, ideology, and the coercive pairs of lies and
false consciousness assume the status of paradigms for linguistic-be-
ing and communicative action generally. If for democracy theorists
the birthing of the individual in language as a citizen defined is the beginning of worlds, for poststructuralists it is the beginning of impris-

onment. "While Amnesty International operates," Barbara Johnson writes, "under the assumption that the arbitrary imprisonment of individuals by governments for reasons of conscience is a transgression of human rights, Foucault, in a sense, sees the evil of such imprisonment as a matter of degree rather than kind, since on some level the very definition of the 'human' at any given time is produced by the workings of a complex system of 'imprisonments.'"[56] Johnson is drawing here upon Louis Althusser's theory of subject interpellation, which depicts the individual as constituted through the ideology and language of a culture in much the same way that a pedestrian is hailed and accosted on the street by a police officer.[57] Language is not the city gate that separates us from violence, as in Arendt; it is instead a prison wall that implies a larger system of threat and coercion. The language that we use for resistance and emancipation is parasitic upon its antecedent capacity for domination. In the end, the myriad corporeal brutalities of organized human interaction from the household to the battlefield appear as cousin to or disclosure of the originary violence of language.[58] It is not the central anxiety of these thinkers, as it was with Chesnut and Melville, to determine how it could be possible for us to represent the manifestations of force in words; the problem instead is how we can escape the violence of language while nonetheless remaining trapped in linguistic existence: Maurice Blanchot's post-Holocaust utopian vision of linguistic possibilities is only one example. He imagines a language based upon the destruction of semantics and syntax as a language that has begun an escape from the constraints and exclusions of violence. "May words," he writes, "cease to be arms; means of action, means of salvation. Let us count, rather, on disarray."[59]

Perhaps the primary example of the violent, disciplinary function of language in nineteenth-century America, to return to our primary case study, would be the function European languages played for African slaves, whose interpellation through a language system that marginalized and pathologized them was both complicit in and inseparable from the brute physical violence they suffered. According to the emancipatory model, in contrast, it would be the original *destruction* of African languages and the annulment of unconstrained communication among all subjects of the system that more dramatically represented the ascendancy of violence in the slave system.[60] In his last autobiography, *The Life and Times of Frederick Douglass*, Frederick

Douglass does indeed tend to equate the absence of dialogue with violence. The "crushing silence" that surrounds the treatment of black prisoners of war in the South is a betrayal that constitutes an extension of the physical violence it hides,[61] and because the South systematically disrupts nonviolent language exchange by using the speech act "threat," and by rejecting communication altogether (refusing, as one man put it, to make any symbolic mark even upon a "blank sheet of paper"), violence becomes an inevitability.[62] In this case, however, violence is desired. "For this consummation we have watched and wished with fear and trembling. God be praised! that it has come at last."[63] Before the war, Douglass wrote with anxious hope on the progress of the antislavery cause. Through communicative action systematic coercion could be abolished: "Rely upon it, we have not written, spoken, or printed in vain—no good word can die, no righteous effort can be unavailing in the end."[64] After 1861, Douglass emphasized the necessity for the demotion of language during times of emergency. "Words are now useful," he wrote during the war, "only as they stimulate to blows. The office of speech now is always to point out when, where, and how to strike the best advantage."[65] Indeed, for those abolitionists interested in promoting an anti-Union revolution, it was a key strategy to emphasize the *mere* textuality of the Constitution: as during the trial of escaped slave Anthony Burns, by setting it on fire, thus revealing it simply to be disposable paper instead of a symbol of a binding normative consensus.[66] Unlike such Garrisonian anti-Unionists, however, Douglass never abandoned his dearly purchased commitment to the Constitution, both as a political instrument of great power and as a document to be cherished as an achievement of language. Indeed, throughout his writings, Douglass fixates reverently upon acts of speech making and upon the physical environments where speeches are delivered (805, 809). He repeatedly points to the language artifact of the Constitution as a bulwark (823) in defense of what he calls "human rights" (811), and even goes so far as to save throughout his life a small Constitution written up by Captain John Brown for his group of guerrilla fighters (755–756). While structured opposition between language and violence is one of Douglass's primary conceptual paradigms, his work is ultimately a useful example for both conceptions of the force-discourse relationship: in his account of the years immediately preceding the war, Douglass repeatedly juxtaposes the "singularly broken" quality of the language of runaway slave Shields Green, whose speeches are restricted to a continual reaffirmation of his willingness to follow Captain John Brown, with the oratorical force and eloquence of the captain, who becomes a poignant symbol through contrast of the systematic silencing of Africans through plantation violence, as well as a symbol of their struggle toward liberation through the valuable work of voices that, as surrogates, partially reproduce this original silencing.[67]

Importantly, both the emancipatory and the disciplinary models of language and violence are hortatory; they make claims upon us. Because conceptions of language are a factor in the invention, obfuscation, or realization of particular social practices, we cannot opt out: to view language merely as an ideologically neutral tool, capable of serving a multiplicity of purposes, is to take a particular sort of stance with a particular set of consequences. Karl-Otto Apel, for instance, argues for the intrinsic ethical value of a collective belief in the force-displacing structure of language-as-communication:

> Human beings, as linguistic beings who must share meaning and truth with fellow beings in order to be able to think in a valid form, must at all times anticipate counterfactually an ideal form of communication and hence of social interaction. This "assumption" is constitutive for the institution of argumentative discourse . . . In my opinion the transcendental-pragmatically justifiable necessity for the counterfactual anticipation of an ideal community of communication of argumentative consensus formation must also be seen as a central philosophical counterargument against . . . a radical antiutopian position . . . For the obligation in the long term to transcend the contradiction between reality and ideal is established together with the intellectually necessary anticipation of the ideal, and thus a purely ethical justification of the belief in progress is supplied which imposes on the skeptic the burden of proof for evidence of the impossibility of progress.[68]

The purportedly unavoidable pragmatic presuppositions of communicative interaction (presuppositions "of the intersubjective availability of an objectively real world, of the rational accountability of interaction partners, and of the context transcendence of claims to truth and moral rightness") are the underpinnings of a postmetaphysical universalist ethics.[69] The pragmatic-utopian discourse ethics of Apel and Habermas is as widely influential today in political and ethical philosophy as it is negated in literary and cultural theory—the opposition of critical orientations is basic. As Thomas McCarthy puts it, contrasting Habermas's and Derrida's views on rationality: "Are the idealizations built into language more adequately conceived as pragmatic presuppositions of communicative interaction or as a kind of structural lure that has ceaselessly to be resisted?"[70] Slavoj Žižek attacks the work of Apel and Habermas as instances of "ideology *par excellence.*" In other words, by treating ideal speech conditions (discourse evacuated of power) as a counterfactual regulative principle of communication, premised upon the necessary and rational principles of intersubjective discourse, rather than as a special case generated by gratuitous conditions or as a narrative construct of power, theorists like Apel and Habermas contribute to the occlusion of the workings of hegemony. It is thus a political burden to theorize and anticipate *nonideal* communication—not simply to treat linguistic action as neutral and hypothetically open to scrutiny but to treat it *first* as a construct of stratified power relations.[71] Judith Butler argues further that existence through language is best understood as a form of trauma inflicted, and that agency itself can be illuminated through the paradigm of subordination: "There is no purifying language of its traumatic residue . . . to be named by another is traumatic: it is an act that precedes my will, an act that brings me into a linguistic world in which I might then begin to exercise agency at all. A founding subordination, and yet the scene of agency, is repeated in the ongoing interpellation of social life."[72] While it would be a mistake to reduce these groups of theorists to easy binaries—Habermas against Butler, Arendt against Blanchot—or to conceptualize as mutually impenetrable the stances they have been invoked to illuminate, one might nevertheless acquire important insights by providing analysis that seeks to highlight macroscopic distinctions and commonalities. The juxtaposition of these works reveals important differences in methods and in basic commitments, explicit and implicit. The adjudication of these differences is one of the primary theoretical objectives of this book.

In the following chapters three primary features in the development of modern violence are examined: first, the multiplication of violence in the Civil War, with its unthinkable body counts and its anguished debate over the moral status of both the individual soldier and the language used to commemorate him; second, the industrialization of violence in World War I, with its startling innovations in weapons technology and its subsequent destabilization of basic moral catego-

ries like caring and harming, intimacy and injury; and third, the rationalized organization of violence in World War II, which saw language
shattered in the centralizing bureaucracies of the military-industrial
complex and reinvented in the rise of international human rights law.
These features of violence are objects of anxiety in particular sites and
in particular moments of cultural production: they become "acting
ideas," as Ezra Pound puts it in his explanation of distinction and repetition in historical analysis. They need not be viewed as "new inventions," "exclusive" to a decade; they are, rather, concerns that have in
special periods "come in a curious way into focus, and have become
at least in some degree operative."[73] Drawing upon legal theory,
moral philosophy, and organizational sociology, this book analyzes
how the pressures of violence in each historical moment gave rise to
important changes in aesthetic forms and cultural discourses, and develops a theory of force and discourse that links specialized modes of
verbalization to the deceleration of violence.

Although each of the following chapters can be read separately,
they are best understood as a totality, developing cumulatively. Inter-
laced throughout are sets of related analytic themes and issues (counting and discrimination, objects and objectivity, autonomy and the
problem of consequences, the solidity of conceptual borders, the referentiality of language) that unite each section's arguments and pull
them together toward the book's summary theoretical argument in
Chapter 6. In this final chapter, I undertake a deep structure analysis
of the international laws of war. Human rights law, because it is a
form of *institutionalized* language, enables a synthetic investigation of
theory and practice that uniquely contributes to current debates over
the nature of language. Offering special insight into the relationships
between force and discourse, documents like the Geneva Conventions
will help us to answer these central questions: given what we know of
the interior structure of language, what can be done to inhibit its
more coercive potentials and to maximize its emancipatory ones?
how can we reconcile contemporary literary theory with a rigorous
elaboration of the features of intersubjective discourse that restrain
violence and promote justice? and how finally should we understand
the relationships among interpretation, pluralism, normativity, and
freedom?

CHAPTER ONE

Counting on the Battlefield: Literature and Philosophy after the Civil War

At the close of the nineteenth century, the English philosopher Francis H. Bradley discovered a conceptual paradox in our understanding of reality that rendered the universe unintelligible. His paradox runs thus. To imagine either a small black circle or a large white square in isolation, against a background of nothing, is impossible. They emerge only through relation: place the small black circle in the center of the large white square and we receive a meaningful image. But here a significant problem follows. To identify the enabling relationship (R) as a third feature in our miniature world (• + R + □) is both necessary and unthinkable. The relationship between the circle and square is either something or nothing, but it must not be nothing, for if there is no relationship the exercise cannot account for the fact of union that it presupposes. And yet if the relationship is something, then its involvement with the circle, as with the square, is itself a relationship (• + r + R + r + □). The relationship's relationships with the circle and square are also either something or nothing: if something, their relationships with the circle, the square, and the relationship must also be something. The simple complex quickly generates an "infinite process." Through numerical accumulation shareable meaning is perpetually deferred. Reality, writes Bradley, "is left naked and without a character, and we are covered with confusion."[1]

For American philosophers after the Civil War, Bradley's paradox was a source of significant anxiety. How might one provide a philosophical foundation for the concept of union? How could one give a coherent account of how the many proceed from and are brought together in the one? William James responded with an aggressive disquisition critiquing philosophical "principles of *dis*union," while Josiah Royce invoked the vision of an infinitely comprehensive yet perfectly unified national map.[2] The philosophical dissension surrounding Bradley's clever, abstract puzzle and the issues it represented was the epiphenomenon of a more pervasive and fundamental cultural anxiety. After the Civil War, large, highly centralized organizations increasingly began to define the lives of individuals. In 1868 the Fourteenth Amendment was ratified, endowing all former slaves with the protections that inhered in citizenship. Five years later in an important dissent to the Slaughterhouse Cases, and in a series of tax cases that followed, Justice Stephen Field used the amendment as the legal premise for granting to corporations select rights and protections of personhood, thereby increasing the extent of corporate immunity to state regulation and facilitating the drive in America toward the bureaucratization of the economic sphere.[3] By the end of the nineteenth century, previously local or communal identities intersected on multiple planes with the forces of expansion and integration, with mass political parties, railroads, national communication networks, an aggressively centralized government, national fraternal organizations, and other large corporations.[4] The proliferation of these organizational formats coincided with the rise of statistics as an epistemological framework. "By the mid-nineteenth century," writes one scholar, "the prestige of quantification was in the ascendant. Counting was presumed to advance knowledge, because knowledge was composed of facts and counting led to the most reliable and objective form of fact there was, the hard number . . . Counting was an end in itself; it needed no further justification."[5] Ian Hacking traces America's enthusiasm for numerical data in the evolution of its census. The first American census, he notes, "asked four questions of each household," while the tenth decennial census posed 13,010 questions on various schedules addressed to individuals and institutions—a 3,000-fold increase in printed numbers.[6] The People had begun to think of itself as a *population,* a statistical group composed of categories and types.

If the nation's self-understanding depended upon a new mathematical organization of reality, so did its power. In the War of 1812,

25,000 American soldiers served; in the Mexican War, 50,000. By the end of the Civil War, an estimated 2.5 million had fought. Survivors of the Civil War had well learned the lesson summed up by the veterans' organizer George Lemon: "Each man is a component part, a scattered drop, of a current which, if united, will sweep to success with a majesty of strength."[7] War had revealed the cohesion and consequently the power made possible through the tendency of numerical accumulation to flatten out difference and distinction. Accounts of cultural power achieved through statistical aggregation competed, however, with accounts of cultural dispersion through the mathematical disorganization of communities.[8] Historian Anne Carver Rose argues that Victorian America's search for meaning after the debacle of war was made urgent by a sharp sense of "personal isolation" due in part to the "anonymity of mass activities." A dissolution of common intellectual and religious standards coincided with the scattering of individuals over distances through the completion of transcontinental settlement, an increasingly travel-oriented leisure sphere, and the replacement of neighborhoods with the transient communities of urban space.[9] Bradley's paradox was thus not simply a matter of abstruse philosophical speculation. Philosophical metaphor encoded the deep anxieties of the age, intensifying and ordering cultural material that was nearly formless in its pervasiveness. The violent scale changes brought about by the reinvention of total war and by postwar developments in social organizations complicated preexisting structures for understanding human interiority and its relationship to the collective. Am I as an individual realized through the mass or am I dissolved into it? Am I with the one or am I among the many? The individual's relationship with the external world was fundamentally a question of how one chose to count.

Crane

Stephen Crane's Civil War short stories provide one index of how these anxieties over the one and many played themselves out in the later nineteenth century. Each is structured as an exercise in counting. In "An Episode of War," Crane examines three ways of looking at a wound: wonder, contempt, and denial. The story, briefly, is about a soldier in the Civil War who is shot. His fellow soldiers react to him with pity and awe, the doctor with distance and disdain, and the soldier himself with blindness, a strenuously willed refusal to see. The first effect of the wound is that it places the lieutenant *outside—hors de combat* and therefore no longer a target as the laws of war have it, but also and more important outside existentially. "A wound gives strange dignity to him who bears it. Well, men shy from this new and terrible majesty. It is as if the wounded man's hand is upon the curtain which hangs before the revelations of all existence—the meaning of ants, potentates, wars, cities, sunshine, snow, a feather dropped from a bird's wing; and the power of it sheds radiance upon a bloody form, and makes the other men understand sometimes that they are little."[10] The lieutenant's journey after his wounding begins from the most external of perspectives, from, so to speak, the God's-eye view. He is able to step back from himself, back from his limited standpoint as "participant," and to look at the "black mass" and "crowds" as if from a great height above (90–91). From this more objective viewpoint, the men appear like figures in "an historical painting" (91)— that is, like *events in the world,* third-person phenomena from which subjectivity is excluded. He remains, for a time, at a tremendous distance from the battle, and all of its men appear includable and small. But when the lieutenant surrenders this transcendent vantage point, he comes across a group of men who have been watching the battle from an even greater distance than he. He himself, he realizes, had been just such an object in the mass, just such an event. He is instantly reduced, as if physically, to a childlike, naive "wonder" (91). As points of view proliferate, the lieutenant is increasingly diminished. Soon he encounters a group of officers, one of whom "scolds" him, and pulls and tucks at his clothes as if he were a child. The lieutenant feels shame and embarrassment: "[he] hung his head, feeling, in this presence, that he did not know how to be correctly wounded" (92). The sphere of the lieutenant's awareness, or rather his image of his own awareness, continues to shrink. When he arrives at the hospital, significantly located in a schoolhouse, he is overwhelmed by a child's panic and struggles like a truant schoolboy against entering. The doctor that he encounters looks upon him as merely one number in an almost infinite series of wounded. In the final diminutive the doctor commands, "Don't be a baby" (92) and draws him roughly in with the accumulated casualties.[11] And it is here, suddenly, that the story changes tone, leaping out of the immediacy of narrative present into the distancing perspective of history. "And this is the story of how the lieutenant lost his arm" (93). The lieutenant's story is over, and the narrator looks back upon him as one looks back upon a small thing at a far distance. The lieutenant stands "shamefaced" and embarrassed at his reduction in scale, and concludes of his own unimportance, "I don't suppose that it matters so much as all that" (93).[12]

The narrative structure of "An Episode of War" is the structure of contempt. Like its master narrative, *The Red Badge of Courage*, it establishes between reader and protagonist the vertical relationship of differential knowledge, thematized by multiple images of distance: objects seen from a great height, the large suddenly becoming small, individuals eclipsed in vast panoramas. Crane's formula of irony provides the basic structure for each of his Civil War short stories, which altogether include "The Little Regiment," "Three Miraculous Soldiers," "A Mystery of Heroism," "An Indiana Campaign," and "A Grey Sleeve." In "The Little Regiment" brothers Billie and Dan maintain toward each other a posture of unremitting hostility, foolishly believing they can hide from each other and the world the depth of their dependence and love. In "Three Miraculous Soldiers" a young woman imagines herself as the heroine in a great POW escape plot only to find herself weeping, helpless, disoriented, and patronized by story's end. In "A Mystery of Heroism" a soldier performs the "courageous" act of obtaining for his comrades a bucket of water from a shell-battered field because he is too cowardly to resist the pressure of their derision: the heroic (as perceived by the characters) is for the reader empty of content as surely as the bucket of water which the author makes certain is upturned by the end. In "An Indiana Campaign" a small village arouses itself with epic self-congratulation to confront the mysteriously sighted single Confederate soldier in the woods, only to find the familiar sight of the town drunk. And "A Grey Sleeve," the love story of a soldier and young woman, is summarized by Crane himself with the simple "Of course, they are a pair of idiots."[13] Each is a narrative of humiliation, in which a cherished self-image is revealed as transparently ridiculous, whether it is a belief that one is emotionally self-sufficient and that one is perceived thus by others, or the belief that one is a hero, or even a sincere and dramatic lover.

"An Episode of War" shares with all of Crane's Civil War short stories not only an ironic humiliation of protagonist culminating in a sudden point of self-revelation, but also a focus upon numerical series, accumulation, and counting. "The Little Regiment" and "The Mystery of Heroism" reproduce the multiplicative structure of "An Episode of War." In each the narrative centers around a single character or a pair of characters moving in and out of focus against the backdrop of uncountable hundreds, enclosing them, so to speak, in the narrative brackets of larger groups. Each shifts unpredictably between the bird's-eye view of bewildering inclusion and the small, familiar perspective of a single human gaze. "Three Miraculous Soldiers," in a slight variation, begins with a single solitary one (daughter), expands the world to include two (mother and daughter, lonely and isolated), expands the world by adding an exciting and unpredictable twelve, and then yet another three, and then yet another group of men too large for a single human to count. "An Indiana Campaign" begins with the one, moves onto the pair, and then exfoliates suddenly into the mass. And at the center of "The Grey Sleeve" is the sudden diminution of number: the backdrop of armies disappears as one is placed in relation to one in a single house—a singularity made poignant by the knowledge of the uncountable armies outside and by the irresistibility of increase even within (how many of the enemy are hidden here? one, two, three?). As in *The Red Badge of Courage,* each short story sets an individual or pair amidst a sea of others, simultaneously incorporating them into the mass as well as singling them out of it, separating them from the "many" into their loneliness as if by a "chasm," as Crane phrases it in "A Mystery of Heroism." Each story is, in a way, the same story told over and over again, a story of irony, death, and numerical increase. To develop most fully what is at stake in Crane's continual return to the same basic structures for his narratives of violence, it will be useful to expand the scope of analysis. I will return to Crane at the end of the chapter; for now, I want to look in greater detail at the representational logic of counting across a variety of nineteenth-century American writing: the remainder of this chapter will thus follow the structure of a cascade, cumulatively developing the issues framed here by Crane through several emblematic pairings, including William Tecumseh Sherman and Ulysses S. Grant, Louisa May Alcott and Walt Whitman, and William James and Josiah Royce.

Sherman and Grant

> "Men and money count so in war."
>
> —MARY CHESNUT

Counting is the epistemology of war. War is bounded by the referential extremes of the prebattle roll call and the postbattle body count, and is constituted within by the mundane and innumerable calculations (days counted, supplies counted, miles counted) that make war in theoretical writings so susceptible to formulation as a mathematical contest, or "war by algebra" as Clausewitz trenchantly puts it. Indeed counting is a speech act so pervasive during war time that it approaches an ideology: it is thus not simply a formal or typological question (What shall I count? How shall I count?) but also a fundamentally ethical one (Who counts? Do I count?).

In the memoirs of battle commanders that proliferated after the Civil War, culminating in *Century* magazine's war series, which ran in the mid-1880s and which contributed to the near doubling of its circulation, the problem of counting and of representing the aggregate is a central generic concern. For General William T. Sherman, whose memoirs of the previous decade were among the first and most widely read accounts of the war by a senior commanding officer, the most effective representational strategies for reconstructing the war are the catalog of names and the chart of the body count. In his *Memoirs,* each battle sequence is recounted as a pattern of making up and taking apart. Each begins with a narrative re-creation of his army: with precision and sweep he details the resources available and positions occupied; he reproduces exactly the orders in correspondence drawn up before the battle and provides extensive lists of the important men (that is, the officers) who make up his army.[14] This exquisitely rendered complex is then subjected to the buffets of war. Resources are consumed, orders fail, positions are lost, and men die. This methodical deconstruction of the army is then followed by a chart of the casualties, which recalls in its cold precision and detachment the accountancy work of Sherman's earlier days as a bank manager. The war that always threatens to burst the seams of narrative clarity is recaptured in an almost aesthetic cleanliness and order. The ones who do not count, so to speak, are merely counted. In a vicious synecdoche the wound replaces the name as the primary bearer of identity, and the wound itself is transformed from the vividly corporeal (a shattered hip, a severed artery) into the abstraction of a mathematical equation, a number in a chart that can be tallied both horizontally and vertically.[15]

The representational strategies used for what Sherman describes as "valuable" men (353) are markedly different from those used for the enlisted. Specific injuries suffered by named officers are accounted for in the battle descriptions (313, 350). Naming is a fundamentally different linguistic act from counting. The body count is an essential tool in the emergency: it slams language into immediate contiguity with mass, thus not merely facilitating action (there are three officers missing, this group is suffering the highest casualties) but also compelling it (ten thousand men have died already in Andersonville prison camp and more are dying each day).[16] And yet if the concentration wavers, if the bodies behind the words are not kept steadily in mind, then numbers can also stagger the imagination, slipping easily into unreality or *mere* numbers.[17] A single death is a tragedy, as Stalin reportedly declared, but a million deaths is a statistic. If naming is a projection of identity, counting is an abstraction out of identity; if naming is an assertion of individuality, counting is an assertion of a category or type. By providing a name (Captain Pitzman) and by detailing experiences that extend temporally beyond the flat present of the battle scene (his hip wound "apparently disabled him for life," 350), Sherman introduces us to a human being with historical volume, a person for whom we can have sympathy.[18] Sherman's staggering and repetitive body counts, in contrast, disable our imaginative and sympathetic capacities. In his aggregations—9,918; 19,452; 32,233—one more or less cannot possibly matter. To the reader, 17,050 dead is little different from 17,049 or 17,051, but is radically different from 17,049 plus a man named Private Wilkinson, whose father had died in Bull Run and whose mother had begged Sherman for the right to see him before the fall of Vicksburg (355–356). Typically, however, the soldiers remain unnamed, and these unnamed, countable units literally disappear from the narrative; they are subsumed instead in the colossal identity of the one named man who represents them.[19] "Morgan was to move to his left, to reach Chickasaw Bayou, and to follow it toward the bluff, about four miles above A. J. Smith" (313). The collective, consequentially, can never suffer death, but rather only minor injury. "Several other regiments were pretty badly cut up" (351). Such simplifying representational strategies are certainly, in part, a practical imperative: the sheer numbers involved would disable any narration that attempted to account for each casualty. Indeed, throughout the *Century* war series, which included over 350 selections by some 230 contributors, nearly every battle account by a high-level commander reproduces to some degree the representational patterns revealed here most dramatically in Sherman. The tactics of compression required by the genre, however, structurally produce unintended narrative effects beyond their purposed goal of expanded descriptive scope. The military narrative replaces the aversive incomprehensibility of war's inhuman scale with a finite collection of clean, containable units of information. By transforming a borderless trauma, which in its resistance to cognition demands a continual repetition and return, into a bordered, consumable, and ultimately disposable piece of information, these rhetorics of substitution enable the integration of an originally meaning-effacing challenge to shared cultural values and symbols into a psychically sustainable quotidian worldview.

Synecdochic logic also enables for Sherman a certain actuarial attitude toward his men, an attitude premised upon counting's strict commensurability of values. Incommensurability is best represented by the notion of ritual sequence: no part of the sequence may be made equivalent to another, and the loss of any unit is the loss of an irreplaceable meaning. Games of chance, in contrast, are premised upon a formula of deducible equivalents: in gambling, for instance, different chips may have different "meanings," but these values are replaceable rather than unique. After the war, Sherman met Confederate generals Johnston and Blair and, on the friendliest of terms, played cards and discussed the "game of war" (507). Throughout his *Memoirs* Sherman explicitly formulates war as a "game" of chance (926, 511). Men are exchangeable, like poker chips; indeed, some are entirely disposable. Speaking of Union citizens living in the South, he writes: "I account them as nothing in this great game of war" (362). In other places, he formulates war as a series of calculated economic purchases that can be "costly" (315) and that might involve the expense of unusually "valuable" officers (353). The epistemology of human commensurability allows Sherman to conceive of men as supplies, thereby blending the body count with the resources checklist: "Here we found much ammunition for field pieces, which was destroyed; also two caissons, and a general hospital, with about two hundred and eighty Confederate wounded, and about fifty of our own wounded men" (264–265). Sherman's paratactic representation enacts the military vector of human into thing: "killed, wounded, and much property" (270). The epistemological violence inherent in the count is manifest in its blending of killed, wounded, captured, stragglers, missing, and surrendered into one "aggregate loss" (358). For Sherman, killed, wounded, and missing are all the same in one important way: they are

all unusable. Again, the military mind is trained by the practical calculations it is forced to make: the use of round numbers in estimating
future dead and wounded, for instance, is a practical imperative with
a value-neutral purpose that at the same time contributes to a value-
oriented function (in this case it trains one to dismiss the value of
the individual unit) (266, 358). Manner of representation determines
one's affect toward the represented.[20] Consequently, the loss of 542
men in the battle of Averysboro' is considered "a serious loss" only
"because every wounded man had to be carried in an ambulance"
(784). With the death of *individuals* excluded from combat equations,
or rather made equivalent to such matters as availability of equipment
and mobility, the problem of the military becomes a matter simply of
keeping an adequate "number" or "supply" of its objects. War is
transformed into a system of productivity and even human improve-
ment: it is a "school" as well as a form of "art" (878). And thus, in the
most startling moment of Sherman's *Memoirs*—at the end, after we
have been subjected to so many body-count charts that it has almost
become a mental reflex to process them—the body count is transformed. In the final chart, the mile replaces the corpse: distance trav-
eled per campaign stands in for casualties. The foot as signifier of
physical vulnerability, as site of war's summary, inescapably near and
present wound (consider Sophocles' *Philoctetes,* Kurt Vonnegut's
Slaughterhouse Five, J. M. Coetzee's *Waiting for the Barbarians,* or
the film *Gallipoli*), is now replaced by the foot as signifier of *distance.*

Writing nearly a decade after its conclusion, Sherman is able to re-
count the war without any significant expression of remorse or self-
doubt, despite its unprecedented slaughter and in particular despite
his unprecedented decision to make war directly upon civilians. Indeed, his *Memoirs* reflects the exhilaration of a "mathematical sublime," which Kant describes as the mind's original abjection in the
face of the seemingly uncountable and its final rapture over the revelation of the totality or infinitude that is its destiny.[21] Reason's ability to
conceive of the inconceivable, to encompass the seemingly infinite
through incremental addition, is a source of power and delight. Thus
at the end of his *Memoirs* Sherman is able to give, with the self-satis-
faction of leaving nothing unaccounted for and with the nearly aesthetic appreciation of seeing a formula produce a final result, one last,
mind-boggling numerical series: "At the close of the civil war there
were one million five hundred and sixteen names on the muster-rolls,

of which seven hundred and ninety-seven thousand eight hundred and seven were present, and two hundred and two thousand seven hundred and nine absent, of which twenty-two thousand nine hundred and twenty-nine were regulars, the others were volunteers, colored troops, and veteran reserves" (903). Through abstraction, aggregation, equivalency, and here, finally, the sublime, the epistemology of counting enables complacency in the face of unquantifiable human suffering. The mathematical formula becomes a sort of teleological narrative, both pointing to an end that is seemingly inevitable and natural and tying together the war's multiply dispersed events with the satisfaction of a coherent and well-told story. History, and with it the possibility for questioning, is closed.

Sherman concludes the main body of his *Memoirs* with the victory parade of the Army of the Potomac. The parade as an exercise in the sublime is both a performance of the army's seamless unity and a breakdown and analysis of its component parts; it is an imagistic re-telling of the story of the war that leads, as naturally as a straight line, to the inevitable end point of its victory (865). Sherman concludes his final two postludal chapters with a closing paragraph that recalls the ritualistic impermeability of this parade, that integrates counting, prayer, and theater: its focus on countable and uncountable types, its evocation of the Prayer of Confession through phrasing and cadence, and its theatrical sense of unreality all combine to make the Civil War the climax in a drama written to end with the final unification of each member of the nation. And most important, a curtain can be drawn upon this performance, so that we can no longer see behind to the cost:

> This I construe as the end of my military career. In looking back upon the past I can only say, with millions of others, that I have done many things I should not have done, and have left undone still more which ought to have been done; that I can see where hundreds of opportunities have been neglected, but on the whole am content; and feel sure that I can travel this broad country of ours, and be each night the welcome guest in palace or cabin; and as "all the world's a stage, / And all the men and women merely players," I claim the privilege to ring down the curtain.
>
> W. T. Sherman, *General* (955)[22]

Sherman and Grant seem a study in contrasts: Sherman's superlatives and rhetorical fire against Grant's understatement and rhetorical precision, Sherman's aggressive politicking and keen sensitivity to his own interests against Grant's quiet impassivity and stated desire to be free of all "interests" in the objective development of his career, Sherman's notorious brutality against Grant's distaste for hunting and inability to eat red meat (he could not stomach the sight of blood).[23] While Grant's *Memoirs* does recapitulate many of the quantifying strategies of Sherman's earlier work, it nonetheless achieves a signal difference in overall tone and affect. Sherman's volume is defined fundamentally by its selective visibility, by its tactics of vindication and justification. His notorious "march to the sea," for instance, is depicted almost as a gamesome venture, with greater attention to the good spirits of the march and to the amusement and "charm" of "foraging" (659) than to the lingering and catastrophic consequences for civilians of his use of starvation as a weapon.[24] Grant's *Memoirs,* in a phrase, is a narrative of control. His autobiography is built word by word, noun by noun; it is a text bristling with referential language, with names, dates, and numbers. Scarcely a paragraph passes without a rhapsodic catalog of facts. His is an attempt to make prose equal to the immediacy and perfect physical referentiality of a map.[25] Grant collected and indeed seemed to think through the structure of maps. As a staff officer in the 1864–65 campaigns noticed, any map "seemed to become photographed indelibly on his brain, and he could follow its features without referring to it again. Besides, he possessed an almost intuitive knowledge of topography."[26] Grant's cartographical representational reflexes (his tight prose, his famously simple and clear written orders, and his stated wish that recorded facts rather than celebratory anniversaries constitute the legacy of war) reproduce his professional military ethic (his direct and unrelenting battle tactics, his uncompromising discipline, and his dutiful if selective respect for the laws of war)—and both together are the epiphenomena of his essential will-to-order.[27]

For Grant, the incommensurability of subjectivity is at best a private adornment and at worst a contributor to all that distorts, exaggerates, renders unclear, or disrupts publicly accessible organizations. This distrust is so strong in him that it leads to the near total suppression of his "private" history, and even in his public roles it flattens out his range of affective response. Grant's will-to-order manifests itself in a desire to achieve comprehensive intelligibility, to transform his prose into a universal language and to make this language absolutely referential and transparent. In his *Memoirs* depersonalized fact prevails: all rumors are identified as such, and all uncertainty is clearly relegated to the category of admitted uncertainty. Objectivity is his touchstone: his *Memoirs* depicts a man continually measuring, counting, and recording. Mathematics is easy for him (32), unsurprisingly, because he understands the world first through the reliability, shareability, and clarity of numbers. An early moment of the *Memoirs* is paradigmatic:

> The next day Mr. Payne, of Georgetown, and I started on our return. We got along very well for a few miles, when we encountered a ferocious dog that frightened the horses and made them run. The new animal kicked at every jump he made. I got the horses stopped, however, before any damage was done, and without running into anything. After giving them a little rest, to quiet their fears, we started again. That instant the new horse kicked, and started to run once more. The road we were on, struck the turnpike within half a mile of the point where the second runaway commenced, and there was an embankment twenty or more feet deep on the opposite side of the pike. I got the horses stopped on the very brink of the precipice. (25)

Why does Grant stifle the potential suspense and excitement of this story by slowing it down at its climax with a series of encumbering details? Is he simply a bad storyteller? Here, in the emergency, when perception is most clouded, memory is most faulty, and emotions are highest, he resorts to the detail of the numerical measurement and to his discipline of mapping.[28] It is narration, so to speak, viewed from a distance, in which one's personal perspective tends to be eclipsed in favor of the objective factual description. There is no depth, uncertainty, or suspense; everything is calmly flattened out and made panoramically visible like the surface of a two-dimensional diagram. It is memory as agent-neutral history; it is prose as a form of counting. As Martha Nussbaum writes of the Greek science of deliberative measurement: "The connection between numbering and knowing, the ability to count or measure and the ability to grasp, comprehend, or control, runs very deep . . . The denumerable is the definite, the graspable, therefore also the potentially tellable, controllable; what cannot be numbered remains vague and unbounded, evading human grasp."[29]

For Grant the war was primarily an experience in helplessness—helplessness in the face of superior numbers, superior orders, chance, or fate. War had shown Grant "how little men control their own destiny" (71) and had taught him the lesson that the future was something "no man could foretell" (143). "Circumstances," he writes at the opening of his *Memoirs*, "always did shape my course different from my plans" (32). "It seems that one mans destiny in this world is quite as much a mystery as it is likely to be in the next" (1117). Grant's notion of agency thus encompasses both the active and the passive senses of the word. "So long as I hold a commission in the Army I have no views of my own to carry out. Whatever may be the orders of my superiors, and law, I will execute. No man can be efficient as a commander who sets his own notions above law and those whom he is sworn to obey" (990). For Grant the agent is both an independent actor and a stand-in or representative for other determinative forces. The personal view of the self, which recognizes our freedom, is yoked together with the sociological view of the self, which recognizes our causal determination or existential passivity. Indeed, Grant *cultivates* passivity and self-effacement—not only as a recognition of his constraints, a recognition of his subservience to the force and will of others, but also as a coping mechanism, a deferral of responsibility to others through an elevation of passive over active agency and a justification of self through reference to a unique role-morality.[30] Grant's passivity is manifest not simply in the frequent references to his suppression of self in favor of obedience to what he perceived as an objective juridical order (for instance, his participation in the Mexican War, which he viewed as deplorable, 41, or his incarceration of a group of sailors whom he nonetheless believed had been falsely charged with mutiny, 46–47) but also in the very construction of his sentences, in his grammatical cloaking of both responsibility and aggression: "firing was continued" (531), "some execution was done" (67), "the troops . . . were moved" (99), "Goliad was at last reached" (54). Grant's passive grammar had a national as well as a personal function, for, like Sherman's, his memoirs are a rhetorical enactment of nation building and reunification. They begin with a detailed family history, which takes the reader through the birthing of America, and end with a semi-Christological invocation of universal community and consensus in the body of a dying Grant himself: "The expressions of these kindly feelings were not restricted to a section of the country, nor to a division of the people. They came from individual citizens of all nationalities; from all denominations—the

Protestant, the Catholic, and the Jew; and from the various societies of the land—scientific, educational, religious, or otherwise. Politics did not enter into the matter at all" (780). A war figured as passively endured rather than aggressively prosecuted is a war that can be incorporated into a vision of reciprocally forgiving union.[31]

The act of writing his *Memoirs* was thus for Grant an act of resistance against the specter of national dissolution. It was also, perhaps more importantly, a striving for order and control against the dissolution of his approaching death. His final notes, written with great effort after his cancer had become almost unbearable, reveal a mind clinging to reason and precision as if to a last hope for salvation: "I will try to observe the effect . . ."; "I was not quite conscious enough to reason correctly about what produced it . . ." (1112); "the time for the arrival of the third [phase] can be computed with almost mathematical certainty" (1111). The effort to control the uncontrollable in his memory, first announced in the preface where he confesses that he is unequal to the task of encircling the war's "thousands" of instances, is reproduced in the scene of writing itself, in which the expansion of memory becomes a counterforce to diminution through bodily pain, and the act of precise recollection becomes all that is left of Grant's agency. "There is nothing more I should do to [my autobiography] now," he writes, "and therefore I am not likely to be more ready to go than at this moment" (1119). Just days before his death Grant wrote a final note to his doctor: "I do not sleep though I sometimes dose off a little. If up I am talked to and in my efforts to answer cause pain. The fact is I think I am a verb instead of a personal pronoun. A verb is anything that signifies to be; to do; or to suffer. I signify all three" (1120). The disease that has reduced him to abject passivity—like a "cross fire" in the war (1117)—teaches him to view himself from the outside, as a function or a thing that happens in the world. Indeed, he represents himself in one place as a useful piece of medical evidence (1119). But it is here, in his last words, that the personal self is most fully evacuated. Here, the verbs bear no subjects; the *I* is replaced by a series of universally exchangeable acts—acts that culminate in the final closure of counting. In death, he becomes the point of universal convergence.

This evacuation of the personal self is not only, and perhaps not at all, a diminishment of self, but rather an expansion: self-erasure is the originary move of objectivity, a move toward increasing control of the world through increases in empirical scope and critical accuracy. The concept of objectivity was central to the major philosophical writings of the period, from the work of William James to late-nineteenth-century neo-Hegelians like F. H. Bradley. Neo-Hegelians believed, in brief, that our capacity to transcend the finite perspective by assuming an impersonal, objective viewpoint was a sign of our relationship to a higher, absolute consciousness.[32] I want to contextualize this notion of objectivity briefly by looking at the current philosophical work of Thomas Nagel. Objectivity, as Nagel describes it in his seminal book *The View from Nowhere,* is a matter of stepping backward from one's original position in order to acquire a viewpoint of greater breadth; it is a matter of looking at the world from behind one's own back, and thereby taking one's self and one's relationship to the world as an object in the world to be assessed in formulating a new, more objective viewpoint. "Only objectivity," he writes, "can give meaning to the idea of intellectual progress." Nagel requires us to consider the distinction between primary and secondary qualities, which he describes as "the precondition for the development of modern physics and chemistry":

> The best account of the appearance of colors will not involve the ascription to things of intrinsic color properties that play an ineliminable role in the explanation of the appearances . . . Things have colors, tastes, and smells in virtue of the way they appear to us: to be red simply *is* to be the sort of thing that looks or would look red to normal human observers in the perceptual circumstances that normally obtain in the actual world. To be square, on the other hand, is an independent property which can be used to explain many things about an object, including how it looks and feels . . . This is a particularly clear example of how we can place ourselves in a new world picture. We realize that our perceptions of external objects depend both on their properties and on ours . . . [This] advance in objectivity requires that already existing forms of understanding should themselves become the object of a new form of understanding, which also takes in the objects of the original forms.

For Nagel, this capacity for objectivity enables us "to escape the limits of the original human situation, not merely by traveling around and seeing the world from different perspectives, but by ascending to new levels from which we can understand and criticize the general forms of previous perspectives."[33] Objectivity, like the lieutenant's development in "An Episode of War," consists in a plurality of perspectives that enables vertical movement; it is the collection and consequent transcendence of subjectivities. Thomas Nagel is seldom put together with William James, because James in the neopragmatist tradition is typically characterized as a philosopher of subjectivity and therefore of some qualified form of relativism.[34] But for James, objectivity is both the primary quality of the philosopher and the enabling condition of truth. Indeed, James partly anticipates Nagel with a rigorous verificationist conception of objective truth as the ineluctable "ultimate consensus" of a wide horizontal sweep of critical perspectives. "Truth absolute," he writes, "means an ideal set of formulations towards which all opinions may in the long run of experience be expected to converge."[35]

Objectivity is the quintessential imperative of war. This statement may at first seem alien, given war's prejudicial division of the world into "friend" and "foe," its sharp demarcation of two sides, each of which must live faithfully and exclusively within the commitments of its own borders. However, when war is conceived not as a competition between political claims but rather as a matter of organizing violence on the battlefield, it becomes clear that the structure of war demands objectivity. The individual situated amidst countless thousands, each with a manifestly limited or even false view of the whole, can no longer take himself as a centering perspective. Indeed, for generals like Grant, such a centered perspective is inherently flawed—only the centerless view can guarantee the survival of some portion of the dispersed thousands. Making sense of the war is an exercise in the limits and fallibility of the individual subject. Soldiers of the Mexican War, he remarks, had small and private viewpoints on the war rather than any macroscopic understanding: they had "little interest" in the results and "little knowledge" of "what it was all about" (82). Grant's expansion of powers, however, depends not upon the exclusion but upon the accumulation and incorporation of just such fallible perspectives. Grant describes the first battle of his first command as a sort of Hegelian synthesis of viewpoints. The enemy

> had been encamped in a creek bottom for the sake of being near water
> . . . I would have given anything then to have been back in Illinois, but I
> had not the moral courage to halt and consider what to do; I kept right
> on. When we reached a point from which the valley below was in full
> view I halted. The place where Harris had been encamped a few days be-
> fore was still there and the marks of a recent encampment were plainly

visible, but the troops were gone. My heart resumed its place. It occurred to me at once that Harris had been as much afraid of me as I had been of him. This was a view of the question I had never taken before; but it was one I never forgot afterwards. (164–165)

Here Grant learns not only to take his subjective experience in battle as a piece of external knowledge in determining an objective battle plan, but also in part to *detach* himself from a subjective or emotive position. "From that event to the close of the war, I never experienced trepidation upon confronting an enemy, though I always felt more or less anxiety. I never forgot that he had as much reason to fear my forces as I had his. The lesson was valuable" (165). By incorporating the view of the individual soldier, the view of the enemy, the view from the front of the lines and the view from the back of the lines (232), Grant endeavors to achieve a bird's-eye perspective, or the view from nowhere in which the world approximates a map upon which men are counted and events happen.[36]

For Grant objective understanding thus combines both the horizontal inclusiveness of James and the vertical ascendance of Nagel. In other words, Grant's objectivity demands both a positive and a negative self-abandon; it demands a self-transcendence that elevates him precisely by treating him as a fallible, potentially expendable object. His narrative range is thus bounded by the epistemological reflexes of composed objectivity and the verbal tics of subjective insecurity: by, for instance, the exquisite mental maps he provides for his readers before each battle scene in the *Memoirs,* the centerless view of the physical site;[37] and by his continual assertions of witness fallibility in the repeated words "I believe," "seem," "probably," in his legalistic "I do not claim to quote Sherman's language; but the substance only," and in the statement to his wife "when I can learn the exact amount of loss I will write and correct the statements I have made if they are not right."[38]

This self emptied of subjectivity, or rather continually outstripping its subjectivity, becomes the model of what public man ought to be. The objective self is *public,* in John Rawls's important sense. In other words, the claims and languages appropriate to the public sphere are only those which are sufficiently exchangeable and translatable, which *each* person can take as a reason for herself without disruptive remainder or residue. The paradigm for intersubjective deliberation is a personality-erasing thought-experiment, in which we view the world from behind a veil of ignorance about ourselves, thereby severing our special connections to "private" interests.[39] Grant's conception of this public self, indeed, is separated even from the demands of personal moral judgment and from the incommensurable experiences of individual joy, grief, or fear: hence Grant's praise of Generals Scott and Lee for their dissociation of private conscience and public function, for their machinelike impermeability (112, 735); hence also the single sentence he allows in his *Memoirs* for mentioning his marriage to his wife (130), the single sentence he allows for reflecting upon his brother's death (144), and, emblematically, his total effacement of any subjective reaction to the possibility of his own death. "Early in this engagement my horse was shot under me, but I got another one from one of my staff and kept well up with the advance until the river was reached" (179). Plato argued that philosophy was a method of preparing to die. In his *Republic,* he offers up an ideal legislator whose self-conception and worldview underscore this relationship between the cultivation of objectivity and death. The legislator's ultimate challenge is the challenge to overcome the notion that, in Nussbaum's words, "the sensations of this piece of flesh have a connection with me that is altogether different from the connection I have with that other piece of flesh over there."[40] Grant—soldier, general, president—chooses to represent himself in just such a tradition at the slow close of his life.

In the final words of his *Memoirs,* Grant presents objectivity, and its concomitant expunging of the private and idiosyncratic, as a formula for universal peace. Grant's ability to step outside himself enabled him to become a "representative" (780) of his nation, and his nation's ability to perceive itself through representative figures enabled it to overcome the incommensurable segregations of the private. The representative figure, like the railroads and telegraphs Grant lingers over throughout his *Memoirs,* traverses all borders: he participates in the "commingling of the people" which dissolves exclusionary language games and regional dialects; and he becomes a symbol and engine of the unification of diverse viewpoints that is the nation's "power" (779). Representation and publicity overcome the problem of dispersion. Indeed, the numerical increase that, for Bradley, destabilized objective perception and that, for Sherman, derealized individual meaning became for Grant an amplification of both. Bradley's radical notion of identifying relations as an object of knowledge thus *generates* objectivity. Bradley's paradox signifies not the infinite deferral of the truth but rather our ability infinitely to refine it.

Alcott and Whitman

Where Sherman's and Grant's encounters with the wounded ended, the work of nurses like Louisa May Alcott and Walt Whitman began.[41] Alcott decided to enlist as an army nurse on her thirtieth birthday: "I want new experiences," she wrote, "and am sure to get 'em if I go."[42] She recorded her experiences at the Union Hotel Hospital in a series of autobiographical sketches that later became a book entitled *Hospital Sketches,* written as the recollections of Tribulation Periwinkle, a doughty New Englander whose preemptively comic name, Elaine Showalter points out, reveals Alcott's fear that female "strong-mindedness would invite ridicule."[43] Installed at Hurly Burly House, a hospital thinly occupied by the diseased and invalided, Periwinkle "had rather longed for the wounded to arrive, for rheumatism wasn't heroic, neither was liver complaint, or measles."[44] Her romantic conceptions of a nurse's duties, predicated upon the domestic scales of a mother nurturing a select and intimate few, did not long survive. She describes her first encounter with the wounded as an encounter with "heaps" (21). Her ability even to count them is overwhelmed from the start: they are "some," "some," "they," "they," and "these" (21–23). She is able to separate out "one" briefly in the beginning only because he is dead; she thereafter quickly collapses into plurals. This encounter with the sheer numbers of the wounded stupefies the sympathetic response: the sight of so many legless and armless "admonished" her, and she "corked up her feelings" (22).[45]

When first stationed at Hurly Burly House, Periwinkle is put in charge of forty beds. Immediately, as both an administrative technique and an emotional distancing mechanism, she begins to distinguish them according to categories: there are a pneumonia, a diphtheria, five typhoids, and a dozen cripples. She transforms individuals into countable types—and the counting, importantly, gives her organizational and emotional control over events that shatter both like steel shatters bone.[46] But the sphere of human contact shrinks: the hospital, like a human abacus, structurally generates *replaceability.*

"This is a very hasty scribble," Alcott writes in a letter from the hospital, "but half a dozen stumps are waiting to be met & my head is full of little duties."[47] Throughout *Hospital Sketches* Alcott depicts how in the emergency the individual is lost in the group: the soldier is "lonely even in a crowd." A man sliding into death is "like a drop in that red sea"; he is unattended because unimportant amidst the accumulation of numbers (28).[48] For Alcott, the tragedy of counting is its paralysis of sympathy. War's ruthlessly mathematical organization of reality allows no space for the incommensurability of the subjective. "Sanitary Commission nurses were trained to be coolheaded, even coldhearted," writes David Reynolds. "One woman associated with the commission advised all nurses to 'put away all feelings. Do all you can and be a machine—that's the way to act; the only way.'"[49] One doctor, Alcott recalls, confessed that "his profession blunted his sensibilities, and, perhaps, rendered him indifferent to the sight of pain" (70). The incommensurability and pure subjectivity of pain cannot be made to fit into the doctor's category-oriented worldview. Alcott censures one doctor in particular whose extreme inability to recognize suffering is matched only by his craftsman's enthusiasm for identifying and mastering certain types of wounds (52).[50] John W. DeForest, going further, points out that many even "acquired a taste" for the sight of surgical bloodletting.[51]

Statistical derealization appalls Alcott, however, not only because it severs the connections between people which are the source of tenderness and care, but also and primarily because it threatens the social perpetuation of meaning. Like the soldiers at Cold Harbor, who before battle pinned to their uniforms scraps of paper bearing their names, Alcott here fears not so much the inevitability of death as the absence of signifying structures surrounding death.[52] Lacking domesticity's tender rituals of witnessing and commemoration—which, like performative speech-acts, help to create the meaning they consecrate—death in the field camp is left uninscribed and incomprehensible.[53] The difference between death surrounded by ritual and death left uncontained corresponds to the difference between mourning and melancholia. For Freud, grief and mourning are correctives, forms of work that bring bereavement under control. Mourning reproduces the structure of the sublime. It is a process of "bit by bit" analysis that identifies, parcels up, and polices the borders of suffering. Melancholia is mourning that lacks an object present to consciousness, mourning that, in other words, remains outside the processes of familiar and coherent articulation. If mourning is bounded melancholia, melancholia is "pathological" mourning; if mourning is a cure, melancholia is a symptom. Melancholia thus appears neither to resemble work nor to actualize closure but rather, as Freud puts it, remains "an open wound."[54]

It is through the narrative imagination of the finite, the small, and the enclosed that Alcott remedies war's disturbing hiatus in meaning.[55] At the heart of *Hospital Sketches* is the story of one man, John, the Virginia blacksmith who suffocates over a period of several days as his lungs fill with blood. His is a "short story and a simple one" (42); he is Alcott's "little boy" (41), and he is killed by a "little wound" (43). The story is rounded and complete: we know who he is, where he has come from, how and to whom his death matters. We linger over his suffering and follow his narrative to its bitter close, when he is made ready for the grave and laid in state for half an hour ("a thing which seldom happened in that busy place," 45). John, Alcott continually emphasizes, is unique; he is not a symbol for the many left unrecognized, and his burial is not a commemoration for all of the previously anonymous dead. Narrative compassion makes such counting impossible, or rather counts only one.

The story-formation itself is for Alcott an exercise in the imagination of the small. A story sets *limits*. As Hayden White observes, despite the peculiar truth that "no set of events attested by the historical record comprises a *story* manifestly finished and complete"—not the life of an individual, an institution, a nation, or a whole people—events, lives, and histories are continually formulated and reconceived in ways that conform to particular story "types."[56] In one tentative digression White argues that psychotherapy and history are equivalent forms of narration or, rather, equivalent forms of *therapeutic* narration: in each discipline trauma is controlled by being "reemplotted" and familiarized. In other words, story-formation like ritual is a recuperative operation, a means of restoring understanding and thereby alleviating the damage of confusion. Linear narration provides *cause*, much as religion establishes stable points of reference and banishes the hobgoblin of the random. And fashioning a linear narration becomes a means of reasserting the primacy of authorship, of agency and self-control. Even as a particular self-narration attests to the impossibility of control, the impossibility of authoring one's own life—

John is killed unexpectedly by a man he has never met in a conflict he does not fully understand—it reasserts by its very telling the control of the author who orders the words.

Narrative sympathy vivifies the singular and private; it realizes for us the subjective viewpoint. The subjective viewpoint does not *fit* into the world of aggregation, countable types, or the statistical imagination. As Nagel argues, it is not that, when the world is viewed from the objective standpoint, subjectivity appears limited and small. When the world is viewed from the objective standpoint, subjectivity does not appear at all; the viewpoints are mutually exclusive. To borrow William James's formulation from the essay "The Importance of Individuals": "Truly enough, the details vanish in the bird's-eye view; but so does the bird's-eye view vanish in the details."[57] Thus the experience of being me, and the singularity and incommensurability of meaning that attaches itself to that experience, cannot be accounted for in a world of mass representation. It is excluded categorically: the subjectivity of an individual encountered in the third person is like the infinity of numbers between one and two that we exclude in a cognitive reflex when counting objects in the real world. From the objective standpoint, subjectivity (or the experience of being me) begins to appear something of a puzzle: others' actions can be processed, but other *minds* are a problem, like an assortment of opaque spheres resistant to the probing of our senses and reason. Taking the irreconcilability of our inner lives as the summary paradigm for disconnection in the universe, James writes that the content of our imaginations "are wholly out of definite relation with the similar contents of anyone else's mind."[58]

For Alcott, sympathy is the suprarational means of penetrating the borders of this fundamental human isolation. Sympathy allows one to enter into the experience of an other, to step into her position upon an economy not of equivalence or exchange but rather of recognition. Periwinkle's first experience comforting the bereaved is with the sister of a soldier who has died unexpectedly in the night. She recalls:

> I pitied her with all my heart. What could I say or do? Words always seem impertinent at such times; I did not know the man; the woman was neither interesting in herself nor graceful in her grief; yet, having known a sister's sorrow myself, I could not leave her alone with her trouble in that strange place, without a word. So, feeling heart-sick, home-sick, and not knowing what else to do, I just put my arms about her, and be-

gan to cry in a very helpless but hearty way . . . It so happened I could not have done a better thing; for, though not a word was spoken, each felt the other's sympathy; and, in the silence, our handkerchiefs were more eloquent than words. (66–67)

Sympathy is an act of recognition, a tribute to the incommensurability of the other's experience. And yet because its interior structure is one of mutuality and reciprocity, sympathy is capable of becoming, as act, a point of shared psychic experience that allows for entry into the position of the other.[59] Periwinkle's sympathy is both a recognition and an instantiation of the meaning of the other's life, just as, to paraphrase William James, a declaration of faith in an athlete's ability can help to make real that athlete's power.

Repetition and increase, however, can diminish and even negate sympathy's validation of individual significance. Immediately upon completing the description of her encounter with the grieving sister, Periwinkle offers it up as a model to be applied generally to the bereaved. Her effective use of tears in this case is a "successful experiment" that can be reproduced for the use of any nurse. "If genuine," Periwinkle asserts, such a performance of sympathy will prove more useful than any other material means of comfort (67). As Periwinkle unself-consciously characterizes it, the sympathetic impulse can be utilized like a tool, as an effective means of producing satisfaction in the wounded and bereaved. Here, communion is replaced by utility, and instrumentality makes suspect the "genuine." Sympathy becomes a means rather than an end. The meaning of an individual's intentions or emotions are rendered secondary to quantifiable consequences in the aggregate.

Hannah Ropes, a nurse who worked with Alcott, summarizes in a single image both the generation of sympathy through acknowledgment of the individual and the degeneration of sympathy through repetition and exchangeability. On first seeing the wounded, she writes: "I thought of Neddie, when he came down from the mountains, and it seemed as though these were he, in fifty duplicates."[60] Sympathy in this formulation is generated through reference to a unique subjectivity, but its extension to multiple others serves to eclipse the unique. Sympathy, it can be argued, becomes a formula for understanding in which one uses samples from one's own life as a means of approaching samples from others'. The econometric exchange of sentimentalism's "experiential equation" allows one to substitute one event for another in order to achieve the simulated intersubjectivity or analogic understanding of sympathy.[61] The sentimental tradition in which Alcott operates, a tradition centrally concerned with the processes of conversion through sentiment, was in large part structured by the inductivity of this sympathetic design. As important studies have revealed, mid-nineteenth-century women's fiction, purposed to elicit sympathy for the individual, proceeded through the invocation of formulaic and readily exchangeable plots;[62] and, at a broader level, the sentimental literature aimed at altering the world by displacing the quantitative, instrumentalizing relations of commerce with the sympathetic, personalizing relations of domesticity ultimately did so by transforming the home, site of the private and the individually attentive, into a generically repeatable model for public reform.[63] The multiplicative element of the sympathetic design, like the asceticism of Max Weber's Protestant spirit, is thus an inherency that proves deformative over time. Because sympathy is a form of transferential narrative, it risks superimposing a simplifying and possibly alien structure upon concrete others. And because sympathy deals in type cases that make it applicable beyond the single unit, it risks departicularizing the subjective that is its origin and intended end point. These risks have serious consequences for the narrative of commemoration; but they are risks that Alcott is willing to take.

The contrast between Whitman and Alcott might be described as the contrast between the statistical and the narrative imagination. Whitman, like Alcott, is keenly sensitive to the hazards of the statistical imagination. His poem "The Wound-Dresser," from his collection of war poems *Drum-Taps,* thematizes dehumanization through a visual sequencing of diminishing sentience. Here, the speaker is an old man, recounting his experiences as a nurse in the war to a group of eager young listeners. The poem begins with the speaker facing a collection of "new faces," attentive children in an active relationship with the speaker; by the end of the second section the sphere of sentience has shrunk from the whole of these collected faces to one pair of "appealing eyes"; as the third section opens the "eye," now singular, is glazed over, unable to express and devoid of sense; as the poem closes, the eyes finally close altogether. The speaker's courageous attempts to attend to "each" of the thousands of wounded means ultimately that he can attend fully to none. As the poem progresses and the wounded

accumulate, panic informs the tempo and the patients are transformed into an unending collection of organs, a staging ground for
the inevitable and horrible amputation pile that Whitman encounters
in *Specimen Days*.[64] With geometric acceleration the wounds absorb
more and more of the speaker's vision, increasing in size like dark objects hurtling toward and filling a camera's lens: one man is identified
as "the crush'd head," whose "poor crazed hand" the speaker ad-
dresses like some hot, clammy animal that has absorbed the last of his
human identity, and the subject of the next encounters are "the neck
of the cavalry-man" and "the stump of the arm."

> I dress the perforated shoulder, the foot with the bullet-wound,
> Cleanse the one with a gnawing and putrid gangrene, so
>   sickening, so offensive,
> While the attendant stands behind aside me holding the tray and
>   pail . . .
> The fractur'd thigh, the knee, the wound in the abdomen,
> These and more I dress with impassive hand, (yet deep in my
>   breast a fire, a burning flame.)[65]

The soldiers become increasingly less human as they are increasingly
identified by their wounds, until finally, in the last stanza, the tone
radically changes. The poem suddenly retreats from the scene of the
hospital crisis back to the safe space of the old man's reflection and
memory. The speaker's vision can only briefly sustain the inhuman
scale of the war hospital. Now, the choppy, quick-moving catalog of
nouns is replaced by the smooth, slow flow of tender and meditative
verbs: "I thread," "I pacify," "I sit," "I recall," "a soldier's loving
arms . . . have cross'd and rested," "a soldier's kiss dwells." Sentimental remembrance and tired equanimity provide a semblance of closure
to the still open wound of past trauma, and the poem closes with the
whisper of parentheses. Framing the hospital crisis within the controlled borders of the old man's act of recollection is a move of limita-
tion that enables control, like Alcott's narrative strategy of the little,
like the stanzas that frame the wounded, and like the dressing that
frames the wound.[66]

In *Specimen Days*, his Civil War diary, Whitman investigates how
the fact of crowding shapes the rhetoric of caretaking and, consequently, trains the perception of the caregiver. "Then went thoroughly
through ward 6," Whitman notes in an emblematic moment,

"observ'd every case in the ward, without, I think, missing one."
"There were thousands," he writes elsewhere, "tens of thousands,
hundred of thousands needing me—needing all who might come.
What could I do?"[67] His cribbed, compressed prose, a match for his
smothering experiences in the hospital, produce the expected results:
he gives a gift to an "amputation," and remarks upon all the "interesting cases."[68] It is sometimes as if he is translating into narrative
form the body-count charts of Sherman's *Memoirs*. The statistical
gaze is a third-person, objective view and thus also an objectifying
one. The rhetorical destabilization of Whitman's account culminates
in an uncanny figurative blending, or mutual substitution, of inorganic and organic matter. He writes:

> *February 23.*—I must not let the great hospital at the Patent-office pass
> away without some mention. A few weeks ago the vast area of the sec-
> ond story of that noblest of Washington buildings was crowded close
> with rows of sick, badly wounded and dying soldiers. They were placed
> in three very large apartments. I went there many times. It was a strange,
> solemn, and, with all its features of suffering and death, a sort of fasci-
> nating sight. I go sometimes at night to soothe and relieve particular
> cases. Two of the immense apartments are fill'd with high and ponder-
> ous glass cases, crowded with models in miniature of every kind of uten-
> sil, machine or invention, it ever enter'd into the mind of man to con-
> ceive; and with curiosities and foreign presents. Between these cases are
> lateral openings, perhaps eight feet wide and quite deep, and in these
> were placed the sick, besides a great long double row of them up and
> down through the middle of the hall. Many of them were very bad cases,
> wounds and amputations. Then there was a gallery running above the
> hall in which there were beds also. It was, indeed, a curious scene, espe-
> cially at night when lit up. The glass cases, the beds, the forms lying
> there, the gallery above, and the marble pavement under foot.[69]

It is important that the wounded—the cases—are *crowded*. Insofar as
we are informed by a bourgeois notion of what it means to be human
(independent, individual, unique), we perceive *crowding* as a particularly inhuman behavior pattern. A crowd is a thing; humans in a
crowd partake of this thingness. Moreover, crowds are dirty and re-
pugnantly physical—insofar as we are part of a crowd we are bodies
contributing to a mass rather than minds or personalities. Animals
and insects crowd; humans do not. Even for Whitman, who most frequently celebrates the crowd as a sort of glittering mosaic, the compression of bodies during wartime can as effectively degrade the hu-

man form as multiply the occasions for its celebration. Thus it is that when Whitman encounters a boatload of "several hundreds" of tormented prisoners-of-war, he reacts as much with disgust and disbelief as with pity: "Can those be *men*—those little livid brown, ash-streak'd, monkey-looking dwarfs?"[70] And yet it is precisely this representation of the mass that Whitman feels he must risk.

Whitman touched the greatest number of lives in the briefest of all ways: "During those three years in hospital, camp or field, I made over six hundred visits or tours, and went, as I estimate, counting all, among from eighty thousand to a hundred thousand of the wounded and sick, as sustainer of spirit and body in some degree, in time of need. These visits varied from an hour or two, to all day or night; for with dear or critical cases I generally watch'd all night."[71] The representation of this crowd—in, for instance, "The Wound-Dresser"—is the representation of narrative fractured; it is a *statistical* vision, a synchronic intersection with multiply developing narrative lines, none of which will ever reach closure (Where did the amputee come from? Where will he end up?). Even in instances when Whitman chooses to illuminate the war with an intense focus on the single individual's life history, he is careful not to let the image remain singular; as if with a verbal reflex, he insistently moves back into the aggregate. In a paradigmatic moment from "Come Up from the Fields Father," Whitman interpolates a multiplicative panorama into the snapshot of a single grieving mother:

> Ah now the single figure to me
> Amid all teeming and wealthy Ohio with all its cities and farms,
> Sickly white in the face and dull in the head, very faint,
> By the jamb of a door leans.[72]

In his most deeply relational and personal accounts of nursing, Whitman likewise presents the individual as embedded in a series of references, as an instance or sample of an organizational pattern. In the diaristic modality, however, the movement from the one to the many takes place not as an act of vision, in the spatialized field of theoretically countable objects, but as an act of narration—or, rather, as an act *out of* narration. He recounts how in one of the wards he "found an old acquaintance transferr'd here lately, a rebel prisoner, in a dying condition. Poor fellow the look was already on his face. He gazed long at me. I ask'd him if he knew me. After a moment he utter'd something, but inarticulately. I have seen him off and on for the last five months. He has suffer'd very much; a bad wound in left leg, severely fractured, several operations, cuttings, extractions of bone, splinters, &c."[73] But here the tender, personal linear narrative is immediately interrupted by the synchronic, statistical array: "I remember he seem'd to me, as I used to talk with him, a fair specimen of the main strata of the Southerners, those without property or education, but still with the stamp which comes from freedom and equality."[74] Memory, the archive of the detail and the story, is transformed through deliberate experiential collection into a matrix of broadly indexed and catalogable types. All the more arresting then are poems like "Vigil Strange," which, because it maintains throughout an intimate, singular focus on the one successfully recovered body, remains one of the salient exceptions in *Drum-Taps*. Even this poem, however, has as its essential backdrop the tragedy of accumulation. As Wynn Thomas observes, the poem's emotional force derives from the unspoken narratives of failure that crowd around it: "The underlying, and as it were sustaining, terror in this case is Whitman's well-documented dismay at the corpses left unclaimed on the battlefield, which were so quickly disfigured and rendered unrecognizable by putrefaction."[75]

For Whitman the competition between the individual and the mass, as it occurred both in the interiorized realm of retrospection and in the exteriorized realm of the political, was an issue of concern that both predated and long survived the war. In later life Whitman would characterize *Leaves of Grass* as war-generated: an expression less true to the facts of production than to Whitman's fervid sense that his artistic and social concerns uniquely resonated with the demands of war representation.[76] As David Reynolds states: "Whitman would long remain haunted by a central question of American democracy: How can the rights of the individual be balanced against those of society? How does the 'simple, separate person' fit into democracy 'en-masse'?"[77] Many have claimed that Whitman's answer is a tendency toward a uniformity composed of deindividualized types and paratactically organized categories—this tendency, however, is often overemphasized. Consider critical reaction to the following passage:

> The groups of newly-come immigrants cover the wharf or levee,
> As the woolly-pates hoe in the sugar-field, the overseer views
> them from his saddle,
> The bugle calls in the ball-room, the gentlemen run for their
> partners, the dancers bow to each other.[78]

According to Betsy Erkkila, the catalog that includes this passage "could operate paradoxically as a kind of formal tyranny, muting the fact of inequality, race conflict, and radical difference within a rhetorical economy of many and one."[79] Critics less nuanced and sophisticated than Erkkila, operating in the tradition of D. H. Lawrence, have argued further that Whitman's relentless juxtapositions erase difference; all identity is made uniform through inclusion in the transcendent statistical union.[80] The three lines above offer contrary evidence: the antagonism they encode is as irreducible as the difference between a quadrille and a fusillade. Here, three classes and two competing orientations in time are represented: the new immigrant class, whose presence will reshape the social and economic contours of America; the African slaves, over whom a war will eventually be fought; and the Southern gentlemen, tragically oblivious to both eventualities, clinging doggedly to their outdated traditions and values, while at the same time running to the military call of a bugle in an unwitting prefiguration of the war that will soon destroy them. Whitman's paratactic style calculatedly enables a layering of interpretive possibilities that preserves the spaces of difference between poetic objects and between readers. Whitman thus cultivates difference and distinction, even while remaining at the level of categories and types.

Alcott, tending toward one representational extreme, believed that the personal introduction and narration was a testament to the individual, a tender act of remembering that elevated understanding and elicited sympathy far more effectively than body counts: encounters at intimate distance—close enough to see, to touch, to name—could be world changing. Whitman agreed but, tending toward the other representational extreme, believed that the narrative imagination was finally inadequate to the task at hand. From Alcott's perspective, private narration is a sufficiently effective social force because, as Davis writes, "public policy is a displaced and expanded form of private feeling . . . the extension of intimate forms of relation into wider political realms."[81] For Whitman, by contrast, private feeling is better conceived of as a distilled and miniaturized form of public discourse, the internalization of external forms of relation in the wider political realm. Whitman turns subjectivity inside out, so to speak, in order to replace the intensely individual with the broadly social. "My idea is a book of the time, worthy the time," Whitman writes against Alcott in the sexist language of scalar critique, "something considerably beyond mere hospital sketches."[82] Whitman believed that through her celebration of irreconcilable narratives, Alcott instituted incoherence and frustrated synthesis. To the degree that we as a culture rely too heavily upon a narrative imagination that can never incorporate the miscellany of experience, "the real war," Whitman believed, "will never get into the books."[83] Whitman's stance is contentious, but useful insofar as it points us toward a set of risks associated with narrative that are often overlooked because of the coercive emotional intimacy (experienced as participatory impulses) that narrative can generate in us. Narrative as structure, it may be argued, can appear to assume all the qualities of fiction, entering into the realm of the constructed, the made-up, the unreliable; narrative builds a teleology, muting agency with inevitability; narrative provides catharsis, which may spend an individual's energy for sympathetic action rather than magnify it; and finally, while narrative certainly does evoke compassion, it evokes a specifically *narrative* compassion not necessarily convertible into the statistical empathy needed to move the individual from the local example toward broader social action. Narration *closes* histories, narration heals; and for the activist, histories must always remain open, like a wound.

Wynn Thomas writes that in later life Whitman "became preoccupied with the responsibility of producing an appropriate personal and national memory out of the war, and was in turn also haunted by the possibility of failure in these respects. Such a failure would have been tantamount to a betrayal of the dead, and their sacred trust."[84] For Whitman, the statistical becomes a means of commemorating the dead by validating the cause for which they died. In an 1864 *New York Times* article, Whitman writes: "As this tremendous war goes on, the public interest becomes more general and gathers more and more closely about the wounded, the sick, the great Government Hospitals. Every family has directly or indirectly some representative among this vast army of the wounded and sick."[85] The whole is unified through representative, sacrificial bodies gathered together in government buildings. Metaphorically conflating the hospital with the structures of representative democracy, Whitman uses the site of the Union's greatest crisis to revivify its legitimating principle of the interchangeability of citizens in a statistically unified nation.[86]

Whitman's poetry and prose is an attempt to create a new genre of war writing, a genre appropriate to the unprecedented multiplicative array of national action. For Whitman, a national memory properly constituted must body forth from a skeletal structure built out of numbers rather than narration, out of counting rather than history:

> The dead in this war—there they lie, strewing the fields and woods and valleys and battle-fields of the south—Virginia, the Peninsula—Malvern hill and Fair Oaks—the banks of the Chickahominy—the terraces of Fredericksburgh—Antietam bridge—the grisly ravines of Manassas— the bloody promenade of the Wilderness—the varieties of the *strayed* dead . . . the clusters of camp graves, in Georgia, the Carolinas, and in Tennessee—the single graves left in the woods or by the road-side, (hundreds, thousands, obliterated)—the corpses floated down the rivers, and caught and lodged, (dozens, scores, floated down the upper Potomac, after the cavalry engagements, the pursuit of Lee, following Gettysburgh)—some lie at the bottom of the sea—the general million, and the special cemeteries in almost all the States—the infinite dead—(the land entire saturated, perfumed with their impalpable ashes' exhalation in Nature's chemistry distill'd, and shall be so forever, in every future grain of wheat and ear of corn, and every flower that grows, and every breath we draw)—not only Northern dead leavening Southern soil—thousands, aye tens of thousands, of Southerners, crumble to-day in Northern earth.
>
> And everywhere among these countless graves . . . we see, and ages yet may see, on monuments and gravestones, singly or in masses, to thousands or tens of thousands, the significant word *Unknown*.[87]

Alcott and Whitman thus represent the two opposed poles of war writing, and indeed of representation in general. If one risks dehumanization, the other risks exclusion. If statistics lose intensity and depth, narrative loses scale, proportion, and breadth. The narrative imagination establishes the reality of persons; the statistical imagination, of conditions. This distinction, as we shall see finally when we return to Crane, has important philosophical ramifications.

Royce, James, and Crane

The problem of "the one and the many," dramatized and particularized by Whitman and Alcott as a problem of commemoration, proved central in its more abstract shape to the philosophical works of and disputes between William James and Josiah Royce. What is the relationship between part and whole, and how can we represent this? How can a unit be part of a conglomerate and yet still remain distinct? Does the individual dissolve into the many, which as a collective gives purpose to each? Or is the many a collection of ones, which each produce their own purpose? These are questions about the possibility of achieving meaning, as we saw at the start with Bradley's paradox, that resolve themselves finally as a matter of counting.

The backdrop for Royce is a "world of brute natural fact" determined by "vain chance" and "caprices," "a chaos of unintelligible fragments and of scattered events" that justifies the most "pessimistic" of philosophies.[88] The world as we are "forced to observe it" is a "mystery"—it defies apprehension and resists the attribution of any coherent meaning (118). In such a world we are all separated, locked away "alone" (150) in compartments of individualism that guarantee only the multiplicity of our isolation and the universality of dissensus. The philosophical resolution, for Royce, is to reduce the confusion of the all to the simplicity and unity of the one (James characterizes such monism as the attempt to relieve the perceived "misery" of our "separation").[89] "The Individual of Individuals, namely the Absolute, or God himself, is," Royce writes. "Just such final determinateness, just such precision, definiteness, finality of meaning, constitutes that limit of your own internal meaning which our theory will hereafter seek to characterize" (133). He explains elsewhere:

> Remember, that truth is in fact your own truth, your own fulfillment, the whole from which your life cannot be divorced, the reality that you mean even when you most doubt, the desire of your heart even when you are most blind, the perfection that you unconsciously strove for even when you were an infant, the complete Self apart from whom you mean nothing, the very life that gives your life the only value which it can have. (105)

The universe, as Royce puts it, is the unified idea of a single creative will. Our tragic separation, the separation that premises counting, is therefore overcome. Royce is able to assert that the universe "is the expression of a meaning" (142) only by making counting impossible, because it is counting, and the confusing multiplicity of possibilities it points to, that challenges the reliability, stability, and singularity of the will's meaning. To illuminate his notion, Royce contrasts the idea of a musical melody with the act of counting ships upon the sea. A melody, even when manifest in the phenomenal world as sound, is an internally generated, meaningful expression of a particular free will. When one counts ships on the sea, in contrast, the idea achieved (that is, the idea "there are nine ships on the sea") is externally generated, imposed upon the will by what happen to be the facts of a contingent external world (122–127). Treated as a paradigm, this commonsense model of descriptive representation, in which the interior idea of the will arrives from the outside, appears a threat to the integrity of the free will as generator of its own meaning. In other words, a meaning may announce itself to the world (as with counting), but each individual will, if it is to be a free will, must still be able to answer the question, "Why ought *I* adopt this meaning for myself?" Counting as a threat to freedom of the will, as a threat to the intelligibility of its possibility for choice, is, as such, also a threat to the unity of meaning itself, for if the free, generative will (as part of the Absolute will that authors the universe) cannot account for the world's elements as completely as a single mind claiming its own invented melody, then it is left with a remainder that can be pointed to and counted *as separate*—the starting point of dispersion. Royce overcomes this problem by reimagining counting as coming from the inside (127–130)—that is, by dissolving the commonsense internal-external binary through the argument that the privileged term (external) is in fact parasitic upon its subordinate—but in so doing he merely reproduces the central paradox of this philosophy as a whole. The problem, which is expressed if inadequately answered in Royce's own writings, imperils the very freedom Royce needs to defend. It is a problem that William James, Royce's friend and primary adviser as well as his most severe intellectual critic, would pick up. As Royce himself writes, "Now all these considerations might seem once more to deprive any finite portion, or aspect, of this conscious universe, of any distinguishable private significance" (155). And earlier: "In consequence of these considerations, our primary question in regard to the finite human individual, in his relation to the divine life, is merely the question, In what sense does the finite Being retain, despite the unity of the whole divine life, any individual significance of his own, and what is the relation of this finite significance to the meaning and plan of the whole?" (144).

Royce's philosophical interest in the one and the many was primarily influenced by his religious beliefs, but it also bore an important relationship to his experience of the Civil War. In a brief autobiographical sketch written late in his life Royce points to the Civil War (he was ten when Lincoln was assassinated) as a notable source for his interests in community, loyalty, and political and social organization—

topics that would remain at the center of his philosophy throughout his life.[90] His first publication, an inquiry into political theory, took the assassination of Lincoln as its framing concern;[91] and shortly before his death, as he called for the development of the "community of mankind" in the face of World War I, he quoted from the debates that preceded the Civil War to argue that "what saves us on any level of human social life is union."[92]

Royce's relationship to the war was a matter of historical contiguity; for William James, by contrast, the war was a defining life event. "It seems in all truth," writes R. W. B. Lewis, "never to have been very far from the mind of that generation of Jameses."[93] William's younger brothers Robert and Wilky served in the war (Wilky returned as a hero after fighting under Colonel Shaw in the famous assault on Fort Wagner), and Henry's failure to serve was the source of significant anxiety throughout his life. William's reaction to the war took three forms: an ardent antimilitarism that received its most characteristic expression in his essay "The Moral Equivalent of War"; a fascination with the soldier as an example of "human nature *in extremis*";[94] and a pervasive sense of guilt and inadequacy for proving too weak, owing to his neurasthenia, to contemplate volunteering.[95] James's philosophical project was deeply informed, I believe, by the peculiar relationship between his self-definition and the war.[96] His writing bears the traces throughout, most obviously in his frequent resort to military examples and war rhetoric in fleshing out his ideas.[97] On several occasions James calls the problem of the one and the many, which the war had made so urgent for American culture, the most important question for all philosophy.[98] Indeed, the monism-pluralism divide cut through at all levels, ranging from issues of space and physical perception to Royce's proclamations of spiritual idealism.[99] It was a question, moreover, at the center of James's early depressive experiences. In his diary in 1870 he asks: "Are . . . the private interests and sympathies of the individual so essential to his existence that they can never be swallowed up in his feeling for the total process,—and does he nevertheless imperiously crave a reconciliation or unity of some sort. Pessimism must be his portion."[100] Despite the temptations of unifying theories, however, James rejects all forms of monism, particularly Royce's. By dissolving individuals into the aggregate, he maintains, we divest persons of uniqueness, significance, and freedom—all those things we experience as true and value in others. James offers instead a form of pluralism in which each unit acquires significance not by becoming a part of a whole but rather by remaining a whole in itself amidst other wholes: this antiabsolutist hypothesis is a philosophical effort to redeem life from captivity to union. Reality, he argues against Royce, exists "in distributive form, in the shape not of an all but of a set of eaches, just as it seems to."[101] In another context, James represents the pluralistic shape of meaning with a mathematical formula: $M + x$, in which M represents the universe as seen from the objective, agent-neutral standpoint that excludes subjectivity, and x represents the seemingly pointlike subjective stance of the individual thinker, "infinitesimal" in relative scope. The x that stands apart and seems to count for so little is in fact the feather weight that, when added in, can change the equilibrium of the most fantastic masses; it is the point from which meaning derives (97–98). As Stanley Cavell puts it in *The Claim of Reason,* there are times when I "rest on myself as my foundation."[102] Or as James writes, expressing the view that he portrayed as helping him to resist suicide in his early years: "This life *is* worth living, we can say, *since it is what we make it, from the moral point of view*" (61).

Royce argued that the pluralism of what he called compartmentalized individuals dissolves into a meaningless, relativistic multiplicity—like a circle breaking down into a scattering of dots. James reacts as strongly against this vision of pure pluralism—he calls it materialism or skepticism—as he does against Royce's opposing monism. The pluralistic world of Bradley's paradox is meaningless; it is "irrationality incarnate."[103] James's pragmatism is an attempt to find a tenable space between totalizing philosophies like Royce's and the foundationless dispersion offered hypothetically by Bradley. By adopting pluralism, he admits, one certainly does risk subverting the unity of meaning, for pluralism points to the diffusion of infinitude:

> The real world as it is given objectively at this moment is the sum total of all its beings and events now. But can we think of such a sum? Can we realize for an instant what a cross-section of all existence at a definite point of time would be? While I talk and the flies buzz, a sea-gull catches a fish at the mouth of the Amazon, a tree falls in the Adirondack wilderness, a man sneezes in Germany, a horse dies in Tartary, and twins are born in France. What does that mean? (118–119)

In a thought experiment on the possibility of moral truth, James points again to the problem numbers pose to meaning: imagine a universe occupied by one person, two people, three people—as the numbers increase the possibility of objective truth decreases (189–192). And yet we have no alternative: the universe's plurality is a fact, and it renders impossible any form of monism, any notion of a single Absolute. The "infinite" potentialities of all possibility, and indeed all of their negations, must make any monism "burst with such an obesity, plethora, and superfoetation of useless information."[104]

The pluralism-monism divide, what might be called the two-worlds view, is essential to an understanding of James's conception of consciousness and the meaningfulness of existence. On the one hand, philosophical monism is intellectually untenable; on the other, to view the universe as entirely "discontinuous," without any unifying philosophic principles, is "intolerable."[105] In his essay "Is Life Worth Living?" James asks whether or not life has any value *as such*—in other words, whether suicide is a matter of preference or value, whether life may be lived or *ought* to be lived. The question was supremely personal for James. "All last winter," he wrote in 1867, "I was on the continual verge of suicide." Months later he queried Wendell Holmes: "What reason can you give for continuing to live? What ground allege why the thread of your days should not be snapped *now*?" James's decision to live, which he represented as a philosophical choice to overcome depression,[106] was based upon "the undetermined hope" of achieving a meaningful life, of living in accordance with unified moral principles discovered to be significant.[107] In his work James relied upon a commonsense notion of the meaning of life. We are getting close to this concept when we ask some familiar questions: What is the point of my actions? Do they count for anything in the scheme of things? Is it worth it? The ascription of meaningfulness to our pursuits is what separates living from mere survival; it is the thin wedge between hope and despair, perseverance and suicide. Absent meaning, James writes, quoting the poet James Thomson, life is "a mockery, a delusion" (36). Skepticism over the meaningfulness of human pursuits, he explains, produces the "suicidal view of life" (39). There is no "intelligible unity" (41) to a universe that holds both our intellectual and spiritual aspirations toward unity and transcendence and what might be called our scientific knowledge that all the material of the universe rolls "together meaninglessly to a common doom" (41–42).

This is an uncanny, a sinister, a nightmare view of life, and its peculiar *unheimlichkeit,* or poisonousness, lies expressly in our holding two things together which cannot possibly agree,—in our clinging, on the one hand, to the demand that there shall be a living spirit of the whole; and, on the other, to the belief that the course of nature must be such a spirit's adequate manifestation and expression. (42)

The universe is logically opaque. There are *no* answers, not even to the most basic questions. Why is there existence? "Why was there anything but nonentity; why just this universal datum and not another?" (72). This lack of transparency lends urgency to the philosophical mission: if we are unable to believe in a structure of truth that gives meaning to our lives, then, because of the way our minds are structured, we might very well prefer to die. "If this life be not a real fight, in which something is eternally gained for the universe by success, it is no better than a game of private theatricals from which one may withdraw at will" (61).

It is not immediately obvious why we might feel motivated to kill ourselves in these circumstances. There may be no "point" to our lives; there may be no relationship between our hopes and dreams and the manner in which our lives unfold; indeed, there may be no necessary relationship between any one event in our lives and any other event—life may lack grammar, so to speak, or, as James puts it, we may live in a "world of mere *withness,* of which the parts were only strung together by the conjunction 'and.'"[108] But is this cause for it to end? God's plan, the good of humanity, the immortality of fame, each of these may justify an existence. But what if God does not exist, and what if the good of humanity and the immortality of fame do not matter? If our justifications themselves require justifications, or are vulnerable to skepticism, then our lives may remain perpetually unjustified. But why should justification matter more than, say, pleasure? And indeed, why should lack of justification destroy pleasure? "A nameless *unheimlichkeit* comes over us," James writes, "at the thought of there being nothing eternal in our final purposes, in the objects of those loves and aspirations which are our deepest energies" (83). James, of course, believed in meaning, and believed that the act of belief itself instantiated meaning. Just as important, however, is what James establishes as the backdrop of his philosophy. The form that he imagines the negation of meaning taking is illuminating. Here, James's rhetoric is important. Life without an arch of meaning is *"vanitas vanitatum"* (107); ungrounded beliefs belong to the "fool's paradise and lubberland" (57). Strangely, there would be something *undignified* about living under such conditions.

The fundamental premise of all philosophy, James writes, is that "the inmost nature of the reality is congenial to *powers* which you possess" (86): "We demand in [the universe] a character for which our emotions and active propensities shall be a match. Small as we are, minute as is the point by which the cosmos impinges upon each one of us, each one desires to feel that his reaction at that point is congruous with the demands of the vast whole,—that he balances the latter, so to speak, and is able to do what it expects of him" (84). The power of creating and discerning meaning is fundamental to us, and if the universe is not responsive to that then we simply do not belong, or rather we embarrassingly *mis*belong. The spectacular gap between our self-conceptions and reality mirrors the structure of comedy or farce.[109] As discussed before, such is Stephen Crane's formula: with brave oratory you prepare your village for a mighty invasion, only to face the arrival of the town drunk; you plot the dashing and heroic rescue of three prisoners-of-war, only to collapse in the face of violence. The word both Crane and James repeatedly use to describe such a condition is "absurd."[110] James uses the word to describe situations in which our humanly aspirations cannot be aligned with what we know to be philosophically true of the world (88). We are "absurd," for instance, if we know the world to be causally determined but nonetheless continue to experience our actions as free—feeling such things as regret (rather than dissatisfaction) or resentment (rather than frustration) (163–164). Just so, it would be "absurd" for an individual alone in the universe to ask himself whether or not the beliefs he held about good and evil were true: that is, it would be a conceptual contradiction for the solitary individual to seek the comforting stability of truth, because he is absolutely alone in the universe, and truth, according to James, "supposes a standard outside of the thinker to which he must conform" (191). Indeed, James's philosophy of belief as a whole reproduces the structure of the absurd. According to James, one must believe in that which one knows to be untrue. What transforms this from an absurdity or a conceptual contradiction into a coherent practice, thus reproducing James's larger philosophical move from skepticism to pragmatism, is James's notion that belief is a performative rather than recognitional act. Belief, in other words, changes the conditions of existence, making real what had previously been neither real nor unreal. James borrows from the absurd, as if to confront and banish it. But philosophical stances that deny humanity's ability fully to circumscribe its environment, while at the same time implicitly acknowledging its desire to do so, are *actually* absurd: thus, from the standpoint of monism, "all pluralism appears as absurd," just as the *regressus ad infinitum* of Bradley's paradox appears "absurd" from the standpoint of phenomenal unity.[111]

Absurdity's "peculiar *unheimlichkeit*" lies in the irreconcilability of indispensable standpoints. According to James, the original source of absurdity (for those who are unable to achieve redeeming belief) is the knowledge of death. Insofar as we continue to cherish all of our small life plans even as we realize their final insignificance, we are tragically absurd. James quotes Arthur Balfour at length in a talk designed to precede his own lecture "The One and the Many":

> The energies of our system will decay, the glory of the sun will be dimmed, and the earth, tideless and inert, will no longer tolerate the race which has for a moment disturbed its solitude. Man will go down into the pit, and all his thoughts will perish. The uneasy consciousness which in this obscure corner has for a brief space broken the contented silence of the universe, will be at rest. Matter will know itself no longer. "Imperishable monuments" and "immortal deeds," death itself, and love stronger than death, will be as though they had never been. Nor will anything that is, be better or be worse for all that the labour, genius, devotion, and suffering of man have striven through countless generations to effect.[112]

How can we be said to count in the face of such truths? It is the pressure of such skepticism (the counterpoint to Royce's idealism) that generates much of James's philosophical project.

These questions of perspectival shifting, violent scale change, and the place of subjectivity are not unique to war but are made urgent, as we saw with Grant, Sherman, Whitman, and Alcott, by war's willful brutality, its crowding, and its devaluation of individual life.[113] The spectacles of violence belittle us. "How contemptible all the usual little worldly prides & vanities & striving after appearances, seems in the midst of such scenes as these," writes Whitman.[114] We return finally to Stephen Crane's "Episode of War." Here, perspectives accumulate like the wounded that fill up the doctor's hospital, and the multiple repositioning of the lieutenant as narrative object renders him increasingly alien. By the story's end, the officer's actions seem thoroughly strange and even pathetic to us. His refusal to acknowledge his wound, attempting to sheath his sword directly after being shot as if nothing has happened; his refusal to accept any assistance from the men; his dilatory and aimless wandering toward the rear; and his final refusal to enter the hospital all bespeak the near stasis of a man hostage to warring motivations. He is compelled, on the one hand, by his acknowledgment of his injury, and on the other, by his refusal to let go of his image of himself as a whole, functioning body, and thereby to abandon the plans, dreams, and desires contingent upon his possession of a sound body. His is a *self-willed* ignorance, a helpless and panicked attempt to change an unwanted reality by simply acting as if it were not so. This two-tiered traumatic consciousness is structurally reproduced in the lieutenant's incorporation into and transcendence out of the "black mass" of the "crowds." Throughout the small space of the story, the lieutenant's perspective thus folds in upon itself repeatedly. With the wound he is diminished, trapped within the confines of the injured and vulnerable body; like a lens inverted, his consciousness suddenly expands seemingly limitlessly, and he achieves a centerless view of the world that is the source of an increasing sense of transcendence and control: "It is as if the wounded man's hand is upon the curtain which hangs before the revelations of all existence . . . the power of it . . . makes the other men understand sometimes that they are little." But just as suddenly, this centerless view reveals to him his own insignificance, his own littleness. He is left as small as he was when the story began—but now he is *aware*. "I don't suppose it matters so much as all that," he says finally of his own tragedy. Knowledge of the fallibility of the individual perspective motivates both the objective expansion of consciousness through the accumulation of perspectives and, simultaneously, derision for the individual standpoint that remains the source and enabling structure of the objective mind.[115] It is not simply that this essentially human capacity to view oneself from outside and above, to think of oneself as an instance of a more general type, is paradoxically the source for both objectivity and meaning-skepticism. Rather, it is that the double bind of consciousness here described reproduces, as a totality, the double-bind structure of absurdity. In other words, absurdity is the deep structure of consciousness itself.

This assertion requires some backtracking. Thomas Nagel has famously summarized the issue of objectivity with a pair of related yet distinct questions: how can Thomas Nagel be me? and how can I be Thomas Nagel?[116] To paraphrase Nagel: if I look at the world objectively (as indeed we are all able to) I am able to see my own particular existence as a certain type of thing amidst countless other instances of this type. When I detach the quality of *me-ness* from my own existence, I am estranged from it: my life appears to me as a fact in the world, a thing that happens or a series of events that can be explained fully without needing recourse to the concept of subjectivity. My experience of freedom in a particular choice is replaced by a "third-person" hypothesis about the event's causal determination; my sense of the importance of being me is replaced by the knowledge of its pure equivalency to other forms of the same type. Viewed objectively, I happen; I am a piece of information to be included in a total conception of the world. The universe is entirely explicable without the addition of my subjectivity—indeed, considered abstractly, there seems to be no place for it, no room for its boundlessness; it simply does not *fit*. My perspective matters, infinitely, as we all experience mattering—but only insofar as it is attached to me. Objectivity detaches that from me—or, rather, it treats the world as if such a quality does not exist, as if *I* doesn't matter. I am thus able to estrange myself from my own subjectivity, to see the absurdity of my attachment to my own particular standpoint and to all that goes along with it. I can see the absurdity of not fear as a fact, but rather my *experience* of fear, not ambitions or dreams as components of the world, but rather the particular way in which I cherish my own. We are able to hold simultaneously, indeed we *must* hold, two mutually exclusive views of the universe, like Henry Fleming from *The Red Badge of Courage*, who alternates between narcissism and abjection throughout the novel.

The narrative logic of *The Red Badge of Courage*, indeed, self-consciously reproduces the perspectival shifts of this objective-absurd vision of consciousness. *The Red Badge of Courage* is both a story about Henry Fleming *and* Henry Fleming's story. The common readerly elision of these discrete stances in the novel obscures its structuring doubleness of viewpoints. As narration *The Red Badge of Courage* stands somewhere between *Tom Jones* and *The Catcher in the Rye*. The novel begins with the external viewpoint of the narrator and descends slowly into the consciousness of the "youthful private."[117] Throughout the novel, expansive objectivity alternates with confinement to subjective apprehension, and a sense of the self's importance in the universe alternates with a sense of its irrelevance. Crane forces us to inhabit both standpoints, to feel each experience, because, as he believes, both are essential to what it means to be a human being. As James puts it repeatedly in *A Pluralistic Universe,* we can conceive of the world as a background of "foreignness" or of "intimacy" (19), a place that was made for us, so to speak, like a home, or a place that is alien to our capacities and drives and to our search for meaning. Crane's ironic duality of perspective is an attempt to get at what is fundamental to the absurd; irony is the primary literary analogue of the absurd or, alternatively, absurdity is irony raised to the level of a philosophy. Absurdity is distinct from irony, however, in one fundamental way: with the absurd, there is no longer a superior position to occupy; the height from which things appear ironic is now not the narrator's position but rather the God's-eye view from which we are excluded. Absurdity is irony inhumanly scaled. Crane uses a variety of other representational strategies to convey the absurd condition, in which subjectivity is perceived not to fit into a universe that excludes meaning: they include an emphasis on distortions of vision, inscrutability, and an inability to see correctly;[118] grammatical structures that convey an alienation from one's own condition (for instance, from *The Red Badge of Courage,* "He thought that he wished");[119] the use of violent scale changes (as in "The Blue Hotel," which through perspectival shifts transforms humans into lice);[120] and an alienation of humanity from the natural environment, the transformation of belonging into exile (see for instance "The Open Boat," as well as Crane's frequent use of the pathetic fallacy, which commemorates our anxious need to imagine continuity between the mind and its external conditions).

We live, Crane insists, in two worlds. We can, so to speak, perceive ourselves through the statistical imagination (as the doctor perceives the lieutenant, as Sherman perceives his infantry) or through the narrative imagination (as the subalterns perceive the lieutenant, as Alcott perceives John). Through a self-willed ignorance we are typically able to maintain the single, coherent view of subjectivity or intimacy—but in unexpected and traumatic crises, such as an encounter with death or with a sudden explosion of numbers, we can be jarred into assuming the objective view, a view that we simultaneously acknowledge and prepare to disown. Our acknowledgment of the view reveals us as trivial; our evasion of it renders us absurd. Hence the final, enigmatic lines of "An Episode of War." Here the lieutenant stands foolish and chagrined at the tears he shares over a meaningless happenstance:

"And this is the story of how the lieutenant lost his arm. When he reached home, his sisters, his mother, his wife, sobbed for a long time at the sight of the flat sleeve. 'Oh, well,' he said, standing shamefaced amid these tears, 'I don't suppose it matters so much as all that'" (323).

It is important that the lieutenant consciously suppresses his awareness of his wound in the first part of the story, and that he has lost his arm by the second. In Crane's phantasmagoria, the figurative is made physical. The lieutenant, in both cases, functions disabled of his full human power, like a *consciousness inherently structured to avoid full awareness of itself.* The lieutenant, unnamed, is a placeholder for all identities and perspectives, including you and me. "An Episode of War" is thus an exercise in contempt not only for the lieutenant, but also for the reader, and the author himself. We are contemptible because we remain attached to our own personal desires, ends, and ambitions when we know that they have been rendered irrelevant not simply by a universe that is malignant and brutal but, more frighteningly, by a universe in which desires, ends, and ambitions—all of those things that give life meaning—have no place.

In one of his later works on the Spanish-American War, Crane returns to the problem of individuality and the damaged body. "The Upturned Face" is the excruciating story of the difficulty two officers confront in burying a comrade and friend: it dramatizes their inability to integrate the knowledge that he is dead into their relationship with his physical body. Like "An Episode of War" it is a story of conflicting perspectives: how a wounded man views battle, how an unwounded man does; how a friend views a corpse, how a stranger views a corpse; how a man who must touch a corpse sees it, how a man who need not does. It is also, like "An Episode of War," a story of shame and embarrassment—but now for very different reasons. In order to bury the body in the middle of a battle, they must treat it as an object. They must assault their friend's autonomy by pulling and pushing his body. They must violate his privacy by removing personal possessions from his pockets. The tension mounts to the final indignity, when they must empty the last shovelfuls of dirt onto his face. The face as source of beauty (symmetry, balance) and source of sentience (language, expression, vision) is also the source of individuality, and it holds us in relationship with the firmness of a moral claim—a claim durable even in death. The embarrassment of "An Episode of War" is a rational embarrassment born of cognitive dissonance; it points to the insignificance of the individual. Here, relationship with a physical body generates an embarrassment almost sensual; it is a nonrational response that commemorates the unalterable sovereignty of the individual subject, a response far more deep and visceral than the countervailing force of objectivity.

"The Upturned Face" is representative of Crane's writing on the Spanish-American War, and its contrast to the cultural memory of the Civil War could not be more stark. In these later stories (generated out of his work as a war correspondent for Pulitzer) bias governs all. Bias against the enemy and in favor of the individual self repeatedly prevents the establishment or maintenance of any objective view of the situation: individuality trumps irony, perhaps even in stories like "This Majestic Lie." The swift, relatively uncostly victory of the United States in its conflict against Spain re-romanticized war. Now the enduring importance of the individual matched the proven importance of the nation: a unique and special meaning could be found in each. It pushed into the past the trauma of the Civil War and replaced the image of conflict as mass slaughter with the image of conflict as a test of individual courage; it replaced the anonymous corpse with the fallen hero.[121] The war was thus the source of a new American confidence to achieve and to overcome combat's material limits through will alone. It was an attitude woefully unfitted for the century of technological and organizational domination that awaited it.

CHAPTER TWO

Care and Creation:
The Anglo-American Modernists

The logic of counting is structural equivalency and personal irrelevance, a logic that does not simply reflect war's massive scale or violence's indiscriminateness but that participates in and reinforces this
pervasive commensurability. From its inception, the law of land war
was designed to work against this representational tendency, to revivify the power of language to discriminate. Indeed, it made this power
to discriminate and to mark difference its primary and essential function: central to the first of the Geneva Conventions (1864) was the
designation of medical personnel with a distinct red cross on a white
background, which signified protected status. With the birth of this
sign, international human rights law received its modern incarnation.
During the American Civil War, shortly before Sherman began his Atlanta campaign, Dr. Francis Lieber drew up for the Union army one of
the world's first national manuals outlining the laws of land warfare—the manual, which underscored the importance of discriminating combatants from noncombatants as well as wanton destruction
from "military necessity," became the model for many other nations,
including the Netherlands, France, Spain, Portugal, and Italy. At the
same time in Geneva, Henry Dunant was establishing an international
committee for treatment of the wounded (later renamed the International Committee of the Red Cross, or ICRC) and was working to
convene an international diplomatic conference to ratify the first of
the Geneva Conventions. The series of language events that followed,

embodied in the law of the Hague and Geneva, worked consistently to resist military representation's tendency to flatten out distinction, to make discrimination impossible.

As they evolved, the international laws of war also functioned to resist the second effect of violence upon representation examined in this book: namely, violence's destabilization of epistemological and moral categories. With World War I in particular, the definitional frameworks of international law were brought into question. Modification and amplification of the laws of war accelerated accordingly. The unusual duration of the war, with its unprecedented number of prisoners taken, and technological advances, including especially the use of chemical weapons, shocked nations into a more vigorous attempt to regulate treatment of prisoners and to control methods of attack.[1] What was the moral status, for instance, of flamethrowers? Or of mustard gas, which caused blistering of the eyes, skin, and lungs in 40,000 soldiers when it was first used in July 1917, and in 400,000 by war's end? Technology, wrote the German veteran Ernst Jünger, made obsolete the aimable weapon. "Giving out the night-flight bombing order, the squadron leader no longer sees a difference between combatants and civilians, and the deadly gas cloud hovers like an elementary power over everything that lives."[2] For jurists and military officials, the technologization and industrialization of combat brought into question received conceptions of categories such as "weapon," "target," "protected noncombatants," "justified reprisal," and "necessary and unnecessary suffering." For the culture as a totality, it brought into question an even more fundamental set of terms.

As Paul Fussell has argued, the trenches of World War I were a murderous parody of the normal, industrial world of "work." Trench sections were organized around ruined architecture like a complex system of familiar city streets: soldiers obeyed ubiquitous traffic signs and bedded down in "Piccadily," "Regent Street" and "the Strand." Men spent most of their time in acts of production, in the work of creation and repair: at night digging parties extended saps; wiring parties repaired wire; carrying parties delivered mail and rations; and all others worked with timbers, stakes, A-frames, and sandbags to rebuild damaged trenches.[3] Jünger, Germany's preeminent chronicler of the front experience, writes: "The image of war as armed combat merges into the more extended image of a gigantic labor process . . . following the wars of knights, kings, and citizens, we now have wars of *workers.*"[4] Indeed, the work of the war was not only urban manual labor but also invention; it was competition not only of sweat and strength but also of technological systems and genius. Technology followed a withering pattern of call and response throughout the war: the invention of the Hiram Maxim machine gun led to the imagination and eventual realization of the tank; poison gas birthed poison gas masks; the need to overcome insuperable trench systems inspired experimentation with aerial torpedoes; and the recently invented Dreadnought class battleship, which had made all previous navies obsolete in an instant, led to the invention of the submarine, which made obsolete the Dreadnought.[5]

The decades preceding the war were a period of unprecedented growth and conspicuous invention, the golden era of the independent inventor as cultural icon. It was the era of Nikola Tesla's garish tower laboratory and his spectacular public displays of electrical transmission, the era of the Wright Brothers, Henry Ford, and most notably Thomas Edison, the Wizard of Menlo Park, the inventor become national symbol.[6] It was also an era of unprecedented material largesse and creativity, an era encompassing the invention and proliferation of cash-and-carry chain stores, advertising agencies, mail-order catalogs, electrified trolleys, department stores, plate-glass windows and window shopping, all of which together "democratized luxury," awakening an ever expanding circle of desire while simultaneously promising that it could always be fulfilled, for everyone.[7] The age is epitomized in the architecture of William Le Baron Jenney, Louis Sullivan, and the Chicago School. Their skyscrapers, like fists jutting to the heavens, became anthropomorphic symbols of human triumph, tributes to creativity's victory over the resistance of the material world.

By the turn of the century, technological euphoria had helped to generate what might be called an industrial worldview, a system of self-description in which all action could be reformulated with reference to the central cultural symbols of making.[8] The benign metaphoric conflations of this industrial worldview were produced by and helped initiate fundamental reconceptualizations of the human condition. In public discourses ranging from the most popular to the most erudite, the human body began to resemble an artifact of industrial creation: William James compares the brain's processes to the production of magnets and the alteration of rubber, and in his essay "Are We Automata?" he repeatedly calls the brain a "machine";[9] Eugen

Sandow, whose bodybuilding course followed the slogan "The Man in the Making," compares the "machinery" of the body to a steam engine;[10] and the efficiency expert F. W. Taylor reconceptualized the individual worker as a piece of machinery, whose every motion could be precisely timed, standardized, and controlled.[11] Free human activity, likewise, began to seem mechanized: in *La Bête Humaine* (1890), Émile Zola associates the most violent extremes of human sexual desire with the "hammer-blows and multitudinous clamourings" of trains;[12] Jack London, who set for himself the factorylike quota of one thousand words per day production, continually emphasizes throughout *Martin Eden* the contiguity between the work of the assembly-line laborer and the work of the writer, the equivalent "machine-likeness of the process";[13] and William James describes habitual behavior like "piano-playing, talking, even saying one's prayers" as "machine-like."[14]

With World War I, the practice of seeing actions and objects first in relation to industrial technology began to lose its benign character. What had previously been a means of expressing a certain cultural fascination, of reanimating and illuminating familiar objects through perspectival change, now functioned primarily to distort perception and obscure reality. For Thomas Edison this technological vision amounted to an imaginative reflex, allowing him to say of a war that had already initiated its eventual 21.5 million person body count: This war, "if the United States engages in it, will be a war in which machines, not soldiers, fight . . . the new soldier will not be a soldier, but a machinist." Indeed, as he phrased it, the new soldier will not bleed on the battlefield; he will sweat in the factory.[15] For others the industrial worldview manifested itself more subtly, as a vocabulary that provided familiar borders to otherwise stupefying traumas and disasters. Frank Richards describes killing a man who shams death as an "ordinary" part of "a runner's work,"[16] Robert Graves describes poison gas attacks on the enemy as a "responsible" "job,"[17] and Ernst Jünger continually reimagines explosive shells as productive engines that "plough" fields.[18] Willa Cather presents the man produced by army machinery as a factory-fresh good, *"a new man"* or "a finished product,"[19] Ernest Jones criticizes clinical psychology's early failures in treating war trauma as a waste in "human material,"[20] and British veteran Siegfried Sassoon, with his standard coping mechanism of gallows humor, compares the nightmarish, factorylike trench system to a large German "Sausage Machine."[21] Sassoon's grotesque image deliberately satirizes this wartime tendency to reconfigure disorder and waste through productive industrial metaphor, but also at the same time relies upon this process of therapeutic reconfiguration— for, however much more sophisticated gallows humor may be than less self-conscious coping mechanisms, it is, nonetheless, a standard coping mechanism.

Peacetime metaphors of creation were enlisted to make sense of an entirely new species of destruction. Peacetime artifacts were enlisted to enable it: World War I saw the application to battle of the telephone, barbed wire, air travel, and safety devices like the guidance and control gyroscope (an innovation that won a 50,000-franc prize for "Safety in Airplanes" now redesigned to make possible the "pilotless flying bomb").[22] In the decades preceding the war, the painstaking care of the inventor, the revelation of travel, and the small, humble objects of the home had been buoyantly imagined as motors and symbols of a global unity achievable through the inclusive embrace of modern material culture.[23] What were the products of creation to be in the twentieth century? After the sinking of the *Sussex* in 1916, the National Academy of Sciences unanimously endorsed the resolution of its foreign secretary, George Hale, to "place itself at the disposal" of the U.S. government for the purposes of war preparation.[24] "This much is clear," wrote Robert Millikan, future Nobel laureate in physics, "If the science men of this country are going to be of any use to her it is now or never."[25] Thomas Edison—who had declared that he would not "invent implements of warfare" and had claimed the dove as his "emblem"—now publicly offered to the American people a plan for industrial combat and promised a profusion of ideas for weaponry.[26] Edison was described at the time as "the one man who can turn dreams into realities,"[27] but the describer, Secretary of the Navy Daniels, had in mind a different sort of dream than what Elaine Scarry calls the "compassion made effective" of domestic invention.[28] What were the products of creation to be in the twentieth century? As an American speaking with Hiram Maxim commented bluntly: "Hang your chemistry and electricity! If you want to make a pile of money, invent something that will enable these Europeans to cut each other's throats with greater facility."[29] Maxim's response was the single most marketable invention of the era, the Maxim machine gun, an invention that helped to produce 60,000 casualties before the end of the first day at the Somme.

By 1914 technology had invented modern war, and modern war

had so effectively blurred the borders between work and waste, between creation and destruction, that spectacular acts of dismantling became for many a source of shameful exultation, the telos of the human will to power. Throughout his diaries and fiction, Siegfried Sassoon luxuriates in the "angry beauty" of battle, in the landscape illuminating flashes of artillery and gunfire,[30] and Ernst Jünger continually celebrates the "fascinating and imposing" signs of the new "machine-made" war, in particular "marvelling" at the unlimited scope of destruction and ubiquitous "beautiful green patina" of gas attacks.[31] For D. H. Lawrence, the zeppelin in combat became the final symbol of the terrible magic of human artifice. Witnessing an assault on London in 1915, he writes:

> Then we saw the Zeppelin above us, just ahead, amid a gleaming of clouds: high up, like a bright golden finger, quite small, among a fragile incandescence of clouds. And underneath it were splashes of fire as the shells fired from earth burst. Then there were flashes near the ground— and the shaking noise. It was like Milton—then there was war in heaven. But it was not angels. It was that small golden Zeppelin, like an long oval world, high up. It seemed as if the cosmic order were gone, as if there had come a new order, a new heavens above us: and as if the world in anger were trying to revoke it . . . It seems the Zeppelin is in the zenith of the night, golden like a moon, having taken control of the sky; and the bursting shells are the lesser lights. So it seems our cosmos is burst, burst at last, the stars and moon blow away, the envelope of the sky burst out, and a new cosmos appeared . . . Everything is burst away now, there remains only to take on a new being.[32]

The war's loss and waste could not obscure the fact that its destruction was also a consummate achievement, an act sublime and gratuitous which, like a celebration of the world's surplus through a border-dissolving festival of consumption, far surpassed the largesse of more familiar, routine, and controlled acts of survival-oriented production. The end of World War I, accordingly, marked the beginning of a sustained cultural meditation on the nature of creation, a meditation made urgent by war's confusion and anxiety, and by the intimacy of cruelty, the realization that exhilaration, seduction, and even care were as natural to acts of violence as they were to compassion.

This chapter traces the concept of creation through various literary registers of the postwar period, establishing the questions that will structure the remainder of this book. What is the relationship between creation and consumption, and what are the links between the sublime and waste? between beauty and damage? What necessary relationship, if any, does the act of creating (creating with objects, creating with words) have with violence? And what processes can be built into the structure of creation to inhibit this potential? What does the created object (tool, weapon, novel, bureaucracy, legal treaty) require of its maker, and what responsibility does the maker bear to the social world? The experience of modern war changed forever the way societies would answer these questions, as well as the way they would ask them.[33]

Modernism

"It was in 1915 the old world ended," D. H. Lawrence agreed.[34] In a series of epistemological maneuvers that matched the war's physical dismantling of civilizations, writers of the Anglo-American avant-garde came upon a new form of truth: the truth of fraud exposed. War had revealed the lies of Western civilization: for Ernest Hemingway the lie of "abstract words such as glory, honor, courage or hallow";[35] for Ezra Pound the "old men's lies" that lured millions to their deaths; and for John Dos Passos the state lies that brought John Andrews to war, desertion, and an anticipated execution in *Three Soldiers,* along with the lies of science and industrialism that generated the "rabies" of war itself.[36] The "lies," wrote Dos Passos, "choke one like poison gas."[37] The social structures humanity had created and believed in were as absurd and malignant as the bureaucracy that imprisoned E. E. Cummings in *The Enormous Room.* On the largest scale, civilization was "botched," as Pound wrote, "an old bitch gone in the teeth."[38]

The literary reaction to war revealed a pervasive fixation on the crisis of what humanity had made and what it could make, with the failed promises of human creation at all its sites—artistic, moral, scientific, biological. Of this fragmented and heterogeneous body of writing only two limited generalizations are possible: first, that the dominant Spencerian-Hegelian concept of teleological evolution vanished; and, second, that it was *not* replaced with the apocalyptic visions of U.S. history that marked much of the literature anticipating and reacting to the national cataclysm of the Civil War—the looming dread of Melville's *Moby Dick,* for instance, or the technological holocaust of Twain's *A Connecticut Yankee in King Arthur's Court.*[39] "We can best identify the special nature of this great catastrophe," writes Jünger, "by the assertion that in it, the genius of war was penetrated by the spirit of progress."[40] The nightmare of World War I, as expressed in Anglo-American modernism, was not that the world was spiraling into indiscriminate butchery and thus to a final end, but rather that the world was spiraling into indiscriminate butchery and that humanity could live with it—indeed, could make an industry of it.[41]

The question of the war's relationship to modernism, an increasingly permeable category of literary-historical analysis, merits some attention. Many critics have argued, for instance, that it was the radical social change associated with the war that brought to full realization the high-modernist aesthetic movement.[42] The methods of the past were increasingly unusable, as T. S. Eliot announced in 1921: the modern poet "must become more and more comprehensive, more allusive, more indirect, in order to force, to dislocate if necessary, language into his meaning."[43] As Virginia Woolf wrote in 1922: "Words have been used too often; touched and turned, and left exposed to the dust of the street. The words we seek hang close to the tree."[44] Much later she connected this effort to revitalize language with the effort to redeem a society structured to produce violence. "We can best help you to prevent war," she writes in *Three Guineas,* "not by repeating your words and following your methods but by finding new words and creating new methods."[45] Paul Fussell makes the connection between war and modernist innovation explicit. Before World War I, he states,

> There was no *Waste Land,* with its rats' alleys, dull canals, and dead men who have lost their bones: it would take four years of trench warfare to bring these to consciousness. There was no *Ulysses,* no *Mauberley,* no *Cantos,* no Kafka, no Proust, no Waugh, no Auden, no Huxley, no Cummings, no *Women in Love* or *Lady Chatterley's Lover.* There was no "Valley of Ashes" in *The Great Gatsby.* One read Hardy and Kipling and Conrad and frequented worlds of traditional moral action delineated in traditional moral language.[46]

As one critic puts it, "modernism after 1914 begins to look like a peculiar but significant form of war writing."[47] Other scholars have disputed this thesis, however, pointing out that "many of the features of style and form we associate with [modernist] fiction had emerged much earlier,"[48] and also that more traditional nineteenth- and early-twentieth-century images and conventions continued to prove useful and were even revitalized after the war.[49] In this debate two points emerge with clarity. First, the cultural dislocations of the war era both abetted developing Anglo-American modernist experimentalism and contributed to its legitimacy as a totemic aesthetic legacy;[50] and, second, modernist concerns and techniques well served those writers inside and outside the high-modernist canon who were interested in creating an appropriate and enduring cultural memory of the war and its aftermath (for instance, Dos Passos's use of fragment, or Cummings's and Cather's interpolations of mythoallegorical and historical resources). In other words, if the war shaped how we remember modernism, then modernism also shaped how we remember the war.

In the remainder of this section I want to focus on three substantive topics in the literary reaction to war. The recurring images and structural patterns I will be underscoring can be simplified and usefully accounted for as a series of three interlocking interests: an interest in enclosure, in the deconstruction of artifacts, and in the failure of human reproduction. While my primary focus is U.S. literature, I will continue to traverse the national borders so fiercely defended by militarists at that time, borders that even now set artificial limits to the intellectual and cultural hybridity of the era.

Enclosure.

Postwar literature was marked by a suspicion of creation exercised at the scale of the public (building industries, cities, nations) and by a concomitant retreat to the diminutive ranges and more controllable outcomes of private creation (making a home, a dinner party, a family, or a work of art).[51] In his *Memoirs*, Sherwood Anderson recalls the terrible anger he felt at being labeled a "great" artist by his friend Waldo Frank:

> It was when the World War was on and I had hidden myself.
> I had got here a room in a working men's quarter of the city. I was hiding there.
> It was a time of too much "greatness."
> Great generals.
> Great statesmen.
> Great hatreds sweeping up through the world.

Great writers glorifying war.

Great diplomats at work.

It was a flood. It was to me terrible, unbearable. I had hidden myself away. More and more I had retreated into an old life I had known before the war came. I wanted passionately now to think not of great soldiers, statesmen, writers, but of being first of all little.[52]

After World War I the literature of production, of Jack London and Theodore Dreiser, gave way to a literature of exhaustion, to a literature of the small, of retreats, frames, and safely bounded spaces. If the defining shape of prewar naturalist literature is the extending line—the assembly line, which makes simultaneous creation and travel, and the railroad track, which extends its penetration into the local—then the defining shape of one major strand of postwar literature is the closing line, or the circle. The circle is the shape of elitism, tribalism, and the solipsism of self-gratification—from Fitzgerald to Dos Passos—but it is also the shape of both shelter and embrace, like a body closing in on itself to cover pain. British war veteran David Jones, who like Hemingway preferred corner seats in restaurants, described his usual mode of painting thus: "I always work from a window of a house if it is possible. I like looking out on the world from a reasonably sheltered position."[53] Eschewing her family's publicly political heritage, its aggressive participation in the dismantling and rebuilding of nations, Gertrude Stein's Alice Toklas writes similarly: "I myself have had no liking for violence and have always enjoyed the pleasures of needlework and gardening. I am fond of paintings, furniture, tapestry, houses and flowers even vegetables and fruit trees. I like a view but I like to sit with my back turned to it."[54] Protective enclosure is especially important to Willa Cather's novel of 1925 *The Professor's House,* which blends local color into the modern with a story about a professor who has lost to the war his brightest student, an idealistic young inventor named Tom Outland. In the book's summary tableau the despairing Godfrey St. Peter contemplates the borderless space of the external world through the small framed window of his workroom retreat, from the safety of an enclosed space. In a letter to a friend, Cather compared her tableaulike stylistics in *The Professor's House* to the interior spaces of Dutch paintings—paintings remarkable, for Cather, because of their common inclusion of a small square window opening out onto the gray sea.[55] Cather conceived of her novel as an accumulation of frames within frames, from the material frames of Godfrey St. Peter's abandoned house to the narrative frames of Tom Outland's story within the story. "Framing," writes Jean Schwind, "is the subject as well as the form of *The Professor's House.*"⁵⁶

The window frame's circumscription of space is the novel's image of both the safety and stability of borders as well as the necessity of apertures for escape. The circle is thus also the shape and end point of retreat. In Claude McKay's *Home to Harlem,* which severally decries "progress," the white man's war, and the mechanical as thematized against the natural, Jake's escape from service during the war is self-consciously doubled in Jake and Felice's retreat from the dangers of Harlem to the safety of Chicago.⁵⁷ Against the safe, loving "circle" of their romance McKay posits the riotous, vicious life of the railroad lines—but it is the circle that closes the novel.⁵⁸ Against the lines of force extending multiply from the industrial North, the writers of the 1929 Southern agrarian manifesto *I'll Take My Stand* privilege the "fixed, closed world" of the South: they romanticize the traditional agrarian structure and "eternal cycles" of the farmer's "orbit," his "spot of ground"; and they defend "provincialism," defined here as "a man's interest in his own center," as the last retreat of the just man.⁵⁹ The postwar reflex toward gestures of enclosure is, however, most emphatically—and ambivalently, for retreat is also surrender—manifest in the myriad (an)aesthetic frames of Virginia Woolf: the assiduously policed borders of Mrs. Ramsay's domestic sphere and the framed space of Lily Briscoe's painting; the seclusion of Clarissa Dalloway's attic, where she reads of the retreat from Moscow, and the window onto the Westminster sky that closes her presence in the novel, reproducing the window of Septimus Smith's final escape from Dr. Holmes;⁶⁰ and the perpetual borders of Orlando's timeless estate, itself the idealized materialization of the need for return and closure that is ironically doubled in the tingling circle on Orlando's finger, a tingling that can be assuaged only by the circle of a wedding band.

A great deal of postwar avant-garde literature depicts failed linearity in association with technoskepticism derived from the war. Faulkner's *Flags in the Dust* is the story of Bayard Sartoris's war trauma and his return to a modernizing South. Its hybrid critique of both the new and the traditional, the invented and the inherited, positions a model of social regress through historical and technological advance against the realities of consuetudinary stagnancy and provincialism.

Its antimodernism manifests itself in paradigmatic juxtapositions. The vainglorious cavalry romances of the Civil War, ceaselessly recounted as the adventures of individual family heroes, are set against the antinarratives of modern airborne combat, experiences relayed "without beginning," and again later, "without beginning or end."[61] In related pairings, Bayard's delirious automobile accident (section 4.4) is immediately juxtaposed to the agrarian, premechanical, and uniquely peaceful lives of the MacCallums (section 4.5), and modern Dr. Alford's arrogance, his urgent fear and surety of the body's weakness, and his aggressive diagnosis of cancer, are contrasted to the calm, fatherly wisdom of Dr. Lucius Peabody, who "had practiced medicine in Yocona county when a doctor's equipment consisted of a saw and a gallon of whisky and a satchel of calomel," and to the folk medicine of Will Falls, who correctly identifies Bayard Sr.'s "cancer" as curable with a salve.[62] The linear progress of history culminates in enervated and useless Horace Benbow, whose glassware art is as sterile and valueless as the cotton speculation that funds the playground of leisure he occupies. The burgeoning of this vacuous leisure class, grotesquely doubled in the "spread" of the Snopeses,[63] displaces the traditional aristocracy and values of the Old South. Organic communities, communities enduring over time, rooted in geographical stability and an unquestioned "natural" order of racist values, are replaced by invented communities—communities become vectors, communities of the moment, of markets, speculation, and a disruptive social mobility that confuses class borders (consider Horace's dismally mismatched marriage to Belle). Speed replaces tradition; artifice assumes the traces of artificial. History's destructive linear acceleration is emblematized in Bayard Sartoris's progress toward suicide, a forward moving journey through increasingly manufactured accidents: from horse, to car, to the final lethal damage of plane.[64]

The Deconstruction of Artifacts.

Dos Passos's singular work novel *The Big Money* (1936), the finale of his epic *U.S.A.*, refigures technoskepticism through a mechanical rather than communitarian nostalgia. Providing an encyclopedic account of postwar America that opens with the return of a group of soldiers from World War I, it traces the decline of work, or the translation of productivity from the actual to the virtual. It is a book of double vision, written during the Great Depression but attributing its cynicism about the system of production to the pre-Depression era. The book is about the deaths of great innovators (Taylor, Ford, the Wright Brothers, Frank Lloyd Wright) and the ascendancy of actors, salesmen, and advertising magnates like J. Ward Moorehouse. Epitomized by the hysterical Florida land boom that closes the novel, *The Big Money* replaces production with talk and identifies that as the nature of America: "This is going to be more than a publicity campaign, it's going to be a campaign for Americanism."[65] It chronicles the transformation of Charley Anderson from war hero, inventor, and mechanic into an enervated and sterile financier, comprehensively alienated from any material production; and it eulogizes the death of the archetypal loyal worker with the dismissive comment, "After all, he was only a mechanic."[66]

If Dos Passos laments the impossibility of work, or rather the emptiness of what is made, Willa Cather laments its brutality. The anticipatory model for Dos Passos's vision of creative degeneration is Cather's *Professor's House*.[67] Cather's book is fundamentally concerned with the act of making, tracing its full process from immaterial idea to material object ("Without capital to make it go, Tom's idea was merely a formula written out on paper")[68] and luxuriating in the expansive range of its possibilities, from the "genesis" (31) of a scientist's airplane engine to an artist's book, from a small, private garden to the lost civilizations of the Blue Mesa. *How* did they build? Cather lingers over an array of tools and designs (89, 238); and she makes the sensuous detail of hands—writing hands, sewing hands, digging hands—a central motif of the book (3, 14, 23, 36, 103, 125, 133, 236, 250 and *passim*). In turn Cather reveals the authorial hand; she turns her own work inside out, exposing the interior of narrative production. It is a book about the process of writing books, from social histories (the professor's *Spanish Adventurers in North America*) to personal memoirs (Tom Outland's diary). Here Cather's penchant for painstaking introductions, building block by block the body of each character as she enters the novel, thematizes the author's role as designer, as builder of body parts. The self-reflexive novel opens with a history of the construction and repairs of the professor's first house from porch inward to bath (paragraphs 1–2), followed immediately by the narrative presentation of the professor's body from bones outward to skin (paragraph 3), followed immediately by his daughter's watercolor representations of his "statue"-like form (paragraph 4), followed immediately by the professor's "making" of a French garden (paragraphs 5–9), returning to his designed spaces inside the house (paragraphs 10–12), and concluding finally with the artificial female bodies from which his housemaid makes dresses (paragraphs 13–15). Each form of artifice blends into another, until, indeed, all forms in the novel begin to reveal themselves as constructed. Each year's students appear as a "new crop"; there is always the danger of feeling that one has "produced" them (42, 50). Likewise Professor St. Peter and his wife are able to see beneath the opera its blueprint. For the aging couple *Mignon* slips easily back and forth between spectacle and mesmerism (the eye of the lover) and program (the eye of the critic). For one who knows how a thing is made, how an illusion is produced—is the female lead "right for the part"? how does the cast compare to the Comique? are the woodwinds off? (77–78)—it takes an effort of imagination to receive it as an organic whole rather than as a made thing of many made parts, each of which can be suitable or not. Indeed, the machinations of the opera's libretto move the St. Peters to consider what they have made of their own marriage, whether they have made it dramatic, beautiful, or even appropriate. Cather scrutinizes especially the artifice of gender. Like opera itself, her women are each a performance; each is a "self-revelatory" "form" like Augusta's female mannequins (10). Cather exposes the "game" (64, 140) of their appearance and behavior, reveals even the training that teaches them how to hold their heads in a properly docile manner when walking (52). Gendered bodies, Cather demonstrates, are *made*, painstakingly, continuously.[69]

As with body so with spirit: even morality is made-up. Indeed, in this particular system morality conforms to the prior value-matrix of artisanship and aesthetics: a well-executed, beautiful, or appropriate thing is "good"; the ugly or inappropriate is "bad." Art and religion are interchangeable (55); "evidences of human labor" are "stirring" (173) and "sacred" (199); and that which is good must also be "glittering" (94). Indeed, at the extremes, morality is *displaced* by the epistemology of making. Attempted suicide is "ugly" (254), a "social misdemeanor" (258); jealousy is physically "ugly" (71), and greed is "unbecoming" (130); overdressing is cruel (70), and an ugly look is "naughty" (146).[70] This conflation of *techné* with morality leads to a mutual demotion, reducing ethics to appearances and beauty to correctness (140). Indeed, if morality is valuable for humans precisely insofar as it is conceived as the sphere of the enduring and transcendent, it is rendered worthless, according to Cather, when tied into the cyclic instability of creation. New houses replace old houses; beauty eventually decays. In Cather's world, few things can be constructed without including in them a vision of their deconstruction. It is for her an abiding concern, manifest as well in her repetition of the famous concluding line of Shakespeare's Sonnet 94 throughout her novel *A Lost Lady*: "Lilies that fester smell far worse than weeds." In *The Professor's House,* while sensuously working up Rosamond's brilliant beauty, Cather inserts within, like a canker in a rose, an alternative vision of her thick, masculine awkwardness (26–27); and her introduction of Professor Horace Langtry as a young man, "with curly brown hair and such a fresh complexion that the students called him Lily Langtry" (41), is undone by Cather's and time's reckless human vandalism in the immediately subsequent description of him as aged, gray, drooping, and cross (41). Cather's deconstructive vision culminates in Outland's discovery of the lost city of the Blue Mesa, where creation and destruction are slammed together and their cycle flattened out. The process of archaeological reconstruction treats simultaneously the flowering and the demise of civilizations: recovered artifacts reveal a people dedicated to "the arts of peace" (197) and exterminated in war for "the mere love of slaughter" (198). Discovery commemorates loss; creation is delayed obsolescence. Even worse, according to Cather, the perpetual cycle of death and renewal represented by the archaeological site is transformed by modern society into a linear process of degeneration. The final outcome of Outland's discovery is desecration: the Blue Mesa is parceled up by a villainous German and its treasures sold as curios. The created object is thus perpetually vulnerable to accident, to the contingent damages of time. And if this exposed, fragile created object is also the primary source of human value, displacing even the sphere of the moral, then lives must always, it seems, end in desecration.

For the novel as a whole, as for the history of the Blue Mesa or the arc of a human body through time, the end point is failure. The book opens, as noted, with a fixation on the optimism of building. The young professor's declaration—"I will do this dazzling, this beautiful, this utterly impossible thing!" (16)—is an anthem not only to writing (his and Cather's), but also to the possibility of building houses that such writing makes possible (23) and to the faith in the future that

building houses implies (28)—indeed, that all effort at making implies. "A man can do anything if he wishes to enough, St. Peter believed. Desire is creation, is the magical element in that process. If
there were an instrument by which to measure desire, one could foretell achievement" (19–20). The book ends, however, with a thorough
repudiation of "achievement." At the novel's close, the professor considers all that he has made with his life—marriage, children, home,
career, self. Weighing it dispassionately, he finds it wanting. Where
was the "mistake" (257) in his design? All that he has made has somehow gone awry, gotten beyond his control, turned into something
other. His labors rise up against him as something alien. His last
attempt to heal himself through working—editing Outland's diary for
publication—he apathetically abandons. Contemplating Outland's
death in combat, and the fortune made by those who recognized during the war the potential uses of his engine (30–31), the professor begins to think himself toward death: a man might do well to die with
the act of creation, he concludes, so that he not be forced to participate in the inevitable perversion of his inventiveness (236–237). The
cycle of creation ends not in obsolescence, he realizes, but in something worse. When the chance for suicide comes unexpectedly, the
professor yields to it.[71]

The Failure of Human Reproduction.

An even more radical form of war anxiety manifested itself as skepticism not only of *techné* but also of its Greek counterpart *genesis*. Like
expanding concentric rings dilating from the common center of still
water's disruption, foreboding generated by the technologies that had
produced war resonated in ever widening circles throughout the fields
of human artifice, from science to industry to art, until finally, and
most radically, it was displaced onto the form of making least separable from the body and thus the nature of persons: the act of human
reproduction. The frequency of postwar representations of birth as
death is uncanny: sex is a way of killing a woman or disfiguring a
body; the production of life demands a death, becomes impossible,
occasions suicide, or represents the triumph of juggernaut Nature
over human freedom. The destructiveness of procreation is central to
the stories of Sherwood Anderson's *Winesburg, Ohio* (published as a
book in 1919, its stories were written during the first years of the
war). For the unnamed woman of "Paper Pills," to have sex is to be

bitten and to bleed; it is the precursor of abortion, which is itself, through the cruelty of narrative parataxis, the precursor of the woman's death. For Ray Pearson in "The Untold Lie" the implacable beauty of the landscape becomes the symbol of the "dirty trick" of Nature, the biological trap of desire and reproduction that renders a man's future sterile. And for Katherine Bentley in "Godliness," the "hard years after the Civil War" are a time of catastrophically depleting labor: "For a year she worked every day from sunrise until late at night and then after giving birth to a child she died."[72] In Faulkner's *Flags in the Dust* (1927), Bayard Sartoris's first wife dies in childbirth while he is at the front;[73] and in Fitzgerald's early novelette *May Day* (1920), while soldiers returning from the war riot, a young man tries unsuccessfully to raise money to pay off a lover who can cause him "trouble," marries her when wildly drunk, and consequently kills himself.[74] In Dos Passos's *Nineteen Nineteen* (1932) Anne Elizabeth becomes pregnant by an American soldier, despairs of the outcome and, seeking death, dies in a technological holocaust when she seduces a drunk fighter pilot into showing her the limits of what his warplane can do.[75] In the sequel *The Big Money*, Margo Dowling (whose mother died when giving birth to her) is raped, later becomes pregnant, considers suicide, and then gives birth to a child that quickly dies from the venereal disease she has passed on to it; and Mary French, likewise, considers suicide when pregnant, has an abortion, and still later has a second abortion.[76] In Hemingway's "Indian Camp" (1925) a man kills himself when he is no longer able to stand bearing witness to his wife's suffering in labor; in a brief sketch of a wartime civilian evacuation from *In Our Time* (1925), the birth of a child in a convoy becomes the symbol of suffering, futility, and tragedy;[77] in *The Sun Also Rises* (1926), Jake Barnes is rendered impotent by a war wound; and in *A Farewell to Arms* (1929) Catherine dies in childbirth, and the surgeon Rinaldi believes he has contracted syphilis, which he calls, transforming intimate human relationship during wartime into an element of a larger mechanical design, an "industrial accident."[78] In Virginia Woolf's *To the Lighthouse* (1927), which critiques the "sterility of men,"[79] Prue Ramsay dies during the war years "in some illness connected with childbirth";[80] in *Mrs. Dalloway* (1925), war veteran Septimus Smith repudiates reproduction and the "filth" of sex because of what the war has taught him;[81] and in *Orlando* (1928) Eusebius Chubb, horrified by the "fecundity" of his era (the profusion of material goods, the expansion of the empire, his garden, and the scale of literature) kills himself during his wife's fifteenth pregnancy.[82] In Thomas Mann's *Magic Mountain* (1924), Dr. Krokowski delivers a lecture series at the sanatorium entitled "Love as a force contributory to disease";[83] in *Blast 2* (1915) Wyndham Lewis equates "the manufacturing of children" with the production of ammunition cartridges;[84] and in H. D.'s *Bid Me to Live* (first written in 1927 and revised throughout the thirties as she underwent psychoanalysis with Freud), Julia's lungs are tainted by poison gas with the kiss of her lover-turned-soldier, and her pregnancy ends with the "crucifixion" of a stillbirth—a fictional reworking of H. D.'s own miscarriage in 1915, which she believed was brought on by the shocking news of the sinking of the *Lusitania*.[85] We were all, H. D. concluded in her account of wartime London, a "still-born generation."[86]

Nathanael West's *Miss Lonelyhearts* (sent in partly completed draft form to Simon and Schuster in early 1930) is perhaps the best example with which to conclude. Here, war plays a surprising role. The novel opens with a letter from "Sick-of-it-all" to Miss Lonelyhearts's newspaper agony column: "I have 7 children in 12 yrs and ever since the last 2 I have been so sick. I was operated on twice and my husband promised no more children on the doctors advice as he said I might die but when I got back from the hospital he broke his promise and now I am going to have a baby and I don't think I can stand it my kidneys hurts so much."[87] The letter, emphasizing the pain and damage of procreation, is a paradigm for the novel and era as a whole. It is immediately followed by a letter recounting the "terrible bad fate" (2) of a girl born without a nose, which is itself followed by a letter written on behalf of a "deaf and dumb" (3) girl raped and possibly impregnated by a stranger. West disdains "the talent to create" (4). He depicts spring as a form of "brutality" that serves to "torture a few green spikes through the exhausted dirt" (5) and mocks the thesis that "Art Is a Way Out" (4). Even "giving birth to groups of words" (45) is a sterile labor, producing confusion rather than understanding. In *Miss Lonelyhearts* foreplay culminates in assault (50), and marital sex is "like sleeping with a knife in one's groin" (21). Throughout the novel the desire to damage and the desire to make love blend together indistinguishably. The novel's logic transforms the final cliché of natural beauty—a rose—into a grotesque vision of mutilation as decoration. "Let me pluck this rose," Miss Lonelyhearts says, tugging sharply at his lover's nipple. "I want to wear it in my buttonhole" (12). When she withdraws, he begins to scream at her. "Instead of answering, she raised her arm as though to ward off a blow. She was like a kitten whose soft helplessness makes one ache to hurt it" (13).

In *Miss Lonelyhearts,* Nathanael West is reluctant to attribute any simple causality to the multiple sorrows of his characters, offering instead only desperate visions of suffering as a natural, uncaused state, impervious to the question "Why?"—why am I a cripple? why is Gracie deaf and dumb? why was I born without a nose? why is my body unable to support the pregnancy that God demands of it? The key exception occurs toward the close of the novel, and here the cause is straightforward: it is war. Just before meeting the man who will shoot him, Miss Lonelyhearts receives a letter from "Broad Shoulders," a woman whose marriage is trapped in a cycle of abuse and reconciliation. She begins: "During the war I was told if I wanted to do my bit I should marry the man I was engaged to as he was going away to help Uncle Sam and to make a long story short I was married to him" (40). In this moment, when marriage is formulated as an act of war, the cliché of domestic warfare is literalized and the quotidian phantasmagoria begins. Her home becomes a murderous parody of the trenches of World War I. Her husband sets an ambush for her, which frightens her so badly that she suffers from hysterical paralysis—a disorder "discovered" in mass in the war. War drives soldier insane drives wife insane. War gives soldier venereal disease gives wife through sex gives son through childbirth. War finally displaces family from home. Hannah Arendt writes:

> Modern enchantment with "small things" . . . has found its classical presentation . . . in the art of being happy among "small things," within the space of their own four walls, between chest and bed, table and chair, dog and cat and flowerpot, extending to these things a care and tenderness which, in a world where rapid industrialization constantly kills off the things of yesterday to produce today's objects, may even appear to be the world's last, purely humane corner.[88]

What has war done to the home? West's startling and dismaying answer is that war, in the broadest scheme, has done nothing. Inverting the standard causality presented in Broad Shoulders' letter, he shows throughout the rest of the novel that, if anything, the war is an *extension* of home. When soldiers in World War I named their particular sections of trench "Regent Street" or "the Strand," they were making the small, very human effort to make a strange and frightening new environment seem more familiar and safe. But for West, they were also, simply, demonstrating a fact. Regent Street leads as naturally to the trenches as desire to violence, as birth to deformity, as inventiveness to destruction. Peace is constrained violence, or violence in slow motion. War is a symptom, not a cause. Searching for an answer to his own exhaustion, Miss Lonelyhearts fixes upon the skyscrapers that menace the horizon. With "tons of forced rock and tortured steel," Miss Lonelyhearts realizes, Americans had "done their work hysterically, desperately, almost as if they knew that the stones would some day break them." They had killed themselves with their work, and their buildings are their funeral pyre. The skyscrapers of Jenney, Sullivan, and the Chicago School—which had symbolized for generations the triumph of creation—are for Miss Lonelyhearts "an orgy of stone breaking"(27).

If the skyscraper is the symbol of the pre–World War I era, then the symbol of the surviving generations is the small hand-tool Broad Shoulders finds in her bedroom. When Broad Shoulders finds a hammer beneath her husband's pillow, she knows it is not a hammer for fixing a bed post or nailing a picture to a wall, but rather a hammer for crushing her skull. In this grotesque reversal of domestic expectations, West announces the cruelty inherent to the process of creation. But for West, creation is not a violent process in which people participate. Creation is violent because violence is the nature of people.

Equipment

A hammer on a workbench is a domestic tale. A hammer beneath your lover's pillow is a gothic tale. The hammer is mute, unbeautiful, morally neutral, and difficult to anthropomorphize, and yet its mere location can shock, can point to the continuity or breakdown of a world. The hammer, as an archetype of man-made equipment, appears in the national flags of Austria, Costa Rica, the People's Republic of the Congo, and the former Soviet Union and East German Democratic Republic.[89] It is a repository of human identity, of the made identities of human communities, and of the potential to imagine and to make that is most extravagantly manifest in the construction of nations. "Your hammer," writes Auschwitz survivor Primo Levi, "can fix everything."[90] The hammer, mute and neutral, whispers a continually evolving story to the world. This fact of human culture is as routine and mysterious as each winter's first snowfall.

Equipment is an extension of the human body, an amplification of its power to alter the world. A shirt changes the temperature of a room; a knife transforms resistant matter into yielding matter; a bag transforms several objects into one object. But equipment is more than physical utility—it is a means of situating oneself in the material universe, of personalizing an otherwise alien physical environment: the particular working subject uses equipment to recreate the earth, to shape it according to his or her desires, and thereby, as Heidegger would explain it, to transform the radically alien earth into a personal world.[91] Using a peasant woman's shoes as a foundational example, Heidegger writes:

> When she takes off her shoes late in the evening, in deep but healthy fatigue, and reaches out for them again in the still dim dawn, or passes them by on the day of rest, she knows all this without noticing or reflecting. The equipmental being of the equipment consists indeed in its usefulness. But this usefulness itself rests in the abundance of an essential Being of the equipment. We call it reliability. By virtue of this reliability the peasant woman is made privy to the silent call of the earth; by virtue of the reliability of the equipment she is sure of her world. World and earth exist for her, and for those who are with her in her mode of being, only thus—in the equipment. We say "only" and therewith fall into error; for the reliability of the equipment first gives to the simple world its security and assures to the earth the freedom of its steady thrust.[92]

If as Heidegger suggests the self comes into being through its world, simultaneously with its world, and if the world is nameable as world only through the reliability of equipment, then equipment is a primary means of creating and sustaining a self.[93] As Elaine Scarry writes, "It is through [work's] movement out into the world that sentience becomes social and thus acquires its distinctly human form."[94]

"Infantrymen, like soldiers everywhere," observes war correspondent Ernie Pyle, "like to put names on their equipment. Just as a driver paints a name on his truck, so does a doughboy carve his name or initials on his rifle butt."[95] War, at the opposite end of human experience from Heidegger's quotidian domestic case, is a clarifying example of the incalculable benefits that equipment brings to the psyche. In traumatic crises the fragility of personality is most dramatically revealed; the need for subjective narrative continuity here overwhelms, and artifacts become the protective containers of threatened personhood. American soldiers storming Omaha Beach, for instance, encumbered themselves with a bewildering variety of personal objects, including banjos and tennis rackets.[96] In such emergencies the process of cathexis is radically compressed, allowing even objects that are newly encountered and empty of significance to become, within the foreshortened temporal brackets of the crisis, sources of stability and continuity.[97] Pyle writes from Omaha Beach:

> I stepped over the form of one youngster whom I thought dead. But when I looked down I saw he was only sleeping. He was very young, and very tired. He lay on one elbow, his hand suspended in the air about six inches from the ground. And in the palm of his hand he held a large, smooth rock. I stood and looked at him a long time. He seemed in his sleep to hold that rock lovingly, as though it were his last link with a vanishing world. I have no idea at all why he went to sleep with the rock in his hand, or what kept him from dropping it once he was asleep. It was just one of those little things without explanation, that a person remembers for a long time.[98]

For Nick Adams in Hemingway's short story "Now I Lay Me," this battle-time emergency is internalized. The emergency's threat to ego coherence shatters temporal limitations and, leaking over into the quotidian, transforms domesticity's transitional states into moments of rupture. For Nick, the loss of the world's objects in each night's darkness initiates the obliteration of self. "I myself did not want to sleep because I had been living for a long time with the knowledge that if I ever shut my eyes in the dark and let myself go, my soul would go out of my body."[99] The eye deprived of light ceases to exist as an eye. Human perception needs a reality, needs a surface against which to discover its own shape. Each night therefore Nick must rebuild the world, imaginatively surrounding himself with a rich array of objects from his past, from the self he remembers being.

In work and through equipment humans create themselves, but equipment has a dual nature. The verb "create," significantly, blends active artifactual production with passive organic growth; in English the word bears the traces of both the Latin transitive verb *creāre* (to produce) and, through the Indo-European base *ker* (to grow), the Latin intransitive verb *crēscere* (to develop or mature). Thus "create" denotes production through human initiative, effort, and cost (after plowing, planting, and tending to my crops, I eventually grew one thousand bushels of wheat) while also connoting a growth as natural and gentle as the blossoming of a flower (the wheat grew taller as if yearning to touch the sun). The two central implications of this etymology are simultaneous and contrary. Thomas Carlyle writes that "True Work *is* Worship. He that works, whatsoever be this work, he bodies forth the form of Things Unseen; a small Poet every Worker is."[100] Karl Marx offers a contrary and startling formulation in his *Grundrisse*. "Production," he states, "is also immediately consumption."[101] Work is "essentially the expenditure of human brain, nerves, muscles,"[102] and therefore human creation is always only a transformation rather than a generation of materials. And in the industrial world, it is a particularly vicious and brutal transformation, a process of making that consumes the body of the maker.[103] As Heidegger writes, *techné* is "ambiguous," enclosing two possibilities: as "poiēsis" it is an extension of our capacity for care and for the unfolding of truth, a revelation of our highest dignity; but in its need for mastery and in its frenzied instrumentality, it is also a "supreme danger," a brutalization of nature and of human experience.[104] This duality of work is reproduced in the material duality of equipment itself: namely, in the dichotomy of the tool and the weapon. The poles of tool and weapon, use and waste, creating and destroying, mark the extreme points of human experience. An arm extends into a saw; an arm extends into a sword. A clear and visible distinction between these two events, between work and war, is the edifice upon which trust is built. It is the beginning of worlds.

In the rest of this chapter I focus almost exclusively on the relationship between people and equipment in Hemingway's *A Farewell to Arms*. Of all the postwar novels discussed so far, it is *A Farewell to Arms* that remains most continually and anxiously engaged with the dialectic of creation, with the limits of work and the momentum of waste. The novel is, moreover and relatedly, centrally concerned with the representation of violent experience through trauma recall and moral evaluation, and with the problem of how such representations can be made to function in a violent world. I look first at the novel's examination of tools and weapons in wartime, and track how for Hemingway their volatility can illuminate questions about our ability to control the social consequences of our material and verbal creations; I then analyze the novel's imbrication with the primary philosophical systems of its time, including rationalist deontology and naturalist consequentialism, in order to understand its claims about our capacity for adequate representation of will, world, and action. In the remaining chapters of the book, I will build upon the ideas developed in these sections by fanning outward from Hemingway, looking in detail at Cather, Cummings, and Dos Passos, and, finally, expanding the scope of analysis to include Faulkner, Heller, contemporary literary and sociological theory, and human rights law.

A Farewell to Arms

The literature of the tool is the literature of production, of Jack London, Theodore Dreiser, and Frank Norris. The literature of the weapon is the literature of waste, the literature of Hemingway, Dos Passos, and Cather. In the postwar literature already discussed war *intersects* with a continuing story; there is a world external to war. In *The Great Gatsby* and *Tender Is the Night* Fitzgerald makes war into background, and in *Mrs. Dalloway* Woolf presents it as a terrible but fading echo: her novel begins with the celebratory cry "the war was over" and ends shortly after the suicide of war veteran Septimus Smith, who disappears into the continuing flow of life like a stone carelessly dropped into a stream.[105] In this liminal literature, poised between creation and destruction, faith and despair, deferral is structurally programmed, and retreat is the only option. Dick Diver's retreat to the lost small towns of America reproduces Nick Carraway's retreat back to the Midwest, and each characterizes the literary shift in America from the nineteenth-century pioneer to the twentieth-century refugee. Exile is, however, rarely without hope. Retreat made positive is figured as escape: George Willard's escape from Winesburg, Ohio, for instance, or Narcissa Benbow's intended escape from the Sartoris legacy, symbolized in her refusal to name her child after its male progenitors. Jake, Orlando, Amory Blaine—all are characterized by the fact of having to depart (from a city, a lifestyle, or a tradition). Their flights entail loss, but they are also the first step in salvaging a world.

In the literature that represents World War I directly, however, where war *is* the world, retreat only furthers destruction. Escape, like the violent unraveling of the Italian army retreating from Caporetto in *A Farewell to Arms*, only amplifies the scope of waste. In Sassoon's

Memoirs of an Infantry Officer, any retreat (whether a temporary withdrawal from the front, a permanent retreat as a conscientious objector, or even a retreat from this estranged perch of protester) is fraught with guilt, futility, and ineffectuality. For Jünger, retreat is a return to a world of banalities that should be razed;[106] for Cather in *One of Ours,* the world of war is the world *to which* we retreat;[107] and for Dos Passos, there is nowhere to retreat *to*—the postwar peace is itself a brutal wasteland, a continuation of war by other means. The plot of *The Big Money* is in large part the transformation of a returning soldier's opening comments from comic aphorism into straightforward prophecy: "We could stand the war, but the peace has done us in."[108]

The end point of the World War I protest novel is waste. In America, often, the texts end with a corpse: Cather's Claude, Hemingway's Catherine, Wharton's George, and Dos Passos's Unknown Soldier. Just as often they begin with workers: Dos Passos's Joe Williams, Wharton's John Campton, and Cather's Wheeler Farm. The question central to these texts is where, and if, a clear division can be drawn between the two. In *A Farewell to Arms,* the problems represented by the contiguity of working and killing, together with Hemingway's personal conviction that the details of skill (bullfighting, boxing, fishing, hunting) blend with the performative requirements of building a self-image, generate a comprehensive analysis of artisanship, personhood, and material and moral deconstruction. Like Whitman, who asserted that "emotions under emergencies" give the "profounder clues" about persons,[109] Hemingway believed that special knowledge could be found at the front, on the battlefield, and in the temporary structures surrounding the site of violence, in the liminal spaces at the fringes of the emergency (the encampment, the hospital, the temporary hotel retreats). Outside naturalized social relations, practiced choices, bounded risk, and given moral worlds, certain cherished illusions become unsustainable. In war as a cultural and in particular technological space, the occluded, interior structures of creation and of injuring are thus exposed. Upon their relationship hangs the very possibility of coherent human morality.

Hemingway considered Stephen Crane the preeminent writer of the Civil War—indeed, Crane was one of the greatest war writers of all time. "That great boy's dream of war," Hemingway wrote, was "truer to how war is than any war the boy who wrote it would ever live to see."[110] But Crane's most "perfect" depiction of battle, *The Red Badge of Courage,* could for Hemingway be a complete account only of premechanized warfare. Alluding to Henry Fleming's terror of advancing in combat, Hemingway wrote: "a mechanized force, not by virtue of their armor, but by the fact that they move mechanically, will advance into situations where you could put neither men nor animals; neither get them up there nor hold them there."[111] As if in tribute to the *ne plus ultra* quality of Crane's work, Hemingway (named for his grandfather, a Civil War veteran) would thus focus in his own war writings almost exclusively upon the twentieth-century adaptation of human perception and behavior to the realities of fully industrialized combat—upon, in Jünger's phrase, our "half-grotesque, half-barbaric fetishism of the machine," summarized in his hybridizing image of a "turbine fueled with blood."[112] Thus Hemingway begins *A Farewell to Arms:*

> The plain was rich with crops; there were many orchards of fruit trees and beyond the plain the mountains were brown and bare. There was fighting in the mountains and at night we could see the flashes from the artillery. In the dark it was like summer lightning, but the nights were cool and there was not the feeling of a storm coming . . . There were mists over the river and clouds on the mountain and the trucks splashed mud on the road and the troops were muddy and wet in their capes; their rifles were wet and under their capes the two leather cartridge boxes on the front of the belts, gray leather boxes heavy with the packs of clips of thin, long 6.5 mm. cartridges, bulged forward under the capes so that the men, passing on the road, marched as though they were six months gone with child.[113]

A Farewell to Arms is about the borders that separate people, their equipment, and the natural environment: the negotiation of these elements determines both the architecture and the metaphysics of the novel as a whole. Here, artillery flashes are like summer lightning, and ammunition belts transform soldiers into pregnant women. What are the implications? Does the comparison of shell fire and lightning reflect the human need to translate the horrifying images of warfare into the safe and familiar images of nature? Or is nature instead posited as a form of warfare? Are ammunition belts redefined by their absorption into the human body—defanged, made harmless? Or is the human body imagined here as a weapon?

The end of a tool is work and making; the end of the weapon is

damaging. Tools, as Heidegger reminds us, bring immeasurable support to the unhoused personality. During a panicked retreat, Frederic
and his men calm themselves by focusing upon their possibilities as
workers: the Tenente volunteers to do the work of an enlisted man, to
use tools upon a machine, and Aymo forgoes a much needed rest in
order to remain connected, at least for the moment, to a reliable kettle
and stove (190). The novel's two central escape scenes are studies in
the startling *range* of equipmental power. In the first, Frederic jumps
into a violent river in order to escape execution during the chaotic retreat from Caporetto. In danger of drowning due to the weight of his
clothes and boots, he clings to a piece of timber that helps him to keep
afloat. This "timber" (225), wood adapted through human labor to
become equipment, is for Frederic both an extension of the caring human hands that shaped it and a stark, crude, but potent amplification
of his own body; in joining itself so seamlessly to his needs, it absorbs
the quality of his own aliveness: the wood is no chance, inert object; it
is his friend, it is "we" (226). Later, in a second water-escape scene,
Frederic and Catherine elude the military police and flee to Switzer-
land. Now the refugees are equipped with a rowboat. In this contrasting depiction, Frederic can afford to ignore his body, to make it, in a
sense, invisible: he is conscious only of the joints between him and
his machine, in the blisters on his hands. The well-made tool allows
Frederic to extend far beyond the limits of his body, thus making possible a social and aesthetic world: he is able to bring Catherine along,
travel many miles, pay close attention to the landscape (271), and
converse. In their progress from the unaided body's friction against
the material world to the artifactually extended body's mastery of it,
these two escape scenes reproduce the accelerating technological arc
that defined the first World War. The complex tool's opening of possibilities is thus vividly contrasted to the blunt assistance of the benign
object.

More central to the novel, however, is the opposition between the
openings of the tool and the radical closures of the weapon. The
weapon is the negation of the tool. It is everything that a tool is not. It
prohibits extension beyond self, isolates the individual, and heightens
consciousness of the body to an obscene, world-extinguishing degree:
for a wounded soldier, Hemingway writes, "all that was happening
was without interest or relation" (60). As Elaine Scarry puts it, physical pain "annihilates not only the objects of complex thought and

emotion but also the objects of the most elemental acts of perception."[114] Tools and weapons, so fundamentally opposed, call into being alternative epistemological and organizational systems; they create within *A Farewell to Arms* two competing theaters of action. A clear dichotomy is established within the first four chapters of the novel between the realm of weapons, of the battleground and the soldier, and the realm of tools, of the hospital and the doctor (and his analogue, the mechanic, who is the doctor of the nonsentient world). These are reciprocally hostile and, at least potentially, mutually exclusive domains: Rinaldi, the doctor, fills his holster with surgical tissue rather than a gun, and the narrator feels shame when entering the English hospital with his weapon (29). Even during scenes of combat the mechanics are shown brandishing tools (a lighter, shaped like a Fiat radiator), which signify their work, rather than guns, which signify wounding (47). As workers, they simply cannot accept weapons: "They were all mechanics and hated the war" (48).[115] *Techné* is posited here as congeneric with morality. *Techné* demands a care for the inorganic world that spills over into the organic. More fundamentally, as Heidegger writes, work is the grounding condition of care and solicitude. It is the means by which we "discover" other human beings not merely as objects instrumental to our purposes but as beings with ends of their own, beings like us: "Thus along with the work, we encounter not only entities ready-to-hand but also entities with Dasein's kind of Being—entities for which, in their concern, the product becomes ready-to-hand, and together with these we encounter the world in which wearers and users live, which is at the same time ours."[116] Work puts us into supportive, mutually legitimating relations with the world. Approaching objects, we find human beings. War deconstructs this world such that, when facing human beings, we see only objects. The tool transforms the other into an I; the weapon transforms the I into an it. The two artifacts require and create alternative worlds.

A Farewell to Arms is structured as a whole according to the movement between these worlds.[117] Book 1 is the world of the soldier. At the climax of this section body damage is described in exquisite detail:

> There was a great splashing and I saw the star-shells go up and burst and float whitely and rockets going up and heard the bombs, all this in a moment, and then I heard close to me some one saying "Mama Mia! Oh, mama Mia!" I pulled and twisted and got my legs loose finally and turned around and touched him. It was Passini and when I touched him he screamed. His legs were toward me and I saw in the dark and the

light that they were both smashed above the knee. One leg was gone and the other was held by tendons and part of the trouser and the stump twitched and jerked as though it were not connected. He bit his arm and moaned. "Oh mama mia, mama Mia," then, "Dio te salve, Maria. Dio te salve, Maria. Oh Jesus shoot me Christ shoot me mama mia mama Mia oh purest lovely Mary shoot me. Stop it. Stop it. Stop it. Oh Jesus lovely Mary stop it. Oh oh oh oh," then choking, "Mama mama mia." Then he was quiet, biting his arm, the stump of his leg twitching. (55)

Traumatic wounds initiate a perceptual-narrative breakdown. The wound's visual incomprehensibility sunders it from the weapon; its obscene intensity, its demand to focus on the now of pain, makes causality irrelevant, makes the wound, so to speak, historyless. Furthermore, it is difficult to cement the weapon to a particular narrative purpose; its plenitude of materializations stifles. The weapon's solidity, cleanliness, and order (the conical simplicity of an unexploded shell, the elegant, handlike pointing of a gun) is so seemingly incompatible with and disproportionate to the wet, gaping disorder of the wound that the two can only be held together in the mind with difficulty. The forever detaching relationship of weapon and wound makes possible and is manifest in the use of guns and knives as children's toys, trophies, and home decorations. Hemingway is careful to prevent this psychic decoupling. In *A Farewell to Arms* the wound is not the breakdown of story but a story in itself. The novel is, in a large part, the causal history of a single wound, from health to weapon to injury to surgery to recovery. Within the scene of wounding itself (a narrative about damage that becomes a damaged narrative, as a student once put it) the ambulance drivers insist upon establishing the narrative accuracy of what has occurred with a quick body count, wound description, and ascription of causality: "It was a big trench mortar shell" (56). The declaration is needless and obvious, but it is a fact amidst chaos, and the soldiers cling to it. "It was a big trench mortar shell." For Hemingway, this declaration reproduces the function of the paratactic beginning to the passage cited in full above, in which a single sentence blends the sounds of shells with the sounds of wounded bodies. Hemingway, vigilant to sustain the aversiveness of perception, here cements the connection between the weapon and its typically effaced end point, the wounded, suffering body. Henceforth one cannot be encountered without evoking the other.

Book 2 undoes the work of Book 1, undoes both the narrative-level violence and the metanarrative attempt to keep fresh the sequence of injury. Book 2 is the realm of tools, of doctor and hospital, and here weapons are made invisible amidst an accumulation of beds and bell cords and thermometers. In the hospital, the trauma of weapons, their dearly purchased signification of wounding, may be alleviated. Healing, the bodily analogue of forgetting, is a means of blurring narrative: the "trench-mortar fragments" that have crippled the narrator may be gradually reimagined as "old screws and bed-springs and things"(85), and X-rays literally lift the wound out of the body, (dis)placing it onto the photographic negative in a prefiguration of the lifting away and replacement of body damage with "wound stripes" (121). The second half of the book as a whole reproduces the damage-healing cycle of the first. Book 3 returns to the battleground, and Books 4 and 5 move to the civilian analogue of the hospital: the hotel, where doctor and nurse are replaced by bartender and concierge, and focus upon body repair is replaced by focus upon body pleasure.

The struggle between these worlds is the struggle of the war itself: local moments of violence between bodies are set within a larger frame of violence between tools and weapons. Nearly twenty years earlier, Jack London had depicted war as a face-to-face encounter between men.[118] Here, Hemingway's narrator configures the approaching first battle as a conflict between equipment more than a conflict between people: the work-power of a "system" of tools ("a new wide road . . . trucks, carts, and loaded ambulances," 24) is pitted against the damage-power of Austrian artillery. The most insistently repeated image of the novel, after all, is not damaged flesh but rather the juxtaposition of guns and damaged houses (6, 10, 45, 163, 181, 185). Wounders and wounded are effaced, at least at the macroscopic level: guns fire themselves (186) and wear jackets like men (230), and hospital equipment is borne away on the vehicles of retreat in place of wounded soldiers (187). Men are involved only insofar as they are extensions of their respective artifacts: they are either "gunners" (weapons) or "drivers" (tools). Hemingway's subject-effacing stylistics (the enemy is typically faceless) is the representational correlative of technological and organizational modernization, which through increasingly powerful weaponry extended the physical and consequently psychic distance between combatants, and through increasingly complex delivery and control systems (communications, transportation, supply) further shifted institutional focus away from the morale of the individual soldier toward higher levels of organization and abstraction. Hemingway is both illuminating the counterintuitive ease with which violence to human bodies can and tends to be effaced in representing modern war and lamenting the shrunken sphere of human presence and personal heroism that technological war allows.[119] Even the trench fields, as John Keegan points out, operated as systems to factor out human initiative. Courage was not required to press on past the enemy's front trench: it was a matter of topography, instinct, and prudence, for the no-man's land behind the troops was an insupportable hazard (retreating was not an option), and the enemy's defenses faced the wrong way (remaining in place was not an option).[120]

In Homer's *Iliad,* the weapon acquires meaning in the narrative by borrowing from the attributes of the man who wields it: "the spear went over his back and stood fast in the ground, for all its desire to tear a man's flesh."[121] The modernization of war reversed this vector of subjectivity. For Hemingway, millennia later, the person assumes the attributes of the weapon. The leading edge of identity for a man encountered at a bar in "Night before Battle" is the mark of his weapon: "His hands were greasy and the forks of both thumbs black as graphite from the back spit of the machine gun. The hand holding the drink was shaking. 'Look at them.' He put out the other hand. It was shaking too." Before he is a named man he is a "tank-man," a shock-absorber and a gyroscope for a firing system.[122] Battle deconstructs the human: a tank man is an artifact ("it takes six months to make a good tank man"), and with continued use a tank man's body is reshaped by his weapon ("it does something to your ears").[123] In this story, then, the true "shape of the battle" is not the gap that separates opposed systems of injuring or even opposed political communities, for one's own leadership is as culpable as the enemy's; it is rather the gap that separates the battlefield's indiscriminate violence from the makeshift reproductions of domestic space—bar, restaurant, washroom—that allow for the reemergence of the human; it is the gap that separates machine-gun posts, antitank batteries, and war-film from soap, drinks, gramophones, and personal photographs.

The objects that sustain the body and the objects that harm it are also employed against each other as enabling symbols in the psyche of the individual combatant. Just as war, as a verbal concept, is transmuted and made bearable through language (battle is a "show," 18, 43), the weapon, a perceptual object, is resisted and made bearable by transmogrifying it into the tool. Perceiving the weapon in its *weaponliness* is to imagine the wound, damage, and disorder; perceiving it in its *preweaponly* nature as a material for making (for instance, as babbitting metal, 182) or indeed reimagining it as a cigarette lighter (75), is to erase the wound, to foreground human control and reliability, and to impute a constructive teleology to the world. Like a crystal that casts new light with each perspectival change, the imaginative faculty can change the world. For those working through the trauma of war, through the aversiveness of witnessing, acknowledging, and enduring pain, language is in the end the most powerful of tools. How does language mediate the soldier's encounter with violence? W. H. R. Rivers was among the first British doctors to recognize the importance of talk and redescription in returning shell-shock victims to normal functioning. The soldier's experience, he writes,

> should be talked over in all its bearings. Its good side should be emphasized for it is characteristic of the painful experience of warfare that it usually has a good, or even noble side, which in his condition of misery the patient does not see at all, or greatly underestimates. By such conversation an emotional experience, which is perhaps tending to become dissociated, may be intellectualised and brought into harmony with the rest of the mental life, or in more technical language, integrated with the normal personality of the sufferer. As a matter of practical experience the relief afforded to the patient by the process of talking over his painful experience, and by discussing how he can readjust his life to the new conditions, usually gives immense relief and may be followed by a great improvement, or even by the rapid disappearance of his chief symptoms.[124]

The intractable bodily phenomena of traumatic stress disorders are contested by the redescriptive power of words, by the transformation into familiar communicability of events experienced as alien to communication. In Hemingway's short story "A Way You'll Never Be," the protagonist's emergency response to psychic and physical trauma is an overflow of speech, a desperate effort to control through language. The story's great poignancy is that in the absence of an explicit understanding of how words can function to revivify agency and derealize resurging aversive memories, the potentially healing verbal response remains disordered and ineffective, more like a scream than a narrative. The story opens with an image of corpses and "scattered papers": postcards, photographs, and "letters, letters, letters." "There was always much paper about the dead and the débris of this attack was no exception."[125] The dispersion of the papers reproduces the dispersion of Nick's speech, and both stand as symbols of what war has done to language.[126] But the power of violence to control our perception and understanding is never complete. In an emblematic moment from *A Farewell to Arms,* Frederic verbally reconfigures shell explosions as flowers, minimizing the concussiveness of battle by blending his description of the Austrian assault into the landscape tableau that immediately precedes it: like strange flowers blossoming in the "wet autumn country," the explosions are "soft puffs with a yellow white flash in the center" (185).[127] The artist's aestheticization of violence stands in for the lexical reinvention of present aversive environments and the therapeutic renarration of traumatic memory. Such meliorative, rehabilitative transformations, however, are difficult to achieve and to sustain. The material world's pressure against language and memory is implacable, like the blood that drips onto Frederic from the soldier helplessly bleeding to death in the stretcher above him. It can be left unnamed ("I felt something dripping," 61), or, in the moments when Hemingway employs metaphorical imagination, it can be analogized to things benign (it is a "stream," or the drops of an "icicle")—but in the end, matter asserts its actuality.

A Farewell to Arms thus foregrounds the friction between language and experience, the friction between the victim's linguistic transmogrification of objects and events and the resistance of the material world. The novel's opening moments document both the benign mutability of the world as experienced (artillery flashes are like summer lightning, and ammunition belts transform soldiers into pregnant women) and the inexorability of the body count (seven thousand died from cholera that winter). In this moment the novel announces questions both about the nature of the bodily environment and about this environment's relationship to language. Are humans, through language at least, able to control their world, or are they the victims of it? Will language hold against "the real," or will it shatter? Perhaps more important, *should* language hold? Metaphorizing aversive stimuli is a method of surviving through displacement or attenuation, but it is also a method of *allowing,* of reducing the unsustainable to the acceptable;[128] literary representation, in the same way, can give voice to suffering, but it can also aestheticize it. The artistic depiction of pain, argues Theodor Adorno, "contains, however remotely, the power to elicit enjoyment out of it." Through the stylization of violence, he

102 · *The Language of War*

warns, "an unthinkable fate appear[s] to have had some meaning; it is transfigured, something of its horror is removed. This alone does an injustice to the victims."[129] As Simone de Beauvoir asks, "Will we not then be inclined to think that if death, misery, and injustice can be transfigured for our delight, it is not an evil for there to be death, misery, and injustice?"[130] The dilemma present in emergency environmental renarration and in artistic representation reproduces the deeper crises of trauma and recovery. As Cathy Caruth argues, the integration of deep shock into a coherent, communicable life history is a method of achieving psychic equilibrium through language that comes with special costs. She acknowledges the requirements but emphasizes the risks of the therapeutic imagination:

> The trauma thus requires integration, both for the sake of testimony and for the sake of cure. But on the other hand, the transformation of the trauma into a narrative memory that allows the story to be verbalized and communicated, to be integrated into one's own, and others', knowledge of the past, may lose both the precision and the force that characterizes traumatic recall . . . The capacity to remember is also the capacity to elide or distort, and in other cases . . . may mean the capacity simply to forget. Yet beyond the loss of precision there is another, more profound, disappearance: the loss, precisely, of the event's essential incomprehensibility, the force of its *affront to understanding*.[131]

For this reason, she concludes, many survivors are reluctant to subject their memory to the operations of speech.

A Farewell to Arms frequently registers suspicion of language's slipperiness and its capacity to distort and to diminish through the translation of event into sign.[132] Immediately after covering over images of human injury by comparing exploding shells to blossoming flowers, Frederic pointedly remarks upon the power of smoke to "distort." Just as immediately before, he presents an image of language detached from material context, and thereby made indecent:

> I was always embarrassed by the words sacred, glorious, and sacrifice and the expression in vain. We had heard them, sometimes standing in the rain almost out of earshot, so that only the shouted words came through, and had read them, on proclamations that were slapped up by billposters over other proclamations, now for a long time, and I had seen nothing sacred, and the things that were glorious had no glory and the sacrifices were like the stockyards at Chicago if nothing was done with the meat except to bury it . . . Abstract words such as glory, honor,

courage, or hallow were obscene beside the concrete names of villages, the numbers of roads, the names of rivers, the numbers of regiments and the dates. (184–185)

The transformative capacity of language is a tool but also a weapon. It subtends therapeutic and emergency responses to aversive stimuli, but it can also serve as a mechanism of ideology complicit in the maintenance of violence, as a subtraction from rather than addition to our referential competence.

The duality of language, and the suture-thin separability of its functions, is reproduced in the duality of equipment. Broad contrast between working and hurting, domestic space and battle sites, peace and war, cannot be read as stable opposition. The worlds of caring and harming infect each other: antiaircraft guns punctuate hospital roofs; civilians duplicate the scene of battle in riots at home (133), and nurses go after scalps (145); losing sums of money at a racetrack is strangely connected to losing sums of men in warfare, if only by the fact of phrasing and juxtaposition (130–133); and sportsmen, expert in the use of tools (skis, luge, toboggan), are also pugilists, using their hands as weapons (311). Indeed, perhaps the most significant and shocking characteristic of tools and weapons is their easy interchangeability.[133] On the one hand, every artifact contains within it the explosive potential of a weapon: a shell cap desired as a souvenir (literally, equipment for the eyes) can become shrapnel that slices the eyes (108); boots that assist walking can also cause drowning (227); a barber's razor can cut a beard or a throat (90); alcohol can produce pleasure or a "self-inflicted" wound (144); and the bicycles that the mechanics dream of wistfully during their retreat (207) can also carry enemy carbines and stick bombs into their homeland (211). Just when a man thinks that he has finally escaped the battleground, the primacy of the weapon in human experience reasserts itself: even a trolling line can suddenly turn against the user, tearing his teeth out by the roots (256).

Weapons, on the other, more optimistic hand, can also become tools. Officers brandish forceps instead of guns (58), and, in the hands of a doctor, a knife entering human flesh becomes a tool, an agent of work. Rinaldi, after all, is an artist of sorts, gentle even when causing pain (166–167). The benign transformation of the weapon, however, is much more difficult psychically to sustain: if one does not keep the concept of work steadily in mind, doctors can suddenly become "butchers" (57). Frederic's attitude toward the doctors of the novel is symptomatic of medicine's deeply ambiguous role in warfare: his hostile, intense distrust of Dr. Varella, the surgeon first assigned to operate on his knee, contrasts sharply with his devotion to Rinaldi, particularly with his fascination with Rinaldi's hands and gloves as sensuous symbols of care (63, 64, 66, 166, 167). Examination is foremost a nurturing union of bodies. When Rinaldi works with Henry's wounded knee, the doctor's own knee becomes a focus of special attention (167). And surgery, as Ira Elliott details it, is like lovemaking.[134] "I would take you and never hurt you," Rinaldi says to Frederic. "I never hurt anybody. I learn how to do it. Every day I learn how to do things smoother and better" (64). But lovemaking blends into violence, and even rape: "There is only one difference between taking a girl who has always been good and a woman," Rinaldi says. "'With a girl it is painful. That's all I know.' He slapped the bed with his glove. 'And you never know if the girl will really like it'" (66). The healer is also a "hog-butcher" (64). "Doctors did things to you and then it was not your body anymore" (231). Decades later, a despairing comedy about the Korean War would juxtapose the bodies of abused women with hospital patients. In *M*A*S*H*, a group of doctors tear down the women's shower to expose and ridicule the proud chief nurse, Major Houlihan (Sally Kellerman). Her violated body—prone, naked, and then covered by nurses with a gown—is uncomfortably similar to the wounded that these doctors enter with the same godlike impunity.[135] In her World War I novel *The Eye in the Door*, Pat Barker likens the gaze of the doctor to an instrument of cruelty. As her protagonist, Dr. Rivers, observes a colleague observing a patient, he reflects that "the same suspension of empathy that was so necessary a part of the physician's task was also, in other contexts, the root of all monstrosity. Not merely the soldier, but the torturer also, practices the same suspension."[136]

John Keegan's description of the competition between martial and medical systems at the Somme seems at first to emphasize their oppositional nature, their fundamental antagonism and cross-purposes:

> despite the intensification of the hazards with which battle threatened the soldier of the First World War, the care which medicine could pro-

vide had been made to keep pace. The infrastructure of the medical service was impressive in scope. Parallel to the complicated networks of supply and communication, emplaced to transport the soldier into battle and provide him with essentials while there—the buried cable system, railheads, roadheads, tramways, Corps and Divisional dumps, workshops, Field Ordnance Parks—was an equally elaborate system to evacuate him from battle if he was hit, treat his wounds and restore him to health.

And yet, in a parenthetical conclusion, cross-purposes become a disturbing complementarity: "an equally elaborate system to evacuate him from battle if he was hit, treat his wounds and restore him to health (and so to the fighting line)."[137] Is the doctor a healer or a butcher? a mechanic or a soldier? a lover or a rapist? Does he save human lives, or simply perpetuate the war by recycling soldiers? The struggle over this question is a struggle over the nature of equipment. It is a struggle engaged throughout the novel: will an artifact be a tool or a weapon? Will an oar be a means of escape or abortion (275)? Are bridges and roads used as tools to move the wounded and allow a retreat, or are they part of the weaponry of an invading army? (211). Is a gas mask a tool for saving lives or preserving weapons? What about a helmet? A doctor? A slogan? A novel?

In its analysis of the organic world, *A Farewell to Arms* offers answers. We return finally to the questions raised at the start of this section about the novel's opening passage: is nature benevolent, something that defangs the horror of weapons? Or is it only another form of weaponry? When troops seek shelter under the "shoulder" of a mountain (23), nature is made equivalent to the human body: it too may find itself in the line of fire; it too may be wounded. And although the river may threaten to drown Frederic, it also carries him to safety. Even the soil acts in an emergency to preserve the body, blocking up a wound and thereby preventing a hemorrhage (57). But this romanticized view of the natural world is finally inadequate. Cholera slaughters thousands, rain and mud conspire with the enemy to impede retreat (197), and mountains, after all, are most appropriately considered as possible weapons (183, 118). In the second escape scene, Frederic uses an umbrella as a sail: the tool here is presented as an extension of the human body, and it is a natural force—wind—that destroys the tool, shattering its "ribs" (272). Nature, in the end, is conflated with weaponry: "In the night, going slowly along the crowded roads we passed troops marching under the rain, guns, horses pulling wagons, mules, motor trucks, all moving away from the front" (188). The reader, consuming the sentence in chunks, first takes guns as an extension of the list of like elements that begins with rain; it is only after reconfiguring the sentence that the words can be reassembled, and their functional separation revealed.[138]

And what of humanity? Are we workers or wounders? Will we rec-reate the world or destroy it? The penultimate moments of the novel are hopeful; creativity is privileged. Frederic and Catherine are secure within a world of tools, a world of boots, umbrellas, keys, and con-cierges (308). Catherine is pregnant, ready to give birth to their first child. But in the hospital, at what would seem to be the ultimate mo-ment of human creativity, the war begins to return. Images become confused. The child is a skinned rabbit, victim of a sportsman's gun (324); Catherine is repaired by a craftsman, a cobbler with a stitching tool (325); forceps recall surgeons from earlier battles (321, 52, 58); Catherine wears a gas mask (316, 11, 77); and the female body recalls the novel's opening page, reinvoking the soldiers pregnant with am-munition.[139] What were humans made to be? Is weaponry eclipsed by the creative power of the body? Or is the weapon generated from *within* the body? The question deferred from the novel's first para-graph is answered: doctors wield knives; Catherine dies. She bleeds to death from wounds inflicted during the birth. The height of human-ity's creative potential is a wounding; the body is a weapon. The urge to make—to make a life together, to make a separate peace, to make a baby—is a "dirty trick" (331). Creativity must materialize itself through the body, but the body is the enemy of the self. "You always feel trapped biologically" (139).[140]

Freedom, Luck, and Catastrophe: Ernest Hemingway, John Dewey, and Immanuel Kant

War slams together violence and productivity; it forces work and waste into a relationship of near seamless contiguity. Radically accelerating the processes of creation and destruction, war transforms their dialectic into a blending, and thereby disrupts the distinct moral values intuitively attributed to each. In *A Farewell to Arms,* violence's capacity to dissolve borders renders untenable the notion that creation-as-care is a moral good and that destruction-as-malice is a moral evil. Creation is instead reconceptualized throughout the novel as a morally neutral act, a use of power to alter the world for unknowable benefits at unforeseeable costs. It is essentially characterized, like destruction, by the quality of largesse, figured negatively as wantonness. Such broad similarity between the two categories makes the act of marking distinctions not only difficult but also, possibly, irrelevant: what is typically understood as the parodic relationship between creation and destruction is thus reconceived as mimetic. The one clear and abiding difference—that creation produces an artifact—can carry no relevant meaning once it is accepted that artifacts themselves are morally neutral. A hammer is possibly a tool but just as easily a weapon, and its creation therefore is also just as easily an early if covert stage of destruction. Carried to its extreme, this erasure of the difference between creation and destruction leads to a disabling epistemological and moral confusion. The ability to separate building from damaging, care from harm, is essential to a moral understanding of the universe and to the trust that builds shared worlds. Lacking this border, we have only war.

Against all that contributes to the dissolution of the borders that establish difference and meaning—against the cognition-disabling facts of bereavement (Catherine is a corpse just as Aymo is a corpse) and against the irresistibility of material consequence as the final arbiter of actions (loving and desiring, just like firing a weapon, produce corpses)—there is the human will. Frail and defiant, like a hand raised against the flash of an explosion, the human will refuses exile, even in war. As long as we are able to retain a sense of the integrity of intention, the world's alteration or even reversal of our plans is of secondary importance. The contingencies of the world do not penetrate the nature of our actions or our selves, if we so believe. And largely we do, primarily because of Immanuel Kant's enormous influence on modern thinking about ethics. Kantian morality elevates the will and its principles over the calculation of effects and utility; it is, broadly, deontological (holding, for example, that it is wrong to lie despite whatever potentially benevolent consequences may result), rather than utilitarian or consequentialist (which would posit, in contrast, that it is permitted to lie if doing so will promote more than harm the measurable satisfactions, desires, or interests of those involved).[1] Most important, Kant argues that the autonomy of the will actualizes itself in active moral choice: in other words, the individual rational will rises above external causalities both as they precede it (as the luck of genetics and environment) and as they follow it (as the luck of contingent consequence) through the universal faculty of inner freedom achievable through the law-giving form of morality.[2] On the causes that follow us, with which we are now concerned, Kant writes:

> Finally, there is one imperative which immediately commands a certain conduct without having as its condition any other purpose to be attained by it. This imperative is categorical. It is not concerned with the matter of the action and its intended result, but rather with the form of the action and the principle from which it follows; what is essentially good in the action consists in the mental disposition, let the consequences be what they may. This imperative may be called that of morality.[3]

According to this will-oriented account of morality, the moral value of an action cannot be determined by weighing worldly consequences, just as the truth of a statement cannot be gauged by calculating the number of people who have heard and believed it. Consequences are, so to speak, accidents of the environment, and are thereby extrinsic to the inherent goodness of an action or decision. The viability of an ethical distinction between creation and destruction, and thus of any distinction worth making, depends upon this notion of the autonomy of the will in moral calculus, its priority, as Kant emphasizes, over consequences. The question remains for Hemingway, and for all those representing contingency at its most violent and coercive: does will *matter?*

In his brilliant phenomenology of war Carl von Clausewitz writes: "In the whole range of human activities, war most closely resembles a game of cards."[4] This counterintuitive formulation is typical of Clausewitz. It does violence to our expectations and to our sense of scale, shrinking the epic to the mundane and reformulating the clash of national wills as a meaningless exercise in calculating chance. "No other human activity," he continues, "is so continuously or universally bound up with chance."[5] Chance and the human effort to overmaster it are central to all of the literatures of war, from King Archidamus's declaration in Thucydides' *Peloponnesian War* that "the course of war cannot be foreseen," despite the "predictions . . . and oracles being chanted,"[6] to the religious talisman Catherine Barkley gives Frederic Henry "for luck" (116), and to the card games and predictions of death that open both Norman Mailer's novel *The Naked and the Dead* and Bao Ninh's account of the North Vietnamese army in *The Sorrow of War.*[7] Contrasting war's unpredictability with the mechanical regularity of domestic life, Clausewitz characterizes it through the concept of friction:

> Everything in war is very simple, but the simplest thing is difficult. The difficulties accumulate and end by producing a kind of friction that is inconceivable unless one has experienced war . . . Countless minor incidents—the kind you can never really foresee—combine to lower the general level of performance, so that one always falls far short of the intended goal. Iron will-power can overcome this friction; it pulverizes every obstacle, but of course it wears down the machine as well.[8]

War is a world of friction, a world where human plans and organization are perpetually vulnerable to the predations of luck, and where the individual will, like the body itself, is eventually broken down by the repetitive strain of the haphazard. The structure of war, and of existence in war, is accident. To be subject to the accidental is to lack control, to be unable to "narrate" the world effectively—that is, to be unable to author a plan and to realize it through actions.[9] If we figure freedom as a series of concentric rings expanding out toward increasing power to act in and successfully alter the environment, then the innermost ring would be the circle of mind, that is, the sphere that includes our desires, intentions, and capacity for choice among bounded givens. In a world of friction and coercive accident this circle is the full reach of freedom, and is itself hotly contested. As Siegfried Sassoon warns, in wartime far more radically than in peace, we are conditioned not only by external causes that intersect with our lives with the force of accident—causes like the line of enemy fire or the commands of a superior—but also by contingent external imperatives meant to be experienced as *internal* choice: "Five sausage balloons were visible beyond the sky-line, peacefully tethered to their mother earth. It was our duty to desire their destruction, and to believe that Corps Intelligence had the matter well in hand."[10] For Sassoon, war is an illumination of the occluded realities of peace, like the radical enlargement of a small section of photograph, and in war belief and feeling are continually turned inside out, exteriorized: the outside world is the source not only of what happens to you, and not only of what you do in response to what happens to you, but also of the motivation that precedes your behaviors; accidental location in the world rather than reasoned decision of the will is the primary determinant of action. Luck is sovereign, and to accept the sovereignty of luck is to accept that we are third-person phenomena, that we are spectators or discoverers of ourselves; it is to accept that all things might just as easily have been otherwise, even those aspects of the self like belief or ethical commitment and choice that are felt to be essential to the continuation of one's existence. Luck is the edge set to freedom; it is the perpetually available extra question that undoes final justifications. And it is the primacy of this experience of luck in war so much more desperately than in peace that makes urgent in writers like Sassoon and Hemingway the need to assert autonomy, to retain some reservoir of self that is not conditioned by chance causes, to make will *matter.*

"Reason's aversion to contingency is very strong," writes Hannah Arendt. "It was Hegel, the father of grandiose history schemes, who held that 'philosophical contemplation has no other intention than to eliminate the accidental.'"[11] For Kant, the only way to free our selves from externalities and therefore luck is to free ourselves from "the impetuous importunity of the inclinations,"[12] or, as Whitman writes in a Kantian excursus, "from the tyrannic domination of vices, habits, appetites."[13] In Kant's striking formulation, that cluster of sensations and desires which we typically conceive of as constituting the "I" is in actuality radically external. Sensuous nature, he argues, is prisoner to the chain of worldly causality. We are able to transcend this sensuous world through the universally accessible capacity for free reason, and the structure of this reason according to Kant is the law of morality. The law of morality, importantly, binds us only insofar as it demands that we be self-legislating, that we act according to rationally chosen principles rather than allowing externalities to determine our actions—in other words, it binds us to accept freedom.[14] Kant thus incorporates no substantive moral values into his conception of law; the categorical imperative of autonomy is content-free and therefore, in Kant's mind, objective rather than culturally contingent. Kant demands only that any self-chosen moral principle have the formal quality of a principle or law (as, by definition, it must): namely, it must be generalizable or, more specifically, conceived of in theory as universally applicable. All moral content is structurally generated from this pure form. If we agree that we must guide our actions through self-chosen principles in order to be autonomous, and if we agree that principles must have general application in order to be principles at all, then certain substantive moral obligations will necessarily follow—obligations that are, as such, the expressions of our freedom. "Subjects of irresistible law," Whitman writes, "we yet escape, by a paradox, into true free will. Strange as it may seem, we only attain to freedom by a knowledge of, and implicit obedience to, Law."[15] Kant summarizes:

Man was viewed as bound to laws by his duty; but it was not seen that man is subject only to his own, yet universal, legislation and that he is bound only to act in accordance with his own will, which is, however, a will purposed by nature to legislate universal laws. For when man is thought as being merely subject to a law (whatever it might be), then the law had to carry with it some interest functioning as an attracting stimulus or as a constraining force for obedience, inasmuch as the law did not arise as a law from his own will . . . I want, therefore, to call my principle the principle of the autonomy of the will, in contrast with every other principle, which I accordingly count under heteronomy.[16]

How are specific, self-imposed constraints derived from the principle of the autonomy of the will? In the classic example, Kant argues that no rational agent could choose as a law for action the principle "I will lie for self-benefit," because it is a conceptual contradiction to imagine a world where such a principle was universally adopted: in this world statements would never be believed, lies would hence be impossible to achieve, and the requirement to lie for self-benefit would be rendered an absurdity.[17]

The details of Kant's complex and counterintuitive argument are not important here. What matters, according to the Kantian conception, is that moral reason, or the ability to articulate ethical difference, is the basis of human freedom, or rather that morality is the experience of freedom. The dictates of morality, unlike those of self-interest, are not hostage to the probabilities of particular outcomes in the world: moral law transcends the sensuous world, and in adopting it for ourselves we also transcend the world. As Kant writes, the universalizing perspective of morality allows us to see the "starry heavens" within us: the visible worlds above may "annihilate" our worth by revealing the absurdity of our animal scale, as Crane saw, but the ethical cosmos within and the objective personality that connects us to it disclose "a life independent of all animality and even of the whole world of sense."[18] Through the moral law we become causes in ourselves and thus, despite all our external constraints and final physical destinies, free. Properly conceived, morality is the one sphere of human activity not instrumentally subordinated to the achievement of consequences in the world. It is not a means to an end but rather an end in itself, the will's final justification against enslavement to luck. "*By acting morally,*" writes Christine Korsgaard, "*we can make ourselves free.*"[19] Thus while it makes sense to conceive of almost any action in the world as subject to luck—in that the external conditions for success may or may not be present—it offends the sense and destabilizes understanding, in the post-Kantian world, to think of any individual as "morally lucky."[20] Nonetheless, it is precisely this unsettling category of luck that conditions and gives coherence to the moral development of *A Farewell to Arms.*

Consequences

A Farewell to Arms provides a powerful analysis of both the deformation and the illumination of morality by war. Throughout all of his work Hemingway is deeply concerned with the concept of skill, that is, with the capacity to control consequences through concentrated activity, whether as a bullfighter, a surgeon, a hunter, or a lover. Skill, as the effort to minimize one's vulnerability to luck in a specific area, is the localization and physicalization of the larger human impulse to know and to do the right thing in the right way. Kant, significantly, uses the notion of skill as a prototype for the structure of morality,[21] and John Dewey, with World War I as his backdrop, tracks how control acquired through "tools" and "technique" functions as a source for our ethical confidence.[22] Skill in each of its manifestations, it can be argued, is an analogue of morality. Put in other words, skill is the morality of a particular physical activity, and morality is the skill of being human. Skill reveals the virtue of doing a thing beautifully, while morality reveals the beauty of doing a thing virtuously. The interior structure of beauty and of the beautifully done thing thus always recalls the original structure of morality.

It is precisely this subfoundational association that Hemingway relies upon to achieve the alienating effect of much of his work. "Killing cleanly," he writes in one paradigmatic passage, "and in a way which gives you aesthetic pleasure and pride has always been one of the greatest enjoyments of a part of the human race."[23] In another passage he describes a soldier's appreciation of skilled artillery combat: "The contact is beautiful. Just where we said. Beautiful."[24] In ancient Greek there is a single word, *kalos,* for the concepts of the beautiful and the morally good. In Aristotle's *Nicomachean Ethics* (3.6–9) it is translated as "noble," which in English still bears the traces of both physical beauty and virtue. Such a conflation is central to American Romanticism, dating from Emerson's dictum in "Nature" that "beauty is the mark God sets upon virtue."[25] It is my contention, then, that Hemingway's overt fixation with the dictates of skill—with cleanliness of result and beauty of execution—is the epiphenomenon of his foundational and more deeply vexed fixation with morality, and with the problem of determining moral value; and moreover, that his conflation of skill, beauty, and morality-as-freedom, as generator "of all significations and value," in Simone de Beauvoir's words,[26] carries with it his concern over language's capacity to render clear the world, to name well, and to articulate the criteria of our actions and choices with minimal distortion. In order to understand the role of the will in determining moral value, we must also understand the nature and quality of our self-representations; we must also ask whether or not we have an adequate moral lexicon and, indeed, whether or not our words can ever be adequate.

Hemingway once reported that he wrote *A Farewell to Arms* after (and in part was enabled to write it *by*) his conversion to Catholicism.[27] Robert Penn Warren calls it "a religious book" centrally concerned with "moral and philosophical" issues; it depicts the attempt "to redeem the incoherence of the world" through moral discipline and self-legislation.[28] *A Farewell to Arms* is the story of an idealistic and sometimes provincially moral protagonist. It is the story of a rule follower in the most generous sense of the term, a flawed and impulsive man who as a strategy of control repeatedly envisions the world as a series of games with strict and clear codes of behavior, and who strives to modulate his behavior in accordance with a concept of duty that transcends his self-interest.[29] Frederic's gestures of selflessness include volunteering to serve as an ambulance driver in the war, not because his interests are involved but because he believes it is the right thing to do, as well as offering to have his wounds treated last in triage because the suffering of others appears to him severe (58). Heroics aside, Frederic is most fundamentally concerned with the mundane requirement of doing the right thing. His grammar is a grammar of *is*'s and *ought*s, of declarative facts and of the obligations of the subjunctive: "he ought to have been baptized"; "you've got to have papers"; "Don't you know you can't touch an officer?" (327, 50, 35, 222). When a subordinate takes a clock from a farmhouse during the chaotic retreat from Caporetto, Frederic orders its return (200). And earlier, after paying a soldier to reserve a seat for him on a crowded train so that he will not be forced to stand after his recent knee surgery, Frederic surrenders it to the first man who protests that it is not fair to save a seat thus. "He was in the right," Frederic concedes (159).

For Frederic, moral value is the only value in war that can be noncontingent. Arguing with the Italian soldiers that they have a duty to continue their service until the war is finished, Frederic is briefly lured into a debate over what the "best" thing to do is. Is it best to win at great cost or to be defeated quickly? How much pain might each bring? In the end Frederic asserts that what is "best" is irrelevant. What matters is that they do what is right, regardless of the pain or pleasure of the consequences. Invoking the language of a higher duty, he concludes the debate by saying: "I know it is bad but we must finish it" (50). The right thing can be calculated simply, indeed, requires no calculation, short-circuits calculation.[30] In evaluating we do not inhabit but rather *rise above* the circumstantial. The right thing is independent of the consequences that follow from it, and by doing the right thing an individual in a like manner becomes independent of the consequences that follow from his actions. As Kant argues, in a deontological moral system obedience to the law makes consequences the responsibility of the law; concomitantly the decision to disregard the law, to attempt to determine what is "best" rather than what is "right," is the decision to take responsibility for consequences unto oneself.[31] After the war John Dewey criticized the philosophical recourse to "universal and necessary law" as an attempt to "deny the existence of chance." The war had revealed that experience is "a gamble," "a scene of risk . . . uncannily unstable"—but the recuperative attempt to achieve clarity through an assertion of universals leaves us "at the mercy of words," he insisted, and should be abandoned for a consequentialist embrace of contingency.[32] For Frederic, the sensation of risk this entails is unbearable. Calculating effects is a form of gambling that puts at stake a bitterly won autonomy, a gambling that, unlike horse racing and cards, hazards freedom on a lucky answer. Deontology and the language of the "right" thus serve to insulate Frederic from the perils of the counterfactual: morality, for Frederic, has the feel of enclosure, like a protective armor. Rule following for the lieutenant is the path of autonomy as freedom from luck.

Against this commanding need for self-sufficiency, clarity, and control, is the special beauty of human openness to chance and risk that perpetually renews itself in the war story's inevitable counterpart, the love story. To love is to make yourself vulnerable to another, vulnerable to a will that is beyond your control and to a body that undertakes sometimes catastrophic risks. Love, like markets, guns, and vice, can "ruin" you (305). Significantly, the risks attendant upon Frederic's love affair with Catherine, epitomized in the reciprocal vulnerability of sexual intercourse, are initially characterized by Frederic as a decision to abandon moral principles and to gamble:

> I thought she was probably a little crazy. It was all right if she was. I did not care what I was getting into . . . I knew I did not love Catherine Barkley nor had any idea of loving her. This was a game, like bridge, in which you said things instead of playing cards. Like bridge you had to pretend you were playing for money or playing for some stakes. Nobody had mentioned what the stakes were. It was all right with me. (30–31)

According to the value system that Catherine's friend Fergy repeatedly invokes, Frederic has seduced a woman recovering from the death of her lover (30), has gotten her into "trouble" (108) during a war when the resources to ensure a safe birth are compromised, and has refused to marry her, leaving her alone with a child to support (247).[33] Catherine, significantly, immediately rejects this paternalistic moralism, asserting her autonomy through her participation in the moral breach. "No one got me in a mess, Fergy. I get in my own messes." Fergy, undaunted, replies, "You're two of the same thing . . . You have no shame and no honor and you're as sneaky as he is" (246–247). By Fergy's measure (which Frederic largely accepts), they have shown a wanton disregard for each other and for the child that will be born into a war; and they have disgraced themselves, choosing not to marry simply because it would lead to unpleasant consequences (Catherine would be sent home for the duration of the conflict, 115). Catherine again rejects this description: like Hester Prynne, she believes that their love has a consecration of its own; they are married in spirit. Catherine is no less concerned with the moral good than Fergy or for that matter Frederic. Depicted throughout the novel as Frederic's double (she is a volunteer like Frederic and asserts frequently, with Frederic, the belief that they are "the same one," 139, 299), Catherine is the female analogue of the self-sacrificing soldier, the type-figure of a moral hero, a lifegiver and servant of the communal good. Her notion of the good, however, diverges markedly from Frederic's. In Hemingway's romantic symbology (dark-haired, dark-skinned male against light-haired, light-skinned female; the mobile ambulance driver against the nurse fixed at her station), their complementarity approaches antithesis. Indeed, from their first meeting, when Catherine forces Frederic to repeat her words, to speak with her voice in a role designed by her (31, 105) their relationship is depicted as a process of contest and conversion.[34] For our purposes, the most significant distinction between the two is the distinction between their moral outlooks. If Frederic's moral logic, like Fergy's, is deontological, or what Max Weber in 1918 called an "ethic of ultimate ends" (the good is that which satisfies the principles of right behavior, and the law absorbs responsibility for consequences), then Catherine's is consequentialist, or what Weber called an "ethic of responsibility" (the good is that which contributes to the general satisfaction, and the individual risks responsibility for the results).[35] Catherine's decision not to sleep with her previous lover is a classic consequentialist utility calculation, in which total predicted satisfaction displaces externally generated rules: she weighs whether it will be good or bad for him and blames herself when his subsequent death proves her prediction to be inaccurate (19—her decision to sleep with Frederic is in no small part a result of her recognition of this earlier utility mistake). Just so, Catherine will consider marriage with Frederic not because it is "right" but rather because it may be "better" (293), may contribute to the general happiness of those around her, including the unanticipated child. "What good would it do to marry now?" she asks Frederic (115); and later she offers, "We'll be married, Fergy . . . if it will please you" (248). If the representative figure for Frederic is Kant, then for Catherine it is the primary American philosopher of the era, the naturalist John Dewey. (I will explain ethical naturalism in detail later; for now we can treat it as equivalent to the broader category of consequentialism.) The divide separating these two thinkers, as representative of the divide mapped out by John Rawls between the umbrella categories of Kantianism and utilitarianism,[36] is the basic divide of all modern moral philosophy and practical moral thought.

Catherine throughout the novel is primarily concerned with risking the achievement of particular good ends; rules for her are of little import at best. The horse racing that is "disgusting" to Fergy because it is "crooked" and flaunts the rules can, for Catherine, become a source of delight as an opportunity to share with her lover (130). But for Catherine rules are not only hindrances to pleasure; when imposed they can do violence to individual autonomy and self-definition by attempting to exclude the risks inherent in self-authorship. As Dewey argues, an individual achieves freedom not through a conception of morality as fixed rule-following (he asserts, against a certain construal of deontology, that this deprives the moral life of its freedom)[37] but rather through the ability to form personal goals and projects and to choose intelligently among means and ends by evaluating their anticipated consequences.[38] "Impartial and consistent foresight of consequences," Dewey argues, is the very basis of ethical action.[39] Indeed, he continues, in each moral decision one is necessarily choosing, committing oneself to, even inventing one's future self *as a consequence:*

> This is the question finally at stake in any genuinely moral situation: What shall the agent *be?* What sort of character shall he assume? . . . The distinctively moral situation is then one in which elements of value and control . . . decide what kind of a character shall control further desires and deliberations. When ends are genuinely incompatible, no common denominator can be found except by deciding what sort of character is most highly prized and shall be given supremacy.[40]

For Dewey, the most prized character (a consequence evaluated according to the consequences it is likely to produce) is one shaped by the "morally invaluable" trait of sympathy,[41] and the most prized virtue is love, for in love the self is "responding with 'complete interest' and intelligent sympathy to the needs of the situation . . . in the pursuit of the ideal possibilities of the situation."[42] The Deweyan moral system—which as self-making Catherine adopts because it is an attractively American practice of daily living, and as other-embracing she adopts because it is extension of her emotional generosity—thus offers up a special marriage of consequentialism and personal integrity: it insists that sympathetic affiliation, responsibility for individual choice, and the anticipated utility of distinctive, communally imbricated life projects supersede preset, anonymous, and departicularized moral rules and constraints.[43] For Catherine generalized moral laws devalue subjectivity in favor of objectivity, contingency in favor of necessity, incommensurability in favor of substitutability; they replace situational evaluation with a belief in the universal applicability of abstract maxims.[44] Catherine rejects this ethics of justice and rights in favor of an ethics of care and responsibility,[45] in part because she experiences the maxims the former produces not only as personal abridgment but also as *mistakes.* Moral rules are a false narrative, so to speak, applied externally, parochially, and inappropriately to the individual. When Frederic offers to redeem Catherine by marrying her, she retorts: "Don't talk as though you had to make an honest woman of me, darling. I'm a very honest woman. You can't be ashamed of something if you're only happy and proud of it" (116; on shame see also 247). Thus her affair with Frederic breaks no rule because for her the only rules are the law of pursuing the good as a consequence (in this case, the good of love), and the law of taking responsibility unto oneself for the unique worlds one builds.[46] Catherine thus reveals to Frederic a new way of evaluating intersubjective action, a generous and other-directed way, which, like the system it opposes, claims to be the source of freedom and self-authorship.[47] This morality of "integrity" is for the lieutenant the opening of worlds. It is also the beginning of risk. It is Catherine, after all, who first opens to Frederic the radical possibility that they might abandon their posts if this would facilitate the good of their relationship (137). When Frederic deserts, he is undertaking an action previously unimaginable to him, an action inspired by his love for Catherine and by the new worldview she provides.[48]

The novel's architecture reproduces its binary ethical divisions. Parallel in importance to the novel's two escape scenes are the two primary moments when Frederic decides to act against his principles, to commit, from his original perspective, a moral crime. The first is his dishonest attempt to seduce Catherine. The second is precisely this decision to desert the army, to forswear an obligation voluntarily undertaken. Initially he tries to justify himself according to his conception of the rules: the contract was broken by the enlisted men who attacked him during the retreat, and therefore he is no longer obligated to serve. He even refuses to accept that he is "in trouble" (eerily like the pregnant Catherine) when approached by a man who identifies him as a possible deserter in need of assistance (238). His redescriptions and justifications quickly fail him, however, and he is forced to accept in the end that he has broken a rule central to his moral self-description. "I know it is bad but we must finish it." Frederic's sense of guilt fails in turn, however, when he is united with Catherine. "A little while later Catherine said, 'You don't feel like a criminal do you?' 'No,' I said. 'Not when I'm with you'" (251). Frederic has indeed abandoned his commitments, but only to fulfill a duty more fundamental to his personal life projects—that is, to support his lover through her pregnancy. He has decided to break the rules and to abandon his post in the army not only because the consequences of this choice will be more satisfying but also because they appear to have moral value of their own. The later effects of his freedom will morally justify his desertion. Mere desertion is never justified; but desertion followed by good acts may be. Like his relationship with Catherine, his decision to leave the army is based upon a new moral calculus, in which the predicted aftereffects of his actions (a loving relationship that protects the interests of his partner and child) retroactively make right the originally wrong act. Consequences enable an ex post facto redescription of the initial decisions (I did not seduce her, I married her in spirit; I did not desert, I undertook a more fundamental obligation) and thereby discredit the relevance of an a priori rule-morality system.

But Frederic is morally unlucky. Catherine dies—dies because he got her into trouble, as Fergy predicted. And he *is* responsible for her death.

> "Aren't you proud of your son?" the nurse asked . . .
> "No," I said. "He nearly killed his mother."
> "It isn't the little darling's fault. Didn't you want a boy?"
> "No," I said. (325)

In blaming the infant, Frederic both displaces his sense of guilt and affirms the logic of his own culpability, directly acknowledging the moral truth of negative responsibility: that is, the notion that we have a special relationship with consequences caused by us, regardless of whether or not we intended or could even control them. As Bernard Williams writes, responsibility

> can extend far beyond what one intentionally did to almost anything for which one was causally responsible in virtue of something one intentionally did . . . The lorry driver who, through no fault of his, runs over a child, will feel differently from any spectator, even a spectator next to him in the cab . . . Doubtless, and rightly, people will try, in comforting him, to move the driver from this state of feeling, move him indeed from where he is to something more like the place of a spectator, but it is important that this is seen as something that should need to be done, and indeed some doubt would be felt about a driver who too blandly or readily moved to that position.[49]

Frederic feels *regret,* the bridge between sorrow and guilt. Contemplating the death of his child, lover, and friends, Frederic ambiguously conflates the aversiveness of bereavement with an acknowledgment that it is he who is the source of these deaths, that without him none of it would have happened: "Poor little kid. I wished the hell I'd been choked like that. No I didn't. Still there would not be all this dying to go through" (327). Not only did consequences *not* end up morally justifying his actions, they positively and permanently *un*justified them. At the end of the novel Frederic is a mere deserter, a fugitive who got a nurse at the front into trouble and thereby brought about her death.

Frederic broke the rules; punishment is the logic of his belief system: "Now Catherine would die. That was what you did. You died. You did not know what it was about. You never had time to learn. They threw you in and told you the rules and the first time they caught you off base they killed you" (327). But the violent disproportionality of cause and effect, transgression and punishment, is senseless.[50] Consequences acquire a significance that blots out all other considerations. And in the end, despite any law, or any obedience, there is only one consequence, and one plot. "They threw you in and told you the rules and the first time they caught you off base they killed you. Or they killed you gratuitously like Aymo. Or gave you the syphilis like Rinaldi. But they killed you in the end. You could count on that. Stay around and they would kill you." As Catherine thereafter formulates it, the notion that we might author our own lives, whether through the moral law and its promise of freedom or through the defense of integrity, is "just a dirty trick" (331). "So now they got her in the end. You never got away with anything. Get away hell! It would have been the same if we had been married fifty times" (320). Initially Frederic believes that something bad has happened because he did the wrong thing; but as he continues thinking he realizes that, on the contrary, *it was the wrong thing because something bad happened.* "It would have been the same if we had been married fifty times."

The Good

Catastrophe is teleological. The rupture moment inverts history: the future is not explained through the past; rather, the past is explained through the future. Catherine's death and *A Farewell to Arms*'s logic of moral evaluation thus reproduce in small and personal detail the mass cultural logic of the war and of representational history itself. The early 1900s even during the war began to be referred to as the prewar years. The disconnected events of that period, each pointing to a different future like light scattered through a prism, were immediately renarrated and unified with reference to the world-defining catastrophe that followed. The prewar years then did not simply precede the war but, by implication, directly and inevitably produced it, as naturally and necessarily as the plot of a well-managed story.[51] The past became itself through the future. The effect determined the nature of the cause. This proclivity of the narrative imagination to redefine the past with reference to a particular chosen end point, to *story* an event, is for Frederic the source of both an increasing consequentialist morality and a decreasing confidence in the possibility of moral evaluation.[52] The two, I will argue, are necessarily connected.

Frederic's morality, at the novel's start predicated upon a confidence in the will as generator of meaning, is replaced at the end by a morality subordinated to the law of consequence and to the rough measures of human utility: that which maximizes and distributes satisfaction is morally good, and that which produces suffering is evil. For what meaning can any idea of duty and justice or any laws of right and wrong have, if they produce as much pain (surely a moral evil) as happiness (surely a moral good)? This was indeed the position taken by the preeminent moral philosophers in postwar America. Partly as a reaction to the war and to earlier deontologists, whose uncompromising absolutist rationalism seemed unsuited to the modern condition, American thinkers formulated a species of consequentialist moral philosophy called naturalism (not to be confused with literary naturalism).[53] One of the seminal works of this diverse movement was R. B. Perry's *General Theory of Value* (1926). Briefly, naturalists held that moral value (that is, any notion of the "good") was contingent upon the particular "interests" of an individual or interpretative community. In Perry's famous definition, the good or what has value is any object of interest. "*A thing—any thing—has value, or is valuable, in the original and generic sense when it is the object of an interest— any interest. Or, whatever is the object of interest is ipso facto valuable.* Thus the valuableness of peace is the characteristic conferred on peace by the interest which is taken in it, for what it is, or for any of its attributes, effects, or implications."[54] A thing is always good "for" something rather than good "simply." In other words, value is "relational,"[55] changing with both time and place, and is dependent not upon any quality inherent in an action but rather upon the intersection between the act and the reflective perception of it. Multiplicity of subject positions and circumstances multiplies notions of good. In a phrase, naturalists replace the closed idea of *"the* good" with the open notion of *"any* good." The limit set to this relativity for moral value is the requirement of the social good, which consists in the harmonious "integration of interests" in a community (and for Dewey, in the realization of self through cooperative social action).[56] For naturalists moral evaluations are thus empirical statements, quantifiable and testable like other natural phenomena through observable outcomes in a community.[57] "A is morally good" therefore means that "the measured consequences of A are consistent with the 'standard-of-harmonious-happiness.'"[58]

The intuitive ease and judiciousness of this utilitarian formulation, however, are misleading. Hemingway illustrates naturalism's special difficulty in moral evaluation with a parable of moral friction that closes the novel. Indifferently watching ants burn in a fire, Frederic contemplates acting the "messiah" by lifting their log out of the flames. He abandons the idea, but when he wishes to put whiskey in his cup he decides to dump out its residue of water onto the log. "I think the cup of water on the burning log only steamed the ants" (328). If moral value ("good" and "bad") resides outside the self in worldly consequences; and if consequences in a world of "friction" are at best unpredictable and at worst uniformly cruel; and finally, if through negative responsibility we are at least partly joined to events in the world external to our intentions and beyond our control—if, in other words, Frederic's worldview at novel's close is valid—then acting morally is impossible. "He did not want any consequences," Hemingway writes of the protagonist from "Soldier's Home." "He did not want any consequences ever again."[59] T. S. Eliot depicts the power of consequences to invert moral expectations in his postwar poem "Gerontion" (1920): "Think / Neither fear nor courage saves us. Unnatural vices / Are fathered by our heroism. Virtues / Are forced upon us by our impudent crimes."[60] In a world where loving can kill, and indeed can be expected to do so (it is for this reason rather than simple jealousy that Fergy cries when Catherine falls in love with Frederic), moral decisions face the problem of infinite regress. Bernard Williams writes:

> One's history as an agent is a web in which anything that is the product
> of the will is surrounded and held up and partly formed by things that

are not, in such a way that reflection can go only in one of two directions: either in the direction of saying that responsible agency is a fairly superficial concept, which has a limited use in harmonizing what happens, or else that it is not a superficial concept, but that it cannot ultimately be purified—if one attaches importance to the sense of what one is in terms of what one has done and what in the world one is responsible for, one must accept much that makes its claim on that sense solely in virtue of its being actual.[61]

To determine the right thing to do in any given situation, you must set an arbitrary limit to those imaginable consequences for which you will take responsibility. But such arbitrary limits have little weight against catastrophe. Could Oedipus, as Williams asks, simply have claimed that it was not his fault?[62] Catastrophe reveals the truths occluded in the mundane: what exactly are you *not* responsible for? If consequences can be infinite, moral decisions require infinite calculation. And if moral law is thus useless as a practical guide to action in the world, then it is irrelevant to the human condition. Its only value is the value of a validity, or truth, that is beyond human reckoning.

Consequentialism fails to supply an adequate account of moral responsibility not only because of its difficulty in setting nonarbitrary limits to moral agency,[63] not only because it makes, so to speak, all actions guilty, but also because its goal-oriented notion of moral value makes all actions *innocent* insofar as they contribute to a preapproved end. Consequentialist morality fosters an attitude of instrumentalization—instrumentalization of self and of the external world. In the consequentialist worldview, all actions and events in the world can be conceived as means toward a desirable end: the more important the end, the greater the number of persons and events that will be judged in relation to it rather than on their own. By midnovel, Catherine is nascently aware that this system thins out any sense of the morally wrong: "I wish we could do something really sinful . . . Everything we do seems so innocent and simple. I can't believe we do anything wrong" (153). But there is of course one fundamental wrong that Catherine does commit—a wrong to herself. Shortly after discussing how a prostitute will do and say whatever a paying customer requests, Catherine equivalently surrenders herself to Frederic: "I'll say just what you wish and I'll do what you wish and then you will never want any other girls, will you? . . . You see? I'm good. I do what you want" (105–106). Catherine believes her subordination is necessary to the primary ideal she pursues throughout the novel: that is, her relationship with Frederic. Their union is for her a good beyond compare, commensurate to a "religion" (116). The chaos and brutality of war make expansive goals futile. In the shrunken space allowed to her for creativity and for good, then, Catherine will cultivate a simple love.[64] But for her this simple love is not only a way to save one man's life (her devotion to him begins in her role as nurse to patient and never significantly departs from this model), it is also a way of preserving the world, a way of defying treachery in one last place. It justifies nearly any sacrifice. Hence the a priori moral wrong that she believes is required by their relationship—the wrong of obliterating her own autonomy, obliterating the "integrity" that her flexible moral code was meant to protect—is transformed through the relentless utilitarian hierarchy into a morally justified and possibly necessary act.[65] As John Rawls writes, "Utilitarianism does not take seriously the distinction between persons."[66] At the same time, this inevitable tendency to aggregate individuals and to view things first insofar as they contribute to the project you have deemed good can also promote a disposition oriented toward *maximizing* perceived self-interest. When there are not enough wounded to justify retaining Catherine at Frederic's hospital, for instance, she complains about the lack. "I hope some will come. What would I do if they sent me away? They will unless there are more patients" (103). As Randolph Bourne argued during the war, the consequentialism of Dewey and like-minded naturalist philosophers is an instrumentalizing vision that justifies "almost any activity" as long as it contributes to a desired end.[67]

Derek Parfit, a leading moral philosopher of the utilitarian tradition, reveals that accepting a certain class of consequentialism can produce moral failure by leading us to understand that collective self-interest is the universal law and that Morality as the embodiment of intrinsic value does not exist. For these consequentialisms, honoring one's commitments or protecting the vulnerable are not right, good, or obligatory in and of themselves, but rather are useful as means, something like rules of thumb that we should obey because, given how our society is constructed, we all have a better chance of a more comfortable existence if most of us remain convinced that this is the proper way to act. That is, moral codes express no truths of immanent right and wrong, for these do not exist; moral codes are, rather, instruments for realizing our rational long-term self-interest. Moral concepts are deployed to describe behavioral conditions determined to be generally favorable for the social organizations we have set up— favorable, that is, as all Prisoner's Dilemma compromises are favorable: any individual might be better off to cheat, but if all cheated all would be worse off.[68] Therefore through a process of social evolution (partly unconscious, partly the result of cultural maintenance by those of superior understanding), contingent behavioral codes are naturalized as a transcendent Morality that people believe they should obey. And so people mistakenly acquire an emotional relationship with wrongdoing *as such* rather than with wrongdoing as calculative data: they feel guilty for being the kind of person who is drawn to selfishness or other sorts of preferentialism, they feel shame for feeling greater attachment to personally adopted ends than to principles of appropriate means, or they suffer from any number of other such forms of false consciousness. But consequentialism, in fact, *can work only if they (wrongly) do so;* the system *requires* that we "make ourselves have false beliefs," as Parfit writes; morality is "deception" and, again, "self-deception."[69] Consequentialism says that we ought to cause ourselves to have the false beliefs and misguided dispositions of nonconsequentialist Morality in order to produce the best overall consequences, because if we believe what consequentialism knows— that other desires and goals should often trump Morality—then as a matter of empirical fact we weaken our consequentially useful desire to avoid wrongdoing and thereby open ourselves to catastrophic calculative mistakes. Catherine, in other words, needs not to believe her own beliefs: to borrow the language of her terminal epiphany, it is all just a "dirty trick" (331). Catherine throughout the novel is the paradigmatic self-transparent consequentialist (or rather naturalist, the predominant form of such consequentialism in postwar America). But in the end, when together with Frederic she begins to see what will follow from their reflectively endorsed actions, the language of moral evaluation explodes. 'Good,' 'bad,' 'should,' 'ought,' 'right,' and 'trouble' proliferate beyond stable and bounded context throughout the novel, but in the last chapter (compared with, for instance, the first four chapters as a parallel unit) they appear with special frequency, often askew of and frequently decontextualized from any moral content: for instance, "give me enough to do some good" (324), "all right" (331), "I'm not any good" (317), or "good luck" (315). Likewise the *ought*s and *must*s Frederic obeyed are now only the alienating and inexplicable commands of the nurses, which, after Catherine's death, he rejects as empty:

> I went to the door of the room.
> "You can't come in now," one of the nurses said.
> "Yes I can," I said.
> "You can't come in yet."
> "You get out," I said. "The other one too."
> But after I had got them out and shut the door and turned off the light it wasn't any good. It was like saying good-by to a statue. After a while I went out and left the hospital and walked back to the hotel in the rain. (332)

"It wasn't any good." What *is* any good? Perhaps the final lesson of the novel is that the naturalist coupling of the concept *good* with the qualifier *any* evacuates the former of all substantive content. For naturalists, the good is considered an indeterminate category until filled out by circumstances: hence, nothing is inexorably good nor inexorably evil—"not even war."[70] For precisely this reason critics assailed the naturalism of R. B. Perry and John Dewey. Dewey was an important supporter of the war (he inveighed against Germany by tracing militarist nationalism back to Kant).[71] With Dewey, Perry justified the war as good by arguing that it contributed to the much desired end of consolidating the norms of international law.[72] Indeed, he asserted, its unprecedented physical terror was our greatest cause for hope, because the new power of "numbers, organization, and science" to destroy revealed a "strength of a higher order" that could be channeled into the creation of institutions and artifacts of "human solidarity" and "international law and equity." "Man must destroy," he wrote, "in order to save."[73] Pacifist Bertrand Russell attacked Perry's instrumentalizing "interest theory" justification of war and argued in detail that the "evil of [this] great war is so stupendous that in itself it outweighs almost any good result that it may achieve."[74] In 1917 Randolph Bourne, a widely read contributor to the *Dial* and the *New Republic,* argued even more forcefully that Dewey's "instrumental" philosophy was so morally unanchored as to be complicit in the war. How could a humane philosopher, he asked, "accept war without more violent protest, without a greater wrench?"[75] Two years later, social critic Harold Stearns blamed the widespread liberal support for war on what he saw as the false promises of Deweyan philosophy.

With Bourne he argued that Dewey's pragmatic, utilitarian confidence in our ability to manage and optimize consequences through experimental observation, along with his conception of the good as a theoretically open variable, made him and other liberals believe (like Catherine) that his philosophical system could effectively manage war, could successfully bring into being *through war* states of affairs situationally understood as good.[76] But in a tragic world consequentialism's promises are deception, as Catherine realizes before dying, and as Dewey himself would come in part to see: not long after the war, he bitterly repudiated his view that positive consequences could be produced by and therefore justify war and joined the international movement outlawing war that culminated in the disappointing 1928 Kellogg-Briand Pact. *It wasn't any good.*

In *Principia Ethica* (1903), a work that set the groundwork for the debates of modern ethical theory and that banished ethical naturalism to the margins of European discourse, G. E. Moore asserted that no moral philosophy can sustain itself without first answering the question "What is good?" Moore argued that ethical naturalism failed in precisely this endeavor. He believed that naturalists confused the natural properties or particular manifestations of good with its nonnatural essence—something like confusing sugar with sweetness.[77] Indeed, for naturalists, good is a revisable concept. In other words, knowledge of the concept *good* is achieved by accumulating particular instances and conceptions of it. Naturalists are left with the formula "A is good," into which can be substituted several equally valid possibilities: "the maximization of happiness for the greatest number is good," "the object of any interest is good," "pleasure is good," or "that which we desire to desire is good." But each of these declarations, Moore asserted, can be transformed meaningfully into a question. Is the maximization of happiness good? Is that which we desire to desire good? No matter how strongly a community may believe that the good is that which we desire to desire, "it may be always asked, with significance . . . 'Is it good to desire to desire A?'"[78] In other words, any naturalist definition of good is open to qualified negation. Each naturalist declaration (the maximization of happiness is good) can be transformed into a contradiction (this maximizes happiness but is not good).[79] Good as a signifier, by this argument, is never equivalent to its signifieds. Indeed, for Moore, it was fundamentally *other* to them at the most deep level: good "is incapable of definition."[80]

The fact that any naturalist conception of the good is both an open-ended question and vulnerable to interior negation was taken by Moore to reveal not only something deep about the inadequacy of such an approach to ethical philosophy, but also something about human accessibility to articulated meaning. Central to Moore's analytic deconstruction of the naturalist good, and equally to Hemingway's in the final pages of his novel, is the somewhat counterintuitive thesis that a sign ("good") which is essential to daily communication, to the meaning of individual lives, and to the structure of society as a whole is unanalyzable and in the end incommunicable. Moore concluded that good is a quality which objectively exists—as real as the physical property of colors—but which, like the subjective experience of yellow, is prior to analysis and definition. He replaced naturalism's relational formula "good for" with the concept "good simply." Good is a quality distinct from those things we experience as good. It is not reducible to any of its multifarious manifestations, nor is it inferable from the appearance of a single characteristic manifestation; it is instead singular, permanent, nonsubjective, and unified. The morally good is therefore rescued from the relativity that follows naturally from the commonsense consequentialism of his day.[81] For Hemingway, such faith in the transcendent unity of the good was untenable. At the same time, however, he was unprepared to reject its possible ideal reality. For without a notion of the good to ground morality, the viability of the will as arbitrator of meanings is subverted, and freedom is lost to luck. If the good does not *exist,* if the good is simply that which we happen to call the good, then the word becomes as meaningless (through surplus of meaning) as any deictic, as contentless (through surplus of content) as the word "any."

"It wasn't any good." In that anguished valedictory remark is manifest both Hemingway's allegorical denial of the existence of good and also his faltering, irresolute, yet finally uncompromising assertion of the concept's potentially transcendent reality. *A Farewell to Arms* is a study in epistemological confusions and deferrals. It is a book of negations: a critique of the primary moral systems articulated in its time from deontology to consequentialism; a critique of violence's senseless waste and of the domestic sphere's sensible, dehumanizing culture of instrumentalization; and a denial of the possibility of freedom, either through moral transcendence or through unlimited realizations of interest (the self in the end is equally slave to each). At the same time, however, the book never fully renounces the search for a sustainable moral form, the necessity of both violence and instrumentalization, or the possibility of individual freedom. In its simultaneous affirmation of the will and its subordination of the will to externality, in its simultaneous sheltering of intact interiors and its opening of the self to the incursions of the sensible, the narrative points beyond the contradiction of sovereignty expressed in Crane's absurdism forward to the dialectic of ambiguity articulated by Simone de Beauvoir, who takes existence's groundlessness itself as a grounding through radical freedom. Beauvoir's ethics seeks not to eliminate ambiguity—"by making oneself pure inwardness or pure externality, by escaping from the sensible world or by being engulfed in it"[82]—but rather, like *A Farewell to Arms*, seeks to disclose it, and to take this disclosure as the inaugural moment of ethics and the assumption of a terrible responsibility. "Meaning is never fixed," Beauvoir writes, so "it must be constantly won."[83]

CHAPTER FOUR

Trauma and the Structure of Social Norms: Literature and Theory between the Wars

Violence destroys fiction: this thesis recurs continuously throughout the literatures of war. The experience of violence puts tremendous pressure on nations, persons, ideas, and language. Violence thus achieves bare truth negatively, by shattering the cherished fictions that structure our routines of life: the daily fictions told by generals, newspapers, and the home front; the deeper fictions of national purpose, history, and identity; and the still more fundamental fictions of moral clarity, a stable self, and the intersubjective availability through language of unified, singular meaning. In landscapes of blasted homes and bloated corpses, words of explanation fall to the ground like brittle and frail autumn leaves.

Foundational epistemological borders—like the borders between care and harm, cause and effect, or the morally permitted and the morally prohibited—are revealed by war to be fragile social fictions. The human will, which through moral intention and declaration stabilizes the borders of these meanings, seems irrelevant and thin when juxtaposed to war's vivid and traumatic material realities. "While they continued to write and talk," writes Erich Maria Remarque, "we saw the wounded and dying."[1] War thus initiates a semantic crisis, a crisis of meaning premised upon disbelief in language's ability effectively to refer to and intervene in the material world. "Words, Words, Words," the protagonist of *All Quiet on the Western Front* declares, "they do not reach me."[2] Remarque depicts a culture exhausted by a language that fails to signify; his American contemporary Ernest Hemingway depicts as a form of obscenity the abstraction of a language disconnected from the actual. For Hemingway, the model of all language beyond the materially referential noun is the model of propaganda. "Abstract words such as glory, honor, courage, or hallow were obscene beside the concrete names of villages, the numbers of roads, the names of rivers, the numbers of regiments and the dates."[3] By destabilizing the routinized meaning-systems of civilization that are so continuously oriented toward the minimization of physical injury, propaganda's hermeneutic spectacle enables catastrophic violence. War legitimates itself through "unanchored language"—*glory, honor, courage, hallow*—and leaves in its wake the tatters of speech and belief that it no longer needs.[4] For Hemingway, it is thus only at the subfoundational level of the deictic, with the capacity of language to name and to count, to match words up seamlessly with their physical referents, that language finds its appropriate place in social practice. Hemingway's vision of solid, bordered, and impermeable referentiality is a retreat from the disorder of interpretation, from the semantic disruption that, for him, is both the cause and the product of violence.

Mikhail Bakhtin has written extensively on the effects of massive cultural change upon literary expression. Engendered by a culture's internal contradictions, he asserts, is a proliferation of crisscrossing language games and a new fluidity of genres. In a period of intense struggle, he writes, "boundaries are drawn with new sharpness and simultaneously erased with new ease; it is sometimes impossible to establish precisely where they have been erased or where certain of the warring parties have already crossed over into alien territory."[5] It is significant that Bakhtin, speaking broadly of language and cultural change, chooses to employ here the metaphor of invasion. War is a paradigm for border crossing, physically, conceptually, and morally. In war the instability of borders between nations (the French desire to reannex Alsace and Lorraine, or Germany's *Drang nach Osten*) is reproduced in the unstable distinction between the body and its external world (Ernst Jünger's narrative of wounds in *The Storm of Steel*, his detailed accounts of the punctured body),[6] which is itself reproduced in the dissolution of borders between individual bodies (Pat Barker's story in *The Ghost Road* of a soldier's collapse into the liquefied belly of a rotting corpse, and of the residue of odor that permanently endures). War precipitates the breakdown of the epistemological and physical integrity of the individual: the soldier, like a miniaturization of his body politic, begins to fragment and to blend into others and objects.

In a like manner, war dismantles the cultures that constitute the individual; it violates the boundaries that structure social meaning. For noncombatants, war is in large measure a matter of transgressing the borders of domestic convention. It is a matter of losing conventions in such a way that you become free, and losing the conventions that make freedom possible. In Louisa May Alcott's autobiographical *Hospital Sketches,* war is an opening of opportunity. The Union's emergency call for nurses frees her from the constraints of tightly bordered domestic space and allows her to exhilarate in free movement, to travel on boat and train, and to walk alone in strange cities. For Mary Chesnut, however, the Civil War initiates the breakdown of the community that enables her to function. Forced to evacuate her home, she can no longer choose where to travel or with whom she will associate; the coercion of scarcity is so pervasive that she cannot even choose what to wear or eat. This dialectic of freedom and necessity reproduces itself over time as a structural component of war. In Dos Passos's *Nineteen Nineteen,* Eveline Hutchins and Anne Elizabeth Trent (referred to by all as Daughter) are both freed from gendered constraints on speech and mobility by the call to service in the war. It is the loss of free speech, however, that characterizes the experiences of a French civilian from the same novel. "C'est la guerre," she explains to an American visitor, referring in guarded, noncommittal, and formulaic language to a public notice that reads "MEFIEZ VOUS LES OREILLES ENNEMIS VOUS ECOUTENT."[7] The notice symbolizes war's breakdown of communicative conventions like transparency and trust, as well as its dissolution of the public-private border that separates private behavior from the interests and invasions of the state. War's disruptive anomie is thus repeatedly figured as both liberating and coercive. As we shall see, this duality is reproduced in the radically opposed hermeneutic theories that developed as a response to the world wars. In the first half of this chapter I will examine the way war's deconstruction of borders determined literary production; in the second half, I will track its shaping effect upon philosophical and cultural theory. What begins as a device of aesthetic theory and practice ends, I will argue, as a theory of the deep structure of language.

The Grotesque

In 1832 Carl von Clausewitz, a favorite among German strategists in World War I, rejected the "geometrical" cleanliness and regularity attributed to war by theorists like Heinrich von Bülow and Antoine Jomini. Against their "war by algebra" Clausewitz describes a war that tends toward maximal disorder, toward the breakdown of linearity and rhythm. "In the conduct of war," he writes, "perception cannot be governed by laws." War produces "a kind of twilight, which, like fog or moonlight, often tends to make things seem grotesque."[8] War dissolves the planes that guide perception. To understand this, he asserts, is to understand the essence of war. It is significant that Clausewitz, who chooses his words with the control and precision of a soldier aiming a weapon, uses here both the image of fog and the word "grotesque." In German Romanticism, the intellectual climate in which Clausewitz wrote, the word "grotesque" referred to a developing, self-consciously unique genre of writing. The literary grotesque—like the fantastic half-plant, half-animal monsters of architectural ornament from which it takes its name (the *grottesche* of the Italian Renaissance)—is marked by the disruption of familiar categories, by unstable oppositions, heterogeneous combinations, and the erasure of formal boundaries. The fog, Wolfgang Kayser notes, is a quintessential grotesque motif, signifying "the disintegration of order in a spatially unified social group."[9] Fog, itself situated somewhere between material and immaterial, commemorates the dissolution of the categories of perception and the disabling of the individual's capacity to discriminate: it wreathes war representation from *The Red Badge of Courage,* which opens with the image of an army emerging from the fog and depicts battle throughout against backgrounds of smoke as pervasive as weather patterns, to Francis Ford Coppola's *Apocalypse Now,* which obscures the viewer's vision from start to end in fog and clouds of smoke and dust. In the key chapter "Snow" of Thomas Mann's *Magic Mountain,* the foreword of which declares that the novel must be understood through its contiguity to the war, the white mist of precipitation that destroys vision, "obliterating all contours," also generates a vertiginous rotation between opposites, between "icy horror" and "joy," between "fatigue and excitement," and between "interest in disease and death" and "interest in life." Perceptions, the protagonist declares, are "two-faced, they are in the highest degree equivocal, everything depends upon the point of view."[10] The novel closes with a brutal reprise of this disintegrating environment, at the scene of battle, with the protagonist lost in twilight, shadows, clouds, and wet air.

In his book *On the Grotesque,* Geoffrey Harpham argues that cultures establish the grotesque "by establishing conditions of order and coherence, especially by specifying which categories are logically or generically incompatible with which others." The hybridity of the grotesque is thus generated by the dynamic interplay and partial fusion of binary opposites: center-margin, legitimate-illegitimate, order-disorder, attraction-repulsion, high-low, known-unknown, and inside-outside. Harpham's emphasis upon the "skewing of logical or ontological categories"[11] draws on the seminal work of Bakhtin's *Rabelais and His World.* For Bakhtin the idea of the grotesque is understood through a particular conception of the body. The grotesque body, he writes,

> is not a closed, completed unit; it is unfinished, outgrows itself, transgresses its own limits. The stress is laid on those parts of the body that are open to the outside world, that is, the parts through which the world enters the body or emerges from it, or through which the body itself goes out to meet the world . . . The body discloses its essence as a principle of growth which exceeds it own limits only in copulation, pregnancy, childbirth, the throes of death, eating, drinking, and defecation.

Bakhtin emphasizes that this "unfinished and open body (dying, bringing forth and being born) is not separated from the world by clearly defined boundaries; it is blended with the world, with animals, with objects."[12] For Bakhtin, the aesthetic grotesque subverts classical notions of beauty that emphasize completion, closure, and symmetry; at a broader level, it bears a reciprocal causal relationship with social practices that, like the carnivals of the politically disenfranchised, offer "liberation from all that is utilitarian" and that parody and disrupt stratified regimes of social order.[13] As Tomas Venclova writes, for worried Soviet authorities Bakhtinian dialogism "raised the specter of a parliament, [and] carnival raised the specter of a revolution."[14] Wolfgang Kayser likewise emphasizes the relationship between the development of literary form and the reception of social practices. He argues that by the twentieth century the grotesque became the source of "widespread phenomena" in art and literature, a style that could be used in combination with the literature of horror to "demolish the categories prevalent in the middle-class world view."[15]

In the post–World War I period, the grotesque developed both as a cluster of literary tropes and as a particular social conception of the fragility of meaning. For literary protest writers, the grotesque became the analogue at the level of image and sentence structure of the broader epistemological confusion generated by collective trauma; it became the means of raising specific questions about cultural givens. The grotesque is a particularly apt form for the representation of war.[16] A specific list of taxonomical correspondences would include the following. First, as already evidenced by Clausewitz, military strategists rely upon images of the grotesque as explanatory paradigms. "War," generalizes Marshal Saxe, "is a science replete with shadows in whose obscurity one cannot move with an assured step . . . All sciences have principles and rules. War has none."[17] Second, in psychiatric casework, war trauma is repeatedly figured in the language of the grotesque, explicitly by Judith Herman, for instance, and implicitly by Freud, who depicts such trauma as a "breach" in "protective" borders, a disruption of inside and outside, and by Dori Laub, who describes trauma as "an event that has no beginning, no ending, no before, no during and no after," an event whose "absence of categories . . . lends it a quality of 'otherness.'"[18] Third, as Elaine Scarry and Paul Fussell argue, war as a field of experiential knowledge is conceptualized as a pervasive set of binary categories in crisis, as "the visible friend and the invisible enemy, the normal (us) and the grotesque (them), the division of the landscape into known and unknown, safe and hostile."[19] Fourth, and relatedly, the passage to war for the soldier reproduces the structure of liminality—that is, the separation of the individual from his familiar place in society, and the ritualistic identification of the individual as transient or outside the borders.[20] In "How to Tell a True War Story," Tim O'Brien emphasizes both Clausewitzian fog and dynamic binarism as essential features of wartime experience:

> For the common soldier . . . war has the feel—the spiritual texture—of a great ghostly fog, thick and permanent. There is no clarity. Everything swirls. The old rules are no longer binding, the old truths no longer true. Right spills over into wrong. Order blends into chaos, love into hate, ugliness into beauty, law into anarchy, civility into savagery. The vapors suck you in. You can't tell where you are, or why you're there, and the

only certainty is overwhelming ambiguity. In war you lose your sense of
the definite, hence your sense of truth itself, and therefore it's safe to say
that in a true war story nothing is ever absolutely true.[21]

For post–World War I writers including Hemingway, Dos Passos,
Cummings, and Cather, the grotesque is used to reveal the primary
features of wartime experience. As we have already in effect seen, the
grotesque is a structuring motif of Hemingway's *A Farewell to Arms,*
which, beneath the surface of its androcentric plot of human agency
and control, deploys images hybridizing the human and the mechanical to tell the story of a world in which tools have taken on a dangerous life of their own. The grotesque is equally the subtext of his later
work *For Whom the Bell Tolls.* This novel, like *A Farewell to Arms,*
destabilizes perception with unexpected metaphors combining the
sentient and the nonsentient: a military truck is described as "sick,"
and a hill under artillery assault is "the breast of a young girl with no
nipple."[22] The novel exposes bodily interiors through the related grotesque motifs of wounding (sharp compact fractures pressing against
taut purple skin, 462), having sex (desire is repeatedly figured as a
swelling of tissue inside the throat), and eating and drinking (hunger
is depicted by the movement of the stomach "inside," 19, and parted
lips leak liquids, 83, or reveal or a "mouth full of roast young goat,"
127). The novel lingers over the openings of the body and their literal
blending of inside and outside; in a like manner it challenges continually the binary distinction between the human and animal, visualizing
humans as composed of animal parts ("his lips made a tight line, like
the mouth of a fish"; her hair grew "like the fur of an animal," 213,
345) or as behaving like animals ("she walks like a colt moves"; "he
saw the gypsy jink like a running boar," 137, 459). If disrupting
the planes that separate the sentient and the nonsentient can arouse
our sympathy by revealing the poignant vulnerability of the material
world, then collapsing the distinction between human and animal reveals one important procedure through which sympathy is abolished.
It is a painstaking process. Soldiers learn to kill only reluctantly: the
human resistance to killing other humans is so strong that, as David
Grossman writes, "in many circumstances, soldiers on the battlefield
will die before they can overcome it." After World War II, Army Bri-
gadier General S. L. A. Marshall released a study showing that, on average, only fifteen to twenty men out of a hundred used their weapons

during combat action—Grossman goes on to argue that this ratio seems relatively stable across time and cultures.[23] This strong, presumptively innate human inhibition against intraspecific violence is effectively overcome by the manipulation of what Erik Erikson identifies as the human tendency to form "pseudo-species": that is, ingroups established through ritual that embody *"the* human identity." Killing is facilitated by the collective reconceptualization of the enemy group as less than fully human and the consequent determination that any individual member of that group of "inimical identities" is a suitable target of lethal violence.[24] *For Whom the Bell Tolls,* which opens with the enemy hunted like "big game" (14), is about learning to kill: it is about learning to shoot in open combat, learning to murder an unsuspecting victim, and learning to injure others theatrically and brutally in acts of retribution. It is thus also, and more basically, about learning to curse, learning to act upon others in speaking, and learning to speak in a murderous tongue. "Damn your bloody, red pig-eyes and your swine-bristly swines-end of a face" (179). And again, cultivating anticipation before shooting a hated enemy: "Look at him walking. Look what an animal. Look at him stride forward" (319). Shortly before his own death the guerrilla fighter Anselmo recalls with quiet resistance the words of his partner Roberto: "How could the *Inglés* say that the shooting of a man is like the shooting of an animal?" (442).

For Whom the Bell Tolls is centrally concerned with the question "What does it mean to be human?" It also asks, with urgency, "What does it mean to be a *specific* human?" In other words, how are the borders that make up a self established, and how are they erased? For Hemingway, all of these questions are tightly coupled with the question of human passion: namely, the conflict between its tendencies toward galvanization, focus, and singularity and its contrary tendencies toward excess, inclusiveness, and diffusion. Hemingway works through these questions with mutually reinforcing examinations of romantic love and guerrilla warfare. Guerrilla fighters disrupt the international laws of war because, lacking a "distinctive emblem," they cannot be identified as combatants and thereby distinguished from the civilian population. They use civilians, in effect, as camouflage, putting at risk both the civilians and more broadly the viability of laws limiting war conduct, laws that depend upon clear and stable definitions.[25] For states guerrillas thus represent cultural breakdown and the shock of lawlessness and terrorism—but for the weaponless they can represent the solidarity of a community's unified resistance, the immersion of each self into the unvanquished collective (the guerrilla's chaos-liberty duality reproduces, significantly, the broader theoretical duality of the grotesque itself). The guerrilla, it is said, disappears into his people like a man into the embrace of the fog or like a fish into the sea. This war story is thus also a love story. War ravishes identity, coercively dissolving the differences between individuals. "I am thee and thou art me and all of one is the other" (262). From the beginning Robert Jordan's relationship with his noncombatant lover, Maria, is marked by the language traces of guerrilla warfare. "Afterwards we will be as one animal of the forest and be so close that neither one can tell that one of us is one and not the other" (262). Robert's beloved is an object of desire only as viscerally as is his cause. "I love thee as I love all that we have fought for. I love thee as I love liberty and dignity and the rights of all men to work and not be hungry. I love thee as I love Madrid that we have defended and as I love all my comrades that have died" (348). Such love exhilarates one with the possibility of a life beyond death, almost as with a soldier living on through his nation ("I will be thee when thou art not there," 263), but also threatens one with the erasure of the distinct, autonomous self, as with a soldier dissolving into his unit ("I do not wish to change. It is better to be one and each one to be the one he is," 263). Love and war share the key feature of human interchangeability. In *For Whom the Bell Tolls* this partial intersection is thematically amplified into a blending. At the extremes of passion, category distinctions are untenable: love is a kind of warfare, as warfare is a kind of love. In the final scene, Robert is left behind to die so that his fleeing compatriots may live. As he gives himself to his comrades, he bequeaths himself to his lover. "Thou art me too now. Thou art all there will be of me" (464). And as the guerrillas flee their base camp to disappear into their people, Jordan disappears equally into his cause and into his lover. "As long as there is one of us there is both of us" (463).

For Hemingway the grotesque illuminates how deep-rooted inhibitions against murder are overcome both negatively, through binary pseudospeciation, and positively, through the refiguration of love and passion. For Dos Passos, the grotesque is elevated from Hemingway's level of individual psychology to the larger matrices of social and economic structure and practice. His war era classic *Nineteen Nineteen*, the second book in his *U.S.A.* trilogy, is a syntax of the grotesque. It is a novel about the elimination of grammatical, physical, and conceptual *spaces between*. Dos Passos structures the novel around the inventions of modern transportation, around the automobiles, airplanes, and sea vessels that eliminate the distances of the globe and replace space with time, promiscuously transporting merchant marines, Red Cross volunteers, and soldiers back and forth between nations. Just so are the spaces between bodies eliminated—eliminated by the shock of sudden fistfights and the unrestrained exchange of sexual partners. Dos Passos's characters are continually marked with the traces of human contact, with contusions, abrasions, and venereal diseases. Intimacy is depicted as a form of costly excess, additional to the novel's excess through alcohol and through speed. Form reproduces content. The multiple "Newsreel" sections indiscriminately combine heterogeneous fragments of the local and international, of news, music, and advertising. And by the novel's closing section, "The Body of an American," even the words begin to run together, the spaces between each eliminated by the pressure of speed and accumulation: ". . . body of an American whowasamemberoftheamerican expeditionaryforceineuropewholosthislifeduringtheworldwarand whoseidentityhasnotbeenestablished . . ."[26] Meaning becomes indistinct, like the identities of soldiers ("and raised in Brooklyn, in Memphis, near the lakefront in Cleveland, Ohio"), which run together in paratactic body counts ("Y.M.C.A. secretary, express agent, truck-driver, ford-mechanic") and which are all finally combined in the vast *one* of the Unknown Soldier, whose body is "scraped up" from the piles of dead.[27]

The grotesque, in *Nineteen Nineteen* and the *U.S.A.* trilogy overall (a fictional history Dos Passos conceived with wars as opening and primary framing events),[28] enabled for Dos Passos an essentially economic critique of the modern world. To contextualize his argument: in the years following the Civil War many Northern intellectuals and veterans lamented that in its move from combat to trade the United States had become weak, instrumental, and passionless; the states of war and peace were perceived to be as distinct and alien to each other as sacrifice and acquisition, generosity and self-interest.[29] This dichotomy preserved for each a quality of virtue: war, however grim, was heroic; and commerce, however mean, was not war. By the close of World War I the relationship between war and peace had been reimagined. Throughout *Nineteen Nineteen* Dos Passos collapses familiar distinctions in a double demotion. He juxtaposes battle reports with the details of labor strikes, and characterizes war as a variable of corporate industrial policy.

> Wars and panics on the stock exchange,
> machinegunfire and arson,
> bankruptcies, warloans,
> starvation, lice, cholera and typhus:
> good growing weather for the House of Morgan.[30]

War in *Nineteen Nineteen* is a matter of jobs and capital investment. It is a continuation of business policy by other means. The accelerations in modern peace and modern war had blurred alarmingly the distinctions between the benign and the brutal, revealing in each a bloodless instrumentality. Far from excluding each other as opposed concepts, war and peace now appeared to operate in tandem.[31]

Disruption of physical borders and conceptual binaries is essential to Dos Passos's grotesque characterization of war. In a letter written during his time as an ambulance driver in France, he presents the misery of war as a matter of "thinking in gargoyles": "If I could sculpt—I'd carve grotesques. The medievals had the right idea—Death is a rollicking dance—Pain writhes into gorgeous jigs about the Arch-Satirist's drunken throne. Gall is as intoxicating as sweet wine—The horror is fun—but don't think: Shriek with laughter along with the gods."[32] Later Wyndham Lewis, in a painful commentary on satire, took the physical and behavioral "disfigurements" of the "shell-shocked man" as quintessential examples of the comic "grotesque,"[33] and Ernest Ludwig Kirchner, a German veteran debilitated by war trauma who offered up bloody, opened bodies in paintings like *Self-Portrait as a Soldier* and woodcuts like *Conflict,* described the war as "a murderous carnival."[34] The carnivalesque is especially important to the work of Dos Passos's pacific college friend E. E. Cummings. Cummings's account of his own war experience, *The Enormous Room,* repeatedly described as "grotesque" in a 1922 review by Dos Passos,[35] presents the structure of war analysis as the structure of the room: inside and outside, belonging and exclusion. During World War I, Cummings volunteered to serve the French army as an ambulance driver for the Red Cross. The most significant portion of his service in Europe was spent in a French prison, where he was detained for suspicious activities: specifically, for cowriting a letter with his friend William Brown that demonstrated a "reluctance to kill Germans," and for subsequent letters written by Brown that referred to the despondency of the French army.[36] The imprisonment, Cummings recalls, was a form of radical exposure. Cummings was accustomed to the fastidiousness of middle-class domestic privacy, which— through the subdivision of domestic space, the multiplication of room into rooms—increasingly hid the necessities, intimacies, and degradations of embodiment. This mapping of space was cruelly reversed in the French prison, which obscenely exposed the practices of the body by dissolving the borders of the domestic interior, transforming spaces into space, and rooms into one, single, enormous room. In *The Enormous Room,* some forty men are collected together like animals in a single pen: together they represent a startling range of nationalities and tongues, including Turkish, French, Belgian, Dutch, Russian, Polish, Spanish, Arabic, Swedish, and German. In their shared humiliation, they manage to form friendships that traverse the borders of ethnicity, nationality, and even language. The novel's emphasis upon cross-ethnic friendships is echoed in its dissolution of genre divisions, in its mixing of prose, poetry, and the graphic arts. The emphasis is echoed likewise in the novel's fixation with the details of bodily functions, which themselves reproduce the structural thematic of the room. As Elaine Scarry writes of domestic space generally, the room is "an enlargement of the body: it keeps warm and safe the individual it houses in the same way the body encloses and protects the individual within; like the body, its walls put boundaries around the self preventing undifferentiated contact with the world, yet in its windows and doors, crude versions of the senses, it enables the self to move out into the world and allows that world to enter."[37] The intact body allows a chaste interaction between interior and exterior. The overflowing pails of mucus, saliva, and urine that are collected each morning in the prison, then, represent the body turned inside out; they are the grotesque symbols of the novel's destabilization and finally total inversion of the categories "inside" and "outside," "incorporation" and "exclusion," and, more broadly, "insider" and "outsider," "friend" and "foreigner," "ally" and "enemy." Writ small in the desacralization of the individual body is the desacralization of the body politic, an insistence upon the natural permeability of borders. Wars are not violence between populations, in Cummings's depiction, but rather violence *upon* populations. Violence is imposed by the tyranny of an alien state (composed of such villains as "Apollyon" and "The Black Holster"), which engineers conflict by propagating artificial divisions among the peoples of the world. Cummings's record of the prison camp, and later of the torture of the conscientious objector in "i sing of Olaf glad and big," are accusations—accusations against nationalism and against the nation-state itself as an organizing principle productive of violence. His alternative vision, biographer Richard Kennedy argues, approaches "political anarchism," a deconstruction of governmental structures in favor of borderlessness.[38]

Willa Cather's novel *One of Ours* (1922) won the Pulitzer Prize and was cited by the author throughout her life as one of her best and most important works. But since Hemingway's derisive declaration that in it war had been "Catherized," the book has been treated as, at best, epiphenomenal to the Cather canon and, at worst, as an uncomplicated artistic embarrassment: "a flat failure," "romantic and naive," "pathetic," and "outrageously idealistic."[39] The novel's platitudinous lexicon and romanticized conceptualizations make it vulnerable to just such a set of judgments. Of all the important American World War I novels discussed, however, it is *One of Ours* that most complexly thematizes boundary crossing and, consequently, it is *One of Ours* that most insistently demands of its readers an interrogation of the stock-in-trade cultural images it deploys. Cather's *One of Ours* is a gallery of the grotesque. Positioned against a select number of classically beautiful characters in the novel are a multitude whose ugliness is depicted as a form of physical damage: characters marked as if through violence by scars, birth defects, crippling obesity, pale and dyspeptic coloring, or red, knobby countenances. Biographer Sharon O'Brien notes Cather's profound personal distaste for injury and infirmity and her simultaneous fixation in her fiction with missing limbs and mutilated bodies.[40] Cather lavishes upon the reader depictions of beauty under attack. Marching soldiers are imagined as once beautiful flowers, now "pretty well wilted,"[41] and the healthy and brave young men who have volunteered to fight in the war are transported to the continent in plague ships: Cather luxuriates in the virulent flu's effects upon the body (the uncontrollable nosebleeds, the discoloration of the eyes), and lingers excessively over death's phlegmatic approach. In one of the novel's paradigmatic moments, Claude's company stumbles upon a grotesque parody of the Nativity: a refugee

mother, consumed by disease and by her nearly cannibalistic infant, is
seeking a place to die (291).

The anti-Nativity scene graphically illustrates what war has done to
the family and to the home. Here the novel seems to be confirming the
pervasive cultural mythology that imagines war as unnaturally
athwart mother-centered domestic space. This gender-oriented
schema depends upon a series of related binaries: female and male,
life-giver and life-taker, peace and war.[42] Cather structures her novel
as just such a binary. The first half, composed of stable, family-ori-
ented spaces, is set against the second half, which is composed of the
multiple transitional sites of war. This dyadic structure, however, is
subverted by the novel's temporal distortions. *One of Ours* is a teleological narrative: the end is implicit in the beginning, and the beginning is rereadable with reference to the end. From the start, we know
that this will be a story of youth sacrificed, of an idealistic young man,
dissatisfied with the constraints of his small town, who will volunteer
and die in the war. Signal moments in the novel thereby acquire double significance: images in the first half of the novel point irresistibly
to the second half, and images of the second half bear the traces of the
first. The "bleeding stump" (25) of young Claude's favorite cherry
tree, destroyed by his father, prefigures the stump of a wounded soldier (271); and the pile of Claude's dead and dying pigs, trapped in the
shelter that has collapsed to become a snow-covered tomb (83), reproduces itself later in the lime-covered corpses of soldiers entombed
together in the former shelter of a dugout (361). These representational vectors are reversed in the second half of the novel. Here, war is
depicted through the images of domestic life: shell-damaged land is
"soft as dough," and corpses are piled "one on top of another like
sacks of flour" (357, 360). Significantly, Claude's service as a soldier
consists primarily of experiences being billeted in different households. The female chaperones and the young soldiers staying with
them form a sort of makeshift family, an emergency copy of mother's
home, now revealed as part of the machinery of warfare.[43]

The first half of the novel is, as much as the second, spotted with
scenes of grotesque consumption and violence: "Mahailey wrung the
necks of chickens until her wrist swelled up, as she said, 'like a puff-
adder'" (132). Claude's childhood anxieties are emblematic: "A funeral, the sight of a neighbour lying rigid in his black coffin, overwhelmed him with terror . . . When he thought of the millions of

lonely creatures rotting away under ground life seemed nothing but a trap that caught people for one horrible end . . . Putrefaction, decay . . . He could not give his pleasant, warm body over to that filthiness!" (43). The worlds of violence and of care blend. The distinctly "feminine" energies of reformism and evangelicalism bear a striking similarity to the idealistic, interventionist attitudes that drive young men to war. Speaking of missionary work in China, Enid explains: "But it is when I pray that I feel this call the strongest. It seems as if a finger were pointing me over there. Sometimes when I ask for guidance in little things, I get none, and only get the feeling that my work lies far away, and that for it, strength would be given me. Until I take that road, Christ withholds himself" (110). Women, idealized in the photographs (of girlfriends), statues (of Lady Liberty) and myths (of Jeanne d'Arc) that encourage Claude and his fellow soldiers, play an important role in the economy of war. It is a role they willingly play. Gladys, the novel's female ideal, warmly supports Claude's decision to fight: "You found your place. You're sailing away. You've just begun" (211). Conflating his mother's and his wife's religious traditions with antique visions of the hero returning from war, Claude reflects: "The more incredible the things [women] believed, the more lovely was the act of belief. To him the story of 'Paradise Lost' was as mythical as the 'Odyssey'; yet when his mother read it aloud to him, it was not only beautiful but true. A woman who didn't have holy thoughts about mysterious things far away would be prosaic and commonplace, like a man" (107). Women, Cather insists, bear responsibility for the production of violence. A wounded soldier who has deserted, abandoning all things of war, suffers a peculiar and significant form of amnesia: wiped clean from his mind are all the women he ever knew (272).

After Claude's absurdly heroic and bloodless death (the bullet holes are "clean" and cause minimal bleeding, and Claude dies with a smile on his face),[44] the narrative returns to the kitchen on Wheeler Farm for the novel's closing pages. Claude's mother reads his letters and takes grim satisfaction in his death. It is tragic, certainly, but beautifully tragic. "For him the call was clear, the cause was glorious. Never a doubt stained his bright faith. She divines so much that he did not write. She knows what to read into those short flashes of enthusiasm; how fully he must have found his life before he could let himself go so far . . . He died believing his own country better than it is, and France better than any country can ever be. And those were beautiful beliefs to die with. Perhaps it was as well to see that vision, and then to see no more" (370). The final words of the novel are given to Mahailey, who felt "superior" for having seen the wounded of the Civil War, and who had warmly praised Claude's decision to fight (191, 178).

> As they are working at the table or bending over the oven, something reminds them of him, and they think of him together, like one person: Mahailey will pat her back and say, "Never you mind, Mudder; you'll see your boy up yonder." Mrs. Wheeler always feels that God is near,—but Mahailey is not troubled by any knowledge of interstellar spaces, and for her He is nearer still,—directly overhead, not so very far above the kitchen stove. (371)

Mother's home, far from being unnaturally disrupted by the intrusion of war, has served its correct function and found its correct place in God's scheme by sacrificing its children. War, Cather writes, is engendered in the "womb" of history (188). Cather deconstructs the artificial separation of male and female spheres not only because it is untenable in fact, a mystification of reality, but also, and more important, because it is morally unjustifiable, because it contributes to a romantic cultural economy that exaggerates the ethic of male violence while at the same time vindicating it through recourse to a morally self-justifying female innocence.[45] If for Hemingway and Dos Passos the grotesque's destabilization of categories functions primarily to signify degeneration, for Cummings and Cather it services moral critique—indeed, it points to idealized reconceptualizations of social organization that promise regeneration. This nascent representational tendency would become vitally important in the years leading up to World War II.

Cultural and Critical Theory

Especially in Europe, at the epicenter of the disaster, war trauma was enduring. Throughout the 1920s and 1930s memory and anticipation of war persisted in shaping rhetorical construction and conceptual framing in basic ways; the continuing integration of trauma into domestic systems of production and knowledge triggered the migration of grotesque forms associated with the war into a variety of disciplines. Roxanne Panchasi, citing a broad cultural fascination with the grotesque in France and Germany, connects Sigmund Freud's 1919 essay "The 'Uncanny'" with the war's mass amputations, the sensation in amputees of "phantom" limbs, and the hybridization of man and machine in prosthetic technology: the uncanny effect generated in special cases by uncertainty about previously certain objects (is this real or imagined, animate or inanimate, alive or dead?) Freud finds in a variety of examples that notably include the experience of being lost in a "mist," as well as encounters with "dismembered limbs, a severed head, a hand cut off at the wrist."[46] Cornelia Vismann, arguing at the level of epistemology, takes the experience of no-man's-land—"the boundary that effaces all boundaries"—as the "primordial scene" for a fundamental schematic shift away from knowledge through universally accessible maps and lines toward knowledge-suspension through the transitionality of destabilized and disputed *zones*. The Great War's deformation of informational geometries, its "negation of all kinds of orders linked with identity," produced discursive changes that were "cognitive as well as psychological, cultural and legal," from exchanges between Ernst Jünger and Martin Heidegger on the nature of order to political theorist Carl Schmitt's work on the "state of emergency."[47]

Freud's work on "war neuroses" offers an especially salient example of the way knowledge would be restructured in the wake of collective trauma. Freud, whose three sons served in World War I, was compelled by the irreconcilability of what he observed in the war's shell-shock victims to revise radically his fundamental psychological principles.[48] The result of his research on the repetition compulsion, *Beyond the Pleasure Principle,* ends with a translation of two lines of the *Maqâmât* of al-Hariri: "What we cannot reach flying we must reach limping . . . The Book tells us it is no sin to limp."[49] Freud connects the limp to the slow advances of scientific knowledge, and one critic asserts that the metaphor must also be applied to the "faltering exposition" of Freud's own work;[50] but most crucially, I think, Freud's closing metaphor points back to the psychic and physical limp of the returning war veteran. Needing to account for the soldier's urge to return to and reenact his original trauma, Freud argues that the pleasure principle is no longer tenable as a theory for explaining human behavior. *Beyond the Pleasure Principle* thus resolves itself into a nearly mystical ambiguity, arguing that persons are guided by the unstably fused binary instincts of life and death (an opposition that, according to Hanna Segal, corresponds to the contest between integration and fragmentation, between structure and structurelessness).[51] War and the death instinct it revealed rehabilitated for Freud the antagonistic dualism that had been displaced by his earlier monistic theorization of narcissism,[52] at the same time that war trauma disrupted the possibility of reliable definitions.[53] "I am not convinced myself," Freud writes, and "do not seek to persuade other people to believe in them."[54] Indeed, as Paul Ricoeur notes, the death instinct—as representative of the "mute" energies that contest the "speech" and "clamor" of life—inserted into theory a certain necessary indecipherability.[55] As Freud concludes elsewhere: "In the confusion of wartime in which we are caught up we ourselves are at a loss as to the significance of the impressions which press in upon us and as to the value of the judgments which we form."[56] Freud's views on hate and love, war and peace, and death and life in *Beyond the Pleasure Principle* are characterized by one critic thus: "Ambivalence goes all the way down to the foundation of life."[57]

After World War II, Simone de Beauvoir asserted such instability of meaning, such commingling of opposites, as the fundamental dialectic of existential morality. Attacking those ethical systems that in her view attempt to deny the contradictory structure of human experience, she writes:

> Those reasonable metaphysics, those consoling ethics with which they would like to entice us only accentuate the disorder from which we suffer. Men of today seem to feel more acutely than ever the paradox of their condition . . . Each one has the incomparable taste in his mouth of his own life, and yet each feels himself more insignificant than an insect within the immense collectivity whose limits are one with the earth's. Perhaps in no other age have they manifested their grandeur more brilliantly, and in no other age has this grandeur been so horribly flouted. In spite of so many stubborn lies, at every moment, at every opportunity, the truth comes to light, the truth of life and death, of my solitude and my bond with the world, of my freedom and my servitude, of the insignificance and sovereign importance of each man and all men. There was Stalingrad and there was Buchenwald, and neither of the two wipes out the other. Since we do not succeed in fleeing it, let us therefore try to look the truth in the face. Let us try to assume our fundamental ambiguity.[58]

Just so members of the Frankfurt School were compelled by the experience of World War I and its aftermath, by the rise of Fascism, and by the final catastrophe of World War II, to reexamine the calcified doctrines and categorizations of modern technological society; they attacked the received meanings of terms as fundamental as "culture," "reason," and even "civilization" itself. The Frankfurt School as a name refers to a diverse group of neo-Marxist thinkers associated with the Institute of Social Research, which was founded in 1923 at the University of Frankfurt (many of its key members—including Max Horkheimer, Friedrich Pollock, Leo Lowenthal, and Herbert Marcuse—entered military service during World War I). The Critical Theory they elaborated throughout the 1930s and early 1940s worked to counter absolutes and impermeable givens, in the end invalidating the very foundations that generated it.[59] Horkheimer and Adorno, writes Martin Jay, the primary historian of the Frankfurt School, opposed all "closed . . . systems"; their philosophy was essentially characterized by its "open-ended, probing, unfinished quality."[60] Inherited language itself was suspect: "It is characteristic of the [contemporary] sickness that even the best-intentioned reformer who uses an impoverished and debased language to recommend renewal, by his adoption of the insidious mode of categorization and the bad philosophy it conceals, strengthens the very power of the established order he is trying to break. False clarity is only another name for myth."[61] Among the established categorizations that their work brought into question was the hierarchical division in modern technological culture between utility and waste. Members of the Frankfurt School were radically suspicious of contemporary configurations of production as exemplified in the notion of the instrument: instrument (tool), instrumental (useful), and instrumental reason (reason used as a tool for strategically achieving particular ends in the world). They notably rejected Kant's distinction between empirical practical reason and pure practical reason—that is, between instrumental/strategic reason and ideal-embodying/norm-revealing reason—arguing that this unyielding "hierarchical construction" and binary separation both mystified and contributed to the total ascendance of the strategic.[62] As Habermas characterizes the position, "In cultural modernity, reason gets definitively stripped of its validity claim and assimilated to sheer power."[63] For Adorno, Horkheimer, and Marcuse, the two world wars had revealed how slight was the difference between cultures of enlightened productivity and cultures of waste and violence, between a tool-centered world and a weapon-centered world.[64] Indeed, they implied a causal relationship between the two. Collectively they attacked what Horkheimer called "the rule of economy over all personal relationships,"[65] along with the scientistic sacralization of instrumental reason and its controlling principles: unity, hierarchization, coercive definition. Technological reason's domination, as Marcuse put it, promotes the degeneration of persons and thinning out of personalities in capitalist society: the prioritization of "operationalism" and "utilization," he asserted, turns human into "thing."[66] Reason envisions the external world as composed of objects instrumental to its purposes: such objectification transforms fellow humans into resources. The related social value of utility justifies not only the manipulation but also the expenditure of these resources. The brutality witnessed in Fascism was thus an extension of rather than regression from the path of modernization.

In *Dialectic of Enlightenment* (written during World War II but conceived before,[67] when Bakhtin was completing his seminal doctoral dissertation on Rabelais) Adorno and Horkheimer characterized the comprehensive ascendance of rationalized domination with a historical narrative describing the administrative transformation of the grotesque medieval carnival into the ordered and decontaminated holiday or vacation.[68] In his work throughout the 1930s, Georges Bataille developed his own criticism of contemporary instrumentality into a philosophy built upon the key features of the grotesque. Dynamic opposition structures Bataille's philosophy, claims one critic: his work draws upon the "violence" of "compressed intimacy or contiguity"; it characteristically establishes the "confrontation of two terms which places in question the ontological status of the space designated by their proximity."[69] Bataille's writing, which makes frequent recourse to the image of the grotesque body, is premised upon the idealization of unboundedness, disruption, and the transcendence of all limiting categories through unchecked consumption.[70] Challenging what he considers to be the alienating economic paradigms of production and scarcity, Bataille reframes the world through a romantic economy of consumption and superabundance. He seeks to replace all forms of constraint—constraint through material scarcity, or constraint through singularity of identity and meaning—with a philosophy of amplification, inclusion, and excess. In a radicalization of the work of Martin Heidegger, who used productivity and physical work as paradigms for understanding human beings and human culture, Bataille makes central to his philosophy the opposition between waste and use, emblematized in the opposition between the weapon and the tool. Dismantling and finally inverting the categories of output and utility, he figures useful exchange as a servile contraction of experience, and waste as a mechanism of transcendence and sovereignty.

In Heidegger's phenomenology a tool is most fundamentally "something in-order-to," an object defined by its "serviceability, conduciveness, usability, manipulability."[71] In use, a tool is something that folds into its end. A tool points away from itself; a tool is self-effacing.[72] It disembodies itself (transferring palpability to the object of its force); it disembodies the present (hurling consciousness every moment into the projects of the future); and it disembodies the worker (dissolving him into the expected products of his work).[73] A hammer always *points*—to an object, an idea, an effect. A tool is oriented forward in time, servicing the imagination. For humans as workers, according to Heidegger, this futurity of the tool springs out of the very nature of our identity—projection is our basic essence: "Above all, he must be able to understand himself not only in that *I am,* but in the possibility that *I can be* . . . to go out beyond himself as he already is to the *possibilities* of his being . . . To be constantly ahead of, in advance of, itself is the basic character of existence."[74] As futurity, instrumentality is the opening of myriad hopes.

The tool, representing the possibility of all ends, is however never an end in itself. Thus if the futurity of instrumentality is vigorously fecund, it can also be insidiously vampiric. Fixing the gaze upon anticipated outcomes can diminish the vivacity of the near-to-hand present; living forward can transform current experience into stock for use, into calculable potential rather than actuality or being. The project/ projection of work, in other words, extends imagination at the cost of presence, forcing humans in contemporary industrialized society to perceive their world through the alienating prisms of "storage," "enframing" and "ordering."[75] It is unsurprising that in Heidegger's vision of modern technology and labor, man "comes to the very brink of a precipitous fall, that is, he comes to the point where he himself will have to be taken as standing-reserve."[76] As his student Marcuse asserted in an interview after World War II, Heidegger depicts Being as overshadowed by death and future-oriented anxiety. For Heidegger, Marcuse emphasizes, the main categories of existence or *Dasein* include "Idle talk, curiosity, ambiguity, falling and Being-thrown, concern, Being-toward-death, anxiety, dread, boredom."[77]

For Bataille a culture is desiccated that encloses Being in future-oriented, accumulative instrumentality, in evasion through "projects";[78] against this pall of calculation he finds salvation in the symbolic logic of the weapon. Occupying the same rhetorical (rather than moral) universe as Ernst Jünger, who depicts war as a transcendent end in itself by virtue of its radical "uselessness,"[79] Bataille asserts that through waste and destruction humans can overcome their demeaning utilitarian relationship with the world.[80] The tool disembodies the individual, surrounding her with artifacts that render the body sensually absent, that promote, as Scarry writes, "bodily evaporation," while the weapon produces wounds that intensify embodiedness, that create an extravagant awareness of both our corporeality and the weapon that magnifies its exquisite sensitivity.[81] The shock of physical waste generates a lavish and charismatic visibility. Waste does not disappear into a purpose but becomes obtrusive in its inability to do so, in its glaring distinctiveness. The weapon is thus conspicuous while the tool is self-effacing: the weapon is a deictic, pointing at others only to point back at its own gratuitous release of force, while the tool is a preposition, always disappearing to take us somewhere further. The bright pain of the weapon is the catastrophic manifestation of our excess over need. As Bataille presents it, violence is a "fundamental ebullition" that expresses the largess and "intimacy" cherished and exalted in sexuality and the sacred.[82] By denying futurity in the moment of waste—representatively, in war, human sacrifice, and the gift—Being no longer takes itself in hand, no longer perceives itself as an object.[83] Through waste, Being denies the alienation of use and achieves true self-consciousness—as Bataille writes, "a consciousness that henceforth has *nothing as its object* . . . Nothing but pure interiority, which is not a thing."[84] Freedom thus begins in the dissolution of our quantifying self-possession, in the obliteration of the agent formulated either as self-legislator or as evaluator of goods. Free choice, the impossible imperative of Kant, Dewey, and Hemingway, is now radically reformulated. We must achieve freedom neither from our sensuous desires nor from the contingencies of luck; rather, we must achieve freedom from all systems of constraining categorization and, more important, from the hegemony of use, best exemplified in the functional imperatives of the increasingly powerful complex organizations that make up the iron cage of modern society.

Pure waste—waste in its ideal form—is difficult to achieve, as Bataille's work reveals. Use is inescapable, and loss is thus often deployed as the extension of domination. Ritual murder, for example, serves to appease gods and redirect potentially negative social energies; the frenzied "glory" of sacrifice in battle is tied into a system of appropriation; and the waste of potlatch confers rank upon the waster: it is a competitive exchange of representations of waste.[85] While Bataille grants the revelatory power of such phenomena (comprehending their lesson of excess and release is, indeed, an obligation: failure to do so "causes us to *undergo* what we could *bring about* in our own way, if we understood"),[86] he never loses sight of his regulating ideal: the moment of preconsciousness, of ecstasy and thoughtless expenditure, in which any consideration of outcome or consequences is effaced, and the spender occupies the uncompromised but sadly untenable space of total waste, total transcendence. This flicker of transcendence is over once it can be recognized, formulated, evaluated. It is a dream that disappears upon waking into linguistic consciousness.

Bataille participated in a transnational ethos dominant between the wars, the traces of which were present in discourses ranging from conservative revolutionary propaganda in Germany to American literary neo-Romanticism: in Ernst Jünger's peculiar association of battle wounds with mouths, stomachs, and eating, and each of these with a heroic beauty;[87] and in what Fitzgerald depicts through a dialogue of "grotesque blending" as an absorption with "the pleasure of losing," the pleasure of drinking, swallowing, and burning, of appreciating beauty only when razing it. The protagonist of his novel *This Side of Paradise* emblematically conceives of violence as an escape from the clichéd instrumentality of society: "He rather longed for death to roll over his generation," Fitzgerald writes, "obliterating their petty fevers and struggles and exultations."[88] Of the "front generation" Hannah Arendt observes:

> The elite went to war with an exultant hope that everything they knew, the whole culture and texture of life, might go down in its "storms of steel" . . . In the carefully chosen words of Thomas Mann, war was "chastisement" and "purification"; "war in itself, rather than victories, inspired the poet." Or in the words of a student of the time, "what counts is always the readiness to make a sacrifice, not the object for which the sacrifice is made."[89]

In an atmosphere in which "all traditional values and propositions had evaporated,"[90] violence and waste seemed to offer the only form of honest transcendence:

The "front generation" . . . were completely absorbed by their desire to see the ruin of this whole world of fake security, fake culture, and fake life . . . it seemed revolutionary to admit cruelty, disregard of human values, and general amorality . . . Destruction without mitigation, chaos and ruin as such assumed the dignity of supreme values . . . the self-willed immersion in the suprahuman forces of destruction seemed to be a salvation from the automatic identification with pre-established functions in society and their utter banality, and at the same time to help destroy the functioning itself.[91]

The literary grotesque of World War I, used as a means of characterizing a perceived reality, became the moral grotesque anticipating World War II, the validation of disruptive reconfigurations most radically expressed in the style and writings of Bataille's favored Marquis de Sade. This grotesque dismantling of inherited moral categories, passively suffered in World War I, was actively championed after World War II. In 1946 Jean Paulhan noted the massive resurgence of interest in Sade, explaining that the incomparable moral iconoclast served as a model for postwar writers who pursued "the inexpressible," who looked "for the sublime in the infamous, for the great in the subversive," and who wished in defiance to utterly "deny artifice."[92]

The post–world war movements against functionality (from Bataille and the revived Sade to the middle and later work of the Frankfurt School) have had an enormous influence upon contemporary literary criticism and cultural studies, particularly upon philosophical critiques of what might be called the hegemony of meaning or the instrumentality of language. Susan Suleiman, identifying Bataille as the "central reference" for "French theorists of modernity" in the 1960s and 1970s, notes that throughout his writings, from the pornographic to the theoretical, the transgression of values functions as an extension of the transgression of language, of "the destruction or 'consumation' of meaning."[93] As Bataille writes, "That sand into which we bury ourselves in order not to see, is formed of words":

Although words drain almost all life from within us—there is almost not a single sprig of this life which the bustling host of these ants (words) hasn't seized, dragged, accumulated without respite—there subsists in us a silent, elusive, ungraspable part . . . They are the vague inner movements, which depend on no object and have no intent—states which . . . are not warranted by anything definable, so that language which, with respect to the others, has the sky, the room, to which it can refer . . . is dispossessed, can say nothing, is limited to stealing these states from attention (profiting from their lack of precision, it right away draws attention elsewhere). If we live under the law of language without contesting it, these states are within us as if they didn't exist. But if we run up against this law, we can in passing fix our awareness upon one of them and, quieting discourse within us, linger over the surprise which it provides us . . . But the difficulty is that one manages neither easily nor completely to silence oneself.[94]

For Bataille, silence and the indefinite—"'slipping' word[s]" and "noises of all sorts, cries, chatter, laughter"—are our only hope for escape from the iron cage of language's "precision" and referentiality, from what Steven Shaviro calls conversational discourse's "culture of utility," and from our related self-blinding drive to, in Bataille's words, "inner hypocrisy, to solemn distant exigencies (such as the morality of Kant)."[95] Language is an impediment to unconstrained communication and authentic experience—indeed, limited to the utilitarian ends of meaning construction, language is directed not toward self- or mutual understanding but toward the extension of networks of power. "All speech is violence," as Maurice Blanchot writes.[96] In the familiar poststructuralist formulation, language constitutes us as subjects through the micro-operations of domination: it enables us for certain functions only insofar as it excludes us from a range of possibilities; it fixes one meaning only by excluding other meanings, by rigidifying the categories into which we are inserted as subjects. Subject interpellation through language is propaganda in the strongest sense of the word, "the propaganda for a definition of reality within which only certain limited viewpoints are possible."[97] The grotesquification of language, in contrast, grinds open fractures that enable lateral movement and escape. The genealogy of contemporary literary theory thus reveals an originary suspicion of referential language as a tool, combined with an advocacy of transgression and a thin theory of agency and autonomy. Words are "quicksand" and "treachery"; we are, Bataille writes, "lost among babblers in a night in which we can only hate the appearance of light which comes from babbling." Bataille's conviction of the "foolishness of all sentences" and the subsequent critical fixation with "the impotence of discourse" was a pervasive yet not inevitable reaction to the rise of Fascism prior to World War II.[98] The extreme range of representational strategies generated by organized violence included difficult, nonreferential work (such as the writings of Maurice Blanchot) designed to function as an opposition to the transparent operations of Fascism, but also the relentlessly clear and direct style of accounts (such as John Hersey's *Hiroshima*) premised upon the idea that establishing a durable, shareable record through referential language is an obligation for the surviving witnesses of atrocity. Throughout the remainder of this book I will trace the development of the two dominant theories of language that have marked our culture since World War II. These theories can be revealed most fully, as we shall see in the next chapter, only through a historically situated analysis of violence and the organizational structuring of language.

CHAPTER FIVE

Language, Violence, and Bureaucracy: William Faulkner, Joseph Heller, and Organizational Sociology

World War II exceeded all boundaries. Dozens of countries entered the war at an estimated cost in material resources of $1.15 trillion. The Axis forces mobilized approximately twenty million men; Allied forces mobilized twice that number. Two million men fought in the battle of Kursk in the Soviet Union; fifty-five thousand civilians were killed in the bombing of Hamburg; forty thousand in Nagasaki; eighty thousand in Hiroshima; one hundred and thirty-five thousand in Dresden; one million died during the siege at Leningrad; and six million Jews were murdered in Axis concentration camps. By 1945 over sixty million people had been killed, as many as half of them civilians. Many of these estimates are considered conservative.[1]

Artists sought a literary style equal to the task of witnessing to the unbounded and unprecedented. The influence of the aesthetics of the grotesque was pervasive: Alain Resnais's film *Hiroshima Mon Amour* opens with a montage that blends the flawless bodies of young lovers with the mutilated and burned of Hiroshima; Kenzaburo Oë's *A Personal Matter* is centered on the birth of an infant, typically the symbol of pure human form, who is now monstrously deformed by radiation; and Thomas Pynchon's *Gravity's Rainbow* uses unrestrained orgies, excessive scatology, and a frequent invocation of category-disrupting monsters to tell the story of a man whose identity can be dissolved and rebuilt without limit.[2] The grotesque also influences the comic dislocations of Joseph Heller's *Catch-22,* which switches names, identities, and even body parts between characters with the rapidity of slapstick;[3] the narrative proliferation of Masuji Ibuse's *Black Rain,* which subtly exfoliates, like an irradiated plant, into multiple genres and subject-positions; and the nonlinear structure of Kurt Vonnegut's *Slaughterhouse Five,* whose protagonist, Billy Pilgrim, comes unstuck in time and space, ultimately finding himself housed in an intergalactic glass zoo so that the private functions of his body might be exposed and observed, stripped of its conventional coverings and facades like the narrative itself.

The first and most characteristic response to the war's chain of disasters, however, was silence. "Impossible to talk about Hiroshima," wrote Marguerite Duras. "All one can do is talk about the impossibility of talking about Hiroshima."[4] Much of the great literature and film about the war was produced long after it had ended. *Hiroshima Mon Amour* was released in 1960, *A Personal Matter* was published in 1964, *Black Rain* was published in 1969, and *Gravity's Rainbow* was published in 1973. Kurt Vonnegut explained that it took more than twenty years for him successfully to complete anything about the war. *Slaughterhouse Five* was published in 1966. Karl Shapiro, speaking of the writers who had fought in the war, wrote: "We all came out of the same army and joined the same generation of silence."[5] Hannah Arendt theorizes this relationship between silence and war's violence as ineluctable. "Speech," she asserts, "is helpless when confronted with violence."[6]

There are two forms of silence, the voluntary and the involuntary. For her model of silence as involuntary trauma, which is based on the premise of the mutual exclusivity of force and discourse, Arendt points to the concentration camp, to its tyranny of violence and its concomitant crippling of referential language. The Holocaust becomes the quintessential example of violence's quest for pure and total silence, in this case through the extermination of all witnesses. Claude Lanzmann's documentary film of the Holocaust, *Shoah,* reveals the logic behind the continually exfoliating nature of Nazi atrocities: original violence is nourished in secrecy and silence; it perpetuates such silence as part of its very nature; and its legacy of incommunicability allows it continually to renew itself. The film, composed entirely of interviews with witnesses (Jewish, Polish, and German), repeatedly points back to the Holocaust's shattering of discourse as its primary enabling condition and also its legacy:

"No one can describe it"; "And let's not talk about that"; "Anyone who uttered the words 'corpse' or 'victim' was beaten"; "It was impossible to say anything—we were just like stoned"; "we were not allowed to talk to each other or to express our views or our minds to each other"; "Re-settlement program. No one ever spoke of killing"; "*You had to take an oath?* No, just sign, promising to shut up about whatever we'd see"; "Well, when the word got around, when it was whispered. It was never said outright. Good God, no! They'd have hauled you off at once!"; "And the key to the entire operation from the psychological standpoint was never to utter the words that would be appropriate to the action being taken. Say nothing; do these things; do not describe them"; "If you lie enough, you believe your own lies"; "I don't think the human tongue can describe the horror we went through in the ghetto."[7]

The micrologic of individual silence reproduces the bureaucratic strategies of the Final Solution as a whole. As historian Raul Hilberg explains, even Göring's infamous July 1941 letter calling for the initiation of the "final solution" proceeds through inference and euphemism. "It was," as Hilberg puts it, "an authorization to invent. It was an authorization to begin something that was not as yet capable of being put into words."[8]

How can one put atrocity into words, at any time? Nadine Fresco, interviewing a group of Jewish men and women born between 1944 and 1948, uncovers a pattern of silences that effectively obliterate the traumatic past. For their parents, she explains, "silence seemed proportionate to the horror that had annihilated members of their families." "If one had to convey such horror to a child," one interviewee offered, "I don't know how one would do it, how one could bring oneself to do it, or what one would use. It's something one can't share with anyone, perhaps with one's child, but then only secretly, without actually saying it."[9] Against the enduring silence that he encounters, Claude Lanzmann is relentless. He continually asks witnesses to describe what they saw "precisely,"[10] as if accuracy were a form of intervention. When one survivor breaks into tears and begs to be left alone, Lanzmann presses:

> *Go on, Abe. You must go on. You have to.*
> I can't. It's too horrible. Please.
> *We have to do it. You know it.*
> I won't be able to do it.
> *You have to do it. I know it's very hard. I know and I apologize.*
> Don't make me go on please.
> *Please. We must go on.*[11]

If coordinated and premeditated violence depends somehow upon the truncation and cessation of speech, then the accretion of referential language becomes, for Lanzmann, an act of resistance. The obligation to bear witness is perceived to transcend personal concerns, to transcend both the right to cover one's pain in mute refusal and the right to surrender. One witness recalls how his wish to commit suicide was rendered impossible by the claims made upon him by those entering the gas chamber: "You must get out of here alive, you must bear witness to our suffering, and to the injustice done to us."[12]

But silence is not only a result of trauma to be resisted. It is also a principled choice, coevolutionary with the deployment of the grotesque, as exemplified in Bataille. This model of voluntary silence, which is based on the premise of the mutually constitutive relationship of force and discourse, is developed in some of the key literature published after World War II. These works, including especially *A Fable* and *Catch-22*, discussed below, and *Slaughterhouse Five*, whose vestal protagonist suffers in speechless sorrow throughout the war, together present silence as a representational act of cutting clarity, while depicting our latticework of words as a screen that occludes both material reality and moral norms. Silence, then, is both imposed and chosen: imposed because language is revealed to be damaged by force, that is, imbricated in a coercive system that batters it into unusability like a stringed instrument frayed to distortion; and chosen because language is revealed to be culpable in this system, a blood-tainted instrument of organizational violence.

Complex Organizations

William Faulkner's novel *A Fable* (1954) begins with the voiceless. It was written during a period of great anxiety for Faulkner, who had begun to doubt his ability to achieve with language because of his advancing age;[13] and it reflects his own experience of inarticulacy in the shadow of a second world war. "Maybe the watching of all this coming to a head for the last year," he wrote in a letter to Robert Haas, "is why I cant write, dont seem to want to want to write, that is."[14] The novel, which revolves around a mutiny in a French regiment during World War I, was described by Faulkner in 1943 and 1944 as an exhortation for universal peace, an exhortation that the tragedies of war obligated him beyond all difficulty to make.[15] *A Fable* opens with a crowd of civilians that has gathered in mute dread for the expected execution of the mutiny's initiators. The quivering, anxious mass is "tongueless"; it "made no sound."[16] The powerless collective is bereft of voice: as if by the weight of the military's inexorable authority, the articulations of the observers' speech are flattened out, made as incapable of carrying complex meaning as "a sigh, an exhalation" (11) or "a wind" (10). Soon, however, their silence is figured differently: it is coupled with the silence of the armistice brought about by the astonishing acts of the mutineers, with the "peace and silence" that signifies their power and that contrasts so sharply with the military's "clash of rifles" and "crash of iron" (11). As the novel progresses peace and silence will be ever more tightly bound, just as violence and the organizations of violence will be accoutered in noise (84). The pairings contravene one another. Against the organization's articulate, instrumental ambition is the inarticulate diffusion of hope.[17] Against the momentum of violence and its accumulation of sound are the bitterly won interruptions of protest: the noise of the guns, which is halted by the silence of nonparticipation, or the ringing speech of the orator celebrating the great general's death at novel's close, which is suspended by the righteous interruption of the former mutineer-battalion runner.[18] More telling, however, is the contest between the general and the chief mutineer, his son the corporal. In their climactic meeting, the general's perorations and invitations to dialogue are consistently broken up by the stubbornly clipped and repetitive replies of the corporal, whose startling refusal to talk is his final evasion of the military's power to coerce and to contaminate morally (289–300). The corporal and his twelve core followers (four of whom, as a matter of fact, cannot be identified as speaking any known language) are repeatedly figured as outside or above language, and thus also, most fully, as outside the control of the large organizations (battalion, army, nation) that are committed to the use of violence.

In *Catch-22,* Joseph Heller's morbid comedy about an American bomber squadron in World War II, mere silence is defeat. Figures of silence are figures of co-optation: Captains Piltchard and Wren, the contentedly dutiful bombers who speak only rarely and inarticulately, for instance (144); the mute MPs, automata of military law who take Yossarian into custody (410); or the dying Communications Colonel, a transmitter of messages reduced to a cipher, whose most salient features are his nearly voiceless lover and his own quiescence (14–15). In a large part the most urgent subject of *Catch-22* is the contest between the institutionalized communicative systems that are structurally distorted by the dictates of propaganda and the subaltern strategies that operate within and resist these systems. When the novel opens its protagonist, Yossarian, is depicted as physically ensnared in the language of the air force bureaucracy. Attempting to escape service by malingering in a hospital bed, Captain Yossarian is pursued and surrounded by the doctors interrogating him, the medical charts tracking his condition, the regulations requiring him to censor the letters of enlisted patients in adjacent wards, and the C.I.D. man who, disguised as a patient, spies on, polices, and writes reports on the censoring activities of the officers in the ward. Yossarian's indiscriminate response reduces communication to tatters: he lies in response to the doctors' questions, and, in his required job as censor, makes "war" on language, each day "obliterating" (8) a separate feature of communication, beginning with the deletion of modifiers and articles and concluding in the switching of signatures and the transformation of paragraphs into linear arrays organized spatially rather than syntactically or semantically. The first chapter sets the pattern for all that follows. Henceforth, it will be ambiguous whether clear communication is damaged by the military bureaucracy or by the voices of protest that have abjured such dialogic axioms as reciprocity, sincerity, and an orientation toward mutual understanding. It is, after all, one of the novel's repeated lessons that in this system the most poignantly vulnerable can begin to protect themselves only when they conceive the possibility of lying (95, 356).

How is it that factual, referential language began to seem unusable, even violent? that silence or distortions of language came to be imagined as robust, liberating alternatives? The remainder of this chapter examines how language functions within a system of institutionalized violence: specifically, how the vertically organized military structures analyzed by Faulkner and Heller produce, regularly and from within, communicative misfires and a destabilization of referentiality. I will *not* be looking at strategies of subversion that developed as a result of language's perceived failure, or at any other externalities that point to effect rather than cause. Instead I will be focusing on the programmatic distortions and normal accidents of communication that complex organizations *structurally* generate. The analysis will proceed at two levels, tracking both dialogic and referential distortions. The dialogic refers to how individuals and groups share information more or less efficiently. Here I will be looking at the communicative frameworks of violence from the perspective of organizational sociology, considering such concepts as roles, communication channels, lexicons, and hierarchies. The referential refers to the ways verbal representations are mapped more or less accurately to the material world. In this section I will examine the interior structure of lies and propaganda.

Organizational euphoria and anxiety increased in the immediate postwar period for a variety of reasons: the Cold War dominance of the increasingly integrated military-industrial complex, the formation of organizations like the United Nations and the International Military Tribunal, the birth of modern organizational sociology in the seminal late 1950s work of Herbert Simon and James March, and the rapid growth in corporate economic structures, which in America always followed the great wars.[19] The postwar years marked the final transformation of America into an *employee* society. Corporate consolidation and expansion reached unprecedented levels through a wave of mergers: *Fortune* magazine estimated that 7,500 mergers were "important enough to be noted by the financial journals" between 1945 and 1953.[20] As Robert Presthus observes, from 1940 to 1950 the labor force increased by over 10 million, but the number of self-employed workers remained roughly constant: 85 percent were now employees, and 9 million of these worked for the 500 largest industrial corporations.[21] Government and government spending increased even more dramatically owing to defense costs. The national debt increased only $4.9 billion from 1924 to 1935, the middle of the Depression. From 1942 through 1945 the debt rose from $72 billion to $258 billion. By 1962 it had reached $280 billion. "The bureaucratic model," Presthus noted that year, is the "major organizational form in our society."[22] Bureaucracies were, indeed, also the major entities of action in the public imagination: during the war and immediate postwar years there was a noteworthy increase in the percentage of the front page of the *New York Times* that discussed corporations as a category of actors.[23] For both Faulkner and Heller, this increasing prominence of organizations was a deep and explicit concern. In his polemical article "On Privacy" (1955) Faulkner makes corporate violations of individual integrity an occasion for lamenting the organizational transformation of the "individual" into an "integer" of a "will-less and docile mass."[24] And in a 1962 interview on *Catch-22* Joseph Heller wonders at the "extraordinary" "amount of waste" and "mistakes in communications" that he sees as inherent to any corporation. "I cannot imagine . . . anybody of any real intelligence," he exclaims, "choosing to place himself within a large organization, where he functions in relationship to dozens or hundreds of other people, because every contact is an impairment of his efficiency."[25]

We now live in a society of organizations; almost no aspect of our lives remains untouched by organizational memberships and structures. But the complex organization is important as a unit of analysis here for several reasons in addition to its historical relevance. Most significant, organizations have been neglected in literary analysis. Relegating specific organizational action to the background even in novels where it plays a central narrative role, like *Catch-22* and *A Fable*, criticism favors character (identity) and cultural context (broad trends and signal moments). When organizational-level social units are invoked they tend to function as symbols of a transdiscursive and encompassing power concept,[26] as figures for the logic of writing, or as units of "over-identity" that nonetheless function as a return to character, a "mapping of the person-concept *over* localism."[27] In analyzing action literary criticism thus moves uneasily back and forth, as if in an endless series of assertions and retreats, between an emphasis upon the individual (what Alan Liu calls the hidden subject or "atom" of high theory)[28] and a reliance upon cultural formations so abstracted and pervasive as to be deterministic (dominant ideologies, episteme, habitus).[29] Organizational analysis, in contrast, is interested in understanding the specific properties of identifiably bounded supraindividual units, the empirical middle points, so to speak, between individual and social action. Looking at organizational dynamics thus helps us to move away from subjective, psychologistic explanations of human action *without* erring toward mystified notions of cultural logic and causality—without, as Jean Howard puts it, deriving "cultural law" from a personalizing anecdote or, as Liu says, building from detail to homogenizing cultural whole with only an "as if" for buttressing argument.[30] Organizationalism's claim is that action cannot be explained effectively through atomistic models of rational, interest-seeking individuals nor through ideological analysis that abstracts away from specific institutional settings in favor of the broader, concept-level categories of "political culture" that stand in for self-interest as the contingent but constitutive elements of identity. Take as an illustrative case the perceived tendency of subordinates in large organizations to tell their superiors only what they want to hear. To paraphrase Charles Perrow, an organizational analysis allows us to translate an explanation oriented toward understanding individual, personal predispositions (the subordinate fears to tell the truth) into a more broadly applicable institutional explanation revelatory of specific macro-unit properties ("truth" is an organizationally established frame of reference, produced in the subordinate through his use of corporate-specific communication channels, lexicons, and forms for processing information) without relying upon class-level ideology explanations that departicularize organizational properties in favor of a dispersed notion of culture/power or a renewed postmodern search for the nature of human character (individual action occurs as a function of hegemonic, transorganizational discursive regimes that constitute the modern subsidiary self by transforming ritualized deference as personal obedience into a performed, impersonal informational subordination).[31]

In the analysis that follows I use a theoretical archive new for literary critics, relying upon organizational sociologists and administrative scientists like James March, Herbert Simon, and Charles Perrow rather than figures like Bourdieu and Foucault, who are more familiar to critics interested in social structure. It is, first, an archive of important historical resonance. Organizational sociology developed as a field symbiotically with the rise of modern bureaucracy, particularly with the expansion of the military-industrial complex. Sociologists were employed in their professional capacities by the U.S. military for the first time in World War II,[32] and, indeed, many of the most important American writers-to-be on organizations and action served in the armed forces at this time, including March, Perrow, Edward Shils, Robert Presthus, Peter Blau, Peter Berger, and Morris Janowitz. Second, despite the great utility of Bourdieu and Foucault for understanding social processes, their theoretical systems present a danger of directing analysis toward certain predictably deterministic conclusions: their concepts of structure have difficulty incorporating a theoretical understanding of change.[33] By emphasizing, within an epistemology interior to the institution, roles rather than identity and organizations rather than ideology, organizational sociology opens a space for a recognizable human agency that is an important corrective to the dominance of post-Foucauldian theorists of action[34]—*without* thereby reproducing a model of unified subjects that precede social interpolation. Third, organizational sociology takes the institution seriously as a subject in its own right, rather than as a sign of other theoretical frameworks or units. In Foucault's homogenizing view of institutions (and in literary criticism derived from Foucault), the specific organization is a site interesting as an example of how externally generated, socially pervasive systems of power/knowledge reproduce themselves: the organization is transformed into a metaphor for culture, and culture, in the critical applications of Foucault, is modeled through the circulation of representations rather than through the causal sequencing of actions.[35] Bourdieu's institutionalism is more rigorous and useful than Foucault's, but the nature of Bourdieu's projects and interests means that specific organizational structure tends to disappear in his theoretical work as multiple institutions are absorbed into various "black boxes" of social reproduction (such as fields or the habitus);[36] and in his empirical work, for instance in *Homo Academicus,* the institution itself is interesting mostly as a receptacle for the data-laden individuals that constitute it.[37] Organizational sociologists, in a contrast of emphasis, treat bureaucracy as an independent (causative) rather than dependent (caused) variable. As fine recalibrators of social structure theory, dedicated to anatomizing organizational particularity, they provide the level of concrete detail, precision of terms, and "agentic orientation" that is needed to match the thickness of description attained in writers on organizations like Faulkner and Heller.[38]

Organizational analysis thus offers a powerful new tool for describing complex arrays of social behavior. It asks specific questions: Are the institutions that enclose the action "tall" or "squat"? That is, are the relevant organizational configurations specialized and subdivided or generalized and unitary? Is communication conducted through conversations or memos? Do decisions require the approval of an executive figure, a committee, or a series of disconnected department heads? Answering such questions is key to answering questions about force and discourse: understanding the relationship between language and violence today *requires* understanding organizations. Organizations are, in essence, a speech act, or rather, a complex layering of speech acts that have become a social fact.[39] Organizations are built by language; in turn, they work to recreate language, not only by altering individual lexicons, but also, more importantly, by altering the social status of words. The efficiency of an organization is determined by its ability to reduce the distance between verbal projections and their realization in the material world. Organizations, in other words, are the place where language is attached to physical force. Organizations see the transformation of words into deeds. Whether they become deeds of violence or deeds of repair, as Faulkner and Heller make especially clear, depends in a large part upon the way each organization allows its members to communicate and the role each assigns to referentiality.

Dialogic Distortions.

Postwar sociological work on the connections among organizations, language, and domination drew primarily from the tradition established by Max Weber. In the years preceding World War I, Weber depicted the state as most fundamentally a monopoly over violence: he characterized the modernization process as a matter of bureaucratizing and expanding the state's war-making powers, and he beheld in the future an iron cage of rationalized coercion through complex organizations. In Germany in the late 1930s, the rise of rationalized violence through the consolidation of Fascist organization seemed to confirm the bleaker elements of Weberian theory, determinatively influencing the Frankfurt School and driving the Weberian Norbert Elias to a study of institutional centralization and the disciplinary restructuring of human personality. Elias, a Jewish veteran of World War I whose mother was murdered in Auschwitz, examined how in Europe the historical expansion of centralized institutional structures (states, courts, administrative centers) functioned to pacify territories and populations.[40] Beginning in the eleventh century, he writes, monopolies over violence, status, and tax began to increase. As localism gave way to spatial and symbolic centralization, unified codes of conduct began to arise, and formerly independent knights were transformed into hierarchically bound subjects. To maintain the favor of the king (the primary dispenser of status) virtuosity in language was required: rituals of courtesy began to displace contests of violence as the primary determinant of a knight's quality.[41] For Elias, social control is realized through the organizational stipulation of language and the minute regulation of the body. He is particularly interested in courtly surveillance, in the development of precise codes for appropriate expression, and in the management of information through secrets and status-determined communication.[42]

For Weber, even more explicitly, the effectiveness of organizational domination is a function of the control of language. His writings on bureaucracy are especially relevant for our purposes. In this seminal work, Weber argues that bureaucratic administration is "capable of attaining the highest degree of efficiency and is in this sense formally the most rational means of carrying out imperative control over human beings."[43] "Bureaucracy as such is a precision instrument that can put itself at the disposal of quite varied . . . interests in domination."[44] According to Weber, this is in a large part because of its control of technologies of "communication," and because of its production of and reliance upon written records ("files") and its capacity for control on the basis of knowledge ("facts" as a "store of documentary material"). As a result of its "striving for power," the bureaucracy establishes monopolies of information.[45] "Every bureaucracy," he writes, "seeks to increase the superiority of the professionally informed by keeping their knowledge and intentions secret."[46] This comprehensive control of "knowledge" is the basis of bureaucracy's superiority over other organizational forms "in precision, in stability, in the stringency of its discipline, and in its reliability." Bureaucracy, he writes, "thus makes possible a particularly high degree of calculablity of results for the heads of the organization and for those acting in relation to it."[47] I will be arguing, however, that bureaucracy's strategies for sustaining such total control over the use of information (both by its subunits and by its competitors) have in particular environments a series of unintended consequences that reflect back upon its purported rationality and efficiency. Both *A Fable* and *Catch-22* are structured according to this critique of organizational coherence. In particular, these novels reveal that nondemocratic dialogic regulation instituted as a dictate of efficiency not only violates the minimal publicity principles that act as important stays against tyranny in certain organizational forms but also, in part *because* of this violation, serves to undermine the very efficiency meant to justify it.

As *A Fable* reveals, language is controlled (and distorted) in very particular ways by organizations skilled in and committed to the use of violence. Information exchange is regulated *across* and *within* the borders of a community. Extraterritorial dialogic communication (barring occasional exceptions) is prohibited. Terms are not translatable: messages and even lexicons are intended only for interior usage. Such nontransparency is essential to the organization's mission of violence. It is not simply a matter of strategy, that is, imposing an information deficit upon the enemy which impedes successful action; it is a matter of creating the enemy as an object, as a thing outside humanizing communication which can then be fully characterized by the stylized interior language of propaganda, by a set of terms that are not usable within the context of and could not withstand scrutiny of intersubjective deliberation.[48] *A Fable's* sustained concern over the truncation of dialogue at national borders is revealed not only in the awkward, distorted conversation between the opposing generals who are attempting to collaborate (awkward not so much because they speak different languages but because they are not accustomed to seeing each other as natural objects of language)[49] but also, and more importantly, in the figure of the corporal, whose movement over enemy lines is presented as almost unimaginable, a form of action outside the capacity of a French-inflected narrative to express that brings about the debilitation of the organizations on both sides (108).

Within tall organizations like the military—that is, organizations characterized by a complex layering of authority, a comprehensive behavioral latticework of rules and regulations, and a concentration upon the technologies of management—*interior* communication channels are regulated both horizontally and vertically. The organization's rigidity is essential to its survival. Lateral communication among the lower members of the organization, in this case the enlisted men, is structurally prohibited. Information is processed vertically and redistributed to various sectors of men from the top down. The only exceptions to this rule are the unauthorized mechanisms of gossip (65) and, again, the disruptive actions of the corporal, who preternaturally manages to travel through and communicate freely with all of the battalions despite restrictions on mobility imposed by a rigorous system of passes and bayoneted MPs.[50] The structures for controlling information that Faulkner focuses upon are so complete and so severe that the commanders cannot conceive how the mutiny was engineered among the men. As the battalion runner puts it when wondering at the ability of the core mutineers to organize: "Unless you've got the right properly signed paper in your hand, it's a good deal more difficult to go to Paris from here than to Berlin" (66). Perhaps, he suggests, betraying through his mystification the fact that he was an officer during the mutiny preparations, the mutineers did not spread the message at all. "Perhaps they didn't even need to go themselves, perhaps just wind, moving air, carried it. Or perhaps not even moving air but just air, spreading by attrition from invisible and weightless molecule to molecule as disease, smallpox spreads, or fear, or hope—just enough of us, all of us in the mud here saying together, Enough of this, let's have done with this" (66). Counterposed throughout the novel to the rigidity of the bureaucracy are such images of occult forces and inexplicably produced, nonlocal effects.

The prohibition of horizontal communication is not simply a matter of social control (segmenting the population and hence making it more amenable to coercion), it is also a matter of organizational efficiency, which in violent organizations is perceived as the capacity for instantaneous responses and quick physical action. It is the military's essential premise that the distribution of information is labor-intensive (hence the elaborate system of message runners and the frantic work of the battalion runner throughout the novel) and that therefore information recipients should be limited to a select few. Moreover, it is assumed that language interferes with action, that unlimited horizontal communication reduces efficiency by inspiring repetitions of deliberation, which consume time and lead to conflicts, which in turn require further deliberation (assumptions represented, again, in the battalion runner, who is simultaneously the novel's figure of mobility, unregulated dispersal of information, and fractious argument). Structural organizational dictates, in other words, require the packaging of information, packaging that functions to withhold vital data (lies of omission) and that minimizes intersubjectivity.

Organizational efficiency also requires regulation of vertical communication, which, relatedly, produces information pathologies and communicative distortions. In this case the perceived problem is not that too many people might receive certain small bundles of information but rather that a small number of people might receive too much unbundled information. In *Catch-22*, to switch texts briefly, Major Major grows despondent as the bureaucracy transforms all of his "simple communications" into "huge manuscripts": each document he signs is distributed to receive endorsements from all other relevant officers and is then returned to him (several pages thicker) for another signature (91). The bureaucracy promotes agent-neutral action (consistency and uniformity) through written guidelines for behavior that are developed through experience and through overlapping levels of seniority-driven supervision: this formalized rule structure is the material expression of an "organizational memory" that, as it deepens, increasingly ensures the stability of a bureau's responses to its environmental input. The highly sedimented organizational memory of older bureaucracies, however, also increases structural complexity and therefore magnifies procedural sunk costs and general inertia.[51] Such bureaucracies, because they tend to consolidate power and status conservatively, also tend to produce members who are blame-averse, seeking collective approval before undertaking nonroutine action.[52] For these reasons communication in an established bureaucracy can tend to proliferate unproductively. Between information and an action decision the bureaucracy inserts a second layer of resource-consuming communication: namely, information about information. As Heller's Major Major reveals, this metainformation can, in fact, partially displace information itself.

The inefficiencies caused by this language-expanding tendency of complex organizations can generate a set of corrective adaptive mechanisms that work to shrink language. The problems that derive, in turn, from this action against language is one of the primary concerns of *A Fable*. At a pivotal moment near the center of Faulkner's novel the old general is portrayed reflecting upon his position at the apex of the great hierarchy.[53]

First and topmost were the three flags and the three supreme generals who served them: a triumvirate consecrated and anointed, a constellation remote as planets in their immutability, powerful as archbishops in their trinity, splendid as cardinals in their retinues and myriad as Brahmins in their blind followers; next were the three thousand lesser generals who were their deacons and priests and the hierarchate of their households, their acolytes and bearers of monstrance and host and censer: the colonels and majors who were in charge of the portfolios and maps and memoranda, the captains and subalterns who were in charge of the communications and errands which kept the portfolios and maps up to date, and the sergeants and corporals who actually carried the portfolios and mapcases and protected them with their lives and answered the telephone and ran the errands, and the privates who sat at the flickering switchboards at two and three and four o'clock in the morning . . . that military metabolism which does everything to a man but lose him, which learns nothing and forgets nothing and loses nothing at all whatever and forever—no scrap of paper, no unfinished record or uncompleted memorandum no matter how inconsequential or trivial. (202)

Because it is Faulkner there is explicit in this series of images the threat of an overwhelming surplus of language, a crowd's cacophony, which, as with the crowds analyzed at the beginning of this chapter, amounts not only to an obliteration of coherent language but also to an obliteration of action.[54] The unstructured collective is always passive and supremely helpless in *A Fable*. The crowd owns nothing but a "reversion in endurance" (204). As the general explains, "They don't want to know . . . they want only to suffer" (199). The military, then, can function actively only because information is filtered out and miniaturized as it passes to higher and higher levels of decision making. For the bureaucracy, in other words, it is rational to limit its own ability to make fully cognizant evaluations and decisions.[55] The hierarchy presented by Faulkner above is as much about the distribution of information as it is about the distribution of power: "communications" are resummarized as increasingly concise "memoranda" and are transported through various levels of sergeants, captains, colonels, and generals. The old general, at the top, is typically depicted behind a border of "clerks and secretaries" (193), in possession of the official "report" (194), receiving an audience of one, and acting without hesitation or consultation. As March and Simon would put it, "uncertainty" is "absorbed" by the structures of information processing.[56] The power to act is preserved but information is impoverished. As Perrow writes: "An organization develops a set of concepts influenced by the technical vocabulary and classification schemes; this permits easy communication. Anything that does not fit into these concepts is not easily communicated . . . This is especially apparent when a body of information must be edited and summarized in order to make it fit into the conceptual scheme—to make it understandable. The inferences from the material rather than the material itself are transmitted."[57] Indeed, information detaches itself from the world. As March and Simon note, for the organization "the particular categories and schemes of classification it employs are reified, and become, for members of the organization, attributes of the world rather than mere conventions."[58]

Communication is structurally distorted: hence what Faulkner emphasizes as the great surprise for all of the commanders when the mutiny is staged. That a conspiracy of hundreds of thousands could remain undetected signifies a near total absence of vertical feedback loops and thus an organizationally generated communicative uncoupling of top from bottom. It is as if at the broadest level of surveillance, with the lower officers and sergeants (sergeants were not included in the mutiny), relevant observers lacked the lexical capacity to translate into the standardized forms of reports and memos the irregular events that were the mutiny's necessary precursors. Indeed, it is as if they were unable even to detect irregularity. The bureaucracy's communication system is composed of necessarily broad classifications of "program-evoking situations."[59] At the levels of both observing and reporting, then, focus is shifted away from the unnamed and unusual toward the identity tags of the familiar. Moreover, as *A Fable* reveals through detail after detail, in steep, efficiency-dominated hierarchies, the subordinates who are objects of control regularly develop an "institutional lingo" designed to exclude superiors from communication;[60] middle managers are structurally motivated to restrict the vertical transmission of information that might be used to evaluate their performance, such as reports on dissension in the ranks; subgroups often fail to report to superiors information not regularly considered relevant to their specialized domain; and high-level decision makers often discredit information and interpretations presented by inferiors, especially in organizations like the military that have a high degree of ritual and symbolism associated with rank.[61] From the bottom of the structure to the top, the hierarchical division that enables action prevents the unformatted dialogue that is necessary to bring fully accurate information into the organizational command from the borders of its environment. This is a key concern for Faulkner: the first sergeant we encounter in the novel is described as having "sold his birthright in the race of man" (9) by assuming a position of command; the battalion runner, because he had once, though briefly, been an officer, "durst not be present even on the fringe of whatever surrounding [enlisted] crowd, even to walk, pass through, let alone stop, within the same air of that small blue clump of hope" (57); and, in one of the most dismaying images of disconnection, the windows of the general's meeting room are open, but the noise and voices of the crowd, "even the sudden uproar of them which the division commander and the chief-of-staff had just left outside in the *Place de Ville,* didn't reach" (192). The leadership appears as detached as the distant, anonymous power in Auden's poem "The Managers." Once again the dictates of organizational efficiency structurally produce debilitating communicative distortions.

The programmatic nature of information and consequently practice means that the intentional action of agents is limited by, or rather
absorbed into, structure. The resultant inflexibility leads to what is
perceived as an irrational misalignment between organization and environment. Organizational rationality can be recalibrated, however,
and hence organizational efficiency, manifest as domination or consensus, can be maximized. Even small breaks in institutional homogenization, Faulkner reveals, can increase an organization's adaptability
and susceptibility to internally generated change. Through the old
general, Faulkner both asserts and challenges a vision of the organization's inevitable stratification and immunity to redirection through
the actions of its agents. The general is both an organizational man
and a charismatic leader with the capacity to evaluate situations from
multiple perspectives. Against stark images of his alienation from subordinates stand the multiple instances when he shatters communicative stratification: he is able, Faulkner reminds us, to talk comfortably
with and remember the name and face of "every man in uniform
whom he had ever seen" (193). The general is thus a symbol of bureaucracy's maladaptive iron cage but also of its capacity for unprecedented nuance and sensitivity in environmental manipulation. He is
able to perform dually, to act with imagination even while he is a
product of an organization that unintentionally constrains speech and
thought, because he has advanced himself through the ranks irregu-
larly, rejecting the conventional career lines that promote conventional thinking and participating in radically exterior organizations
(211–215). As Perrow argues, under some conditions bureaucracies
can be structured to allow more frequently for such nonlinear training
and thus can more effectively rejuvenate themselves.[62] Perspectival
proliferation can break down the cognition barriers typical of place-
ment within a hierarchy and can maximize individual agency within a
structure.

As this case demonstrates through negation, organizational dysfunctionality is a result not only of communicative stratification but
also of military premise-setting, which amounts to a regularization of
involuntary silence.[63] One of the most important features of any organization is its capacity to reproduce itself—but the very same mechanisms that provide adaptive durability are also a source of maladaptive organizational inertia. Combat, once begun, must be able to
sustain itself in the face of extreme discouragement. To be functional
violent organizations must therefore make themselves dysfunctionally

resistant to change; control must be exerted over members and stake-holders so that they do not question the organization's assumptions. In other words, the fact of combat must be made into a social *institution*, a way of life, so to speak, a background against which decisions are made (Brecht's *Mother Courage* is a brutal analysis of this fact). "The same war," Faulkner writes, "which we had come to believe did not know how to end itself" (63). It is for this reason that wars so frequently continue to be fought past all rational limits, that wars as institutions overlive their purposes. There is no need for implausible psychosocial arguments extrapolated from individualist models of experience that explain war's counterintuitive stability through self-perpetuating cycles of repression-release or revenge, through collective delight in destruction or collective impulses toward self-destruction, through uniquely amplified cultural tenacity, or, as Simone Weil explains it, through existential paralysis.[64] There are several specific strategies that violent organizations use to control their agents and to achieve inertia: the direct, coercive control of enforceable rules: non-coercive bureaucratic control such as role specialization and motivation through rewards; and the more total control of cognitive premise-setting.[65]

The first set of strategies is built upon a model of rules as prohibitions; the second and third sets upon a model of rules as possibilities (for example, the rules of chess). Direct controls (obey or you will be punished) are effective but costly.[66] As Faulkner repeatedly points out, they are increasingly inefficient as the scale of membership grows:

> Even ruthless and all-powerful and unchallengeable Authority would be impotent before that massed unresisting undemanding passivity. [The battalion runner] thought: *They could execute only so many of us before they will have worn out the last rifle and pistol and expended the last live shell,* visualising it: first, the anonymous fringe of subalterns and junior clerks to which he had once belonged, relegated to the lathes and wheels to keep them in motion rifling barrels and filling shell-cases; then, the frenzy and the terror mounting, the next layer: the captains and majors and secretaries and attachés . . . among the oil cans and the flying shafts; then the field officers: colonels and senators and Members; then, last and ultimate, the ambassadors and ministers and lesser generals themselves frantic and inept among the slowing wheels and melting bearings, while the old men, the last handful of kings and presidents and field marshals . . . fired the last puny scattered and markless fusillade as into the face of the sea itself. (57)

Once instituted, noncoercive bureaucratic controls are more a product of organizational structure than of vigilant managerial intention or subordinate pliability—their indifference to personality increases their scope and efficiency.[67] Role specialization, for instance, effectively induces conformity to organizational objectives by shrinking the volume of decisions and compass of information for which particular members are responsible. Concomitant membership compartmentalization and stratification, further, impede suborganizational consensus building and grass-roots innovation.[68] The most effective control, however, is cognitive. As Walter Powell and Paul DiMaggio have pointed out, rational-choice theorists argue that technical interdependence and physical sunk costs are key causal elements in organizational inertia; neoinstitutionalist sociologists argue, however, that "these are not the only, or the most important, factors. Institutionalized arrangements are reproduced because individuals often cannot even conceive of appropriate alternatives (or because they regard as unrealistic the alternatives they can imagine). Institutions do not just constrain options: they establish the very criteria by which people discover their preferences." In sum they argue, "some of the most important sunk costs are cognitive."[69]

In *A Fable*, the ending of war does not become a live option for the enlisted men because they are unable to think of it as such, unable to think and speak beyond the bounds of the combat institution. *"It's not that we didn't believe: it's that we couldn't, didn't want to know any more. That's the most terrible thing they have done to us. That's the most terrible"* (61). This negative consensus is not the result of failings in individual decision-making capacities; it does not result from actors' preferences and choices but rather derives from the organization's minimization of information sources and its maximization of uncertainty absorption.[70] Mutiny is not chosen as an option in the action that precedes the novel because information is not a given, because human decisions do not conform to individualistic, rational-choice models, and in particular because group action is not determined, as behavioralists would argue, by the aggregate consequences of individual choice: the soldiers are not individuals with coordination problems; coordination brings them into being as individuals.[71] Faulkner wants both to acknowledge and to challenge this social fact. Thus he emphasizes that only one man (a Christ figure transcending human limitations)[72] had the capacity to conceive the thought of nonparticipation and practical rebellion, even after so many years, but also that one was enough to verbalize it and hence create it as a shareable conceptual possibility:

> "Wasn't it just one before?" the old porter said. "Wasn't one enough then to tell us the same thing all them two thousand years ago: that all we ever needed to do was just to say, Enough of this—us, not even the sergeants and corporals, but just us, all of us, Germans and Colonials and Frenchmen and all the other foreigners in the mud here, saying together: Enough. Let them that's already dead and maimed and missing be enough of this—a thing so easy and simple that even human man, as full of evil and sin and folly as he is, can understand and believe it this time." (56)

The unclassifiable corporal is a symbol of the inevitability of institutional overdetermination, and thus of the possibility, however small, of creative action. In the "total institution" detailed by Erving Goffman (armies, prisons, asylums), physical and cognitive barriers are used to prevent members from acquiring or retaining actively competing organizational roles; authorities thereby instill in their subjects a singular, comprehensive institutional identity.[73] "Role dispossession"—a crucial element in the centralized restructuring of persons—is effected in the individual through procedures of mortification: physical appearance, posture, language, and the activities of work and self-care are publicized and programmed, thereby evacuating personality and autonomy from bodily practices, while in admission and evaluation regulations the self's vital "informational preserve" is routinely violated. The inmate, writes Goffman, is continually "made to display a giving up of his will."[74] But the social complexity of personhood is durable, as Faulkner reveals, even under these extreme circumstances. However deeply submerged, prior institutional and community affiliations can in transitional or crisis moments bring out important cleavages in role identities and therefore in cognition. Contradiction, in other words, disaggregates "identity" into "roles." Enlivening the enlisted soldiers' sense of their multiple external commitments and roles, the corporal enables them to challenge the self-evident character of the military's basic premises;[75] and by establishing the basic organizational interconnectedness minimally required for social movements (detailed by Faulkner as an excruciating grass-roots campaign), the corporal enables them to *act* on this challenge, to build from what Sidney Tarrow calls "the work of 'naming'" to the construction of "collective action frames" that both constitute and are constituted by structurally muted alternative affiliations, affiliations that when operative can transform ineffective individual protest into politically effective practice.[76] As the passage quoted above shows, the corporal's soldiers are not just members of a national military institution, realized through a vertical command network. They are also members of specific religious institutions and tightly bound in-groups of a subordinate class ("enlisted"), all of which make synecdochic membership claims horizontally across national borders. The military works to achieve a monopoly over the models of identity that are available to its members. Models derived from other cultural and organizational frameworks can be, as the enlisted mutiny shows, directly threatening to its unchecked monolithic functioning. As Arendt notes in her study of totalitarianism, domination is maximized when individuals are atomized and decontextualized: fascism, perpetually jealous of its organizational sovereignty, is vulnerable in the presence of autonomous communal bonds and cultural practices.[77] Plurality promotes innovation: hence the Perrowian argument that developing an array of permeable bureaucracies with different interests, limited power, and diverse information sources and monitors will enhance both individual agency and organizational responsiveness to diverse societal interests. As Emirbayer and Mische put it in an argument for a fractured conception of structure, *"Actors who are positioned at the intersection of multiple temporal-relational contexts can develop greater capacities for creative and critical intervention."*[78]

In Milo Minderbinder, perhaps the bleakest literary characterization of cognitive bureaucratic control, Joseph Heller deletes Faulkner's considerations of agency through institutional fractions in favor of a fuller exploration of role structure, domination, and the organizational contraction of personality. Organizational rigidity in *Catch-22* is exaggerated to an absurd extreme. The details of communicative stratification, for instance, are emblematized in Colonel Korn's rule that "the only people permitted to ask questions were those who never did" (35; see also 78) and in the policy of Major Major, who permits subordinates to consult him in his office only when he is not in his office (271). Milo is the paradigmatic product of this compartmentalizing system. His role in sustaining combat is the procurement

and delivery of food to the armed forces. This insulating specialization forces him to see all elements of war, including combat and
death, only insofar as they relate to the gargantuan business ventures
that have developed out of his duties as mess officer. One example (illuminating both the organizational pattern and its dysfunctionality)
will suffice. Milo, seeing no contradiction, coordinates an enemy attack upon his own troops in order to increase the business revenues
that sustain his food gathering enterprise (248–254). Agents are constituted by multiple practical identities and often competing moral
claims. To operate effectively according to its structuring-efficiency
conception, Heller asserts, the military must as much as possible reduce its members not merely to one primary institutional identity, as
in Faulkner, but to *one function*. Alternative conceptions of action,
the possibility of contradiction, must remain unimaginable. Milo is
thus continually figured as an automaton, unable to think or speak
past his specialized role and in the grip of forces beyond his control.
On a mission to rescue an abandoned child, Milo stumbles upon a
plan to raise revenue by smuggling tobacco:

> Milo . . . started toward the door as though in a spell . . . "Stay here and
> help me find her," pleaded Yossarian. "You can smuggle illegal tobacco
> tomorrow." But Milo was deaf and kept pushing forward, nonviolently
> but irresistibly, sweating, his eyes, as though he were in the grip of a
> blind fixation, burning feverishly, and his twitching mouth slavering. He
> moaned calmly as though in remote, instinctive distress and kept repeat-
> ing, "Illegal tobacco, illegal tobacco." Yossarian stepped out of the way
> with resignation finally when he saw it was hopeless to try to reason
> with him. (402)

How does the institutionalization of violence affect language? The organization's efficiency-oriented stratifications of communication and
specializations of identity are in war so radically amplified that they
self-consume: the reciprocal and innovative capacities of language are
central casualties. For all of his actions Milo is, finally, a man of one
act; and for all of his talk Milo's language is, finally, as radically trun-
cated and repetitive as Aarfy's, which throughout the novel is depicted
as an empty collection of clichés impervious to response (his inability
to hear Yossarian during flight is one of Heller's heavier symbols,
146–147).

Organizations are driven to reproduce themselves, but short-term survival often works at cross-purposes with long-term adaptability. According to the organizational theories of Chester Barnard, theories that prevailed in America throughout the 1940s and early 1950s, organizations are "cooperative systems where the organizational and the individual objective must coincide."[79] It is in part the function of reward structures to bring about this ideal, but in complex organizations, particularly organizations composed of multiple sectors and subunits, the mechanisms of norm building and the norms themselves are sometimes uncoupled: often rewards do not promote an orientation toward organizational goals as much as they promote an orientation toward reward seeking.[80] Also, the formation of subgoals around which departments are then built as part of organizational division of labor produces conflicting goals within the macro-organizational structure itself: as the case of Milo shows, departmental subgoals (means) can begin to compete with and even displace an organization's primary goals (ends).[81] For Heller, then, Barnard's organizational symmetry is an impossibility. Both sectors and individuals learn to process information and perceive problems differently according to their particular frames of reference; and perhaps more important, they invidiously compete for control of organizational resources, because organizational subunits like the organization as a whole are structured to reproduce themselves, to guarantee their own flourishing.[82] Colonel Cathcart, for instance, does not worry over whether or not he is a good commander, indeed he does not even concern himself with what "good" might in this context mean. Instead, he spends time and resources currying the favor of his superiors, an activity that, because the organization is violent and thus necessarily authoritarian, is most effective when appeal is made to immediate personal rather than abstract organizational interests (185–186). General Peckem (representing Special Services) formulates strategy not against the Germans but against General Dreedle (representing combat operations) in order to increase his sector's and therefore his personal share in organizational power: "Dreedle's on our side, and Dreedle is the enemy. General Dreedle commands four bomb groups that we simply must capture . . . I keep invading his jurisdiction with comments and criticisms that are really none of my business, and he doesn't know what to do about it. When he accuses me of seeking to undermine him, I merely answer that my only purpose in calling attention to his errors is to strengthen our war effort by eliminating inefficiency" (316–317).

Departments and departmental action are shaped not by the requirements of organizational function but rather by competing intra-
organizational "interests." The result, as Heller illustrates, is organizational irrationality and inefficiency: the scheming, duplicitous,
"goddam memorandums" (383) engendered by Peckem's sectional
competition lead to the final ascendancy of the aptly named General
Scheisskopf, whose most remarkable features are his incompetence
and his dysfunctional obsession with parades (which are, importantly,
a simulation of work). In complex bureaucracies, the mechanisms of
goal reproduction that are necessary for survival structurally undermine the efficiency and adaptability that are necessary for survival.

Such organizational irrationality, for Heller, is ultimately a problem
of language. Information is embedded in power structures, and the
differential distribution of the information can either promote or hinder the interests of particular subunits within the organization. Thus,
to be the generator of new names and informational categories is to
increase the share of one's organizational control. General Peckem,
citing one of his great successes in displaying (and thus, by the military's logic, expanding) his authority,[83] explains, "A *bomb pattern* is a
term I dreamed up just several weeks ago. It means nothing, but you'd
be surprised at how rapidly it's caught on. Why, I've got all sorts of
people convinced I think it's important for the bombs to explode close
together and make a neat aerial photograph. There's one colonel in
Pianosa who's hardly concerned any more with whether he hits the
target or not. Let's fly over and have some fun with him today . . . It
drives General Dreedle insane to find out I've been inspecting one of
his installations while he's been off inspecting another" (318). The
structurally generated results of organizational norm building range
from linguistic nontransparency and internal censorship of communication to outright deception. Structural dialogic deformations also include the establishment of unofficial communicative hierarchies that
work counter to the already limited exchange of information within
the organization. Because ex-Pfc. Wintergreen is so low in the organization that he is involved in the actual physical transfer of information (working in a mail-sorting cubicle), he becomes an important figure in the Peckem-Dreedle competition: he can destroy and misdeliver
information as it suits his purposes. Heller's summary example of the
distortion of communication in the military comes early in the novel
with the floating signifier "T. S. Eliot." A memo from Peckem's office

rhetorically asks if there is any poet who makes money; Wintergreen anonymously calls the office and, before hanging up, says simply "T. S. Eliot"; Peckem's office, in a combination of exploratory mischief and alarm, anonymously calls Dreedle, announces "T. S. Eliot," and hangs up; Dreedle, fortuitously, anonymously passes the message back; Peckem, now panicked, questions whether or not it is a new code and, searching for answers, closes the sterile circle by having his office contact Wintergreen. In the fruitless conversation that proceeds, Wintergreen criticizes the prose of Peckem's memos as "too prolix" (37).

The disaffected participate as well in the disintegration of communication. Men like Yossarian, trained into distrust of how language and logic work in the military (the law Catch-22, like the declaration of Daneeka's death, is as physically threatening as the enemy's weapons), resort to a disruption of its basic elements as a means of resistance. The bureaucracy's conformity-promoting educational seminars, for instance, are brought to an end when Yossarian and other alienated pilots dismantle its question-and-answer sessions with a series of seemingly insoluble questions: "Who is Spain?" "Why is Hitler?" "When is right?" (34). Subversives challenge the system by challenging the language that it speaks, shattering grammar (the products of which are either ineffective as protest or complicit) at the same time that they shatter its justifying premises: What is a nation, that we should identify with it? What is the function for us of identifying the enemy as Hitler? And does just cause in entering a war justify all subsequent actions throughout the duration of a war? Explanatory language is and has always been a ruse. Yossarian, the novel declares, was ready to "pursue" the educational officer "through all the words in the world to wring the knowledge from him if he could" (35).[84]

Implicit in this analysis of the inevitability of internal organizational fractures is thus also an acknowledgment of the fragility of totalizing control in complex structures and the opportunities this gives subordinates for independent action.[85] In this context Heller provides not a theory of the self but rather a diagrammatic understanding of the relationship between structure and action. Indeed, Heller works assiduously to prevent narrative's traditionally vivid attention to the individual from overshadowing organizational dynamics: he deploys a confusing assembly of secondary characters to distract attention from the central figures, and works to minimize

readerly identification by flattening out his characters into stereo-
types. Faulkner, for a like purpose, tends to leave his characters unnamed, referring to them by their organizational title and thereby allowing particularity to fade into deindividualized allegory or type. At
the same time, however, neither author minimizes the presence of the
individual as a social actor as radically as many postmodern writers
(consider Italo Calvino's *Invisible Cities*), precisely because an organizational focus disallows not only overemphasizing but also *under-
emphasizing* the individual as a component of social structure. Hence
one might replace the reading offered earlier of Milo as an extreme instance of the subdepartmental personality with a reading of Milo as
someone operatively independent of the organization. His business
activities—pitting against each other the needs of various buyers and
sellers in the military—are, after all, seldom coincident with the military's interests, often illegal, and always self-promoting in a way that
grotesquely maximizes his agency (for bringing the egg trade to Malta
he is appointed assistant governor general of the region; he is also designated the caliph of Baghdad, the mayor of Palermo, and in some re-
gions the corn god, 230–233). By this argument, Milo as an action
type symbolizes how the power of elites is limited by their bounded
rationality and by the structures they create and need, and how these
limits (manifest here as the potential for goal conflicts) offer to subordinates opportunities for control and change. However, one important claim of organizational theory is that in complex organizations
individuals who feel creative and effective are often highly reproductive of institutional givens, whereas individuals who feel frustrated
and blocked by organizational limits are often forces for radical reconstruction.[86] Against the preceding recuperative reading, then, one
might argue that Milo's choice between the conflicting roles offered
by the international trade syndicate and by the air force is in fact a
false choice, as both institutions are controlled by the same elites, and
both offer the same range of social options. Despite his democratizing
claim that his rise will contribute to a more just redistribution of
wealth ("Everybody has a share"), the only real change that Milo
brings about in the end is his own entrance into the class of elites that
runs the war. His exploitation of cross-cutting organizational cleavages enables him to rise in the organizational hierarchy but not to
imagine anything outside it. The neo-Weberian vision of agency and
social dynamism through organizational diversity is rendered impos-

sible when the existing array of institutional frameworks offers only *apparent* contradictions.

Heller's view of the organizational structuring of action incorporates both readings. *Catch-22* does not present a deterministic view of the essential impossibility of effective agency, or even a depiction of a stable agency-structure dichotomy within which human action occurs. Rather, it depicts a world of social actors within changing temporal and situational contexts where degrees and types of agency (from Milo's successful but merely instrumental actions to Yossarian's frustrated actions but fully realized capacity to imagine alternatives to his given condition) are realized through location in multiple specific organizations and through the tactical utilization of internal organizational fractures. The important questions for Heller, then, are not whether our actions subvert power or are contained by it, nor whether identity is fractured or coherent. Heller is interested not in constructing a model of identity formation, but rather in asking how different institutional contexts support or preclude particular "agentic orientations" and, most important, how the interest networks of tightly bound elites can be maximally disaggregated.[87]

Referential Distortions.

As Milo's sterile self-promotion demonstrates, the contingently achieved but nevertheless durable consolidation and alignment by elites of various organizations minimize our capacity to imagine alternatives to given social realities. The parallel at the level of language is lexical consolidation. Two facts about organizations are key here: their capacity to achieve monopolistic control over language and communication patterns is extensive; their tendency to do so is inherent. In a context where violence is the default means and discursive competition is absent, the resulting communicative strictures can have catastrophic effects. The limit case for the damage that organizationally programmed language can effect upon the public sphere is revealed in Hannah Arendt's *Eichmann in Jerusalem*. I will return to Faulkner and Heller after this clarifying example. The bureaucratic mass-murderer Eichmann, Arendt notes, was an incessant talker.[88] In thirty-five days of interviews with the police he produced 3,564 typewritten pages from seventy-six recorder tapes of talk: "he was in an ebullient mood, full of enthusiasm about this unique opportunity 'to pour forth everything . . . I know.'"[89] However, as the Israeli judges quickly accused, Eichmann's testimony was all "empty talk." "Officialese," he said in performative self-deprecation, "is my only language."[90] Arendt is more expansive:

> Eichmann, despite his rather bad memory, repeated word for word the same stock phrases and self-invented clichés (when he did succeed in constructing a sentence of his own, he repeated it until it became a cliché) each time he referred to an incident or event of importance to him. Whether writing his memoirs in Argentina or in Jerusalem, whether speaking to the police examiner or the court, what he said was always the same, expressed in the same words. The longer one listened to him, the more obvious it became that his inability to speak was closely connected with an inability to *think,* namely, to think from the standpoint of somebody else. No communication was possible with him, not because he lied but because he was surrounded by the most reliable of all safeguards against the words and the presence of others, and hence against reality as such.[91]

The cliché, in other words, is a way of *not* talking; it is a way of avoiding the mutual cognitive vulnerability of intersubjective deliberation.[92] The cliché (and here I use "cliché" to signify a range of prescripted or rigidified discursive forms) manipulates reality to fit a predetermined form rather than manipulating form to approximate reality. The cliché is a textual snare that immobilizes thought; it is a linguistic device that forces the programmatic reproduction of specific and limited interpretive patterns, formatting the new and strange according to familiar achromatic paradigms and rendering impossible both precise representation and supple dialogue. As Martha Gellhorn reveals in her depiction of her experiences in Nazi-occupied Czechoslovakia, the memorization of scripts enables members of coercive bureaucracies to interact with the objects of their coercion without becoming pregnable to the normative ethical force of unconstrained conversation (a force I will discuss more fully in the next chapter).[93] The logic of the cliché is reproduced most nakedly in Eichmann's continual unwillingness to see—his resistance to visiting the killing installations and, when forced to, his refusal to watch.[94] Fascism reproduced upon the body politic as a whole a similar crippling of discernment, exchange, and comprehension. Slogans and catchphrases displaced searching expression, and an elaborate system of "language rules" systematically enforced the widest of possible slippages between signifiers and signifieds, thereby rendering official public lan-

guage as empty of referential content as lies. "Extermination," "liqui-
dation," and "killing" were, in paradigmatic instances of what
Arendt later chillingly called "defactualization,"[95] officially rede-
scribed as "evacuation," "change of residence," and "resettlement."
"For whatever other reasons the language rules may have been de-
vised," Arendt writes, "they proved of enormous help in the maintenance of order and sanity in the various widely diversified services
whose cooperation was essential in this matter."[96]

Eichmann is structured by the grotesque euphemisms provided for
him: the referential distortions he embraces like the rules of a game alter his affective relationship to what he knows. The protagonists of
Faulkner and Heller are violated by the lies told them. However
quickly successive experiences of being deceived may follow upon
each other during war, an epistemologically structuring expectation
of sincerity allows us to experience each one as a breach.[97] And yet,
while deception in war may thus remain subjectively exterior, exceptional, or actlike, it nonetheless assumes in us, as Faulkner reveals, interior, structuring and rulelike features.

A Fable is a catalog of lies. Indeed, the whole of the novel's plot is
oriented around the final unmasking of one collective, monument-
alized, agentless deception. The story of the unknown soldier's identity was the originating idea of A Fable and remained throughout its
development the primary narrative engine. Through his lack of a separate, discrete identity, the unknown soldier signifies the imagined
universalizability within the nation of selfless devotion to the indefea-
sible cause. But here, in fact, the corpse of the unknown soldier is the
corpse of the chief mutineer, the Christ figure who has revealed the
war's illegitimacy and who dies because he will *not* consent.

Faulkner presents two categories of lies in the novel: internal lies, or
lies of strategy, and external lies, or lies of legitimation and condition.
As Elaine Scarry has demonstrated, war making is inextricable from
lying. A key feature of its most basic operations is deceit and the confusion of reference. Codes, for instance, "are attempts to make meaning irrecoverable," and in camouflage "the principle of lying is carried
forward into the materialized self-expression of clothing, shelter, and
other structures." "Strategy," she concludes, "does not simply entail
lies but is essentially and centrally a verbal act of lying."[98] In war lying
governs external relations with the enemy; lying is also necessary to
produce and maintain the symbols of cultural exchange that are con-

stitutive of a community. Wars are a legitimation crisis. To justify excruciating sacrifice, nations or national claims whose legitimacy have been brought into serious question must rely upon a counterfactual image of robust legitimacy; in other words, legitimacy is required to make a nation sacrifice, but at the same time this sacrifice is being called for in order to create the required legitimacy. Emblematic for Faulkner is the elaborate conspiracy that transforms a French general from a symbol of the mutiny into a symbol of heroic sacrifice: he is executed in secret—"by a kraut bullet"—so that he can be offered up in a narration of unfaltering and just belief. Internal unity is maintained through false symbols of internal unity; consent is revealed as manufactured through a structure of lies. When the commander of the troops that have mutinied argues that they must all be executed, he claims extravagantly that it is the primary duty of the war leaders to preserve the rules they have created. "We shall enforce them, or we shall die" (45). But his own commander corrects him, explaining that it is not the maintenance of a particular system of order which is their primary duty: it is instead the maintenance of a particular illusion, the constitutive illusion of war's crushing necessity.[99]

> We can permit even our own rank and file to let us down on occasion; that's one of the prerequisites of their doom and fate as rank and file forever. They may even stop the wars, as they have done before and will again; ours merely to guard them from the knowledge that it was actually they who accomplished that act. Let the whole vast moil and seethe of man confederate in stopping wars if they wish, so long as we can prevent them learning that they have done so. (45)

Violence is made possible by denying the articulation of, and thereby negating, the agency of social actors.[100] Deception in *A Fable* is thus not merely a strategy of war, it is the necessary enabling condition. It is a rule in the deep sense: not a guideline for action in a preexisting game, but that structuring element which brings the game into being, which, like gravity to a human body, determines the structure of its organs and the possibilities of its environmental field. Acts of war do not generate lies, by this argument: lies generate acts of war.

A Fable looks at social practices built with lying; *Catch-22* analyzes the interior structure of the lie. Lies and propaganda can be characterized by two complementary rulelike qualities: first, the signifier is made identical to or displaces the signified (in other words, names are too easily attached to their objects); second, the signifier is readily detachable from its signified by competing signifiers (in other words, names are too easily removed from their objects). *Catch-22* presents a language system in which the dictates of authority rather than referentiality determine manner of representation.[101] History as the "official report" (424, 433) determines organizational action, but does so in the absence of evidentiary rules. Things are so because they are claimed to be so, and the material world does not effectively push back. One case is representative. When Doc Daneeka's name appears on the flight roster of a plane that has crashed, he is officially determined to be dead despite his heated protests (335). In Heller's violent organizations, moments of description are transformed into performative speech acts. Here, as elsewhere in the novel, the military bureaucracy is capable of divesting individuals of personhood through simple acts of declaration. In such a system, where language provides no resistance, where it is fully manipulable by organizational hierarchy, persons have no protection from arbitrary force. Writing in 1940 after the fall France, Simone Weil defined force as "that x that turns anybody who is subjected to it into a thing."[102] This is, in fact, the "ideal" (in Clausewitz's sense) form of force, which is achieved only when language is stripped of its countercoercive potential, its stubborn referentiality. The maximization of force, as tyrants have always understood, depends upon an uniform "thinness" of definitional structures. The thinnest of all definitions, as *Catch-22* reveals, is the tautological: a traitor or spy is he who is called a traitor or spy. Intersubjectively elaborate or "thick" definitions defy the sovereignty of force because of the particular way they establish the identity of signifier and signified: such definitions have multiple elements that require multiperspectival empirical confirmation before the signifier can attach itself. Therefore, once it passes the threshold for attachment, it is simultaneously both difficult to detach (each act of assembling counterevidence multiplies opportunities for argument, resistance, and delay) and theoretically always potentially detachable (the signifier, because provisionally fastened, is reformable).

The positive strategic value of this formulation will become clear in the next chapter, where the role of intersubjective deliberation in producing moral norms is examined. For now it is only important to detail Heller's negative conception. In his send-up of the workings of military language even personal names are easily detachable: identity is so "thin" in this system that mere physical coincidence with an organization's official marker (sitting in another man's hospital bed behind his medical charts, 181, 285–286) is enough to effect a transformation, and form letters of condolences ("Dear Mrs., Mr., Miss, or Mr. and Mrs.: Words cannot express the deep personal grief I experienced when your husband, son, father or brother was killed, wounded or reported missing in action," 275) are considered a sufficient address to personal loss. Language is so emptied of enduring referential content that the vow, a speech act important precisely because it retains a clear, singular, and durable meaning over time, is reduced to a temporally finite physical act: Captain Black's plan to force soldiers to sign and pledge loyalty oaths unceasingly throughout the day (because only this can in fact guarantee continuity of allegiance) is aptly entitled the Continual Reaffirmation program (113). The broken vow or lie becomes the default or background in a merely instrumental language system. But of course it is Catch-22 itself, the law justifying arbitrary assertions of military authority, which is most fully and tragically representative. At the heart of the law Catch-22 is the evacuation of empirical content from the word "insanity": Catch-22 will ground an insane pilot who requests to be grounded, but any pilot who requests to be grounded must be, by virtue of his reasonable request, sane. The organization's words of explanation need follow no laws of coherence because its definitions are self-consuming. Indeed, what Catch-22 points to is the final disappearance of language. When military authorities forcibly evict a group of young women from their only home, they cite Catch-22 as their justifying authority:

> "Didn't they show it to you?" Yossarian demanded, stamping about in anger and distress. "Didn't you even make them read it?" "They don't have to show us Catch-22," the old woman answered. "The law says they don't have to." "What law says they don't have to?" "Catch-22." (398)

> Yossarian . . . strode out of the apartment, cursing Catch-22 vehemently as he descended the stairs, even though he knew there was no such thing. Catch-22 did not exist, he was positive of that, but it made no difference. What did matter was that everyone thought it existed, and that was much worse, for there was no object or text to ridicule or refute, to accuse, criticize, attack, amend, hate, revile, spit at, rip to shreds, trample upon or burn up. (400)

The witnessing of organizationally generated deconstructions of language and communication is a primary cause for postwar skepticism toward language; a second equally important cause, as *Catch-22* shows, is related not to language's moments of breakdown but rather to its moments of intentional material accomplishment. Organizations are the place where norms are created and where they acquire their legitimacy. Organizations need not use force to achieve these ends; nevertheless, their declarations acquire a forcelike quality. Organizational language is composed of mystified performatives: in other words, the organization's language itself is treated as endowed with force rather than the institutional field within which it is deployed; consequently, the effects of its speech acts are deemed to reveal something about the nature of language rather than about organizational goals and structures. The end result in time of war, when material accomplishment tends to the production of violence, is an undifferentiated sense of language's inherent violence and an ambient desire for alternatives.

In the post–World War II era, two possibilities have been recognized. The first is an antiorganizational response suspicious of the performative in language. The war-related glorification of silence and incoherence from Bataille to Heller is a part of this tradition. The second, opposite response depends upon the organization for an *amplification* of performativity. Arendt's analysis of Eichmann is useful here as well: it is her thesis that the impoverishment of referential language contributed to the execution of atrocities only as effectively as the stabilization of language, through accurate reporting and witnessing, would have prevented it. Arendt insists that we can achieve binding interpretative consensus through evidentiary rules of objective accuracy and through suasive appeals designed to revivify submerged moral norms. Nazi hegemony depended upon a fragile combination: for perpetrators, upon the painstaking disabling of language's capacity to refer effectively; and for victims, upon the assumed *incapacity* of linguistically constructed norms to refer. Arendt illustrates the latter with the testimony of a German clergyman (Propst Grüber) who had frequently encountered Eichmann:

> Dr. Servatius . . . asked the witness a highly pertinent question: "Did you try to influence him? Did you, as a clergyman, try to appeal to his feelings, preach to him, and tell him that his conduct was contrary to moral-

ity?" Of course, the very courageous Propst had done nothing of the sort, and his answers now were highly embarrassing. He said that "deeds are more effective than words," and that "words would have been useless"; he spoke in clichés that had nothing to do with the reality of the situation, where "mere words" would have been deeds, and where it had perhaps been the duty of a clergyman to test the "uselessness of words."[103]

I will elaborate what is at stake in Arendt's critique of Propst Grüber more fully in the next chapter by inverting our standing premises. How can organizationally imbricated language function to stabilize referentiality and maximize dialogue? How can it function to minimize violence, and what principles should we abstract from this? Visions of escaping from bureaucratized action are utopian. What is important to understand is how we can create *networks* of differently motivated organizations to regulate action according to our reasoned moral judgments. Equally important is to understand how language recreates itself within its inevitable organizational structures, and how much control social actors can exert over this. The answers to these questions bring us to contemporary theories of the deep structure of language and to the promise of international law, with which this book began. Each of these discourses is best understood, as we shall see, as originating with the question raised by Hemingway at the beginning of Chapter 4 about the power of language to name.

CHAPTER SIX

Total War, Anomie, and Human Rights Law

Naming is violence. Among poststructuralist theorists this is an essential and commonly invoked critical maxim. The act of naming is a matter of forcibly imposing a sign upon a person or object with which it has only the most arbitrary of relationships. Names produce an Other, establish hierarchies, enable surveillance, and institute violent binaries: naming is a strategy that one deploys in power relations. The violence cuts through at all levels, from the practically political ("They are savages," "You are queer") to the ontological (one critic writes of "the irreducibility of violence in any mark").[1] Discussing the naming practices of Nambikwara children in *Of Grammatology,* Jacques Derrida identifies naming as an act of "originary violence" that is productive of both the disciplinary violence of the law and the cognate violence of its infractions: "war, indiscretion, rape."[2] Naming is authority's attempt to categorize and control difference.[3] For Derrida as for others, this is at the core of poststructuralist logic.

Contrast this cluster of antifoundationalist arguments (let us call it "theory" for simplicity's sake) to the International Covenant on Civil and Political Rights (ICCPR). Article 16 of the ICCPR reads: "Everyone shall have the right to recognition everywhere as a person before the law."[4] Subsequent articles detail some of the freedoms contingent upon this recognition of personhood, including freedom of thought, conscience, and religion. Shortly thereafter, Article 24 establishes the fundamental duties required of each state to promote the dignity and worth of the children within its territory. What steps must states take to ensure the recognition of the personhood of their children? Section 2 of Article 24 reads: "Every child shall be registered immediately after birth and *shall have a name.*"[5] To be named is to suffer violence; to be named is the foundation of human dignity.[6] This juxtaposition calls attention to one of the most pressing ethical questions asked today of literary and language theory.

I should begin with a word about my own attempts to categorize and control through naming. In this chapter I use "theory" as a term both broad and narrow in its application. It denotes a particular stance toward referentiality that manifests itself variously throughout the antifoundationalist practices (deconstruction, neopragmatism, constructivism, postmodernism) generated by late 1960s poststructuralism. Of course, to define theory in such a way, that is, inclusively by virtue of particular dominant features, is on one level already to position oneself against it: this characterization, which glosses over radical differences between thinkers, has historically signified an intention to discredit the whole. Remaining aware of this potential conceptual injustice I nonetheless want to begin by using the word "theory" in this special sense, although as the chapter progresses I will complicate the definition by considering its potential interpenetration with the discourse of rights to which I have opposed it. For now, however, I want to treat "theory" and "rights discourse" as basic terms signifying fundamentally divergent accounts of the nature of language and its relationship to social practice.[7]

"Rights discourse" refers to a set of claims (outside the positivist tradition) that hypothesizes the existence of universal, morally binding rights that inhere in the individual by virtue of a natural, rational, or pragmatic necessity. The philosophical grounding of rights can take many forms: the most influential include neo-Kantian social contract theory, which locates the source of moral obligation in individual autonomy; variants of Habermasian ethics,[8] which ground our reciprocal obligations in the enabling principles of intersubjective discourse; and the "capabilities" approach developed more recently by Amartya Sen and Martha Nussbaum, which argues for a set of basic human capabilities from which cross-cultural obligations can be derived.[9] Theory, in a contrast of premises to such postmetaphysical universalism, advances a claim about the contingency of meaning that renders impossible both the endorsement and the construction of universalizing evaluative hypotheses. Because of this aggressive anti-foundationalism/contextualism, theory has found itself placed by critics in opposition to a variety of cultural movements and academic disciplines,[10] but most important for our purposes is its presumed opposition to the human rights community. Tzvetan Todorov writes: "I am simply saying that it is not possible, without inconsistency, to defend human rights with one hand and deconstruct the idea of humanity with the other."[11] Terry Eagleton, more impatiently, caricatures deconstruction by ventriloquizing it thus: "I am not *for* socialism; but I am not *against* it either. Neither am I *neither* for nor against it, nor simply for or against the whole opposition of 'for' and 'against.'"[12] The essential charge for both is that theory functions as an apology for political quietism.[13] At the very least, rights-oriented thinkers argue, theory can be condemned for the rhetorical larceny of claiming the language of political terror. Its arguments and lexicon thin out notions of violence to such a degree that the term loses all of its normative force. If, as two literary critics characterize the position, "writing is not so much about violence as a form of violence in its own right," then violence is something with which we can and indeed must live.[14]

That theory is difficult to reconcile with a vigorous defense of human rights may not be an unbeatable argument, but it is currently the argument to beat. In this chapter I will evaluate the case made against theory by analyzing the role of language in social action. In the next section I will more fully characterize the theory-rights conflict and will briefly rehearse the political and hermeneutic claims of theory by looking at the writings of Maurice Blanchot and Paul de Man. I choose these thinkers not because they are generally representative but because they are exemplary of the features of theory I want to emphasize. In the third and fourth sections I will turn to the work of human rights law: I will examine the norm-building function of argument and analyze in detail the specific linguistic strategies that underpin rights work. At the conclusion of the chapter, in the second half of the fourth section, I will return to the questions and claims of theory and will test them against the rights-oriented model of political and linguistic action developed herein. Does the collision between theory and rights lead to the diminution of one or to the mutual alteration of both of their claims? In answering this question I will focus upon the international laws of war and in particular the Geneva Conventions, both because war and internal armed combat are the sites of our most pressing human rights concerns and because the international laws of war, as we shall see, call into question most dramatically the relationship between theories of language and the initiation of violence.[15]

Theory and Rights

The presumed theory-rights conflict manifests itself most dramatically in what might be called the cultural relativism debate. When the Commission on Human Rights created under the United Nations Charter in 1947 began considering proposals for a declaration on basic human rights, the executive board of the American Anthropological Association issued a thinly disguised preemptive critique of the expected document based upon the premise that *"standards and values are relative to the culture from which they derive."*[16] This cultural relativist critique of human rights initiatives can be delivered in at least three ways: first, that human rights disproportionately tend to be premised upon the values of Western liberalism, particularly upon mythologies of the social contract and the prioritization of the individual;[17] second, and more deeply, that the concept of rights itself is a Western invention that cannot be imposed upon other cultures without harming them, much like the Christianity of earlier centuries;[18] third, and deeper still, that right and wrong do not exist objectively but are rather the expression of particular cultural practices that consequently ought to be considered immune to external critique. Theory in its strong form is associated by critics with deep cultural relativism, and to that degree it is considered by many to be hostile to the promotion of human rights.[19]

Interrogatories skeptical of theory come in a variety of forms. Does theory undermine for resistance movements the possibility of political and rhetorical unity in the face of tyranny?[20] How can theory deconstruct totalizing systems of thought without also rendering impossible any notion of the "truth" of history—a notion useful for the condemnation of atrocity?[21] Does theory subvert the universalizing idea of human rights without offering any effective alternatives for promoting certain widely shared conceptions of human dignity?[22] Questions of this sort have been taken very seriously by literary and cultural critics and have received a variety of answers in a variety of contexts. Stanley Fish, for instance, has argued from the perspective of legal pragmatism for the nonexistence of a conflict: antifoundationalism's observation "that practice is not after all undergirded by an overarching set of immutable principles, or by an infallible and impersonal method, or by a neutral observation language" has no significant practical applications, and certainly none that interfere with the pursuit of rights.[23] For Gayatri Spivak and Diana Fuss, however, the local pressures of perceived theory-rights conflicts necessitate an exploration of the possibilities and limits of a strategic essentialism;[24] Chantal Mouffe, alternatively, embraces *anti*essentialism as "the necessary condition" for a radical democratic politics and rejects "appeals to universality, impartiality and individual rights" as now irrelevant and possibly even harmful to the furthering of emancipation.[25] Barbara Herrnstein Smith, insisting that the charge of quietism illuminates not theory's inability to support moral action but rather the foundationalist's inability to see theory *from the inside,* argues that relativism can coherently structure both action and the exchange and judgment of reasons;[26] Drucilla Cornell has conceptualized deconstruction as a utopian project oriented toward a justice that remains forever "beyond";[27] and Derrida in his later work writes that "deconstruction is justice."[28] Indeed, it is asserted by many that a practical relevance to politics and to questions of ethical value is one of poststructuralism's foundational premises. Before moving into my discussion of the laws of war, I want to analyze briefly the viability of this thesis.

Contemporary theory, no doubt, is in large part rooted in an ethically engaged response to the atrocities of Fascism and the Holocaust. The experience of World War II generated a sense of bewildered disillusionment with previously unquestioned cultural assumptions now revealed to be constructed artifacts (here bearing the traces of "artifice," "artificial," and "artful");[29] concomitantly, it generated among intellectuals a pandemic suspicion of the impulse to elevate any subsequent system of discursive "artifice" to the "true," "reliable," or "right." In the later work of Maurice Blanchot, a writer and critic whose prewar involvement with the anti-Semitic, nationalist right in France has been the source of extended debate,[30] the Holocaust is figured as the "*absolute* event of history," the moment when humanity was bound in cords of silence, when books were burned and "meaning was swallowed up."[31] Henceforth, he writes, "any text . . . is empty—at bottom it doesn't exist" (10/23). Blanchot argues that humans are not the structurers of language but are themselves structured by it. Because language is internally different—that is, since there is a fundamental and arbitrary disjuncture between our sign system and the world it describes—we can rely upon no ontological certainties. After all, every foundation is itself linguistically constructed. Even "existence," which we typically think of as preceding language in some fashion, is itself a linguistically constructed concept that needs to be questioned.[32] The fundamental questions we can ask of the universe are thus epistemological rather than ontological: in other words, the important question is not "What do we know?" but rather "How do we know?"

Blanchot's point, however, is not *merely* philosophical. As John Treat writes, "When someone argues that a literature of atrocity is a priori impossible because words do not, will not, suffice, that person is also insisting that he steadfastly refuses to cooperate with any such attempt and means for that stubborn insistence to suffice as its own message."[33] For Blanchot, the logic of the Holocaust is a vicious double bind: it shatters society's frail, communally constructed meanings by shattering language and, moreover, makes impossible any efforts at redemption through language by revealing that it was the very systems of meaning destroyed by the Holocaust that enabled and fostered its crimes.[34] "Writing is per se already (it is still) violence" (46/78). "Speaking," he explains, "propagates, disseminates [errors] by fostering belief in some truth" (10/22). Even the smaller claims of language—its promise temporarily to alleviate hurt, to relieve loneliness and confusion—are for Blanchot radically suspect. Writing about the disaster is necessarily a lie: it gives limits to the limitless, sense to the senseless. Writing presents the "danger that the disaster acquire meaning instead of body" (41/71). He writes, "But the danger (here) of words in their rhetorical insignificance is perhaps that they claim to evoke the annihilation where all sinks always, without hearing the 'be silent' addressed to those who have known only partially, or from a distance the interruption of history" (84/134).[35]

Meaningful language is suspect because it contributes to the establishment and consolidation of regimes of power, but also because it attempts to present as "real" an experience inaccessible to reality, insofar as reality consists of what we can understand through our socially preprogrammed conceptual categories. How then are we to communicate in the shadow of the Holocaust? The only response available to humanity is linguistic guerrilla warfare: as one critic puts it, "to speak a language that power doesn't know."[36] Blanchot's an-

swer is thus an escape into history's wreckage of syntax, into its dilap-
idated heaps of verbiage and belief systems. He calls foremost for passivity and lassitude, which is "the desire for words separated from
each other—with their power, which is meaning, broken, and their
composition too, which is syntax or the system's continuity . . . [Lassi-
tude] is intensity without mastery, without sovereignty, the obsessive-
ness of the utterly passive"(8/11, 18/23). Blanchot's text is a collection
of fragments, of words fallen together, as poignant as cries of pain.
Like cries of pain, the text is both meaning-saturated and meaning-
resistant, both urgent and indecipherable. It is language made into
a puzzle, gesturing toward sense but never enclosing it, assaulting
meaning (and thereby power) through paradox and a splintering of
grammar. It is a text that resists the reader, that refuses to open itself. Its most simple anthem, offered up with the vulnerability of
prayer, contradicts its own enunciation: "May words cease to be
arms; means of action, means of salvation. Let us count, rather, on
disarray" (11/25).[37]

Paul de Man, like Blanchot writing under the sign of the Holocaust,[38] argues for the inevitability of rhetoric's destabilization of
meaning and function. He tracks relentlessly the proclivity of language toward metaphor and catachresis—that is, toward unrestricted
proliferation, monstrous combination, and the grotesque mixing of
modes. Stable meaning, he asserts, is continually subverted by the uncontrollable allusiveness of the figurative language upon which it depends. Language, he writes, "reintroduces the elements of indeter-
mination it sets out to eliminate."[39] De Man's analysis of metaphor is
pockmarked by the ruptures of violence, by the traces of the war he
lived through. He lingers over examples that include abortion, man-
slaughter, and parricide (40–41), examples that culminate in describing the abstraction manufactured by language as "a monster on
which [one] then becomes totally dependent and does not have the
power to kill" (44). He speaks of "epistemological damage" (34),
of "policing the boundaries" (39) of words, of impressions being
"locked up" by understanding in a "potentially violent and authoritarian way" (44), of the "directly threatening" (46) aspect of our metaphorical construction, and finally of the "disfiguring power of
figuration" (49) that is set against "totalizing systems" (49) of meaning (meaning now permanently stained with the traces of the totalitarian). Playing on the double meaning of "passage" (the act of passing

and a section of text), de Man writes: "Motion is a passage and passage is a translation; translation, once again, means motion, piles motion upon motion" (38). Translation creates only "the fallacious illusion of definition," for the translation itself may be translated, and meaning is thus perpetual motion (38).[40]

For many literary and cultural critics following de Man the discovered motion and free play of language has functioned as a sometimes implicit, sometimes explicit normative value. Contingency is taken to represent a complex form of liberation; identification of a lack has become a celebration.[41] This is a core concern for those who experience the dissolution of meaning through the slippage of language as a threat. If Blanchot's antimanifesto is perceived as quietistically redefining the political prisoner's silence and structured social alienation as a sort of moral victory,[42] then certain rhetorics derived from de Man seem unintentionally to sanction power's victory over meaning by validating the communicative misfires and slippages that render so difficult the faltering human effort toward consensually shared rather than externally imposed values and order.[43] These are important concerns, both for the concept of norm and for critique. But what if we turned away from arguments thus bounded by a reactive framework? What would it mean instead to invert theory's premises, and to pursue its questions by turning them inside out? Is language violent because it names, or is violence released precisely when language fails to name effectively? As we shall see, force assiduously defends its right to be arbitrary against the concretized discursive structures that challenge and attempt to constrain it. Excessively pliable hermeneutics, therefore, might very well play into the cultural logic of violence. In the sections that follow I will investigate this possibility by looking at discursive strategies and language artifacts that, like photographic negatives of theory's dismantling of referentiality, depend upon and celebrate language's capacity effectively to refer and which demand of their readers a "less moveable" hermeneutic practice.[44]

The Laws of War

Theories of language that bear upon the fragility of meaning and the breakdown of intersubjective consensus are, at their extreme, intimately connected to theories of war. Elaine Scarry has called war a "crisis of substantiation," a conflict in which previously shared meanings have become so derealized and confused that they can no longer be resolved through argument and negotiation.[45] When language and the agreements dependent upon it are divested of force (such force being based upon the broad consensual agreement to *perceive* the language as a form of force), then violence becomes, often, the first resort in reachieving clarity and agreement. One primary response to the historical ascendance of force over discourse, as we have seen, has been to treat language as frail and suspicious. An alternative response has been to seek methods of employing language that make it more likely to resist derealization,[46] and also to reinscribe violence itself within the bounds of language, to make war (a state of transitionality or suspension of meaning—literally, meaninglessness) into a site of unalterable meanings, agreements, and definitions. It is to this realm of covenants and rights that I now turn.

Silent enim leges inter arma.[47] Cicero's maxim translates: "In time of war the law is silent." War impairs the human power to describe, define, or narrate. At the broadest level, war interrupts history. Is the Confederate soldier a patriot or a traitor? History as description can recommence only after the conflict, when war's "reality duel" or "contest to out-describe" has ceased, and the victor can promulgate the official version.[48] War interrupts intersubjective evaluation and, at the most personal level, interrupts self-narration.[49] What is the moral significance of reprisal executions of prisoners designed to prevent further executions of one's own captured soldiers? Or the bureaucratic decision to bomb a munitions factory in an area dense with civilians? And what moral code can guide *my* behavior? Am I "good" to kill a man ("brave," "heroic") and "bad" to show mercy ("cowardly," "treacherous")? Familiar moral codes cease to apply at the outbreak of hostilities. Many interpret this absence of a guide as a license to act without restraint. The impossibility of describing an event (good or bad, legal or illegal, heroic or treacherous) is the enabling condition of war's entropic cruelty. *Silent enim leges inter arma.*

Shortly after he assumed control of Atlanta, General William T. Sherman ordered the expulsion of all Southern families from the city. "War is cruelty," he declared in a public letter directed to Mayor James Calhoun and his two councilmen, "and you cannot refine it" (601). In a bitter response to Sherman's then unprecedented decision to make civilians into targets of the war, Confederate General J. B. Hood asserted, "the [mass expulsion] you propose transcends, in studied and ingenious cruelty, all acts ever before brought to my attention in the dark history of war" (593). The forced exodus, he argued, contradicted the customs of war and "the laws of God and man" (595). Sherman countered by characterizing all of war's brutalities as "inevitable": "You might as well appeal against the thunderstorm as against these terrible hardships of war" (601). "If we must be enemies," he writes, "let us be men, and fight it out as we propose to do, and not deal in such hypocritical appeals to God and humanity" (594–595).[50] Often cited as natural truths of war, Sherman's brutal aphorisms are better described as a statement of deliberate policy, as mystifications of agency designed to justify the *choice* to make the theater of war a site of maximal moral chaos and lawlessness. Earlier in the war, in a private letter to General Halleck, his superior at the time, Sherman found it necessary to argue strenuously in favor of amplifying and exaggerating the hardships of war. In place of the magisterial pronouncements of his Atlanta declaration we find here a series of conditionals and subjunctives: "In accepting war, it should be 'pure and simple' as applied to the belligerents. I would keep it so, till all traces of the war are effaced; till those who appealed to it are sick and tired of it, and come to the emblem of our nation, and sue for peace. I would not coax them, or even meet them half-way, but make them so sick of war that generations would pass away before they would again appeal to it" (365). Sherman was aware of the rhetorical subterfuge of his Atlanta declaration. He was also aware that the subterfuge was likely to work, that civilians would be poorly equipped to resist the superimposition of his particular narrative model—that is, his invasion is more like a "thunder-storm" than like a "crime."[51] Civilian vulnerability to the strategic narrative manipulations of warfare is due primarily to the essential epistemological confusion of war, but also to the paucity of publicly sanctioned, alternative narrative models available to the disempowered populace. The tyrannical violence of war in its emergency disrupts borders and epistemological categories; it also mutes the human creativity that enables us continually to reconceptualize our world in ways that make it amenable to our shaping.

As Hood's rejoinder to Sherman illustrates, one primary response to this narrative bewilderment, as old as war itself, has been the attempt to regulate conduct in war through preestablished customs and agreements—that is, to transform war into a self-narrating event by establishing inviolable categories of persons and actions that can stand as a guide to the incidents of war. Posed against war's chaos is the human will to order, manifest most dramatically in what are called the laws of war. In instances when such laws are publicly validated and accessible, resistance is possible. In the context of an inter-subjective consensus on normative discourse, the act of articulation becomes an experience in constraint. "Moral talk is coercive," as Michael Walzer argues.[52] It forces us to tell a very special story to justify our actions, a story that is vulnerable to all the rules of evidence and credibility. An invasion that is called just is not, to paraphrase Walzer, an invasion that simply enjoys approbation; it is an invasion that enjoys approbation for particular reasons, and anyone asserting its "justice" is required to provide particular sorts of evidence.[53] Moral talk constrains what we can say, even in the face of what might be our overwhelming and unrelenting power. One year before the sacking of Atlanta, Francis Lieber drew up for the Union army the first national manual outlining the laws of land warfare, issued as General Order 100 of the Adjutant General's Office. Article 22 reads, "the unarmed citizen is to be spared in person, property, and honor as much as the exigencies of war will admit."[54] Article 23 continues, "the inoffensive individual is as little disturbed in his private relations as the commander of the hostile troops can afford to grant."[55] The details of regulations throughout are accompanied by the language of moral responsibility: "As Martial Law is executed by military force, it is incumbent upon those who administer it to be strictly guided by the principles of justice, honor, and humanity—virtues adorning a soldier even more than other men, for the very reason that he possesses the power of his arms against the unarmed";[56] "Men who take up arms against one another in public war do not cease on this account to be moral beings, responsible to one another and to God."[57] Resistance for the citizens of Atlanta was thus possible. Overlapping vocabularies between North and South opened up a space for argument, a language event that much like violence can forcibly bring about outcomes in the world but that does so, unlike violence, without the use of injury.[58] Argument can function, moreover, to vivify normative values: one reinforces the legitimacy of particular moral obligations even if one enters into rational discourse only to assert, disingenuously, that one has not violated them. At the conclusion of Sherman's public epistolary debate with Hood (the letters were published in Macon newspapers), the Northerner was forced to acquiesce. He did so partially, tersely, and negatively—cruelty *could be* refined; he was not free to do anything—by acknowledging the potentially "binding" power of the laws of war in a denial that he had violated the requirements of the texts. "I was not bound by the laws of war to give notice of the shelling of Atlanta, a 'fortified town, with magazines, arsenals, founderies, and public stores;' you were bound to take notice. See the books" (602). With all the power of an absolute dictator, Sherman was forced to retreat, to abandon his previously abstract characterizations of war and respond to the precise, publicly accessible charges of his enemy.[59]

The international laws of war have a long history, dating back to the religious contracts of the Middle Ages and the birth in Europe of international law with writers like Giovanni da Legnano and Hugo Grotius. Their appearance as we know them, in the shape of binding multilateral agreements like the Geneva Conventions, is much more recent. In 1862 Henry Dunant published *Un Souvenir de Solferino,*[60] a harrowing account of his experiences attending to the thousands of French and Austrian troops wounded in the battle of Solferino. The book detailed the primitive, haphazard conditions of field medicine and exposed to the public the disastrous consequences of the Napoleonic Wars, which had brought to an end the customary practice of treating enemy wounded and medical personnel as neutral parties. Now they were simply easy targets: armies regularly shelled field hospitals and fired upon doctors and stretcher bearers.[61] Medical personnel thus often were forced to retreat at the approach of the enemy, leaving the wounded to lie where they fell, untended and helpless. Dunant's exposé, and the necessary reforms indicated therein,[62] had a prodigious influence in mid-nineteenth-century Europe. With Dunant's leadership it took less than two years to form an international committee for treatment of the wounded (the ICRC) and to convene an international diplomatic conference that quickly adopted the first of the Geneva Conventions. The 1864 Convention for the Amelioration of the Condition of the Wounded in Armies in the Field was an international watershed: it reestablished the neutrality of medical personnel, dictated that all wounded soldiers be collected and cared for equally, and introduced the custom of distinguishing medical personnel from combatants with the use of flags and armbands bearing a red cross on a white ground.[63]

Two humanitarian imperatives, corresponding to two legal traditions, have developed out of the original conventions. The law of
Geneva concerns the targets of attack, or whom one can legitimately
aim at: it dictates that a distinction be drawn between combatants
and persons "hors de combat" (civilians, wounded, and so on) and requires that every effort be made to spare the lives of the latter. The law
of the Hague concerns the method of attack: it prohibits, for instance,
the use of weapons that "uselessly aggravate" the suffering of the enemy or that "render their death inevitable."[64] Since 1864 these principles have been expanded and reaffirmed in a series of conventions
that have increased limitations on methods of attack and augmented
protections for noncombatants. By the mid-1950s, four major
Geneva Conventions had been passed (dealing with the wounded and
sick on land; the wounded, sick, and shipwrecked at sea; prisoners of
war; and protected civilians), and the law of the Hague had been expanded with bans on chemical and bacteriological weapons and a
convention for the protection of cultural property during wartime.

The originary principle of *jus in bello* laws of war is, as the ICRC
summarized it in 1965, that "the right of the parties to a conflict to
adopt means of injuring the enemy is not unlimited."[65] The radical,
counterintuitive nature of this formulation is underscored when juxtaposed to more familiar arguments of "realists" like Clausewitz,
who wrote in the early 1800s: "Attached to force are certain self-
imposed, imperceptible limitations hardly worth mentioning, known
as international law and custom, but they scarcely weaken it."[66] Importantly, it has been a widely shared philosophical premise of the
Geneva Conventions that the protections granted to soldiers and civilians are *rights* inhering in the individual rather than indulgences
granted out of the pity or benignity of states.[67] The law is not formulated to maximize a particular conception of social welfare but rather
to respect the obligations of justice. It is a matter not of pursuing the
good but rather of demanding the right. This is, for many, the premise
of all international human rights law, which posits itself (again, outside the positivist tradition) as a series of binding norms that transcend state interests rather than as a series of agreements derived from
the consent of the states involved.

Prior to World War II, international law had affirmed the notion
that we are, in R. B. J. Walker and Saul Mendlovitz's phrase, citizens
first and humans second—indeed, that our status as humans is in

some way contingent upon membership in a state.[68] "We are not people," an unnamed character from Martha Gellhorn's *Stricken Field* says flatly. "We are exiles."[69] The galvanization of the universal human rights movement after the atrocities of World War II led to a radical rethinking of the scope of international law and to a reimagination of the organizing principles of the world's people. The notion of the world as a collection of reified, absolutely independent states fiercely protective against encroachments upon their sovereignty began to be replaced by the idea of a society of societies, a community of mutually dependent states institutionally imbricated through a variety of international bodies (anticipated in the post–World War I League of Nations). This modern invention of transnationally binding human rights has generated two very different views of the potency and relevance of international law. Judge Antonio Cassese, the first president of the International Criminal Tribunal for the former Yugoslavia, writes that universal human rights (in conjunction with the doctrine of the self-determination of peoples) "have subverted the very foundations of the world community, by introducing changes, adjustments and realignments to many political and legal institutions." Like a "powerful corrosive," rights theory must over time dissolve the "pillars of traditional power."[70] Raymond Aron, however, characterizes the force of human rights law differently. International society, he argues, is "an anarchical order of power" where violence settles questions of what is right.[71] Treaties lacking enforcement mechanisms are irrelevant to global processes. Or, as Thomas Hobbes wrote: "Covenants without the Sword are but Words, and of no strength to secure a man at all."[72] It is precisely this radical disparity between viewpoints that makes international law so relevant to the considerations of literary theory. It is the limit case of the relationship between words and actions, between discursive structures and the dictates of physical violence.

In *The Bridge on the River Kwai* (1957), a classic representation of the treatment of prisoners of war and an unparalleled film study of the relationship between unrestrained force and unenforceable law, a captured British company is brought to a Japanese prison camp in the heart of an impenetrable forest. When the camp commander, Colonel Saito (Sessue Hayakawa), orders the British officers to perform manual labor alongside their men, the British commander, Nicholson (Alec Guinness), confidently informs him that such a directive is expressly forbidden by the Geneva Conventions. He hands to Colonel Saito his own well-worn copy of the conventions as evidence. Colonel Saito patiently reads it, rolls it up and strikes Nicholson in the face with it, throws it into the dirt, and orders his soldiers to shoot Nicholson and his fellow officers on the count of three. The line of blood which runs down the center of Nicholson's face physically doubles the bright red spine of his copy of the conventions. In this moment the man has become the document, but the document no longer represents the accumulated weight of national wills. It is, instead, disposable paper. "Do not speak to me of rules," Colonel Saito says with contempt. "This is war. This is not a game of cricket." In short, the laws of war are widely regarded as a laudable exercise at the same time that they are seen in practice as essentially futile and perhaps even pathetic. The effectiveness during wartime of any prewar convention is certainly open to question, for in war it is precisely this right to mandate law that is being struggled for through violence. While Sherman may have been philosophically and morally wrong to claim that one cannot refine the cruelty of war, he may have been for all practical purposes empirically right. The record of modern war's infamy is compelling argument. Yet the salience of revealed violations (torturing prisoners, executing the wounded, shelling civilian neighborhoods) combined with the moral unobtrusiveness of compliance (refraining from harming prisoners or the wounded, circumventing a civilian neighborhood) creates a distorted picture. Furthermore, the tortured lengths to which state governments go in order to argue that they are *not* in violation of the laws of war evidence the effective pressure of these laws, if only negatively.[73] In an early 1950s conflict between the Netherlands and Indonesia, for example, the Netherlands defended its refusal to apply the Prisoners of War Convention of 1949 to captured Indonesian infiltrators because, as it argued, *both* nations chose not to recognize the dispute as an armed conflict. The law stated that the convention should apply "even if the state of war is not recognized by one of [the parties]"—it did not say "one *or more*."[74] This revision was made shortly after the Indonesian conflict, as the language struggled to keep pace with the efforts to obfuscate it.[75] In the end, at the ICRC's insistence (an insistence entirely lacking in "realist" enforceability), the Dutch government retreated from its position and began to apply the convention to Indonesian prisoners. Why? Why would any nation struggling for its vital interests and in some cases

even survival inhibit itself at the request of a disinterested and unforti-
fied third party? The power of the laws of war is the power, small and
defiant, of speech in the face of overwhelming physical force. The
documents of international jurisprudence, and the extreme pressure
brought to bear upon them by the outbreak of war, thus reveal much
not only about the relationship between language and physical violence, but also about the interior structure of each.

The Geneva Conventions

The laws of war are derived from the notion that language, deployed
in a particular fashion, can be made equivalent to force—or, rather,
can so effectively inhibit the reflex toward violence that disputes can
be resolved, as Jürgen Habermas has put it, through the "unforced
force of the better argument."[76] As a reference point of communal
judgment, the Geneva Conventions achieve effectiveness in a variety
of ways: binding nations to certain behaviors by standing as a re-
minder of their consent to be bound thus, for instance,[77] or providing
interested parties with universally accepted standards and vocabularies for mounting critiques (critiques that implicitly threaten resistance
by and ostracism from the community of nations).[78] As isolated textual artifacts rather than as tools of institutionally imbricated communal interaction, however, the conventions rely upon far different
strategies of self-realization: namely, a structure of repetition and a
style of comprehensiveness and referential clarity.

A paradigmatic requirement of the Geneva Conventions is the directive that the text of the conventions be posted in prisoner-of-war
camps, "in the prisoners' own language, in places where all may read
them."[79] Such imperatives, a genre of command that might be called
the "communicative directives" of the Geneva Conventions, are
among the most common of its requirements. They are also the least
immediately intrusive and costly, and thus the least plausibly dis-
obeyed on economic grounds—contrast, for instance, the regulation
requiring medical inspections each month for each prisoner. In Article
41 the language seeks to assure only its own reproduction, to repeat
and multiply itself like tangling verbal weeds in the field of war—in
effect acknowledging its simple visibility as a primary source of its
own enforcement. During war language is censored, encrypted, and
euphemized; imperatives replace dialogue, and nations communicate

their intentions most dramatically through the use of injury rather than symbol; talks are broken off, individuals are reduced to silence by traumatic experience, and witnesses are exterminated. War's violence shrinks language and damages communication; this diminishment of discourse (arguments, pleas, justifications, appeals for sympathy) in turn enables further violence. The conventions thus prioritize the basic forms of language itself, defending the rights of prisoners to communicate, for instance, or insinuating themselves into the behavior of belligerents by requiring exercises in language (trials, warnings) to precede exercises in force (executions, bombings).[80] The conventions replace discourse-as-coercion—as threats, intimidation, or lies—with morally coercive discourse. They use language to interfere with force, to create gaps and pauses that break up the momentum and self-amplification of violence. Examples abound. One provision, important because it is so minutely prescriptive, requires that a belligerent publicly declare if a certain locality is nondefended, requires then that the perimeter of this territory be marked with agreed-upon signs, requires in turn that the opposing belligerent acknowledge receipt of this declaration, and requires finally that this same latter belligerent make a public declaration if it later ceases to interpret this locality as meeting the written stipulations for nondefended status.[81] In a sense what is most important about the Geneva Conventions is not their substance but rather their procedure: in other words, not their catalog of rights but rather their interior mechanisms for guaranteeing their own discursive proliferation. Their effects derive from their magnification of language and multiplication of opportunities for discourse. Thus, as important as any specific declaration they make about the rightness or wrongness of conduct during war is their exhortation that the text as a linguistic artifact be disseminated and repeated both in wartime and in peace.[82] For their repetition as a whole reproduces on a larger scale the microfunction of accumulating bits of language in any particular theater of action. Hence the article, repeated identically in each of the four conventions, which demands that contracting states "disseminate the text of the present Convention as widely as possible"—as if through unrelenting visibility the conventions finally could be internalized in belligerents, like a reflex; as if through the sheer weight of verbal repetition the conventions could achieve material force.[83]

Self-actualization proceeds not only through repetition and procedural deceleration but also through clarity, or rather clarity as visibility, as a form of pure intelligibility epitomized in the conventions' tendency toward producing discrete physical signs and distinctive emblems: a red cross on a white ground (for medical personnel), three orange circles placed on the same axis (for protected objects), an equilateral blue triangle on an orange ground (for civil defense).[84] These sign systems establish inviolable categories of persons, actions, and objects, thereby standing against the confusion and border-disruption of war. Moreover, they create a universally accessible, morally coercive language that works to counter war's disarticulations, silences, and translation barriers.

The Geneva Conventions are a collection of definitions, a dictionary of war with tirelessly detailed and comprehensive explanations of seemingly self-announcing states and objects. A "mercenary," for instance, is a belligerent who is recruited from an uninvolved party and is rewarded financially—the definition as written in the convention, however, extends to sixteen lines.[85] Other typical definitions include "shipwrecked" (eight lines), "religious personnel" (twelve lines), "medical units" (ten lines), "medical personnel" (sixteen lines), and "wounded" (eight lines).[86] The last, strangely, recalls the disruptive logic of *A Farewell to Arms,* listing pregnancy as a condition that constitutes "wounding."[87] In fact, though, through their plethora of definitions the conventions work directly *against* the object confusion of war that is emphasized in *A Farewell to Arms.* They place special emphasis, for example, upon establishing the principles that distinguish civilian objects (tools) from military objectives (weapons)— hence discriminating between a munitions depot and a food storage center, or even between a bridge used for offensive purposes and a bridge used for civilian purposes.[88]

At the center of the Geneva Conventions are these clear, comprehensive definitions—definitions that, importantly, *precede* moral injunctions.[89] The institutionalization of definitions is an attempt to maximize language's fixed continuity with the material world. The conventions, writes Frits Kalshoven, offer "protection [not] against the violence of war itself, but against the arbitrary power which one belligerent party acquires in the course of the war over persons belonging to the other party."[90] The conventions set themselves up against arbitrary or unprincipled power: in other words, against power unconstrained by the limits of definitions—hence their harsh treatment of "perfidy," "feigning," and especially spies, who, because they disrupt the clarity of signifiers upon which the law depends, are denied many of the protections granted to prisoners of war.[91] With their hundreds of pages of definitions and explanations—clarified, expanded, and repeated time and time again over the decades—the Geneva Conventions offer themselves as a sort of unmovable textual monument.

These points about rights language would be triumphantly clear if, in contrast, the language of war consisted only of grunts and staccato commands. But war broadly construed, as a cultural event that extends beyond the battle theater to include domestic practice, is decidedly full with rich and complex language, with indoctrination, elaboration, justification, and propaganda. It might be argued here that the conventions, in fact, borrow from the structure of propaganda (a discourse type essential to the theory of Blanchot). There are important distinctions between the two, however, that are related not only to the discursive procedures that produce them but also to the discursive procedures that they in turn produce. War language and rights language differ both in their treatment of certain widely recognized, minimal moral norms and in their treatment of three key features of communicative legitimacy: intersubjectivity, objectivity, and referentiality. The Geneva Conventions might thus best be viewed as producing a counterlanguage to war, distinct for three reasons: first, because it is directed toward establishing an overlapping vocabulary between belligerents rather than simply enforcing linguistic conformity within a community (intersubjectivity, or susceptibility to nonexclusionary argument); second, because it attempts to make transparent its structuring reasons and to correct for limited positional biases through the inclusive deliberation that precedes its entry into force (objectivity, or partial situational independence); and third, because it signifies consistently, clearly, and narrowly rather than freely as the dictates of the moment demand (referentiality, or interpretive constraint through the prioritization of preestablished external criteria).[92] The conventions are a porous discourse: they set boundaries to the play and "motion" of meaning but, at the same time, avoid consolidating an impermeable epistemic power. That is, they remain adaptive to context and susceptible to change both in their application (by creating a communicative structure within and between belligerent parties where alternative interpretations can be tested)[93] and in their development (by establishing a tradition of revisability that is based upon a consensus-oriented dialogue between nations)—but they do so within a practice of referential fixity.

The Geneva Conventions, like battle commanders attempting to control the uncertainty of the future with a painstaking matrix of controlled language in the present,[94] establish in expansive detail the meaning of combatant, attack, civilian, or prisoner, as if with this multitude of definitions they can render the chaos of war susceptible to the control of language. Unlike battle commanders, however, the conventions seek to control the development of war not by controlling a synchronic array of disconnected speech acts but by controlling the constitutive language system of the war makers. If we call the Germans "enemy," "criminal," or "animal," we enable ourselves to feel about and act toward them in a certain way; if we instead call them "combatant," "prisoner of war" or "civilian" (agent-neutral terms that could easily be used to describe us or our own families), we are forced by the pressure of our own lexicon to think about and act toward them in a drastically different fashion. Those like Sherman who would point to the emptiness of any concept of law in war argue that people in danger are naturally selfish, frightened, and murderous. War devolves into savagery because humans, stripped naked and freed from the constraints of civilization, are essentially vicious.[95] The culture of laws, in contrast, depends upon no strong theory of human "nature." The institutional discourse of rights, like any ideology, is a lived relation to the real; it provides a structure of intelligibility to experience that is increasingly naturalized as the persuasive force of representations accumulate. It is thus the premise of the Geneva Conventions, in a contrast to Sherman's "realism" which is not, importantly, idealistic, that war devolves into savagery not because savagery is the nature of humans but rather because war *confuses* us. In war we are strangers in a strange land, bereft of language and of the borders that regulate social meaning; we are removed from our familiar habitat of verbal space and put under the dominion of injury and violence, where, as Weil puts it, catastrophe appears as the "natural vocation" of the victim.[96] The routine human rights violations of war,[97] an attorney of international law might argue, are thus in many cases not so much inevitable viciousness as they are *mistakes*—mistakes born of the same epistemological disruption and reversals that allow soldiers to understand killing an enemy as "ending the war" and that allowed

American commanders successfully to conceptualize the bombing of civilian neighborhoods in Japan as "saving American lives."[98]

The laws of war are about avoiding conflation and making clear distinctions; they are about the moral imperative to discriminate and about the morality enabled by the act of discrimination.[99] In 1968 the General Assembly of the United Nations adopted Resolution 2444, which endorsed what it considered to be the three most fundamental, incontrovertible principles of the laws of war.[100] Two of the three concerned the "principle of distinction": namely, that combatants are required to discriminate between military objectives and civilians and are prohibited from targeting the latter.[101] This principle received its most recent restatement in Article 51 of the 1977 Geneva Protocol I:

> The civilian population as such, as well as individual civilians, shall not be the object of attack . . . Indiscriminate attacks are prohibited. Indiscriminate attacks are . . . those which employ a method or means of combat the effects of which cannot be limited as required by this Protocol; and consequently, in each such case, are of a nature to strike military objectives and civilians or civilian objects without distinction.[102]

Any attack is by nature indiscriminate if it disrupts the conceptual borders established in the law, either by treating "as a single military objective a number of clearly separated and distinct military objectives," or by causing excessive "incidental loss of civilian life, injury to civilians, damage to civilian objects, or a combination thereof."[103] This protocol restatement is actually a radical revision of the inherited principle of distinction. Earlier formulations centered on the concept of *aiming,* thus prohibiting the subjective intent directly to harm particular categories of noncombatants.[104] In other words, you were permitted to kill civilians as long as you could successfully argue that you had not consciously intended to make them a direct target of your assault. It had been the strategy of lawmakers since the inception of the ICRC and the Geneva Conventions to eschew the murkiness of such subjectivity, to resist slipping into an idiom of culturally specific appellations and subjective evaluations by instead constructing a language of universal categories and objective measurements.[105] The revision in Article 51 ingeniously overcame distinction's vexed problem of subjectivity by pointing to the "method and means of combat" rather than the intent of the combatant as the relevant evidence in determining the threshold of discrimination.[106] The attacking soldier as thinking human becomes irrelevant, or rather his thoughts are now deemed transparent, regarded as taking shape through the weapons that give his subjectivity content. This is a striking moment; it gives us the opportunity for a thought experiment: namely, to trace the logic of a literary theoretical critique of the law's language, and to evaluate its methods and results. In this almost imperceptible textual rupture, one might argue, the article mandating distinction proceeds by treating civilians and civilian objects *without* distinction: "military objectives and civilians or civilian objects"—and again, "or a combination thereof." Here the text seems vulnerable to hermeneutic practices instrumentally oriented toward the destabilization of referentiality. The easy substitutability and hierarchy-erasing nature of Article 51's "or" (a civilian or an object) reproduces its earlier "objective" elision of the combatant into the weapon. Thinning out the distinctions between humans and their objects, Article 51 describes the site of war by using categories so broad and inclusive (weapons of attack and objects of attack) as to be "indiscriminate."

This rhetorical slippage points to an associated set of larger category crises in human rights discourse. Replacing the particular with the general, the private with the common, and the subjective with the objective, international law (it can be argued) invokes the participation of selves devoid of personhood, and of cultural and linguistic thickness. It therefore creates an ethics based on achromatic duty rather than respect; it institutes an empty formalism that obliterates the space of difference, of the individual, the unique, and the context-dependent. Relatedly, international law's use of language and concepts abstract enough to be widely applicable and inclusive of widely divergent cultures and cultural formulations (a universalism of the lowest common denominator) works counter to its effort to reify moral borders through precise and impermeable classification and specification. Here, in Article 51, the law's "universality" bears the traces of the grotesque. The battleground is a junk heap of objects and weapons that deploy themselves, as in a scene from a Hemingway novel. And the individual will is displaced as arbiter of meaning by the consequences deemed inherent to the equipment there employed. The logic of war *against which* the conventions set themselves is this very tendency to devalue individual subjectivity, to make humans into collectible, countable, and disposable things. And yet here, unexpectedly, a strange confluence is revealed between the two. For a striking and suggestive moment, the conventions seem to operate not so much athwart as within the assumptions of war. The humanitarian treaties and organized butchery work together: war's instrumentalization/dehumanization and law's universalization/departicularization both serve to *objectify* (to make into an object, to make objective). Violence and its other, in a word commingled, achieve grotesque synthesis.

There is, indeed, a long history to international law's kinship with its infractions. The contemporary international laws of war spring in a large part from the early Christian Church's effort to codify a notion of "the just war." This essentially theological tradition of *jus ad bellum* laws, dating from the works of Saint Ambrose and Saint Augustine, establishes rigorous standards for determining when it is justifiable to enter into a war.[107] The *jus ad bellum* tradition is generally characterized as a matter of prohibiting certain forms of war—a humanitarian endeavor, by all accounts. Analyzed in the context of the church's earliest history, however, it must be seen that the tradition developed instead as a means of *permitting* and even *facilitating* certain types of warfare.[108] Early Christianity was strictly pacifist: believers, Origen wrote, were permitted to fight for the king only "by offering . . . prayers to God."[109] It was only after Constantine adopted Christianity and Theodosius I designated Catholic Christianity the state religion of the Roman empire, only after the formerly marginalized believers found themselves repositioned at the center of the state apparatus, that Christian thinkers adulterated their pacific beliefs—essentially in order to make themselves amenable to the needs of a militaristic empire.[110] The laws of war from their inception functioned as much to justify violence as to prohibit it. Centuries later, things are much the same. The United States, for instance, managed to quell much of the criticism and dissent against its war with Iraq by asserting through selective video evidence that its use of "smart" weapons complied fully with Geneva restrictions—indeed, complied to such an unprecedented extent that the war could be imagined as "clean" and almost casualty-less.[111] The conventions can be turned into a weapon for any military's propaganda arsenal.

More radical critiques argue, however, that it is not the strategic *misuse* of the laws of war but rather their essential nature that facilitates violence. Clausewitz argued that war executed without pity or hesitation achieved "absolute perfection." His aesthetics of war, produced with the painstaking moral neutrality of the pure observer, nonetheless encloses within itself a counterintuitive ethical argument: were all wars fought with the merciless speed of Bonaparte, he implies, they would be both shorter and scarcer.[112] Echoing Clausewitz, Sherman wrote: "If the people raise a howl against my barbarity and cruelty, I will answer that war is war, and not popularity-seeking . . . Indeed, the larger the cost now, the less will it be in the end; for the end must be attained somehow, regardless of loss of life and treasure, and is merely a question of time" (585, 367). Sherman denied the notion of civilian neutrality and treated the Confederacy instead as a "nation-in-arms." Using starvation as a weapon and taking the war to civilians, the logic goes, broke the will of the Confederacy and, by ending the war early, saved the lives of thousands of conscripted and confused young men. During the Vietnam War, American frustrations and anxieties over the notion of limitations in war manifested themselves in a plenitude of diverse cultural texts. Among the most widely disseminated was *Star Trek*'s "A Taste of Armageddon" television episode: here, explorers encounter a civilization that has circumscribed so radically the conduct of one particular war that, despite its inordinate casualties, it is no longer perceived as unbearable and so is never brought to a close. This popular allegory of the Geneva Conventions trenchantly contrasts honest, *human* barbarism with the measured and bloodless scientific detachment of those aliens who would quantify "appropriate" levels of carnage.[113] Frits Kalshoven, legal adviser on international affairs to the Netherlands Red Cross Society, acknowledges this concern: "Does . . . the very existence of the humanitarian law of armed conflicts perhaps contribute to perpetuating the phenomenon of war? Would war made 'unbearable beyond endurance' make mankind realize that the situation cannot go on unchanged and that war in all its manifestations, no matter how just its cause, must be effectively banned from the face of the earth?"[114] The rhetorical slippage in Article 51 over persons, tools, and weapons emblematizes war's continuing disruption of epistemological and linguistic borders, recalling the grotesque thematic of Hemingway's *Farewell to Arms* detailed in Chapter 2. The disturbing referential destabilization and category dissolution of wartime experience manifests itself not only in the particular shreds of language I have analyzed, but also in the larger purposes of the conventions themselves. Just as a doctor may become a butcher and a penis a gun, just as any tool may become a weapon, so may law become propaganda, and so may a treaty of peace become an instigator of war. The unpredictably multiple functioning of all artifacts, including these treaties, forces the question: are the conventions tools to minimize violence or weapons to justify it? Is there, finally, any way to tell the difference?

Many in the human rights community perceive theory as a threat.[115] But has not this theoretically generated analysis identifying the possible prolongation of atrocities through the laws of war shown otherwise? Could not a recognition of the radical heterogeneity of signification enable a deep-structure critique of certain unquestioned discourses that might actually be contributing to human rights violations? A compelling defense for a selectively deployed theory might be made along these lines. Although I believe the substantive argument and the textual distortions that generated it are unacceptable and unsound (both as method and as morals), a revised form of their interior logics need not be. Theory as social practice might be conceived minimally as a plea for humility, as an injunction to continually reexpose our assumptions to critical analysis, to question our terms and even to leave them perpetually open to the possibility of resignification. Theory, as thought experiment, is the pause between consideration and judgment. But is not such a procedurally supplemental theory then just a version of Ernest Gellner's "Enlightenment rationalism" in grandiose rhetorical disguise?[116]

A difference remains. As proponents of tolerance we may wish for the theoretical pause to be as long and rich as possible, but in the end a judgment must be made. Postmetaphysical universalists and poststructural contextualists alike, of course, accept this last point.[117] They disagree, however, in their *characterization* of this act of judgment. Universalists accept the embodied and embedded nature of human identity, but they also insist upon our capacity to distinguish, based upon inclusive procedures of argumentation, between the "social validity of norms" and "their hypothetical validity" from the shareable standpoint of "justice, fairness, impartiality";[118] they argue for a subject that is situated in rather than an extension of various local linguistic and social practices, and for the possibility of validity claims that extend to the category "human."[119] Antifoundationalists/contextualists, in contrast, assert that judgments across cultures or language games can have no moral or philosophical *legitimacy,* insofar as this connotes the possibility of universal reasons or evaluative standpoints capable of rising above the conditions of their own enunciation.[120] In the absence of a concept of normative justification, such judgments must instead be conceived of as questions of interest rather than of right: we must abandon the counterfactual regulative ideals of universal consensus and the rational harmonization of different ends through procedures of deliberation, and we must instead accept the purely immanent nature of critique[121] and, as Mouffe and Laclau argue, the ineradicable antagonism and violence that constitutes the realm of the political, along with the social bifurcations engendered in all identity formation.[122] Can we force "them" to be like "us," and is it worth it? The ambiguity of "force" here is deliberate—it incorporates the wide spectrum of persuasion, manipulation, and coercion.[123] This blending generates resistance from human rights activists, justifiably, for their project depends upon taking very seriously the distinctions among the three. A deeper criticism from rights thinkers like Seyla Benhabib, however, argues that the retreat to incommensurable local knowledges and to the exclusive position of immanent critique only reinscribes the question of evaluation: because language games of any scope and cultures extending over any domain, however bounded, are irreducibly heterogeneous, the social critic is never exempted from the task of "evaluative, ideal-typical reconstruction" and from the resolution of conflictual justificatory criteria.[124] Moreover, as Amy Gutmann and Dennis Thompson argue, the metalevel critique that no validity claims across belief systems are susceptible to comparative assessment of reasonableness is itself a claim that rests upon moral considerations with a built-in universal applicability and upon the presumption that the metalevel claim itself is more reasonable than those it rejects, judged by some shareable procedures or standards.[125]

Relatedly, it is asserted, the antifoundationalist theory of judgment is incompatible with almost *any* particular antifoundationalist's system of belief. Antifoundationalists do not merely experience belief; they endorse their beliefs. They do not merely discover their moral values; they choose them. In other words, antifoundationalists feel compelled to abhor atrocity not because they recognize it as incompatible with the values of their contingent cultural indoctrination (an indoctrination they can recognize but not rise above), but rather because they *believe* it to be wrong.[126] If antifoundationalists are comfortable with an incompatibility between their beliefs and their beliefs about their beliefs, which Simon Critchley has called "an impossible psychological *bi-cameralism,*" then human rights activists are not, if only because such ironic determinism is a "recipe for political cynicism" rather than for action and sacrifice.[127] Ernesto Laclau, responding to such concerns, has argued with lyrical force that the "historicist recasting of universalism" and the perception of the gratuitous rather than necessary character of Enlightenment values can in fact revivify our political commitment: the precious fragility of what we now recognize as contingent creations will make us "more ready to engage in their defence."[128] In other words, a theoretical commitment to value dispersion can promote the practical commitment to particular values that many assert it disallows. But just so, rights thinkers counter, a theoretical commitment to context-transcendent validity claims can promote the practical commitment to contextual ungovernability and meaning surplus that many assert it disallows. It is precisely the consensus-disrupting power of truth claims, writes Thomas McCarthy, "that opens us up to the alternative possibilities lodged in otherness and difference," and it is precisely the idealizing moment of unconditionality that generates its own critique. The commitment to universal intersubjectivity implicit in validity claims draws us together through irreducible heterogeneity and promises the hope of an alternative to "resolving differences through coercion."[129]

Is the naming function of language emancipatory or disciplinary? Is it recognitional or constrictive? Is it the clarion of rights or the instrument of domination? The bulk of this chapter has been devoted to identifying and justifying the urgent sense in the human rights community that collective goals of the highest priority, which revolve around the protection of the most vulnerable, depend upon a concerted and continuous effort to stabilize our most basic moral categories along with the language that constitutes them. Whether or not one finally accepts these moral categories as objectively valid or universal in scope, procedurally grounded in the workings of our autonomy as Kant argued or in the interactive structure of discourse as Habermas argues,[130] it is at the very least in our collective self-interest to treat them as if they were so.[131] As William James would have argued, it is the act of treating them as real that makes them real. Lacking the signatures of belief and reaffirmation, words do indeed require Hobbes's sword for actualization. But treated as real in the overlapping consensus of a nonexclusionary intersubjective discourse, they become real: real without coercion, and with the key feature of susceptibility to argument.

Requiem
(1935–1940)

> *No foreign sky protected me,*
> *no stranger's wing shielded my face.*
> *I stand as witness to the common lot,*
> *survivor of that time, that place.*
> —ANNA AKHMATOVA, 1961

Notes

Introduction

1. Throughout this book I will take war as an exemplary case of violence and will contrast it to existence under the rule of law during times of peace. Violence in war has unique features (scope, organization, technology) that distinguish it from other forms of violence, but just as important as their differences are their commonalities. Violence in war and violence in domestic affairs, particularly in private, unregulated spaces like the household, can be mutually illuminating. Judith Herman has argued that one of the most striking facts about trauma recovery is the overlap "between rape survivors and combat veterans, between battered women and political prisoners, between the survivors of vast concentration camps created by tyrants who rule nations and the survivors of small, hidden concentration camps created by tyrants who rule their homes." *Trauma and Recovery* (New York: Basic Books, 1992), p. 3.

2. For an analysis of war's effect upon language, see Elaine Scarry, *The Body in Pain: The Making and the Unmaking of the World* (New York: Oxford University Press, 1985), pp. 133–137.

3. Hannah Arendt, *On Revolution* (New York: Viking, 1963), p. 9. See also Hannah Arendt, *The Human Condition* (Chicago: University of Chicago Press, 1989), pp. 26–27. Arendt invokes the paradigm of a two-model theory of language in her effort to distinguish violence (coercion) from power (the human capacity to act in concert): she provides a synopsis of the tradition that implicitly understands social organization through a vision of language as violence (commands, threats) and counterpoises this to her own emancipatory view, which is premised on the idea that language is fundamentally an instrument of power (deliberation, consent). See, for instance, *On Violence* (New York: Harvest, 1970), pp. 37–41. More recently, Judith

Butler has relied upon a similar, generalized theoretical duality (language threatens the body, language sustains the body) as a starting point for her own nuanced disciplinary theory in *Excitable Speech* (New York: Routledge, 1997), pp. 5–6. Explicit distinctions made by various theorists concerning the force-discourse relationship have been lucidly reprised by Beatrice Hanssen in a talk that elegantly tracks this dichotomous structure in language theory: "The Violence of Language," Bunting Institute, Harvard University, 1998.

4. Simone Weil, *The Iliad, or, The Poem of Force* (Wallingford, Pa.: Pendle Hill, 1956), p. 25.

5. For the most comprehensive analysis available of the world-building power of language, see Scarry, *The Body in Pain,* pp. 1–59. See also *Confronting the Heart of Darkness: An International Symposium on Torture in Guatemala* (Washington, D.C.: Guatemala Human Rights Commission, 1992). G. Elliot Smith and T. H. Pear emphasized during World War I the importance of talking as both a cure and a form of personality restoration for victims of war trauma in *Shell Shock and Its Lessons* (Manchester: University of Manchester Press, 1917), p. 66. On conceptions of language as violence and language as healing, see James Dawes, "Narrating Disease: AIDS, Consent, and the Ethics of Representation," *Social Text,* 13, no. 2 (1995): 27–44.

6. Jürgen Habermas, *Moral Consciousness and Communicative Action,* trans. Christian Lenhardt and Shierry Weber Nicholsen (Cambridge, Mass.: MIT Press, 1990). See Thomas McCarthy, *The Critical Theory of Jürgen Habermas* (Cambridge, Mass.: MIT Press, 1994), pp. 272–333; and John B. Thompson, *Studies in the Theory of Ideology* (Cambridge: Polity Press, 1984), p. 71. See also Seyla Benhabib, "The Utopian Dimension in Communicative Ethics," *New German Critique,* 35 (1985): 83–96.

7. Norman Mailer, *The Armies of the Night* (New York: New American Library, 1968), pp. 262, 274.

8. Bao Ninh, *The Sorrow of War,* trans. Vo Bang Thanh, Phan Thanh Hao, Katerina Pierce, and Frank Palmos (London: Secker and Warburg, 1993), pp. 105, 135, 213–217.

9. Albert Speer, *Inside the Third Reich,* trans. Richard Winston and Clara Winston (New York: Macmillan, 1970), pp. 33, 364, 376, 408.

10. Albert J. Von Frank, *The Trials of Anthony Burns: Freedom and Slavery in Emerson's Boston* (Cambridge, Mass.: Harvard University Press, 1998), p. 260.

11. James M. McPherson, *What They Fought For, 1861–1865* (New York: Anchor Books, 1994), pp. 27–46. Thomas Gustafson analyzes pre–Civil War conceptions of the promises and perils unique to a government by words, built upon a written constitution and the *vox populi:* see *Representative Words: Politics, Literature, and the American Language, 1776–1865* (Cam-

bridge: Cambridge University Press, 1992), pp. 21, 38–40, 43, 49–50, 54–55, 57, 65, 285, 324.

12. Abraham Lincoln, "The Perpetuation of Our Political Institutions," in *The Collected Works of Abraham Lincoln,* ed. Roy P. Basler, vol. 1 (New Brunswick: Rutgers University Press, 1953), p. 112. See Mark E. Neely Jr., *The Last Best Hope of Earth: Abraham Lincoln and the Promise of America* (Cambridge, Mass.: Harvard University Press, 1995), p. 17.

13. Neely, *The Last Best Hope of Earth,* p. 109.

14. James M. McPherson, *Abraham Lincoln and the Second American Revolution* (New York: Oxford University Press, 1991), p. 109.

15. Senator Wilson, and the Resolutions of the Legislature of Massachusetts, 23 May to 13 June 1856, in *The Congressional Globe: Containing the Debates, Proceedings, Laws, Etc., of the First and Second Sessions, Thirty-Fourth Congress,* ed. John C. Rives (Washington, D.C.: Office of John C. Rives, 1856), pp. 1400, 1386.

16. The quotation comes from David Donald, *Charles Sumner and the Coming of the Civil War* (New York: Alfred A. Knopf, 1960), p. 287.

17. *The Congressional Globe,* 1856, pp. 1399–1403.

18. Donald, *Charles Sumner and the Coming of the Civil War,* pp. 303, 301.

19. *The Congressional Globe,* 1856, pp. 1414–1417.

20. *The Congressional Globe, Second Session of the Thirty-Sixth Congress,* ed. John C. Rives (Washington, D.C.: Congressional Globe Office, 1861), 31 January 1861, pp. 665, 663.

21. *The Congressional Globe,* 1861, p. 659. Relatedly, see James Brewer Stewart, "Joshua Giddings, Antislavery Violence, and Congressional Politics of Honor," in *Antislavery Violence: Sectional, Racial, and Cultural Conflict in Antebellum America,* eds. John McKivigan and Stanley Harrold (Knoxville: University of Tennessee Press, 1999), pp. 167–192.

22. Letter to James Lawson, Woodlands, 4 July 1861, in *The Real War Will Never Get in the Books: Selections from Writers during the Civil War,* ed. Louis P. Masur (New York: Oxford University Press, 1993), p. 218.

23. Quoted in Daniel Aaron, *The Unwritten War: American Writers and the Civil War* (New York: Alfred A. Knopf, 1973), p. 219. For more instances of authors explaining that the Civil War destroyed their desire and capacity to write, see pp. 44, 150, 152. See also George M. Fredrickson, *The Inner Civil War: Northern Intellectuals and the Crisis of the Union* (Urbana: University of Illinois Press, 1993), p. 173; Edmund Wilson, *Patriotic Gore* (New York: W. W. Norton, 1994), pp. 753–754; and Gerald F. Linderman, *Embattled Courage: The Experience of Combat in the American Civil War* (New York: Free Press, 1987), p. 269.

24. Mark Twain, *Mark Twain's Letters, 1853–1866,* ed. Edgar Branch, Michael Frank, and Kenneth Sanderson, vol. 1 (Berkeley: University of California Press, 1988), p. 239.

25. Walt Whitman, *Prose Works 1892, Specimen Days,* ed. Floyd Stovall, vol. 1 (New York: New York University Press, 1963), p. 24.

26. Walt Whitman, *Leaves of Grass* (New York: Vintage Books, 1992), pp. 419–420. I am thankful to Deborah Martinez for her enlightening discussions of this poem.

27. Ambrose Bierce, *The Complete Short Stories of Ambrose Bierce,* ed. Ernest Jerome Hopkins (Lincoln: University of Nebraska Press, 1984), p. 318.

28. Whitman, *Specimen Days,* p. 118.

29. Ibid., p. 116. Sherwood Anderson bitterly represented the "endless war talk" of Civil War veterans as "mysterious mutterings," "blustering, pretending," "chattering and shouting," "raving" and "lying": the talk of men like his father was empty of content, an impediment to communication. "No real sense of [the war]," he wrote, "has as yet crept into the pages of a printed book." *Windy McPherson's Son* (Chicago: University of Chicago Press, 1965), pp. 12–14, 23, 16.

30. Quoted in John Treat, *Writing Ground Zero: Japanese Literature and the Atomic Bomb* (Chicago: University of Chicago Press, 1995), pp. 40–41. See also p. 81.

31. Aaron, *The Unwritten War,* p. 256; Wilson, *Patriotic Gore,* p. 279; C. Vann Woodward, "Mary Chesnut in Search of Her Genre," *Yale Review,* 73, no. 2 (1984): 200. For an analysis of Southern women's war diaries, see Jane Schultz, "Mute Fury: Southern Women's Diaries of Sherman's March to the Sea," in *Arms and the Woman: War, Gender, and Literary Representation,* ed. Helen Cooper, Adrienne Munich, and Susan Squier (Chapel Hill: University of North Carolina Press, 1989), pp. 59–96.

32. Mary Chesnut, *Mary Chesnut's Civil War,* ed. C. Vann Woodward (New Haven: Yale University Press, 1981), pp. 715, 718, 761.

33. Ibid., pp. 416–418.

34. Ibid., p. xl.

35. William Kerrigan, "Death and Anxiety: The Coherence of Late Freud," *Raritan,* 16, no. 3 (1997): 67. See also Eric L. Santner, "History beyond the Pleasure Principle: Some Thoughts on the Representation of Trauma," in *Probing the Limits of Representation: Nazism and the "Final Solution,"* ed. Saul Friedlander (Cambridge, Mass.: Harvard University Press, 1992), p. 144.

36. Herman Melville, "Shiloh," in *Collected Poems of Herman Melville,* ed. Howard P. Vincent (Chicago: Packard and Company, 1947), p. 41.

37. Stanton Garner, *The Civil War World of Herman Melville* (Lawrence: University Press of Kansas, 1993), p. 441.

38. Edwin Haviland Miller, *Melville* (New York: George Braziller, 1975), pp. 312, 309. Even Timothy Sweet, whose compelling work is extremely sensitive to Melville's doubleness of vision, has characterized the function of pastoralism in "Shiloh" by referencing postwar works that "naturalize the events and especially the outcome of the war, evading the reality of histori-

cal forces in its legitimation of the ideology of the victor." *The Traces of War* (Baltimore: Johns Hopkins University Press, 1990), p. 190. After this quick reference to "Shiloh," however, Sweet goes on to discuss in elaborate and convincing detail instances of the deconstruction of pastoralism in other poems from *Battle-Pieces*. On the interplay of pastoralism and realism in "Shiloh," see Garner, *The Civil War World of Herman Melville,* pp. 141–142.

39. Helen Vendler, "Melville and the Lyric of History," *Southern Review,* 35, no. 3 (1999): 579–594, 588, 584. See also Rosanna Warren, "Dark Knowledge: Melville's Poems of the Civil War," *Raritan,* 19, no. 1 (1999): 100–121.
40. Melville, "The Armies of the Wilderness," in *Collected Poems of Herman Melville,* ed. Howard P. Vincent (Chicago: Packard and Company, 1947), p. 69.
41. Kerry C. Larson, *Whitman's Drama of Consensus* (Chicago: University of Chicago Press, 1988), p. 225.
42. Carl von Clausewitz, *On War,* trans. Michael Howard and Peter Paret (Princeton: Princeton University Press, 1976), p. 605.
43. Sidney Lanier, *The Centennial Edition: Tiger-Lilies and Southern Prose,* ed. Garland Greever, vol. 5 (Baltimore: Johns Hopkins University Press, 1945), p. 96.
44. For "My Maryland" see *The Columbia Book of Civil War Poetry,* ed. Richard Marius (New York: Columbia University Press, 1994). "A Cry to Arms" may be found in Henry Timrod, *The Poems of Henry Timrod* (Boston: Houghton, Mifflin, 1899), pp. 144–146.
45. *The Columbia Book of Civil War Poetry,* p. 53.
46. Sir Walter Scott, *Old Mortality* (New York: Penguin Books, 1975), p. 240.
47. Ibid., p. 242.
48. W. B. Gallie, *Philosophers of Peace and War: Kant, Clausewitz, Marx, Engels, and Tolstoy* (Cambridge: Cambridge University Press, 1978), p. 121.
49. Ibid., pp. 120–121.
50. Jürgen Habermas, *The Theory of Communicative Action,* trans. Thomas McCarthy, vol. 1 (Boston: Beacon Press, 1984), pp. 273–338. Habermas also gives attention to the ideological functioning of language: see *Moral Consciousness and Communicative Action,* p. 360.
51. For poststructuralists, writes Meili Steele, "the discursive is the oppressive so that linguistic structures are not enabling but ensnaring." *Theorizing Textual Subjects: Agency and Oppression* (Cambridge: Cambridge University Press, 1997), p. 30. See Pierre Bourdieu, *Language and Symbolic Power,* trans. Gino Raymond and Matthew Adamson (Cambridge, Mass.: Harvard University Press, 1991), pp. 23, 24, 105, 113, 116, 121, 122, 209–214. In an interview with Bourdieu, Terry Eagleton characterizes *Language and Symbolic Power* as emphasizing that "language is as much—or is per-

haps more—an instrument of power and action than of communication." Agreeing that he tends to depict practice through language as a "war," Bourdieu insists that "a struggle for domination" determines most human interaction. "The undistorted communication referred to by Habermas is always an exception." Pierre Bourdieu and Terry Eagleton, "Doxa and Common Life: An Interview," in *Mapping Ideology,* ed. Slavoj Žižek (New York: Verso, 1994), pp. 265–277, 265, 271. Bourdieu's extensive and nuanced arguments do, however, acknowledge the power of what he calls heretical discourse to subvert the original falsifications of language as enchantment (e.g., pp. 127–130). See the discussion of symbolic violence in Thompson, *Studies in the Theory of Ideology,* pp. 63–64, 67–71. On dominant languages, see also pp. 56–58. On the contrast between Foucault's view of communication and Habermas's, see Thomas McCarthy, *Ideals and Illusions: On Reconstruction and Deconstruction in Contemporary Critical Theory* (Cambridge, Mass.: MIT Press, 1991), p. 66.

52. Catherine A. MacKinnon, *Only Words* (Cambridge, Mass.: Harvard University Press, 1993), pp. 105, 109. See also Nancy Fraser, "Politics, Culture, and the Public Sphere: Toward a Postmodern Conception," in *Social Postmodernism: Beyond Identity Politics,* ed. Linda Nicholson and Steven Seidman (Cambridge: Cambridge University Press, 1995), pp. 289–290.

53. Jonathan Culler, "Communicative Competence and Normative Force," *New German Critique,* 35 (1985): 140. Against Habermas see Jean-François Lyotard, *The Postmodern Condition: A Report on Knowledge,* trans. Geoff Bennington and Brian Massumi (Minneapolis: University of Minnesota Press, 1984), pp. 10, 16, 60, 65–66; against Lyotard's critique of Habermas, see Peter Dews, "Editor's Introduction," in Jürgen Habermas, *Autonomy and Solidarity,* ed. Peter Dews (New York: Verso, 1992), pp. 1–32.

54. Butler, *Excitable Speech,* p. 18. Butler herself is suspicious of the value of conflating speech and conduct; when emphasizing hate speech's illocutionary status one should not fail, she cautions, to take account of its possible infelicity (19, 102).

55. For Butler on Bourdieu's idea of the "hexis," see ibid., pp. 154–156.

56. Barbara Johnson, Introduction, *Freedom and Interpretation: The Oxford Amnesty Lectures, 1992,* ed. Barbara Johnson (New York: Basic Books, 1993), p. 6. On the functions of citizenship, see Brook Thomas, "China Men, United States v. Wong Kim Ark, and the Question of Citizenship," *American Quarterly,* 50, no. 4 (1998): pp. 689–717. For a feminist appraisal of contemporary theories of the violence of language, see Beatrice Hanssen, "Elfriede Jelinek's Language of Violence," *New German Critique,* 68 (1996): 79–112. On Foucault's blending of violence and discourse, war and politics, see Beatrice Hanssen, "On the Politics of Pure Means: Benjamin, Arendt, Foucault," in *Violence, Identity, and Self-Determination,* ed. Hent De Vries and Samuel Weber (Stanford: Stanford University Press, 1997), pp. 250–251.

57. Louis Althusser, "Ideology and Ideological State Apparatuses (Notes towards an Investigation)," in *Lenin and Philosophy and Other Essays,* trans. Ben Brewster (New York: Monthly Review Press, 1971), pp. 173–174.

58. Although the examples with which I began this introduction were each presented as illustrations of the emancipatory linguistic model, they could just as coherently be analyzed from the disciplinary perspective: Mary Chesnut's indirection in the hands passage represents language's complicity in violence because it hides the brute reality of war's physical injuries; Walt Whitman's "Beat! Beat! Drums!" is a recruiting poem intended to motivate people to violence; and Ambrose Bierce's "Chickamauga," with its image of soldiers crawling in swarms like injured insects, naturalizes violence through dehumanization of its victims.

59. Maurice Blanchot, *The Writing of the Disaster,* trans. Ann Smock (Lincoln: University of Nebraska Press, 1995), p. 11.

60. For a brilliant example of such an argument, see Ann Kibbey and Michele Stepto, "The Antilanguage of Slavery: Frederick Douglass's 1845 *Narrative,*" in *Critical Essays on Frederick Douglass,* ed. William L. Andrews (Boston: G. K. Hall, 1991), pp. 166–191.

61. Frederick Douglass, *Life and Times of Frederick Douglass* in *Frederick Douglass: Autobiographies* (New York: Library of America, 1994), p. 784.

62. Ibid., pp. 767, 771.

63. *Douglass' Monthly,* 3, no. 12 (May 1861): 450.

64. David W. Blight, *Frederick Douglass' Civil War: Keeping Faith in Jubilee* (Baton Rouge: Louisiana State University Press, 1989), p. 5.

65. Douglass, *Life and Times of Frederick Douglass,* pp. 778–779; see also p. 799. Cited hereafter in the text. "Human governments," Douglass writes, "rest not upon paper, but upon power" (quoted in Blight, *Frederick Douglass' Civil War,* p. 71; see also p. 99).

66. Von Frank, *The Trials of Anthony Burns,* pp. 279–280. For more on the demotion of language in favor of force and on the rhetorical deployment of a words-deeds binary, see pp. 59, 104–105, 224, 260.

67. Douglass, *Life and Times of Frederick Douglass,* pp. 757, 759–61.

68. Karl-Otto Apel, "Ethics, Utopia, and the Critique of Utopia," in *The Communicative Ethics Controversy,* ed. Seyla Benhabib and Fred Dallmayr (Cambridge, Mass.: MIT Press, 1990), pp. 46–47.

69. McCarthy, *Ideals and Illusions,* p. 3

70. Ibid., p. 231.

71. See Žižek in his *Mapping Ideology,* p. 10. Relatedly, see Michael Hardt and Antonio Negri, *Empire* (Cambridge, Mass.: Harvard University Press, 2000), pp. 33–37, 404; and Stanley Rosen's critique of Habermas in his *Hermeneutics as Politics* (New York: Oxford University Press, 1987), pp. 11–16. Žižek proposes that we seek an understanding of the reach of ideology (mystified domination) in the limit set to language: the Real, or the nonsymbolized. See *The Ticklish Subject: The Absent Centre of Political Ontology* (New York: Verso, 1999); *Mapping Ideology,* p. 21. The trau-

matic Real as key to ethics is also "the internal stumbling block on account of which the symbolic system can never 'become itself', achieve its self-identity . . . the Real cannot be positively *signified;* it can only be *shown,* in a negative gesture, as the inherent failure of symbolization." Žižek, *The Plague of Fantasies* (New York: Verso, 1997), p. 217.

72. Butler, *Excitable Speech,* p. 38. Butler's is a qualified and nuanced view that nonetheless tends both to give the priority of antecedence to the moment of insult-assault in language and to surrender domain-formation to inter-subjective discourse conceived as constraint. She writes: "Bound to seek recognition of its own existence in categories, terms, and names that are not of its own making, the subject seeks the sign of its own existence outside itself, in a discourse that is at once dominant and indifferent." "And yet," she continues later, "the social categorizations that establish the vulnerability of the subject to language are themselves vulnerable to both psychic and historical change." *The Psychic Life of Power: Theories in Subjection* (Stanford: Stanford University Press, 1997), pp. 20–21.

73. Ezra Pound, "Affirmations VI: Analysis of This Decade," *New Age,* 16, no. 15 (11 February 1915): 409, 410.

1. Counting on the Battlefield

1. Francis Herbert Bradley, *Appearance and Reality* (Oxford: Clarendon Press, 1968), pp. 29, 16–29.

2. Josiah Royce, *The World and the Individual* (Gloucester, Mass.: Peter Smith, 1976), pp. 502–507; William James, *Essays in Radical Empiricism* (Cambridge, Mass.: Harvard University Press, 1976), pp. 26–27, 52–53; see also William James, *A Pluralistic Universe* (Cambridge, Mass.: Harvard University Press, 1977), p. 41.

3. Morton Horwitz, *The Transformation of American Law, 1870–1960* (Oxford: Oxford University Press, 1992), pp. 19–70.

4. Alan Trachtenberg describes the concentration of capital and the development of centralized, powerful organizations in the post–Civil War era in *The Incorporation of America: Culture and Society in the Gilded Age* (New York: Hill and Wang, 1982). See also Alfred D. Chandler Jr., *The Visible Hand: The Managerial Revolution in American Business* (Cambridge, Mass.: Harvard University Press, 1977); C. Wright Mills, *The Power Elite* (New York: Oxford University Press, 1956), pp. 102, 271–272; Stuart McConnell, *Glorious Contentment: The Grand Army of the Republic, 1865–1900* (Chapel Hill: University of North Carolina Press, 1992), pp. 1–52; George M. Fredrickson, *The Inner Civil War: Northern Intellectuals and the Crisis of the Union* (Urbana: University of Illinois Press, 1993), pp. 176–180, 225–228. See also Gerald F. Linderman, *Embattled Courage: The Experience of Combat in the American Civil War* (New York: Free Press, 1987), pp. 19–21, 36–37, 39, 75, 247, 289. For important commen-

tary on the anxiety over corporations in the second half of the nineteenth century, see Brook Thomas, *American Literary Realism and the Failed Promise of Contract* (Berkeley: University of California Press, 1997), pp. 231–269.

5. Patricia Cohen, *A Calculating People: The Spread of Numeracy in Early America* (Chicago: University of Chicago Press, 1982), p. 205. See also Theodore Porter, *The Rise of Statistical Thinking, 1820–1900* (Princeton: Princeton University Press, 1986).

6. Ian Hacking, *The Taming of Chance* (New York: Cambridge University Press, 1990), p. 2. For an analysis of statistical discourse as it relates to questions of embodiment in the late nineteenth century, with special reference to Stephen Crane, see Mark Seltzer, *Bodies and Machines* (New York: Routledge, 1992), pp. 91–118.

7. McConnell, *Glorious Contentment*, p. 139.

8. Lewis Saum asserts that in the late nineteenth century the conceptual framework of probability began to displace traditional, community-bound meaning. After the war, he argues, "luck," "chance," and "fortune" began to replace "Providence" in popular discourse. *The Popular Mood of America, 1860–1890* (Lincoln: University of Nebraska Press, 1990), p. 29. Kenneth Cmiel tracks postwar anxiety over the leveling of culture and the erasure of traditional social hierarchies in the work of conservative language critics who sought to regulate "proper" language use and thus preserve "the lines between the few and the many." *Democratic Eloquence: The Fight over Popular Speech in Nineteenth-Century America* (New York: William Morrow, 1990), p. 124.

9. Anne Carver Rose, *Victorian America and the Civil War* (New York: Cambridge University Press, 1992), pp. 236, 58, 110, 13. Elizabeth Stuart Phelps's novel *The Gates Ajar* (1868), which was written, according to the author, in response to the mass bereavement of the war, evidences throughout an intense anxiety over the dissolution of the individual into the mass. *The Gates Ajar* (Cambridge, Mass.: Belknap Press of Harvard University Press, 1964), pp. 55, 130, and *passim*. In *Looking Backward, 2000–1887* (1888) Edward Bellamy imagines a new model of corporatist social organization, an "industrial army" modeled on the paradigm of the military regiment (New York: Penguin Books, 1982, pp. 224–225, 89). The prioritization of the aggregate here leads to a conception of human character lacking in individual thickness. Bellamy's protagonist, for instance, is able to abandon without pause the relationships of love and friendship that define his preutopian life (158). More telling, however, is the emblematic interchangeability of his beloved Ediths (211–213). See Walter Benn Michaels, "An American Tragedy, or, The Promise of American Life," in *The New American Studies*, ed. Philip Fisher (Berkeley: University of California Press, 1991), pp. 171–200; and Fredrickson, *The Inner Civil War*, pp. 225–228.

10. Stephen Crane, "An Episode of War," in *Stephen Crane: Tales of War,* ed. Fredson Bowers (Charlottesville: University Press of Virginia, 1970), p. 90. Cited hereafter in the text.

11. The doctor is elevated by viewing the sublime of the battlefield. Edmund Burke writes that self-opinion swells when "we are conversant with terrible objects" without suffering exposure to danger ourselves, "the mind always claiming to itself some part of the dignity and importance of the things which it contemplates." Quoted in Thomas Weiskel, *The Romantic Sublime: Studies in the Structure and Psychology of Transcendence* (Baltimore: Johns Hopkins University Press, 1986), p. 98.

12. For a brilliant study of perspectivism in Crane's war writing, see David Halliburton, *The Color of the Sky: A Study of Stephen Crane* (Cambridge: Cambridge University Press, 1989), pp. 98–181; see also Robert Rechnitz, "Depersonalization and the Dream in *The Red Badge of Courage,*" *Studies in the Novel,* 6, no. 1 (1974): 76–87. Patrick Dooley's study on pluralism and ethics in the writing of Stephen Crane was brought to my attention too late to incorporate into this project; those with further interest should see *The Pluralistic Philosophy of Stephen Crane* (Urbana: University of Illinois Press, 1993), especially pp. 26–79.

13. Stephen Crane, *Stephen Crane: Letters,* ed. R. W. Stallman and Lillian Gilkes (New York: New York University Press, 1960), p. 99.

14. William Tecumseh Sherman, *Memoirs of General W. T. Sherman* (New York: Library of America, 1990), p. 338 and *passim.* Cited hereafter in the text.

15. Body counts, unsurprisingly, were frequently disputed; their precision was a form of fiction. For the military professional, whose job in Harold Lasswell's phrase is "the management of violence" (Samuel P. Huntington, *The Soldier and the State,* Cambridge, Mass.: Harvard University Press, 1985, p. 11), numerical exactitude is an essential step in maintaining control.

16. Elaine Scarry, *Literature and the Body: Essays on Populations and Persons* (Baltimore: Johns Hopkins University Press, 1988), Introduction; Elaine Scarry, *The Body in Pain: The Making and the Unmaking of the World* (New York: Oxford University Press, 1985), pp. 192, 269–270.

17. Linderman describes in detail the response of witnesses to the unprecedented number of casualties encountered in Civil War battles (*Embattled Courage,* pp. 125–126). See also Frederickson, *The Inner Civil War,* p. 84. On waste and the management of numbers in the Civil War, see Martha Banta, *Taylored Lives: Narrative Productions in the Age of Taylor, Veblen, and Ford* (Chicago: University of Chicago Press, 1993), pp. 42–46; on the pleasure of war as passionate spectacle, see Bill Brown, *The Material Unconscious: American Amusement, Stephen Crane, and the Economics of Play* (Cambridge, Mass.: Harvard University Press, 1996), pp. 134–135.

18. Edmund Wilson points out how, amidst a "morass of agony," an individual instance of suffering could move Grant to a sudden "impulse of pity." *Patriotic Gore* (New York: W. W. Norton, 1994), p. 156.

19. On the function of displacement in war, see Scarry, *The Body in Pain,* pp. 71–72.
20. During the Atlanta campaign Sherman reported that he had begun "to regard the death and mangling of a couple of thousand men as a small affair, a kind of morning dash" (Linderman, *Embattled Courage,* p. 207).
21. For more on the mathematical sublime, see Weiskel, *The Romantic Sublime,* pp. 38–39.
22. Lincoln's linguistic practice stands behind much of the language about violence in the later nineteenth century. Analyzing the Gettysburg Address, Gary Wills explains how Lincoln's rhetoric worked to derealize the fact of particular injuries and deaths. "The stakes of the three days' butchery are made intellectual," he writes, "with abstract truths being vindicated." And later: "The draining of particulars from the scene raises it to the ideality of a type." *Lincoln at Gettysburg: The Words That Remade America* (New York: Simon and Schuster, 1992), pp. 37, 54. For more on how damage to bodies is occluded in Civil War writing, see Lisa A. Long, "The Corporeity of Heaven: Rehabilitating the Civil War Body in *The Gates Ajar,*" *American Literature,* 69, no. 4 (1997): 781–812.
23. Whitman said of Sherman that he possessed "something of grandeur, hauteur, haughtiness," and described Grant as "quite another man," who "liked to defy convention by going a simple way, his own." (Quoted in David S. Reynolds, *Walt Whitman's America: A Cultural Biography* (New York: Vintage Books, 1996), p. 437.
24. Timothy Sweet argues that Melville's poem "The March to the Sea" is an explicit critique of the tendency to obfuscate and naturalize the brutality of Sherman's tactics. *The Traces of War* (Baltimore: Johns Hopkins University Press, 1990), pp. 192–193.
25. Mark Twain, William Dean Howells, and Matthew Arnold (grudgingly) all praised the precision, compression, and control of Grant's writing. See Daniel Aaron, *The Unwritten War: American Writers and the Civil War* (New York: Alfred A. Knopf, 1973), pp. 179, 131; Wilson, *Patriotic Gore,* p. 140. See also Henry James, *The American Essays,* ed. Leon Edel (Princeton: Princeton University Press, 1989), pp. 208–210; John Keegan, *The Mask of Command* (New York: Penguin Books, 1987), pp. 199–202.
26. Keegan, *The Mask of Command,* p. 213.
27. Grant, *Memoirs and Selected Letters* (New York: Library of America, 1990), pp. 95, 115, 160–161, 164–166. Cited hereafter in the text.
28. See Edmund Wilson's account of Grant's "deliberate flatness" in presenting the capture of Vicksburg, as well as his claim that Grant's objectivity functions to efface the tragedy and terror of violence (*Patriotic Gore,* pp. 151–153).
29. Martha C. Nussbaum, *The Fragility of Goodness: Luck and Ethics in Greek Tragedy and Philosophy* (Cambridge: Cambridge University Press, 1986), p. 107.
30. In public speeches like his Second Inaugural Address, Lincoln like Grant de-

picted himself as the passive agent of superior forces. "And the war came," he proclaims, subtracting human agency. See for instance Mark E. Neely Jr., *The Last Best Hope of Earth: Abraham Lincoln and the Promise of America* (Cambridge, Mass.: Harvard University Press, 1995), pp. 154–155. In a typical moment in 1864, Lincoln said in response to a story about a Confederate plan to assassinate him: "I am but a single individual, and it would not help their cause or make the least difference in the progress of the war. Everything would go right on just the same." Charles Royster, *The Destructive War* (New York: Alfred A. Knopf, 1991), p. 292; see also pp. 287, 284–295. In his journal Ralph Waldo Emerson figures the war as an agent beyond individual and institutional control: "We watch its course as we did the cholera." *The Real War Will Never Get in the Books: Selections from Writers during the Civil War,* ed. Louis P. Masur (New York: Oxford University Press, 1993), p. 134.

31. Publicly shared retrospectives of battle were explicitly perceived as an effective means of revivifying national unity. The editors of *Century* magazine wrote that their war series, "through peculiar circumstances, has exerted an influence in bringing about a better understanding between the soldiers who were opposed in that conflict . . . Coincident with the progress of the series during the past three years, may be noted a marked increase in the number of fraternal meetings between Union and Confederate veterans, enforcing the conviction that the nation is restored in spirit as in fact, and that each side is contributing its share to the new heritage of manhood and peace." *Battles and Leaders of the Civil War,* ed. Robert Underwood Johnson and Clarence Clough Buel, vol. 1 (New York: Century Company, DeVinne Press, 1887), p. ix. Relatedly, see Evelyn Cobley's analysis of the ritualized mystification of violence in World War I: "Violence and Sacrifice in Modern War Narratives," *SubStance,* 23, no. 3 (1994): 75–99.

32. Jennifer Welchman, *Dewey's Ethical Thought* (Ithaca: Cornell University Press, 1995), p. 28.

33. Thomas Nagel, *The View from Nowhere* (New York: Oxford University Press, 1986), pp. 75–77.

34. See Hilary Putnam's lucid critique, *Pragmatism: An Open Question* (Oxford: Blackwell, 1995), pp. 74–75, 8–12, 20–22.

35. William James, *The Meaning of Truth* (Cambridge, Mass.: Harvard University Press, 1975), pp. 144, 143.

36. In "Chattanooga," Melville captures both a sense of Grant's panoramic vision and his studied self-suppression: "Grant stood on cliffs whence all was plain, / And smoked as one who feels no cares; / But mastered nervousness intense / Alone such calmness wears. / . . . / He, from the brink, / Looks far along the breadth of slope, / And sees two miles of dark dots creep." *Collected Poems of Herman Melville,* ed. Howard P. Vincent (Chicago: Packard and Company, 1947), p. 59.

37. See Carl von Clausewitz's description of the imaginative genius and nearly

aesthetic sensitivity, combined with the capacity for objective inclusiveness, required for a military comprehension of locality and topography. *On War,* trans. Michael Howard and Peter Paret (Princeton: Princeton University Press, 1976), pp. 109–110.

38. Grant, *Memoirs and Selected Letters,* pp. 354, 911, 59, 232, 33, 34, 767, 534, 20, 26, 32, 43, 46, 52, 461.

39. On one level, war is the place where one is least able to make sense of Rawls's concept of the veil. For intelligibility, one must add the important qualification that the "public" here is restricted to the borders of a community mobilized to the war effort.

40. Nussbaum, *The Fragility of Goodness,* p. 160.

41. Traditionally women's writing on the Civil War has received scant attention from literary critics. Recent work that has begun to analyze the contribution of women to the war literature of the nineteenth century includes Kathleen Diffley, *Where My Heart Is Turning Ever: Civil War Stories and Constitutional Reform, 1861–1876* (Athens: University of Georgia Press, 1992), and Elizabeth Young, *Disarming the Nation: Women's Writing and the American Civil War* (Chicago: University of Chicago Press, 1999). For Young on Alcott, see pp. 69–108.

42. Louisa May Alcott, *The Journals of Louisa May Alcott,* ed. Joel Myerson, Daniel Shealy, and Madelene Stern (Athens: University of Georgia Press, 1997), p. 110.

43. *Alternative Alcott,* ed. Elaine Showalter (New Brunswick: Rutgers University Press, 1988), pp. xxvi–xxvii.

44. Ibid., p. 21. Cited hereafter in the text.

45. Later, in a fever delirium from the typhoid she contracted at the hospital, Alcott would suffer, without the mediation of conscious desensitization, the continual reprise of a nightmare where she tended "millions of sick men who never died or got well" (*The Journals of Louisa May Alcott,* p. 117).

46. See also Hannah Ropes, *Civil War Nurse: The Diary and Letters of Hannah Ropes,* ed. John R. Brumgardt (Knoxville: University of Tennessee Press, 1980), p. 120.

47. Louisa May Alcott, Letter to Miss Stevenson, 26 December 1862, *M.H.S. Miscellany,* 65 (1996): 4.

48. For one of the most vivid fictional depictions of the overcrowded field hospital, see John W. DeForest, *Miss Ravenel's Conversion from Secession to Loyalty* (New York: Harper and Brothers, 1939), pp. 257–262.

49. Reynolds, *Walt Whitman's America,* p. 431. Fredrickson writes of the Sanitary Commission: "Brutally stated . . . the commission saved the soldier in the hospital so that he could die a useful death on the battlefield. This much might have been expected. What is surprising is that some of the commissioners not only accepted the necessary agonies of war but welcomed them as good in themselves." One of the founders, Frederickson notes, carried a hip bone and a skull as souvenirs from the Bull Run battlefield and was sur-

prised that some found his display in poor taste (*The Inner Civil War,* pp. 102–103).

50. On Civil War medical culture and the elevation of the specific injury-category over the complete physiological reactions of patients, see Richard Shryock, "A Medical Perspective on the Civil War," *American Quarterly,* 14, no. 2 (1962): 167.

51. DeForest, *Miss Ravenel's Conversion,* p. 264.

52. On patterns of grieving in mid-nineteenth-century America, see Lewis O. Saum, "Death in the Popular Mind of Pre–Civil War America," in *Death in America,* ed. David Stannard (Philadelphia: University of Pennsylvania Press, 1975), p. 41.

53. The War Department estimated after the war that up to 25,000 soldiers had never been buried. Phillip Shaw Paludan, *"A People's Contest": The Union and the Civil War, 1861–1865* (New York: Harper and Row, 1988), pp. 316, 325, 366. Clara Barton's research led to the conclusion that 45 percent of Northern graves were marked unknown (Linderman, *Embattled Courage,* pp. 248–249). On ritual and the framing of meaning, see Mary Douglas, *Purity and Danger: An Analysis of the Concepts of Pollution and Taboo* (London: Routledge, 1991), pp. 62–67.

54. Sigmund Freud, "Mourning and Melancholia" (1917), in *The Standard Edition of the Complete Psychological Works of Sigmund Freud,* ed. James Strachey, vol. 14 (London: Hogarth, 1957), pp. 245–259, 253.

55. According to Robert Davis, Florence Nightingale's *Notes on Nursing: What It Is, and What It Is Not* provided the dominant paradigm for nursing in the Civil War. It was a process of therapy and healing premised upon closed systems and the elimination of disorder. "The goal of Nightingale's hospital was perfect containment, what medical historians have termed 'a sanitary code embodied in a building.'" See Davis, *Whitman and the Romance of Medicine* (Berkeley: University of California Press, 1997), p. 46. According to Davis, Alcott's carnivalesque, topsy-turvy episodic sketches function to disrupt this disciplinary regime in order to emphasize transgressive sexuality. Davis makes a convincing argument, but it is also true that when Alcott's sketches turn to the central story of the central section "A Night," her narrative manner transforms itself and becomes the correlative of Nightingale's enclosing systems, figured now not as a disciplinary form but rather as a tender embrace.

56. Hayden White, *Tropics of Discourse* (Baltimore: Johns Hopkins University Press, 1978), pp. 90, 86–87.

57. William James, *The Will to Believe and Other Essays in Popular Philosophy* (New York: Dover Publications, 1956), p. 256.

58. William James, *Pragmatism* (Cambridge, Mass.: Harvard University Press, 1975), p. 77. See especially Frank Lentricchia, "On the Ideologies of Poetic Modernism," in *Reconstructing American Literary History,* ed. Sacvan Bercovitch (Cambridge, Mass.: Harvard University Press, 1986), pp. 237,

245. Elsewhere James comments upon our built-in "blindness" to the special beauty and value of those in the multitude that surrounds us. "What Makes a Life Significant?" in *The James Family: Including Selections from the Writings of Henry James, Senior, William, Henry, and Alice James,* ed. F. O. Matthiessen (New York: Alfred A. Knopf, 1947), p. 405.

59. "The therapist's act of bearing witness provides a social context that allows the story to cohere both because of the emotional meaning of receiving another's empathic attention and because it invokes the tacit dimension of shared (or public) history. Even fragments can be read as a story if a larger narrative context is supplied by an audience primed by history." Laurence J. Kirmayer, "Landscapes of Memory: Trauma, Narrative, and Dissociation," in *Tense Past: Cultural Essays in Trauma and Memory,* ed. Paul Antze and Michael Limbek (New York: Routledge, 1996), p. 186.

60. Ropes, *Civil War Nurse,* p. 53.

61. Philip Fisher, quoted in Davis, *Whitman and the Romance of Medicine,* pp. 78–80, 83. For more on the work of the sympathetic imagination, see Philip Fisher, "Democratic Social Space: Whitman, Melville, and the Promise of American Transparency," in *The New American Studies,* ed. Fisher (Berkeley: University of California Press, 1991), pp. 89–91.

62. Nina Baym, *Woman's Fiction* (Ithaca: Cornell University Press, 1978).

63. Jane Tompkins, *Sensational Designs: The Cultural Work of American Fiction, 1790–1860* (New York: Oxford University Press, 1985). For more recent work on domesticity and power, see Lora Romero, *Home Fronts* (Durham: Duke University Press, 1997).

64. Whitman, *Prose Works 1892, Specimen Days,* ed. Floyd Stovall, vol. 1 (New York: New York University Press, 1963), p. 32.

65. Walt Whitman, *Leaves of Grass* (New York: Vintage Books, 1992), p. 445.

66. On Whitman's pattern of attending to the individual while always reasserting absorption into the whole, see Whitman in Masur, *The Real War Will Never Get in the Books,* pp. 256, 259, 272. "Let me tell his story—it is but one of thousands"; "He is one of the thousands of our unknown American young men in the ranks about whom there is no record or fame, no fuss made about their dying so unknown." For more on Whitman's fraught efforts to realize the corpses that threaten to disappear in the abstraction of taxonomy, see Katherine Kinney, "Making Capital: War, Labor, and Whitman in Washington, D.C.," in *Breaking Bounds: Whitman and American Cultural Studies,* ed. Betsy Erkkila and Jay Grossman (New York: Oxford University Press, 1996), pp. 174–189.

67. Whitman, *Specimen Days,* p. 35; *Walt Whitman's Civil War,* ed. Walter Lowenfels (New York: Alfred A. Knopf, 1960), p. 15.

68. Whitman, *Specimen Days,* p. 36.

69. Ibid., pp. 39–40.

70. Ibid., p. 100.

71. Ibid., pp. 112–113.

72. Whitman, *Leaves of Grass,* p. 437.
73. *Walt Whitman: November Boughs,* in *Walt Whitman: Complete Poetry and Collected Prose,* ed. Justin Kaplan (New York: Literary Classics of the United States, 1982), pp. 1216–1217.
74. For one of the innumerable additional examples one could cite showing how Whitman moves from the individual to the sample, see Whitman, *Walt Whitman: The Correspondence,* ed. Edwin Haviland Miller, vol. 1 (New York: New York University Press, 1961), p. 205. "One poor boy (this is a sample of one case out of the 600) . . ." Even when he explicitly emphasizes that he will focus on the individual, he does so with an invocation of the multiple elements he is temporarily bracketing. *Specimen Days,* p. 97; see also section 7 of "When Lilacs Last in the Dooryard Bloom'd"; on the latter, see Betsy Erkkila, *Whitman the Political Poet* (New York: Oxford University Press, 1989), p. 228. For an analysis of Whitman's war poetry and the problems of aggregation, see Davis, *Whitman and the Romance of Medicine,* pp. 72–94, 64, to which I am generally indebted. See also Wynn Thomas, *The Lunar Light of Whitman's Poetry* (Cambridge, Mass.: Harvard University Press, 1987), p. 212, 217–221; and Roy Morris Jr., *The Better Angel: Walt Whitman in the Civil War* (Oxford: Oxford University Press, 2000).
75. Thomas, *The Lunar Light of Whitman's Poetry,* p. 208.
76. Ibid., pp. 252–255.
77. Reynolds, *Walt Whitman's America,* p. 50. War and its aftermath does seem to have affected Whitman's presentation of the individual. The 1867 *Leaves of Grass,* Reynolds notes, opens with "One's Self I sing, a simple separate person, / Yet utter the word Democratic, the word En-Masse," which reads more objectively (and, according to Reynolds, more desperately) than the earlier individualistic chant "I celebrate myself" (*Walt Whitman's America,* p. 467).
78. Walt Whitman, *"Leaves of Grass": A Textual Variorum of the Printed Poems,* vol. 1, *Poems, 1855–1856,* ed. Sculley Bradley, Harold W. Blodgett, Arthur Golden, and William White (New York: New York University Press, 1980), p. 17. "Such was the war," wrote Whitman. "It was not a quadrille in a ball-room" (*Specimen Days,* p. 117).
79. Erkkila, *Whitman the Political Poet,* p. 103.
80. See, for instance, Quentin Anderson, *The Imperial Self* (New York: Alfred A. Knopf, 1971), pp. 88–118.
81. Davis, *Whitman and the Romance of Medicine,* p. 75. As Davis argues, this is the premise of the effectiveness of individualized sentimentality. The counterargument is that in an increasingly diversified and complex society, civic function and private feeling are separated by multiple layers.
82. Walt Whitman in Masur, *The Real War Will Never Get in the Books,* p. 274.
83. Whitman, *Specimen Days,* p. 115.

84. Thomas, *The Lunar Light of Whitman's Poetry,* p. 221. Kerry Larson characterizes Whitman's representational anxieties as generated by the conflict between his resistance to making the war uncomplicatedly intelligible through reference to a higher cause and his countervailing resistance to allowing it to remain mute. *Whitman's Drama of Consensus* (Chicago: University of Chicago Press, 1988), pp. 220, 240. On Whitman's attempt to "confront the true suffering of war" without "idealizing the damage done to real bodies"—an attempt John Carlos Rowe calls into question—see *At Emerson's Tomb: The Politics of Classic American Literature* (New York: Columbia University Press, 1997), p. 160; see also Sweet, *Traces of War,* pp. 46–77. Whitman, Sweet argues, "mobilized an organicist poetics to heal or hide the wounds of the Civil War and to idealize the conservation of the Union effected by the war" (78).

85. Walt Whitman, *Prose Works 1892,* vol. 1, p. 302.

86. On the "interchangeability of selves," see Philip Fisher, "Democratic Social Space," in *The New American Studies,* ed. Fisher (Berkeley: University of California Press, 1991), pp. 70–77. Davis refers to the wounded soldier here as "a representative in Whitman's Hospital Congress" (*Whitman and the Romance of Medicine,* p. 83). Whitman strains toward the idea that radical difference need not fracture community: with the help of the poet, the drive for consensus need not violate the dignity of the individual. Relatedly see Larson, *Whitman's Drama of Consensus,* and Allen Grossman, "The Poetics of Union in Whitman and Lincoln: An Inquiry toward the Relationship of Art and Policy," in *The American Renaissance Reconsidered,* ed. Walter Benn Michaels and Donald Pease (Baltimore: Johns Hopkins University Press, 1985), pp. 183–208. For a brilliant contrasting analysis of the role of democratic interchangeability and incommensurability in Whitman's work, see Wai Chee Dimock, *Residues of Justice: Literature, Law, Philosophy* (Berkeley: University of California Press, 1996), pp. 96–139.

87. Whitman, *Specimen Days,* pp. 114–115. For Whitman's pained sense that the unknown would be forgotten and unrecorded in history, see Thomas, *The Lunar Light of Whitman's Poetry,* pp. 233–239. For accounts that convey the brutality of the Civil War through overwhelming numbers, see Aaron, *The Unwritten War,* p. 266.

88. Josiah Royce, *The Philosophy of Josiah Royce,* ed. John K. Roth (New York: Thomas Y. Crowell, 1971), pp. 118–119. Cited hereafter in the text. See especially *The Religious Aspect of Philosophy* (Boston: Houghton Mifflin, 1913).

89. James, *Pragmatism,* p. 75.

90. Josiah Royce, *The Hope of the Great Community* (New York: Macmillan, 1916), p. 125.

91. John Clendenning, *The Life and Thought of Josiah Royce* (Madison: University of Wisconsin Press, 1985), p. 36–37.

92. Royce, *The Hope of the Great Community*, p. 52. William Kluback points out that Royce believed that the absorption of the individual into "the beloved community" is a crucial step in countering the spread of violence. "The Problem of Christianity," in *Josiah Royce: Selected Writings*, ed. John E. Smith and William Kluback (New York: Paulist Press, 1988), pp. 27–32.

93. R. W. B. Lewis, *The Jameses: A Family Narrative* (New York: Farrar, Straus and Giroux, 1991), p. 553. For Henry's relationship to the war, see Wilson, *Patriotic Gore*, pp. 664–665; see also Aaron, *The Unwritten War*, pp. 106–112.

94. The phrase is from William James, "What Makes a Life Significant?" in *The James Family: Including Selections from the Writings of Henry James, Senior, William, Henry, and Alice James*, ed. F. O. Matthiessen (New York: Alfred A. Knopf, 1947), p. 408. In this essay on the heroism of the quotidian James refers back to the soldier as an emblem of virtue and idealism. R. B. Perry notes "a common thread running through James's observations on religion, neurasthenia, war, earthquakes, fasting, lynching, patriotism—an interest, namely, in human behavior under high pressure, and the conclusion that exceptional circumstances generate exceptional inner power." *The Thought and Character of William James,* vol. 2 (Westport, Conn.: Greenwood Press, 1974), p. 273.

95. Lewis describes William's "guilt at not having taken any active part in the great national conflict; at not having proven his manhood by the confrontation of mortal danger as Wilky (and of course others of William's acquaintance, like Captain Wendell Holmes) so conspicuously had done . . . the effects of the war years upon William's intellectual life and actual behavior were to be very long-lasting indeed" (*The Jameses,* pp. 156–157). William himself wrote: "The grit and energy of some men are called forth by the resistance of the world. But as for myself, I seem to have no spirit whatever of that kind, no pride which makes me ashamed to say, 'I can't do that.'" Lewis comments: "These were painful utterances to make to a father who set such store by manliness, and in the wake of fraternal examples of vigorous 'grappling with external circumstances'" (175). For more on James's relation to the war, see R. B. Perry, *The Thought and Character of William James,* vol. 1 (Westport, Conn.: Greenwood Press, 1974), pp. 202–203; 2:270–279.

96. See Frederickson, *The Inner Civil War,* pp. 229–238.

97. See, for instance, James, *The Will to Believe and Other Essays in Popular Philosophy,* pp. 260, 213, 205, 198, 168, 152, 109, 93, 61, 37, and *passim.* Cited hereafter in the text.

98. For the implicit link between James's pluralism and his antiimperialist militarism, see Frank Lentricchia, "On the Ideologies of Poetic Modernism," in Bercovitch, *Reconstructing American Literary History,* p. 230.

99. See for instance William James, *Essays in Psychology* (Cambridge, Mass.: Harvard University Press, 1983), pp. 62–64, 74–75.

100. Perry, *The Thought and Character of William James,* 1:322.

101. James, *A Pluralistic Universe,* p. 62.

102. Stanley Cavell, *The Claim of Reason* (Oxford: Oxford University Press, 1979), p. 125.

103. James, *A Pluralistic Universe,* p. 96.

104. Ibid., p. 62.

105. Ibid., p. 94.

106. On the misleading romantic notion that James overcame his depression through pragmatic philosophy, see Louis Menand, "William James and the Case of the Epileptic Patient," *New York Review of Books,* 17 December 1998, 81–94.

107. Lewis, *The Jameses,* p. 185.

108. James, *Pragmatism,* p. 76–77.

109. For the paradigmatic modern expression of the absurd, see Albert Camus, *The Myth of Sisyphus and Other Essays,* trans. Justin O'Brien (New York: Alfred A. Knopf, 1955), p. 29. See also Thomas Nagel, *Mortal Questions* (Cambridge: Cambridge University Press, 1979), pp. 11–23.

110. See also Stephen Crane, "The Open Boat," in *Tales of Adventure,* ed. Fredson Bowers (Charlottesville: University of Virginia Press, 1970), p. 77.

111. James, *A Pluralistic Universe,* pp. 35, 51, 37.

112. James, *Pragmatism,* p. 54.

113. Camus relates war to the structure of the absurd. See *The Myth of Sisyphus and Other Essays,* p. 93.

114. Whitman in Masur, *The Real War Will Never Get in the Books,* p. 267.

115. Perspectival objectivism as a component of the late-nineteenth-century quantifying mentality bears an important relationship, it might be argued, to the development of literary realism. For analyses of American realism that emphasize the causal factors of post–Civil War accelerations in urbanization and industrial capitalism, see Eric J. Sundquist, "Introduction," and Alan Trachtenberg, "Experiments in Another Country: Stephen Crane's City Sketches," in *American Realism: New Essays,* ed. Eric J. Sundquist (Baltimore: Johns Hopkins University Press, 1982), pp. 3–24 and 138–154, respectively; and Amy Kaplan, *The Social Construction of American Realism* (Chicago: University of Chicago Press, 1988). David Shi points specifically to the Civil War and to the rise in statistics as elements contributing to the ascendance of realism. *Facing Facts: Realism in American Thought and Culture* (New York: Oxford University Press, 1995), pp. 45–66, 71–73.

116. Nagel, *The View from Nowhere,* p. 55.

117. See Christine Brooke-Rose, "Ill Logics of Irony," in *New Essays on "The Red Badge of Courage,"* ed. Lee Clark Mitchell (New York: Cambridge University Press, 1986), pp. 129–146.

118. See for instance Halliburton, *The Color of the Sky,* pp. 11, 105.

119. Stephen Crane, *The Red Badge of Courage* (New York: Lancer Books, 1967), p. 113.

120. Stephen Crane, "The Blue Hotel," in *Tales of Adventure,* ed. Fredson Bowers (Charlottesville: University of Virginia Press, 1970), p. 442. See also David Halliburton's analysis of the "little" in Crane's fiction (*The Color of the Sky,* p. 111).
121. See, for instance, Frederickson on Theodore Roosevelt, *The Inner Civil War,* pp. 224–225.

2. Care and Creation

1. Frits Kalshoven, *Constraints on the Waging of War* (Geneva: ICRC, 1987), pp. 10, 16.
2. Ernst Jünger, "Total Mobilization," in *The Heidegger Controversy: A Critical Reader,* ed. Richard Wolin (Cambridge, Mass.: MIT Press, 1993), p. 128.
3. I have borrowed from Paul Fussell's description of life in the trenches. See *The Great War and Modern Memory* (New York: Oxford University Press, 1975) pp. 40–43, 47. For another account, see Robert Graves, *Good-Bye to All That: An Autobiography,* ed. Richard Perceval Graves (Providence: Berghahn Books, 1995), pp. 109–113.
4. Jünger, "Total Mobilization," pp. 126, 128. See also Ernst Jünger, *The Storm of Steel,* trans. Basil Creighton (New York: Howard Fertig, 1975), p. 59.
5. On technology and war, see Thomas Hughes, *American Genesis* (New York: Viking Penguin, 1989).
6. As John Kasson notes, "the record of 23,000 patents issued during the decade of the 1850s . . . was approximated if not excelled during every single *year* from 1882 on." *Civilizing the Machine: Technology and Republican Values in America, 1776–1900* (New York: Grossman Publishers, 1976), pp. 183–184.
7. Daniel J. Boorstin, *The Americans: The Democratic Experience* (New York: Vintage Books, 1974), pp. 107, 101–135, 334. Prewar optimism in the capacity of society to perfect itself manifested itself as renewed faith even in social inventions and artifacts like international law. "With that naïve optimism that pervaded all peace movements in the first decade of the twentieth century," writes Joseph Wall, "the deed [for the Carnegie Endowment for International Peace], at Carnegie's direction, provided that 'when the establishment of universal peace is attained, the donor provides that the revenue shall be devoted to the banishment of the next most degrading evil or evils, the suppression of which would most advance the progress, elevation and happiness of man.'" *Andrew Carnegie* (New York: Oxford University Press, 1970), p. 898.
8. For an analysis of the naturalist fascination with "the body-machine complex" to which I am indebted, see Mark Seltzer, *Bodies and Machines* (New York: Routledge, 1992). Excitement over technological development and

the dominance of the machine as a perceptual paradigm also played into the conflation of art and automated, mechanical spectacle. In a mid-nineteenth-century lecture entitled "The Importance of the Mechanic Arts," Edward Everett compared the noise of American machines to "the richest strains of poetry, eloquence, and philosophy." *Orations and Speeches on Various Occasions,* 5th ed. (Boston: Little, Brown, 1859), pp. 246–247, 255. Through the mid-nineteenth century, the word "arts" signified all skilled crafts, including invention, and through the second half of the nineteenth century, as John Kasson argues, the "pleasures of viewing machinery" competed with and even superseded what was increasingly known as the "fine" arts (*Civilizing the Machine,* p. 140). The aesthetic spectacle of the machine, its power and the mystery of its process, generated what Kasson has called a "technological sublime" (166), that is, a sense of awe and dread as well as beauty. In the latter half of the nineteenth century, he argues, it was a primary aesthetic response (139–180).

9. William James, *Principles of Psychology,* vol. 1 (Cambridge, Mass.: Harvard University Press, 1981), pp. 110–112. William James, "Are We Automata?" in *Essays in Psychology* (Cambridge, Mass.: Harvard University Press, 1983), pp. 43, 54.

10. Eugen Sandow, *Strength: And How to Obtain It,* 3d ed. (London: Gale and Polden, 1905), pp. 146, 30–33; *Sandow on Physical Training,* ed. G. Mercer Adam (New York: J. Selwin Tait and Sons, 1894), p. 178.

11. For a comprehensive analysis of the cultural influence of scientific management, see Martha Banta, *Taylored Lives: Narrative Productions in the Age of Taylor, Veblen, and Ford* (Chicago: University of Chicago Press, 1993).

12. Émile Zola, *La Bête Humaine,* trans. L. W. Tancock (New York: Penguin Books, 1977), pp. 319, 328, 220, 64–65 and *passim.*

13. Jack London, *Martin Eden* (New York: Penguin Books, 1984), pp. 161, 115–122, 131–138, 241–275 and *passim.* For more on the professionalization of literature, and its transformation into a labor for a market, see Christopher Wilson, *The Labor of Words: Literary Professionalism in the Progressive Era* (Athens: University of Georgia Press, 1985). See also Bill Brown's provocative analysis of machine-body intersections in various forms of popular discourse, "Science Fiction, the World's Fair, and the Prosthetics of Empire, 1910–1915" in *Cultures of United States Imperialism,* ed. Amy Kaplan and Donald E. Pease (Durham: Duke University Press, 1993), pp. 129–163.

14. James, *Principles of Psychology,* p. 19.

15. *New York Times,* 16 October 1915, p. 4.

16. Frank Richards, *Old Soldiers Never Die* (Sleaford, Eng.: Phillip Austen, 1994), p. 255.

17. Graves, *Good-Bye to All That,* pp. 137, 130.

18. Jünger, *The Storm of Steel,* pp. 95, 99.

19. Willa Cather, *One of Ours* (New York: Vintage Books, 1991), pp. 315, 280.

242 · *Notes to Pages 72–75*

20. Ernest Jones, *The Treatment of Neuroses* (New York: William Wood, 1920), p. 208.
21. Siegfried Sassoon, *Memoirs of an Infantry Officer* (New York: Collier Books, 1969), p. 156.
22. On air travel, aerial torpedoes, and the gyroscope, see Hughes, *American Genesis,* pp. 101–116, 127–130.
23. As an advertisement for the Singer Sewing Machine put it: "American machines, American brains, and American money are bringing the women of the whole world into one universal kinship and sisterhood" (Boorstin, *The Americans: The Democratic Experience,* p. 96). On the imagined communities of the commodity, see also Philip Fisher, "Democratic Social Space: Whitman, Melville, and the Promise of American Transparency," in *The New American Studies,* ed. Philip Fisher (Berkeley: University of California Press, 1991), pp. 75–76.
24. Daniel J. Kevles, *The Physicists: The History of a Scientific Community in Modern America* (New York: Alfred A. Knopf, 1978), pp. 109–111.
25. Ibid., p. 117.
26. *The World* (New York), 30 May 1915, p. E1; *New York Times,* 16 October 1915, p. 4. See also Hughes, *American Genesis,* pp. 118, 125.
27. Hughes, *American Genesis,* p. 119.
28. Elaine Scarry, *The Body in Pain: The Making and the Unmaking of the World* (New York: Oxford University Press, 1985), p. 291.
29. Hughes, *American Genesis,* p. 104. See also Sandra M. Gilbert and Susan Gubar, *No Man's Land: The Place of the Woman Writer in the Twentieth Century,* vol. 2 (New Haven: Yale University Press, 1989), p. 259.
30. Siegfried Sassoon, *Diaries, 1915–1918,* ed. Rupert Hart-Davis (London: Faber and Faber, 1983), p. 163; see also pp. 48, 70, 73, 157.
31. Jünger, *Storm of Steel,* p. 109, 83. On the joy of battle and delight in killing, see Niall Ferguson, *The Pity of War* (London: Allen Lane, Penguin, 1998), pp. 357–366.
32. D. H. Lawrence, 9 September 1915, in *The Letters of D. H. Lawrence,* ed. George J. Zytaruk and James T. Boulton, vol. 2 (Cambridge: Cambridge University Press, 1981), pp. 389–390. See also Douglas H. Robinson, *The Zeppelin in Combat: A History of the German Naval Airship Division, 1912–1918* (London: G. T. Foulis, 1962), p. 331. On the pleasures of the tank, see Trudi Tate, *Modernism, History, and the First World War* (New York: Manchester University Press, 1998), pp. 120–146.
33. The antecedents of modernist disillusionment with creation can be found in countercultural reactions to the Civil War and to post–Civil War industrial development: the mechanical genocide of Twain's *A Connecticut Yankee in King Arthur's Court,* Henry Adams's antimodernism, and the late-century "Arts and Crafts ideology," which blamed modern nervous prostration on technological growth. See T. J. Jackson Lears, *No Place of Grace: Antimodernism and the Transformation of American Culture, 1880–1920*

(New York: Pantheon Books, 1981), pp. 66–70; see also Kasson, *Civilizing the Machine,* pp. 187–191; and Alan Trachtenberg, *The Incorporation of America: Culture and Society in the Gilded Age* (New York: Hill and Wang, 1982), pp. 38–69. The Civil War was arguably the world's first modern war. It was a total war in which armies regularly demanded unconditional surrender and made a policy of targetting civilians. It was also a war that generated numerous military innovations, including the telegraph, railroad delivery systems, ironclad battleships, hand grenades, land mines, rifled muskets, and trench warfare. See for instance Paul Fussell, "On Modern War," in his *The Norton Book of Modern War* (New York: W. W. Norton, 1991), p. 17. Some critics have argued, however, that the North's victory reaffirmed rather than subverted the value of industrial and technological progress, strengthening assumptions about development and proving the judiciousness of the Victorian "tendency to equate material and moral progress" (Lears, *No Place of Grace,* p. 12); see also Kasson, *Civilizing the Machine,* pp. 184–185; and James McPherson, *Abraham Lincoln and the Second American Revolution* (New York: Oxford University Press, 1991), p. 11. Indeed, the antimodernist critique was itself often premised, as Lears argues, on a belief in civilization's linear climb to a "higher moral organization" (*No Place of Grace,* p. 100). The danger of progress, by this account, was the danger of overcivilization or feminization, of progressing to the point of banality. Reactions to the experience of war, Lears argues, were peculiarly tied into both a presumption of progress and a martial idealism that together made war the promise of "both social and personal regeneration" (*No Place of Grace,* p. 98). See also Michael Rogin on the conservative response to the Civil War, which saw the violence as a source of moral and social cleansing and unification. *Subversive Genealogy* (New York: Alfred A. Knopf, 1983), pp. 264–265.

34. D. H. Lawrence, *Kangaroo,* ed. Bruce Steele (Cambridge: Cambridge University Press, 1994), p. 216.
35. Ernest Hemingway, *A Farewell to Arms* (New York: Collier Books, 1957), p. 185.
36. John Dos Passos, "A Humble Protest" (1916), in *John Dos Passos: The Major Nonfictional Prose,* ed. Donald Pizer (Detroit: Wayne State University Press, 1988), p. 34.
37. Townsend Ludington, *John Dos Passos: A Twentieth Century Odyssey* (New York: E. P. Dutton, 1980), p. 136.
38. Ezra Pound, "Hugh Selwyn Mauberley," in *Selected Poems* (New York: New Directions, 1957), p. 64.
39. Paul Boyer, in a history of premillennialism in America, finds that after an intense spike during World War I apocalypticism declined throughout the 1920s as it began to diverge from mainstream religious views. *When Time Shall Be No More: Prophecy Belief in Modern American Culture* (Cambridge, Mass.: Harvard University Press, 1992), pp. 104–105. For the

"imagination of disaster" in the latter half of the nineteenth century, see Kasson, *Civilizing the Machine*, pp. 189–191. On the relationship between *A Connecticut Yankee* and the Civil War, see Daniel Aaron, *The Unwritten War: American Writers and the Civil War* (New York: Alfred A. Knopf, 1973), pp. 140–145.

40. Jünger, "Total Mobilization," p. 123. For the German postwar antitechnological ethos, see Hanna Hafkesbrink, *Unknown Germany: An Inner Chronicle of the First World War Based on Letters and Diaries* (New Haven: Yale University Press, 1948), pp. 65–70; and Max Weber, "Science as a Vocation," (1918) in *From Max Weber: Essays in Sociology,* trans. and ed. H. H. Gerth and C. Wright Mills (New York: Oxford University Press, 1946), p. 142. "Mechanized warfare," Hafkesbrink writes, "negated all personal values to a generation . . . eager to regain those very values" (69). On the preoccupation with violence in British representation preceding the war, from E. M. Forster to Vorticism, see Bernard Bergonzi, *Heroes' Twilight* (Manchester: Carcanet, 1996), pp. 17–32. Before World War I, war was seen as "fulfillment and deliverance" for many (27). The Futurist celebration of cultural reinvention through violence and technological advance preceded the war and powerfully influenced the Anglo-American avantgarde. For Futurism's relationship to violence, the disruption of language, war, and surplus, see Peter Nicholls, *Modernisms: A Literary Guide* (Berkeley: University of California Press, 1995), pp. 84–111; and Marjorie Perloff, *The Futurist Movement* (Chicago: University of Chicago Press, 1986).

41. World War I accomplished the industrialization and professionalization of armed combat and the creation of a permanent military industry. See C. Wright Mills, *The Power Elite* (New York: Oxford University Press, 1956), p. 179.

42. Tyrus Miller calls the war the "generative matrix" of *late* modernism in *Late Modernism: Politics, Fiction, and the Arts between the World Wars* (Berkeley: University of California Press, 1999), p. 27. For more on the war and modernism, see Michael North, *Reading 1922* (New York: Oxford University Press, 1999), pp. 15, 57–58.

43. T. S. Eliot, *Selected Essays* (New York: Harcourt, Brace, 1950), p. 248.

44. Virginia Woolf, *Jacob's Room* (London: Hogarth, 1971), p. 92.

45. Virginia Woolf, *Three Guineas* (London: Hogarth, 1968), p. 260; see also pp. 146, 184, 186, 248, 250. George Steiner treats the modernist project to reinvent language as a by-product of the war in *Martin Heidegger* (Chicago: University of Chicago Press, 1989), pp. vii–xi. Randy Malamud argues that an important aspect of modernism generally, which predates but was amplified and galvanized during the war, was a frustration with the limits of the inherited language's "false Victorian stability." *The Language of Modernism* (Ann Arbor: UMI Research Press, 1989), p. 3. Distinguishing between modernism and irrationalism, he insists that language experiments which

disrupted traditional understanding were meant to rebuild and reshape rather than destroy language.

46. Fussell, *The Great War and Modern Memory,* p. 23.

47. Tate, *Modernism, History, and the First World War,* p. 3. See also Samuel Hynes, *A War Imagined: The First World War and English Culture* (London: Bodley Head, 1990), pp. 337–348.

48. Malcolm Bradbury, "The Denuded Place: War and Form in *Parade's End* and *U.S.A.,*" in *The First World War in Fiction,* ed. Holger Klein (New York: Harper and Row, 1977), p. 193. See also "Modernist Culture in America," special issue of *American Quarterly,* 39, no. 1 (1987); and Malcolm Bradbury and James McFarlane, "The Name and Nature of Modernism," in *Modernism: 1890–1930,* ed. Malcolm Bradbury and James McFarlane (New York: Penguin Books, 1976), pp. 30–35.

49. Jay Winter, *Sites of Memory, Sites of Mourning: The Great War in European Cultural History* (Cambridge: Cambridge University Press, 1995).

50. Malcolm Bradbury and James McFarlane write, "Modernism is our art" because it is the art "of the destruction of civilization and reason in the First World War . . . It is the literature of technology . . . It is the art consequent on . . . the linguistic chaos that ensues when public notions of language have been discredited and when all realities have become subjective fictions" ("The Name and Nature of Modernism," pp. 26–27). See also John Limon, *Writing after War: American War Fiction from Realism to Postmodernism* (New York: Oxford University Press, 1994), p. 106.

51. Max Weber observes: "Our greatest art is intimate and not monumental . . . Today [it is] only within the smallest and intimate circles, in personal human situations, in *pianissimo,* that something is pulsating that corresponds to the prophetic *pneuma,* which in former times swept through the great communities like a firebrand, welding them together" ("Science as a Vocation," p. 155).

52. Sherwood Anderson, *Memoirs: A Critical Edition,* ed. Ray Lewis White (Chapel Hill: University of North Carolina Press, 1969), p. 448. Artist-photographer Paul Strand wrote in 1917: "It seems impossible to get away from the war—it touches everybody now, and everyone finds the same resentment and lack of enthusiasm. The mere idea of trying to create anything nowadays seems so mad." Quoted in Henry Allen, "Strand's Great Moment," *New York Review of Books,* 14 May 1998, p. 26.

53. Fussell, *The Great War and Modern Memory,* p. 144.

54. Gertrude Stein, *The Autobiography of Alice B. Toklas* (New York: Vintage Books, 1990), pp. 3–4.

55. Willa Cather, *On Writing* (New York: Alfred A. Knopf, 1949), p. 31.

56. Jean Schwind, "This is a Frame-Up: Mother Eve in *The Professor's House,*" in *Cather Studies,* ed. Susan J. Rosowski (Lincoln: University of Nebraska Press, 1993), p. 32. For more on Cather's use of framing spaces and how

this relates to Cather's sense of self-fashioning, see Sharon O'Brien, *Willa Cather: The Emerging Voice* (New York: Oxford University Press, 1987), pp. 70–71, 201–202.

57. Claude McKay, *Home to Harlem* (New York: Harper and Brothers, 1928), pp. 155, 267, 331–332, 169–170, 280.

58. Ibid., p. 311.

59. John Crowe Ransom et al., *I'll Take My Stand: The South and the Agrarian Tradition* (New York: Peter Smith, 1951), pp. 137, 125, 212, 19, 343. The writers of *I'll Take My Stand,* including Allen Tate and Robert Penn Warren, repeatedly compare industrial expansion to a hostile military invasion (23, 234). War veteran John Crowe Ransom, for instance, describes industrial production as "an unrelenting war on nature" (7).

60. Virginia Woolf, *Mrs. Dalloway* (New York: Penguin Books, 1992), pp. 33–34, 163–164, 203.

61. William Faulkner, *Flags in the Dust* (New York: Vintage Books, 1974), pp. 280, 367.

62. Ibid., pp. 102, 262–268.

63. Ibid., p. 181.

64. Bayard's car, significantly, is described as "a machine a gentleman of [his father's] day would have scorned" (Faulkner, *Flags in the Dust,* p. 119).

65. John Dos Passos, *The Big Money,* in *U.S.A.* (Boston: Houghton Mifflin Company, 1960), p. 438.

66. Dos Passos, *The Big Money,* p. 288.

67. In her earlier war novel, *One of Ours,* "the machine is a recurrent symbol of disaster," according to E. K. Brown, *Willa Cather: A Critical Biography* (New York: Alfred A. Knopf, 1953), p. 220.

68. Willa Cather, *The Professor's House* (New York: Vintage Books, 1990), pp. 118–119. Cited hereafter in the text.

69. "From her mother Willa Cather learned that being a lady was a performance," Sharon O'Brien writes (*Willa Cather: The Emerging Voice,* p. 38). Analyzing Cather's transformation from tomboy into stereotypical female angel through a paradigmatic photograph, O'Brien comments: "As this photograph suggests, the lady's role is a social construct mothers impose upon daughters: Willa is transformed into a 'little woman' by the proper costume and hairdo" (43).

70. On the conflation of religion and art, see Brown, *Willa Cather: A Critical Biography,* pp. 246–247.

71. David Stouck reads the professor's desire for isolation and finally death as a stand against the corrupt acquisitiveness and materialism of modern society. *Willa Cather's Imagination* (Lincoln: University of Nebraska Press, 1975), pp. 100–103.

72. Sherwood Anderson, *Winesburg, Ohio* (New York: Penguin Books, 1976), p. 67.

73. Faulkner, *Flags in the Dust,* p. 79. See also Graves, *Good-Bye to All That,* p. 295.

74. F. Scott Fitzgerald, "May Day," in *The Short Stories of F. Scott Fitzgerald,* ed. Matthew Bruccoli (New York: Charles Scribner's Sons, 1989), pp. 97–141.

75. John Dos Passos, *Nineteen Nineteen* (New York: Signet Classic, 1969), pp. 407–415.

76. Dos Passos, *The Big Money,* pp. 146, 219–220, 131, 400.

77. Ernest Hemingway, *The Complete Short Stories,* Finca Vigía Edition (New York: Charles Scribner's Sons, 1987), p. 71. Edmund Wilson argues that a fundamental "butchery" links the world of Hemingway's Michigan stories and that of his war stories. *The Wound and the Bow: Seven Studies in Literature* (New York: Oxford University Press, 1947), p. 215.

78. Hemingway, *A Farewell to Arms,* p. 175.

79. Virginia Woolf, *To the Lighthouse* (New York: Harcourt Brace Jovanovich, 1989), p. 83.

80. Ibid., p. 132.

81. Woolf, *Mrs. Dalloway,* p. 97.

82. Virginia Woolf, *Orlando* (New York: Harcourt Brace Jovanovich, 1956), pp. 229–231.

83. Thomas Mann, *The Magic Mountain,* trans. H. T. Lowe-Porter (New York: Alfred A. Knopf, 1977), p. 116.

84. Wyndham Lewis, "The European War and Great Communities," in *Blast 2,* ed. Wyndham Lewis (Santa Barbara: Black Sparrow Press, 1981), p. 16.

85. H. D., *Bid Me to Live (a Madrigal)* (New York: Grove Press, 1960), pp. 39, 46. Regarding sexuality and death in *Bid Me to Live* I am indebted to Claire Tylee, *The Great War and Women's Consciousness* (London: Macmillan, 1990), pp. 231–244.

86. H. D., *Palimpsest* (Carbondale: Southern Illinois University Press, 1968), p. 117.

87. Nathanael West, *Miss Lonelyhearts and The Day of the Locust* (New York: New Directions, 1962), p. 2. Cited hereafter in the text.

88. Hannah Arendt, *The Human Condition* (Chicago: University of Chicago Press, 1989), p. 52.

89. On tools (and in particular the hammer) in flags, see Scarry, *The Body in Pain,* p. 367, n. See also pp. 172–176, for the distinction between tools and weapons that I will utilize throughout this chapter. Note that I will elide Scarry's distinction between the tool and the artifact (310). Hence, by my provisional categorization, tools would include, for example, not only hammers and nails but also shoes, trucks, and boats (tools for enhancing man's power to move), as well as clothes and houses (tools for re-creating the environment).

90. Primo Levi, *The Monkey's Wrench,* trans. William Weaver (New York: Penguin Books, 1995), p. 18.

91. On "earth" and "world," see Frederic Jameson, *Postmodernism, or, The Cultural Logic of Late Capitalism* (Durham: Duke University Press, 1991), p. 7.

92. Martin Heidegger, "The Origin of the Work of Art," in *Martin Heidegger: Basic Writings,* ed. David Farrell Krell (San Francisco: Harper and Row, 1977), pp. 163–164.

93. See Martin Heidegger, *The Basic Problems of Phenomenology,* trans. Albert Hofstadter (Bloomington: Indiana University Press, 1982), pp. 158–161.

94. Scarry, *The Body in Pain,* p. 170.

95. Ernie Pyle, "Battle and Breakout in Normandy," in *Reporting World War II,* vol. 2, *American Journalism, 1944–1946,* ed. Samuel Hynes, Anne Matthews, Nancy Caldwell Sorel, and Roger J. Spiller (New York: Library of America, 1995), p. 198.

96. Ernie Pyle, "Omaha Beach after D-Day," in *Reporting World War II* (see preceding note), p. 149.

97. On the importance during crises of "transitional objects"—small mementos such as letters or photographs—see Judith Lewis Herman, *Trauma and Recovery* (New York: Basic Books, 1992), p. 81.

98. Pyle, "Omaha Beach after D-Day," pp. 149–150.

99. Ernest Hemingway, "Now I Lay Me," in *The Complete Short Stories,* p. 276.

100. Thomas Carlyle, *Past and Present* (New York: New York University Press, 1977), p. 205.

101. Karl Marx, "The *Grundrisse,*" in *The Marx-Engels Reader,* 2d ed., ed. Robert C. Tucker (New York: W. W. Norton, 1978), p. 228.

102. Ibid., p. 320. On the contiguity of labor and consumption, see Arendt, *The Human Condition,* pp. 134–135, 100.

103. For a deep analysis of the concept of work in nineteenth-century British novels, see Elaine Scarry, *Resisting Representation* (New York: Oxford University Press, 1994), pp. 49–90.

104. Heidegger, "The Question Concerning Technology," in *Martin Heidegger: Basic Writings,* ed. David Farrell Krell (San Francisco: Harper and Row, 1977), pp. 314, 315, 308, 283–318.

105. Woolf, *Mrs. Dalloway,* p. 4. For extensive analysis of Virginia Woolf's relationship to war, see *Virginia Woolf and War,* ed. Mark Hussey (Syracuse: Syracuse University Press, 1991).

106. For a trenchant analysis of Jünger's era, see Hannah Arendt, *The Origins of Totalitarianism* (New York: Harcourt Brace, 1973), pp. 326–332.

107. See Josephine O'Brien Schaeffer, "The Great War and 'This Late Age of Experience' in Cather and Woolf," in Hussey, *Virginia Woolf and War.*

108. Dos Passos, *The Big Money,* p. 6.

109. Walt Whitman, *Prose Works 1892, Specimen Days,* ed. Floyd Stovall, vol. 1 (New York: New York University Press, 1963), p. 116.

110. Ernest Hemingway, *Men at War,* ed. Ernest Hemingway (New York: Crown, 1955), Introduction, p. xvi.

111. Hemingway, *Men at War,* p. xvii.
112. Jünger, "Total Mobilization," pp. 129, 137. On Hemingway and the uniqueness of modern technological war, see Stanley Cooperman, *World War I and the American Novel* (Baltimore: Johns Hopkins University Press, 1967), pp. 181–206, 214–220.
113. Hemingway, *A Farewell to Arms,* pp. 3–4. Cited hereafter in the text.
114. For a detailed analysis of the relationship between pain and consciousness, see Scarry, *The Body in Pain,* pp. 33–38.
115. Mechanics are trained to be skilled with machinery, but frequently in Hemingway's stories their inability to apply these skills to war is emphasized. In "Night before Battle," for instance, Hemingway writes: "They're mechanics, but they couldn't learn to soldier" (*The Complete Short Stories,* p. 443).
116. Martin Heidegger, *Being and Time,* trans. John Macquarrie and Edward Robinson (New York: Harper and Row, 1962), pp. 100, 153–163. George Steiner writes that *Being and Time* is in an important way a product of the catastrophe of World War I (*Martin Heidegger,* pp. vii–xii, 75–76).
117. For a related structural analysis tracing the novel's movement between "regenerative" and "destructive" cycles in nature, see Michael Reynolds, *Hemingway's First War* (Princeton: Princeton University Press, 1976), pp. 263–270.
118. Jack London, "War," in *Jack London: Novels and Stories,* ed. Donald Pizer (New York: Library of America, 1982), pp. 914–919.
119. For the German reaction to the diminution of agency in World War I, see Hafkesbrink, *Unknown Germany,* pp. 68–70.
120. John Keegan, *The Face of Battle* (New York: Vintage Books, 1977), p. 279.
121. Homer, *The Iliad,* trans. Richmond Lattimore (Chicago: University of Chicago Press, 1951), p. 420.
122. Hemingway, *Complete Short Stories,* pp. 439, 438.
123. Ibid., pp. 444, 442.
124. W. H. R. Rivers, "Freud's Psychology of the Unconscious," *Lancet,* 16 June 1917, p. 914. G. Elliot Smith and T. H. Pear, also physicians from the World War I era, explain that doctors can intervene in the early stages of war neurosis by helping the soldier "correctly to interpret his unusual experiences by explaining to him their origin and nature." *Shell Shock and Its Lessons* (Manchester: University of Manchester Press, 1917), p. 23. They emphasize that a contest of stories determines treatment: the soldier's "I am going mad" against the doctor's "You suffer from a temporary and common condition that is unrelated to your essential character" (16–25). For more on the importance of the talking cure, see pp. 30–31, 44–46. In casework with Holocaust survivors, Henry Krystal observes that patients were most effectively treatable "if they were especially endowed with literary or artistic talents that permitted them to develop or reconstruct damaged functions." "Trauma and Aging," in *Trauma: Explorations in Memory,* ed. Cathy Caruth (Baltimore: Johns Hopkins University Press, 1995), p. 97.
125. Hemingway, *Complete Short Stories,* pp. 306–307.

126. On aphonia (also indexed as mutism) produced by war trauma in World War I, see E. E. Southard, *Shell-Shock and Other Neuropsychiatric Problems Presented in Five Hundred Eighty-Nine Case Histories from the War Literature* (Boston: William Leonard, 1919), *passim*.

127. In "Night before Battle," Hemingway mocks such aestheticization in the character of a flyer who describes opening parachutes as "big beautiful morning glories" (*Complete Short Stories*, p. 456).

128. On a poem by Paul Celan, Shoshana Felman writes: "The violence is all the more obscene by being thus *aestheticized* and by aestheticizing its own dehumanization, by transforming its own murderous perversity into the cultural sophistication and the cultivated trances of a hedonistic art performance." Shoshana Felman and Dori Laub, *Testimony: Crises of Witnessing in Literature, Psychoanalysis, and History* (New York: Routledge, 1992), p. 31. See also Hayden White, "Historical Emplotment and the Problem of Truth," in *Probing the Limits of Representation: Nazism and the "Final Solution,"* ed. Saul Friedlander (Cambridge, Mass.: Harvard University Press, 1992), p. 40.

129. Theodor Adorno, "Commitment," in *The Essential Frankfurt School Reader,* ed. Andrew Arato and Eike Gebhardt, intro. Paul Piccone (New York: Continuum, 1982), pp. 312–313. On Adorno, see Felman and Laub, *Testimony*, pp. 33–34.

130. Simone de Beauvoir, *The Ethics of Ambiguity,* trans. Bernard Frechtman (New York: Citadel Press, 1994), p. 77.

131. Cathy Caruth, "Recapturing the Past: Introduction," in *Trauma: Explorations in Memory,* ed. Caruth (Baltimore: Johns Hopkins University Press, 1995), pp. 153–154. The literature of atrocity, John Treat explains, suffers "a nagging doubt that it may somehow constitute a moral betrayal." The "pleasure" of form, he argues, "is to be distrusted: a belief in the human instinct for form may make us think that the well-executed lyric or novel can restore coherence, through its own internal order, to even a disintegrating world." *Writing Ground Zero: Japanese Literature and the Atomic Bomb* (Chicago: University of Chicago Press, 1995), pp. 43, 39; see also pp. 40–41, 81. Claude Lanzmann argues that "there is an absolute obscenity in the very project of understanding." "The Obscenity of Understanding," in *Trauma: Explorations in Memory,* ed. Cathy Caruth (Baltimore: Johns Hopkins University Press, 1995), p. 204.

132. Robert Lewis argues in *Hemingway on Love* (Austin: University of Texas Press, 1965), pp. 37–54, that *A Farewell to Arms* is saturated with images of camouflage (deceit, disguise, misreading) and that Frederic's disillusionment with war propaganda is doubled in his deeper disillusionment with the false promises of romantic love.

133. For an explanation of how they become interchangeable, see Scarry, *The Body in Pain,* p. 174.

134. Ira Elliott, "*A Farewell to Arms* and Hemingway's Crisis of Masculine

Values," *Lit: Literature Interpretation Theory,* 4, no. 4 (1993): 297–304. I am also indebted to Elliott for his analysis of Rinaldi's gloves.

135. Twentieth Century Fox, 1969.
136. Pat Barker, *The Eye in the Door* (New York: Plume, 1995), p. 164.
137. Keegan, *The Face of Battle,* p. 266.
138. For similar human-other conflations, see pp. 194, 232, 118.
139. For a more thorough analysis of Hemingway's conflation of childbirth and war, see Gayle Whittier, "Childbirth, War, and Creativity in *A Farewell to Arms,*" *Lit: Literature Interpretation Theory,* 3, no. 4 (1992): 253–270.
140. The novel's climax may also be read as the silencing of the feminine voice, a male author's ritual obliteration of the possibility of female creativity (see Whittier, "Childbirth, War, and Creativity," pp. 253–270). Catherine could be considered a model of a threatening female independence; but her role as nurse, as selfless caregiver and natural other, could be perceived as playing into the essentialized, stereotypical views of women that are prevalent in war writings and war culture. For trenchant feminist criticism of the treatment of Catherine, see Judith Fetterley, *The Resisting Reader: A Feminist Approach to American Fiction* (Bloomington: Indiana University Press, 1978), pp. 46–71; James McKelly, "From Whom the Bull Flows: Hemingway in Parody," *American Literature,* 61, no. 4 (1989): 554–556; Sandra Whipple Spanier, "Hemingway's Unknown Soldier: Catherine Barkley, the Critics, and the Great War," in *New Essays on "A Farewell to Arms,"* ed. Scott Donaldson (Cambridge: Cambridge University Press, 1990), pp. 75–108. See also Cooperman, *World War I and the American Novel,* pp. 181–182. For a detailed analysis of the role of women in war, see Jean Bethke Elshtain, *Women and War* (New York: Basic Books, 1987).

3. Freedom, Luck, and Catastrophe

1. Kant famously wrote in "On a Supposed Right to Lie Because of Philanthropic Concerns" that "to be truthful (honest) in all declarations is, therefore, a sacred and unconditionally commanding law of reason that admits of no expediency whatsoever." *Ethical Philosophy,* 2d ed., trans. James W. Ellington, intro. Warner A. Wick (Indianapolis: Hackett, 1994), p. 164.
2. I am thankful to Christine Korsgaard for her formulation of causality in Kant's thought.
3. Kant, *Grounding for the Metaphysics of Morals,* in *Ethical Philosophy,* p. 26.
4. Carl von Clausewitz, *On War,* trans. Michael Howard and Peter Paret (Princeton: Princeton University Press, 1976), p. 86.
5. Ibid., p. 85.
6. Thucydides, *The Peloponnesian War,* trans. John H. Finley Jr. (New York: Modern Library, 1951), pp. 90, 88.
7. Bao Ninh, *The Sorrow of War,* trans. Vo Bang Thanh, Phan Thanh Hao,

Katerina Pierce, and Frank Palmos (London: Secker and Warburg, 1993), pp. 6–11. "Grinker and Spiegel observed that soldiers in wartime responded to the losses and injuries within their group with diminished confidence in their own ability to make plans and take initiative, with increased superstitious and magical thinking, and with greater reliance on lucky charms and omens." Judith Herman, *Trauma and Recovery* (New York: Basic Books, 1992), p. 46.

8. Clausewitz, *On War,* p. 119.

9. That faith is "true and adorable," Oliver Wendell Holmes writes, "which leads a soldier to throw away his life in obedience to a blindly accepted duty, in a cause which he little understands, in a plan of campaign of which he has no notion, under tactics of which he does not see the use." *Speeches by Oliver Wendell Holmes Jr.* (Boston: Little, Brown, 1934), p. 59. Charles Royster comments: "Holmes's metaphor—an uncomprehending soldier acting blindly in the incomprehensible battle—was the antithesis of narrative, the negation of a clear story of events subject to comprehension and control." *The Destructive War* (New York: Alfred A. Knopf, 1991), p. 282.

10. Siegfried Sassoon, *Memoirs of an Infantry Officer* (New York: Collier Books, 1969), p. 50. It is important to maintain the distinction between contingency (that is, luck or the unpredictability of consequences) and constraint (the abridgment of freedom). The two intersect most interestingly in the notion of the contingency of self. In recognizing the luck that has produced one as one is or, rather, in perceiving the givens of the self (one's socioeconomic position, health, or temperament), one sees the degree to which the will is not free to be anything other than what it is. Even if external environmental constraints are not fully determinative, might not internal, constitutive constraints be? According to Kant, it is impossible to prove that they are not. He asserts, however, that while freedom can never be established as a certainty and may indeed seem impossible, it is nonetheless the only conceivable self-perception for us to act upon, particularly in our capacity as moral actors (*Grounding for the Metaphysics of Morals,* pp. 49–61). Indeed, it is the perception we all in fact *do* act upon (the "experience" of freedom in making decisions) despite any belief we may have about our determinedness (the sociological knowledge of our constraint). As Christine Korsgaard writes: "In the phenomenal world, because it is temporal and causality is temporal succession according to a rule, every event has a cause, and there can be no freedom. But the noumenal world does not exist in time and a spontaneous causality is possible, though not knowable, in it. This leaves room for belief in the freedom of the will, which is the foundation of morality." *Creating the Kingdom of Ends* (Cambridge: Cambridge University Press, 1996), p. 11; see also pp. 159–229. I want to invert the order of this free will problem. The initiating question is thus not whether we are free but whether moral value is determined by unconditioned intention or contingent consequences. For thinkers like Kant who argue that morality is the structure of reason and therefore the means of

achieving freedom, accepting the latter answer—that moral value is determined from the outside—would mean that not only morality but also freedom does not exist in any relevant sense. Self-preservation in war is thus as much ontological as it is physical.

11. Hannah Arendt, "Lying in Politics," in *Crises of the Republic* (San Diego: Harcourt Brace Jovanovich, 1972), p. 12.

12. Immanuel Kant, *Critique of Practical Reason,* 3d ed., trans. Lewis White Beck (New York: Macmillan, 1993), p. 167.

13. Walt Whitman, "Notes Left Over," *Walt Whitman: Complete Poetry and Collected Prose,* ed. Justin Kaplan (New York: Library of America, 1982), p. 1073.

14. As Christine Korsgaard puts it: "The moral law does not impose a constraint on the will, it merely says what it has to do in order to be an autonomous will at all. It has to choose a law" (*Creating the Kingdom of Ends,* p. 166).

15. Whitman, "Notes Left Over," p. 1073.

16. Kant, *Grounding for the Metaphysics of Morals,* p. 39; see also pp. 12–13, 43; Kant, *Critique of Practical Reason,* pp. 28, 64, 167. See also Thomas Nagel, *The View from Nowhere* (New York: Oxford University Press, 1986), pp. 134–137; Korsgaard, *Creating the Kingdom of Ends,* pp. 159–187; and Charles Taylor, *Sources of the Self: The Making of the Modern Identity* (Cambridge, Mass.: Harvard University Press, 1989), pp. 363–367.

17. Kant, *Grounding for the Metaphysics of Morals,* pp. 14–15.

18. Kant, *Critique of Practical Reason,* p. 169.

19. Korsgaard, *Creating the Kingdom of Ends,* p. 176.

20. For the seminal articles on moral luck, see Thomas Nagel, *Mortal Questions* (Cambridge: Cambridge University Press, 1979), pp. 24–38; and Bernard Williams, *Moral Luck* (Cambridge: Cambridge University Press, 1981). The question of moral luck is especially urgent during war. "But one has to win out," writes Simone de Beauvoir. "Defeat would change the murders and destruction into unjustified outrage, since they would have been carried out in vain; but victory gives meaning and utility to all the misfortunes which have helped bring it about." *The Ethics of Ambiguity,* trans. Bernard Frechtman (New York: Citadel Press, 1994), p. 111. Relatedly, see Hannah Arendt, "Lying in Politics," and Jean-Paul Sartre, *The War Diaries: November 1939–March 1940,* trans. Quintin Hoare (New York: Pantheon Books, 1984), p. 30. For a compelling analysis of the relationship between luck and Kantian ethics, see Wai Chee Dimock, *Residues of Justice: Literature, Law, Philosophy* (Berkeley: University of California Press, 1996), pp. 96–140.

21. Kant, *Critique of Practical Reason,* p. 18; *Grounding for the Metaphysics of Morals,* pp. 25–27. On *techné* and ethics, see Martha Nussbaum, *The Fragility of Goodness: Luck and Ethics in Greek Tragedy and Philosophy* (Cambridge: Cambridge University Press, 1986), pp. 86–121.

22. John Dewey, *Experience and Nature* (Chicago: Open Court, 1926), p. 44.

23. Ernest Hemingway, *Death in the Afternoon* (New York: Simon and Schuster, 1996), p. 232. On Hemingway's ambient blending of rules, skill, morality, and beauty, see pp. 159, 21.

24. Ernest Hemingway, "How We Came to Paris," in *Reporting World War II*, vol. 2, *American Journalism, 1944–1946*, ed. Samuel Hynes, Anne Matthews, Nancy Caldwell Sorel, and Roger J. Spiller (New York: Library of America, 1995), p. 245.

25. Ralph Waldo Emerson, *Essays and Lectures* (New York: Library of America, 1984), p. 16. See also Taylor, *Sources of the Self*, pp. 422–423.

26. Beauvoir, *The Ethics of Ambiguity*, p. 24.

27. A. E. Hotchner, *Papa Hemingway* (New York: Random House, 1966), pp. 50–51. On Hemingway and Catholicism, see James Mellow, *A Life without Consequences* (New York: Houghton Mifflin, 1992), pp. 323–324.

28. Robert Penn Warren, "Ernest Hemingway," in *Ernest Hemingway*, ed. Harold Bloom (New York: Chelsea House, 1985), pp. 54, 47, 59.

29. The idea of "the hero and the code" in Hemingway's fiction received its most characteristic expression in the work of Philip Young. The code, as developed by precontemporary critics, is a wartime ideal that demands self-denial and control in the face of adversity. Young argued that all of Hemingway's fiction, even his explicitly nonwar work, is best understood as a patterned reaction to war trauma. The autobiographical moment of wounding in *A Farewell to Arms* is the determinative moment that establishes the basic design for his subsequent characters and fiction. See Philip Young, *Ernest Hemingway, a Reconsideration* (University Park: Pennsylvania State University Press, 1966). Biographer Kenneth Lynn has attacked this war thesis, arguing that Hemingway's troubled relationship with his mother was far more important to his fiction than his combat experience. *Hemingway* (Cambridge, Mass.: Harvard University Press, 1987), pp. 103–107, 386; for a response to Lynn and a qualified defense of the war thesis, see Matthew Stewart, "Ernest Hemingway and World War I: Combating Recent Psychobiographical Reassessments, Restoring the War," *Papers on Language and Literature*, 36, no. 2 (2000): 198–217; and Malcolm Cowley, "Hemingway's Wound—and Its Consequences for American Literature," in *The Pushcart Prize, X: Best of the Small Presses*, ed. Bill Henderson (New York: Pushcart Press, 1985), pp. 32–50. While a plausible argument can be made identifying a set of characteristics common to most of Hemingway's protagonists, attempting to identify a single psychological source for the phenomenon is perhaps impossible. Hemingway, for that matter, was unusually deeply disturbed by literary critics like Young, who, he believed, minimized the uniqueness of each of his works while in search of an overarching theory of imaginative cause. For my purposes, it is not necessary to identify a "source" for the code hero, or to argue that it was necessarily the war that generated this ideal of conduct. It suffices to say that the conceptual space of war, with its particular set of moral risks and imperatives, was

especially well suited to the creation and artistic elaboration of characters thus constituted. For more on control and value in Hemingway's work, see Nancy Comley, "Hemingway: The Economics of Survival," *Novel,* 12, no. 3 (1979): 244–253.

30. Calculation, as a utilitarian balancing of positive and negative situational quanta in the effort to maximize a goal, is replaced by Kant with judgment—that is, with the capacity, not susceptible to rulelike formulation, to apply a priori rules wisely in the effort to embody an ideal. Immanuel Kant, *Critique of Pure Reason,* trans. Norman Kemp Smith (New York: St. Martin's Press, 1965), pp. 177–179.

31. Kant implies the necessity of taking responsibility for consequences when one has chosen to act independently of the law in "On Our Supposed Right to Lie Because of Philanthropic Concerns," in *Ethical Philosophy,* p. 164. Kant at the same time acknowledges that the deontological moral system is not impenetrable by the extreme contingency of consequences. Christine Korsgaard writes: "If the motivating thought of morality is that freedom means that we can make a difference in the world, but we then find that we have no control over the form this difference ultimately takes, then the motivating thought is genuinely threatened." Kant overcomes the problem of the unpredictability of consequences with a gesture of faith in God and the Highest Good, which causes all to work for the best in the end (*Creating the Kingdom of Ends,* pp. 169–170).

32. Dewey, *Experience and Nature,* pp. 41, 44.

33. For a negative moral analysis of Frederic, see Scott Donaldson, *By Force of Will* (New York: Viking, 1977), pp. 151–161; and Donaldson, "Frederic Henry's Escape and the Pose of Passivity," in *Hemingway: A Revaluation,* ed. Donald Noble (New York: Whitston, 1983), pp. 180–185. For an alternative appraisal, see Charles J. Nolan Jr., "Shooting the Sergeant: Frederic Henry's Puzzling Action," *College Literature,* 11, no. 3 (1984): 269–275.

34. On the reversal of roles between Frederic and Catherine, see Michael Reynolds, *Hemingway's First War* (Princeton: Princeton University Press, 1976), pp. 253–259. Kenneth Lynn argues that the two protagonists represent "two halves of an androgynous whole" (*Hemingway,* p. 389). Relatedly, on androgyny in Hemingway's fiction, see Gerald Kennedy, "Hemingway's Gender Trouble," *American Literature,* 63, no. 2 (1991): 187–207.

35. Max Weber, *From Max Weber: Essays in Sociology,* ed. H. H. Gerth and C. Wright Mills (New York: Oxford University Press, 1946), p. 120.

36. John Rawls, preface, *A Theory of Justice* (Cambridge, Mass.: Harvard University Press, 1971), pp. vii–viii. In this chapter I will attempt to illuminate Dewey's ethics with reference to utilitarianism; I do not wish, however, to conflate the two. Dewey's ethics shares key features with utilitarianism but also differs in crucial ways, most notably in its rejection of ultimate ends or singular guiding principles.

37. Against the model of morality as rules, John Dewey writes: "Morals is not a catalogue of acts nor a set of rules to be applied like drugstore prescriptions or cook-book recipes." *The Middle Works, 1899–1924,* 15 vols., ed. Jo Ann Boydston (Carbondale: Southern Illinois University Press, 1976–1983), 12:177. See also John Dewey, *The Quest for Certainty: A Study of the Relation of Knowledge and Action* (New York: Minton, Balch, 1929), pp. 277–278. On Dewey's belief that an absolutist conception of ethical laws deprives the moral life of freedom, see Steven C. Rockefeller, *John Dewey: Religious Faith and Democratic Humanism* (New York: Columbia University Press, 1991), pp. 418–419; see also Jennifer Welchman, *Dewey's Ethical Thought* (Ithaca: Cornell University Press, 1995), p. 155. In a critique of Kant, Dewey writes that with naturalism "the standard of judgment has been transferred from antecedents to consequents, from inert dependence upon the past to intentional construction of a future . . . The old center was mind knowing by means of an equipment of powers complete within itself, and merely exercised upon an antecedent external material equally complete in itself. The new center is indefinite interactions taking place within a course of nature which is not fixed and complete, but which is capable of direction to new and different results through the mediation of intentional operations. Neither self nor world, neither soul nor nature (in the sense of something isolated and finished in its isolation) is the center, any more than either earth or sun is the absolute center of a single universal and necessary frame of reference" (*The Quest for Certainty,* pp. 289–291).

38. Rockefeller, *John Dewey,* pp. 433. See also John Dewey, *The Later Works,* vol. 13, ed. Jo Ann Boydston (Carbondale: Southern Illinois University Press, 1988), pp. 41–42.

39. Dewey, *The Middle Works, 1899–1924,* 14:170.

40. Dewey, *The Middle Works, 1899–1924,* 5:194–195. See also Welchman, *Dewey's Ethical Thought,* pp. 178, 156; Rockefeller, *John Dewey,* p. 430. On Dewey's belief that such choosing of the self is the basis and experience of freedom, see Rockefeller, *John Dewey,* p. 432.

41. Rockefeller, *John Dewey,* pp. 412–414.

42. Ibid., p. 415.

43. Ibid., p. 420.

44. Margaret Urban Walker writes in a critique of universalist methodology: "Adequacy of moral understanding decreases as its form approaches generality through abstraction. A view consistent with this will not be one of individuals standing singly before the impersonal dicta of Morality, but of human beings connected in various ways and at various depths responding to each other by engaging together in a search for shareable interpretations of their responsibilities, and/or bearable resolutions to their moral binds. These interpretations and resolutions will be constrained not only by how well they protect goods we can share, but also by how well they preserve the very human connections that make the shared process necessary and possi-

ble." "Moral Understandings: Alternative 'Epistemology' for Feminist Ethics," in *Justice and Care: Essential Readings in Feminist Ethics,* ed. Virginia Held (Boulder: Westview Press, 1995), pp. 144, 139–152. See also Joan C. Tronto, "Women and Caring: What Can Feminists Learn about Morality from Caring?" in the same volume, pp. 109–110, 101–116.

45. Carol Gilligan and others have discussed the thesis that such distinctions in moral thinking and practice correspond to traditionally constructed gender divisions. See Virginia Held, *Feminist Morality: Transforming Culture, Society, and Politics* (Chicago: University of Chicago Press, 1993); Held, *Justice and Care* (cited in previous note); and Seyla Benhabib, "The Generalized and the Concrete Other: The Kohlberg-Gilligan Controversy and Feminist Theory," *Feminism as Critique: On the Politics of Gender,* ed. Seyla Benhabib and Drucilla Cornell (Minneapolis: University of Minnesota Press, 1987), pp. 77–95.

46. For Dewey on responsibility, see Rockefeller, *John Dewey,* p. 420.

47. Geoffrey Harpham discusses how ethical models that associate disinterested rationality and an interest in duty with men, while associating inclination with women, support a sexist paradigm. *Getting It Right* (Chicago: University of Chicago Press, 1992), pp. 15–17. Sandra Gilbert and Susan Gubar point to the economic and social independence women began to acquire with the war, and how this was represented in fiction by men like Hemingway as a "sinister" sexuality and a "disturbing power." *No Man's Land: The Place of the Woman Writer in the Twentieth Century,* vol. 2 (New Haven: Yale University Press, 1989), p. 287. Combining these two arguments, some might propose to read *A Farewell to Arms* as a depiction of how newly liberated women were reabsorbed into the dominant patriarchal paradigm through (socially programmed) morality as self-construction, through morality as gendering.

48. Many critics have commented on Catherine's role as moral teacher for Frederic. See Robert W. Lewis, "Manners and Morals in *A Farewell to Arms,*" in *Hemingway up in Michigan: Perspectives,* ed. Frederic J. Svoboda and Joseph J. Waldmeir (East Lansing: Michigan State University Press, 1995), p. 158; and James Phelan, "The Concept of Voice, the Voices of Frederic Henry, and the Structure of *A Farewell to Arms,*" in *Hemingway: Essays of Reassessment,* ed. Frank Scafella (New York: Oxford University Press, 1991), p. 226.

49. Williams, *Moral Luck,* p. 28. For Dewey and his collaborator J. H. Tufts on the ill luck of unforeseen consequences, and the responsibility consequentialists must take for error, see Welchman, *Dewey's Ethical Thought,* pp. 180–181.

50. The disproportion between cause and effect is an essential feature of trauma. Recovery is a matter of reestablishing the link between the two. Writes Henry Krystal: "The heart of the work of psychoanalysis [is] . . . the acceptance of the inevitability and necessity of every event which was part

of one's life as having been *justified by its causes.*" "Trauma and Aging," in *Trauma: Explorations in Memory,* ed. Cathy Caruth (Baltimore: Johns Hopkins University Press, 1995), p. 83. For an analysis of anomie in *A Farewell to Arms,* see Gerry Brenner, *Concealments in Hemingway's Works* (Columbus: Ohio State University Press, 1983), pp. 27–41. See relatedly John Limon, *Writing after War: American War Fiction from Realism to Postmodernism* (New York: Oxford University Press, 1994), pp. 95–98.

51. D. A. Miller theorizes the nature of teleological narration thus: "Once the ending is enshrined as an all-embracing cause in which the elements of a narrative find their ultimate justification, it is difficult for analysis to assert anything short of total coherence." *Narrative and Its Discontents: Problems of Closure in the Traditional Novel* (Princeton: Princeton University Press, 1981), p. xiii.

52. As Derek Parfit has noted, consequentialist moral systems can vary widely because they can appeal to a variety of guiding principles. The relevant consequence in moral evaluation could be happiness, equality, the avoidance of sin—some consequentialist principles could even, Parfit explains, refer to past events, to "consequences" that precede the action under investigation. *Reasons and Persons* (Oxford: Clarendon Press, 1984), p. 26. Consequentialism as a philosophical category is supple and broad; as a term used in this chapter it is limited: it fills in a particular space in Hemingway's moral dichotomy.

53. See Harold Larrabee, "Naturalism in America," in *Naturalism and the Human Spirit,* ed. Yervant Krikorian (New York: Columbia University Press, 1944), p. 351.

54. Ralph Barton Perry, *Realms of Value: A Critique of Human Civilization* (Cambridge, Mass.: Harvard University Press, 1954), pp. 2–3. Dewey distinguishes his theory of value from prevailing views by emphasizing the difference between the "valued" and the "valuable." Something that is in mere social fact valued can be deemed normatively valuable only after withstanding a particular sort of naturalistic scrutiny (that is, a reflective inquiry modeled on the scientific method that weighs the utility of consequences) (*The Quest for Certainty,* pp. 254–286).

55. Perry, *Realms of Value,* pp. 12, 121.

56. Ibid., pp. 92, 104–106. For Dewey's view on the constitutive role of social integration in moral agency, see Welchman, *Dewey's Ethical Thought,* pp. 164–167.

57. On Dewey's pragmatic version of naturalist consequentialism, see Welchman, *Dewey's Ethical Thought,* pp. 163–164; see also Rockefeller, *John Dewey,* pp. 404–410, 418.

58. Perry, *Realms of Value,* p. 121.

59. Ernest Hemingway, *The Complete Short Stories,* Finca Vigía Edition (New York: Charles Scribner's Sons, 1987), p. 113.

60. T. S. Eliot, "Gerontion," in *The Complete Poems and Plays: 1909–1950*

(New York: Harcourt Brace Jovanovich, 1980), p. 22. On "Gerontion" and the war, see Lynndall Gordon, *T. S. Eliot: An Imperfect Life* (New York: W. W. Norton, 1998), p. 167.

61. Williams, *Moral Luck,* pp. 29–30.

62. Ibid., p. 30.

63. For more against consequentialism, see Bernard Williams, "A Critique of Utilitarianism," in J. J. C. Smart and Bernard Williams, *Utilitarianism: For and Against* (Cambridge: Cambridge University Press, 1973), pp. 77–150.

64. See Sandra Whipple Spanier, "Hemingway's Unknown Soldier: Catherine Barkley, the Critics, and the Great War," in *New Essays on "A Farewell to Arms,"* ed. Scott Donaldson (Cambridge: Cambridge University Press, 1990), p. 76.

65. According to Kant, "perfect" duties forbid us to "subordinate the value of our person and qualities to any casual purpose" (Warner Wick, Introduction, *Ethical Philosophy,* p. li).

66. Rawls, *A Theory of Justice,* p. 27.

67. Randolph S. Bourne, *War and the Intellectuals, Essays 1915–1919,* ed. Carl Resek (New York: Harper and Row, 1964), p. 61. See also Harold Stearns, *Liberalism in America: Its Origin, Its Temporary Collapse, Its Future* (New York: Boni and Liveright, 1919), p. 184. For more on Bourne's critique of Dewey's instrumentalism, see Rockefeller, *John Dewey,* pp. 304–305.

68. William Poundstone, *Prisoner's Dilemma* (New York: Doubleday, 1992).

69. Parfit, *Reasons and Persons,* pp. 41, 42, 23, 28.

70. Welchman, *Dewey's Ethical Thought,* p. 201; see also pp. 184, 200. See also Rockefeller, *John Dewey,* pp. 291–294. For Dewey's writing on the war, see Dewey, *The Middle Works, 1899–1924,* 10:211–215, 260–264. Ernest Hemingway called the first World War "the most colossal murderous, mismanaged butchery that has ever taken place on earth." *Men at War,* ed. Ernest Hemingway (New York: Crown, 1955), Introduction, p. xiii.

71. Alan Ryan, *John Dewey* (New York: W. W. Norton, 1995), pp. 191–192.

72. See *The Ethics of War: Bertrand Russell and Ralph Barton Perry on World War I,* ed. Charles Chatfield (New York: Garland, 1972), Ralph Barton Perry, "What Is Worth Fighting For?" pp. 830, 827, 308–309.

73. Ibid., pp. 831, 830, 826.

74. Perry writes: "The moment any human achievement of body, mind or character is taken to be good, then war of self-preservation is in principle justified." "Non-Resistance and the Present War, a Reply to Mr. Russell," in Chatfield, *The Ethics of War,* p. 310); see also Perry, "What Is Worth Fighting For?" pp. 826, 830. Bertrand Russell, "The War and Non-Resistance," in Chatfield, *The Ethics of War,* p. 26.

75. Bourne, *War and the Intellectuals,* p. 56 (Dewey used his influence to have Bourne excluded from both publications; see Ryan, *John Dewey,* p. 203). On Dewey's "relativism," see Rockefeller, *John Dewey,* pp. 284–285, 409–410.

76. Stearns, *Liberalism in America*, pp. 178–189. For more on Bourne, see Welchman, *Dewey's Ethical Thought*, p. 200.
77. George Edward Moore, *Principia Ethica* (Cambridge: Cambridge University Press, 1954), pp. 10, 14, 40.
78. Ibid., p. 15.
79. Ibid., pp. 15–17. I am indebted to Kai Nielsen for my characterization of naturalism.
80. Ibid., p. 9.
81. H. J. Paton, "The Alleged Independence of Goodness," in *The Philosophy of George Moore*, ed. P. A. Schilpp (New York: Tudor, 1952), p. 113. For Perry's response to Moore, see *General Theory of Value* (New York: Longmans, Green, 1926), pp. 127–137.
82. Beauvoir, *The Ethics of Ambiguity*, p. 8.
83. Ibid., p. 129.

4. Trauma and the Structure of Social Norms

1. Erich Maria Remarque, *All Quiet on the Western Front*, trans. A. W. Wheen (New York: Fawcett Crest, 1958), p. 13.
2. Ibid., p. 173.
3. For a socioliterary analysis of language's failure to signify in Hemingway's fiction, see Robert Weimann, "Text, Author-Function, and Appropriation in Modern Narrative: Toward a Sociology of Representation," *Critical Inquiry*, 14, no. 3 (1998): 431–447.
4. Elaine Scarry, *The Body in Pain: The Making and the Unmaking of the World* (New York: Oxford University Press, 1985), p. 133.
5. Mikhail Bakhtin, *The Dialogic Imagination: Four Essays by M. M. Bakhtin*, trans. Caryl Emerson and Michael Holquist (Austin: University of Texas Press, 1981), p. 418.
6. Ernst Jünger, *The Storm of Steel*, trans. Basil Creighton (New York: Howard Fertig, 1975), pp. 314–315, 77, 135, 230.
7. John Dos Passos, *Nineteen Nineteen* (New York: Signet Classic, 1969), p. 153.
8. Carl von Clausewitz, *On War*, trans. Michael Howard and Peter Paret (Princeton: Princeton University Press, 1976), pp. 76, 152, 140. See also pp. 214–215, 27–40. For the original German, see *Vom Kriege* (Bonn: Ferd. Dümmlers Verlag, 1980), p. 289.
9. Wolfgang Kayser, *The Grotesque in Art and Literature*, trans. Ulrich Weisstein (New York: Columbia University Press, 1957), pp. 19–99, 67. See also Mikhail Bakhtin, *Rabelais and His World*, trans. Helene Iswolsky (Bloomington: Indiana University Press, 1984), pp. 1–58, 303–367.
10. Thomas Mann, *The Magic Mountain*, trans. H. T. Lowe-Porter (New York: Alfred A. Knopf, 1977), pp. 479, 495, 484–485.
11. Geoffrey Galt Harpham, *On the Grotesque* (Princeton: Princeton University Press, 1982), pp. xx, 10.

12. Bakhtin, *Rabelais and His World,* pp. 26–27.

13. Ibid., e.g., pp. 276, 273–277.

14. Tomas Venclova, "The Pluralist," *New Republic,* 18 May 1998, p. 30. See Katerina Clark and Michael Holquist, *Mikhail Bakhtin* (Cambridge, Mass.: Harvard University Press, 1984), pp. 306–312. For a thorough history of Bakhtin's reception in ethical and political criticism, see Caryl Emerson, *The First Hundred Years of Mikhail Bakhtin* (Princeton: Princeton University Press, 1997).

15. Kayser, *The Grotesque in Art and Literature,* pp. 130, 142.

16. In theorizing the grotesque, Harpham draws repeatedly upon images of war to explain what is at stake in this perplexing generic phenomenon (*On the Grotesque,* pp. 7, 9, and *passim*). The grotesque's relationship to war is also seen in the work of philosophers and sociologists who, according to Dennis Wrong, reflexively conflate epistemological disorder with war. *The Problem of Order: What Unites and Divides Society* (Cambridge, Mass.: Harvard University Press, 1994), pp. 81–82. See also Robert Davis, *Whitman and the Romance of Medicine* (Berkeley: University of California Press, 1997), pp. 1–8, 70–71.

17. Samuel P. Huntington, *The Soldier and the State* (Cambridge, Mass.: Harvard University Press, 1985), p. 29. The primary thesis of Edward Luttwak's analysis of policy and practice in war is that strategy induces "*the coming together and even the reversal of opposites.*" *Strategy: The Logic of War and Peace* (Cambridge, Mass.: Harvard University Press, 1987), p. 5.

18. Judith Herman describes the psychic experiences generated by trauma as "grotesque." *Trauma and Recovery* (New York: Basic Books, 1992), p. 146; see also p. 41. Sigmund Freud, *Beyond the Pleasure Principle,* trans. James Strachey (New York: W. W. Norton, 1961), p. 23; Shoshana Felman and Dori Laub, *Testimony: Crises of Witnessing in Literature, Psychoanalysis, and History* (New York: Routledge, 1992), p. 69. On the binary structures associated with accounts of trauma, see *Trauma: Explorations in Memory,* ed. Cathy Caruth (Baltimore: Johns Hopkins University Press, 1995), including Krystal, "Trauma and Aging," p. 85; Cathy Caruth, "Recapturing the Past: Introduction," p. 152; Bessel van der Kolk and Onno van der Hart, "The Intrusive Past," p. 166; and Robert Lifton's explanation of identity doubling, "Interview," p. 137. See also Herman, *Trauma and Recovery,* p. 87, and L. L. Langer, *Holocaust Testimonies: The Ruins of Memory* (New Haven: Yale University Press, 1991), p. 95.

19. Scarry, *The Body in Pain,* p. 88; Paul Fussell, *The Great War and Modern Memory* (New York: Oxford University Press, 1975), pp. 75–80. Clausewitz likewise structures his analysis of war according to a series of binaries in crisis: "War and politics, attack and defense, intelligence and courage . . . are never absolute opposites; rather one flows into the other" (Introduction, *On War,* p. 16). Elsewhere he writes that war is "a half-and-half production, a thing without a perfect inner cohesion." *On War,* ed. Anatol Rapo-

port, trans. J. J. Graham (New York: Penguin Classics, 1968), p. 369. See W. B. Gallie's analysis in *Understanding War* (New York: Routledge, 1991), pp. 56–60.

20. See Eric Leed, *No Man's Land: Combat and Identity in World War I* (Cambridge: Cambridge University Press, 1979), pp. 1–33.

21. Tim O'Brien, "How to Tell a True War Story," in *The Things They Carried* (Boston: Houghton Mifflin, 1990), p. 88.

22. Ernest Hemingway, *For Whom the Bell Tolls* (New York: Charles Scribner's Sons, 1940), pp. 448, 309. Cited hereafter in the text.

23. David Grossman, *On Killing: The Psychological Cost of Learning to Kill in War and Society* (Boston: Little, Brown, 1995), pp. 4; 1–16.

24. Eric H. Erikson, "Ontogeny of Ritualization in Man," *Philosophical Transactions of the Royal Society, London*, B251 (1966): 340, 346, 337–349. Hemingway writes that "most men die like animals, not men." The details of the death scene recall for Hemingway the deaths of rabbits and cats. *Death in the Afternoon* (New York: Simon and Schuster, 1996), p. 138–139.

25. The laws of war in this way favor the interests of states and other powerful organizations over those of communities, groups, or collectives lacking vertical centralization: they "seem to reflect the values of those who have gained by stability." See Alfred R. Rubin, "Is the Law of War Really Law? War and Law Since 1945," *Michigan Journal of International Law* (1996): 647.

26. Dos Passos, *Nineteen Nineteen*, p. 462.

27. Ibid., pp. 462–464. See William Solomon on Dos Passos's stylized breakdown of the synecdochic trope of the Unknown Soldier as antimilitarist protest. "Politics and Rhetoric in the Novel in the 1930s," *American Literature*, 68, no. 4 (1996): 799–818. I am thankful to Jojo Liu for her discussion of related points.

28. See Townsend Ludington, *John Dos Passos: A Twentieth Century Odyssey* (New York: E. P. Dutton, 1980), pp. 257–258.

29. George M. Fredrickson, *The Inner Civil War: Northern Intellectuals and the Crisis of the Union* (Urbana: University of Illinois Press, 1993), pp. 217–238; T. J. Jackson Lears, *No Place of Grace: Antimodernism and the Transformation of American Culture, 1880–1920* (New York: Pantheon Books, 1981), p. 100.

30. Dos Passos, *Nineteen Nineteen*, p. 341; see also p. 147. Cited hereafter in the text.

31. For an analysis of the development of Dos Passos's war novels, culminating in a treatment of *Nineteen Nineteen* as a charge of broad social complicity in the instigation and maintenance of war, see John Rohrkemper, "Mr. Dos Passos' War," *Modern Fiction Studies*, 30, no. 1 (1984): 37–52. It is a primary thesis of John Limon's *Writing after War* that war literature reveals a continual conflation of peace and war experience.

32. Quoted in Ludington, *John Dos Passos: A Twentieth Century Odyssey,* p. 129. The phrase "thinking in gargoyles" is from Ludington. See also p. 128.

33. Wyndham Lewis, *Men without Art* (Santa Rosa: Black Sparrow Press, 1987), pp. 91–93. For analysis, see Tyrus Miller, *Late Modernism: Politics, Fiction, and the Arts between the World Wars* (Berkeley: University of California Press, 1999), pp. 26–64.

34. See *War, Violence, and the Modern Condition,* ed. Bernd Hüppauf (Berlin: Walter de Gruyter, 1997), in which Richard Cork, "'A Murderous Carnival': German Artists in the First World War," p. 269, quotes Kirchner.

35. John Dos Passos, "Off the Shoals," *Dial,* 73, no. 1 (July, 1922): 100–101.

36. Richard S. Kennedy, *Dreams in the Mirror: A Biography of E. E. Cummings* (New York: Liveright, 1980), p. 147.

37. Scarry, *The Body in Pain,* p. 38.

38. Kennedy, *Dreams in the Mirror,* p. 216. Cary Nelson comments on Cummings's willingness to "satirize all forms of political conviction" in *Repression and Recovery* (Madison: University of Wisconsin Press, 1989), p. 122.

39. See Edmund Wilson, "Two Novels of Willa Cather," Granville Hicks, "The Case against Willa Cather," H. L. Mencken, "Four Reviews," and Sinclair Lewis, "A Hamlet of the Plains," all in *Willa Cather and Her Critics,* ed. James Schroeter (Ithaca: Cornell University Press, 1967). See also John H. Randall, *The Landscape and the Looking Glass* (Boston: Houghton Mifflin, 1960), p. 169; Dorothy Van Ghent, *Willa Cather* (Minneapolis: University of Minnesota Press, 1964), pp. 25–26; James Woodress, *Willa Cather: Her Life and Art* (New York: Pegasus, 1970), pp. 192–193; Josephine Jessup, *The Faith of Our Feminists* (New York: Richard Smith, 1950), p. 64; Elizabeth Shepley Sergeant, *Willa Cather: A Memoir* (Lincoln: University of Nebraska Press, 1963), p. 155; Stanley Cooperman, *World War I and the American Novel* (Baltimore: Johns Hopkins University Press, 1967), pp. 29–33, 76, 136–137. For more recent work that has begun to argue for the artistic integrity and complexity of *One of Ours* and to make it more central to the Cather canon, see Jean Schwind, "The 'Beautiful' War in *One of Ours,*" *Modern Fiction Studies,* 30, no. 1 (1984): 53–71; Sharon O'Brien, "Combat Envy and Survivor Guilt: Willa Cather's 'Manly Battle Yarn,'" in *Arms and the Woman: War, Gender, and Literary Representation,* ed. Helen Cooper, Adrienne Munich, and Susan Squier (Chapel Hill: University of North Carolina Press, 1989), pp. 184–204; Susan J. Rosowski, *The Voyage Perilous: Willa Cather's Romanticism* (Lincoln: University of Nebraska Press, 1986), pp. 95–113; and Michael North, *Reading 1922* (New York: Oxford University Press, 1999), pp. 173–192. On the challenges women faced when writing about the Great War, and their exclusion from canonical literary history, see Margaret R. Higgonet, "Not So Quiet in No-Woman's Land," in *Gendering War Talk,* ed. Miriam Cooke and

Angela Woollacott (Princeton: Princeton University Press, 1993), pp. 205–226.

40. Sharon O'Brien, *Willa Cather: The Emerging Voice* (New York: Oxford University Press, 1987), pp. 89, 92.

41. Willa Cather, *One of Ours* (New York: Vintage Books, 1991), p. 356. Cited hereafter in the text.

42. On this issue see Schwind's important article "The 'Beautiful' War in *One of Ours*," pp. 53–71. Schwind argues at the close for an economy of violence that is resisted by the feminine and the domestic. The novel concludes, she notes, with an image of a woman by a kitchen stove. Against the war machine the novel celebrates the "humble homecrafts" (71) that affirm life. Schwind thus argues that *One of Ours,* often read as a romantic confirmation of war's glory, should instead be read as an ironic distancing from war enthusiasm. For opposing views on the relationship between domesticity and war, and on Cather's war sentimentalism, see Jean Bethke Elshtain, *Women and War* (New York: Basic Books, 1987), pp. 216–218; 163–193.

43. Frederick Griffiths, analyzing Cather's self-conscious blending of the male and female experiences of war, draws attention to her strategy of creating self-consuming binary structures. "The Woman Warrior: Willa Cather and *One of Ours,*" *Women's Studies: An Interdisciplinary Journal,* 11, no. 3 (1984): 261–285.

44. Schwind argues in "The 'Beautiful' War in *One of Ours*" that Claude's death is heroic and beautiful only for Claude, and that readings to the contrary fundamentally misunderstand the novel. See also Griffiths, "The Woman Warrior."

45. Jean Bethke Elshtain brilliantly traces this tendency throughout war representation. See *Women and War, passim.* See also Helen Cooper, Adrienne Munich, and Susan Squier, "Introduction" and "Arms and the Woman," in their *Arms and the Woman,* pp. xiii–xx, 9–24. For a pertinent analysis of femininity in *One of Ours,* see John Limon, *Writing after War: American War Fiction from Realism to Postmodernism* (New York: Oxford University Press, 1994), pp. 200–205. Relatedly, see Anne Goodwyn-Jones, "Male Fantasies? Faulkner's War Stories and the Construction of Gender," in *Faulkner and Psychology / Faulkner and Yoknapatawpha* (Jackson: University of Mississippi Press, 1994), pp. 21–55. Cather had been trained to see the world as divided into domestic, female space and nondomestic, male space. Throughout her life she attempted to disrupt this division. As Sharon O'Brien notes, Cather claimed as her artistic heritage the writings of Kipling and Crane and, as an adolescent "surveying the family tree for a suitable ancestor, she chose to claim her military heritage and decided she had been named for her soldier uncle." Cather writes: "When a woman writes a story of adventure, a stout sea tale, and manly battle yarn, anything about wine, women and love, then I will begin to hope for something great from them, not before" (*Willa Cather: The Emerging Voice,* p. 13; see also pp. 68–69, 98, 156, 166, 97, 107–109, 162, 100). For more on gender, sexuality, and

the movement of names in Cather, see Judith Butler, *Bodies That Matter* (New York: Routledge, 1993), pp. 143–166.

46. Roxanne Panchasi, "Reconstructions: Prosthetics and the Rehabilitation of the Male Body in World War I France," *Differences*, 7, no. 3 (1995): 109–140; Sigmund Freud, "The 'Uncanny,'" in *The Standard Edition of the Complete Psychological Works of Sigmund Freud*, ed. James Strachey, vol. 17 (London: Hogarth, 1955), pp. 237, 244. See also Robert Weldon Whalen, *Bitter Wounds: German Victims of the Great War, 1914–1939* (Ithaca: Cornell University Press, 1984), pp. 44–45.

47. Cornelia Vismann, "Starting from Scratch: Concepts of Order in No Man's Land," in Hüppauf, *War, Violence, and the Modern Condition*, pp. 55, 62, 57, 53. See also Bernd Hüppauf, "Walter Benjamin's Imaginary Landscape," in *"With the Sharpened Axe of Reason": Approaches to Walter Benjamin*, ed. Gerhard Fischer (Oxford: Berg, 1996), pp. 33–54.

48. Lisabeth During argues that for Freud "the category crisis which is coterminous with Modernism begins on the battlefield, where the European psyche, late in its career, began to doubt that there was anything fundamental and absolute about the binaries of its culture." "The Failure of Love: A Lesser Theory of the Great War," in Hüppauf, *War, Violence, and the Modern Condition*, p. 200.

49. Freud, *Beyond the Pleasure Principle*, p. 58.

50. William Kerrigan, "Death and Anxiety: The Coherence of Late Freud," *Raritan*, 16, no. 3 (1997): 71. On the Great War as source for *Beyond the Pleasure Principle*, see Ernest Jones, *The Life and Work of Sigmund Freud*, ed. Lionel Trilling (New York: Basic Books, 1961), p. 406; Frank J. Sulloway, *Freud, Biologist of the Mind: Beyond the Psychoanalytic Legend* (Cambridge, Mass.: Harvard University Press, 1992), pp. 394–395.

51. See Hanna Segal, *Psychoanalysis, Literature, and War* (London: Routledge, 1997), p. 7. Dennis Wrong writes that for Freud "love and hate, life and death, creation and destruction" are "fused in varying unstable compounds in all concrete motivations and actions, thus accounting for what Rieff calls 'the law of primal ambivalence' governing human experience" (*The Problem of Order*, p. 135).

52. See Sulloway, *Freud, Biologist of the Mind*, p. 396.

53. On the "crisis of knowledge" war precipitated (exemplified in Freud's work by the breakdown of borders between self and world, fantasy and reality), see Jaqueline Rose, *Why War?* (Oxford: Blackwell, 1993), pp. 15–40.

54. Freud, *Beyond the Pleasure Principle*, p. 53. Relatedly, on Freud's theories of war, see Jean Bethke Elshtain, "Freud's Discourse of War/Politics," in *International/Intertextual Relations: Postmodern Readings of World Politics*, ed. James Der Derian and Michael J. Shapiro (New York: Lexington Books/Macmillan, 1989), pp. 49–67.

55. Paul Ricoeur is citing Freud's language: see *Freud and Philosophy* (New Haven: Yale University Press, 1970), p. 294.

56. Sigmund Freud, "Thoughts for the Times on War and Death," (1915), in

The Standard Edition of the Complete Psychological Works of Sigmund Freud, ed. James Strachey, vol. 14 (London: Hogarth, 1957), p. 275.

57. William Kerrigan, "Death and Anxiety," p. 71.
58. Simone de Beauvoir, *The Ethics of Ambiguity,* trans. Bernard Frechtman (New York: Citadel Press, 1994), pp. 8–9.
59. See Jürgen Habermas, *The Philosophical Discourse of Modernity,* trans. Frederick Lawrence (Cambridge, Mass.: MIT Press, 1987), pp. 116–119.
60. Martin Jay, *The Dialectical Imagination: A History of the Frankfurt School and the Institute of Social Research, 1923–1950* (Berkeley: University of California Press, 1973), p. 41. See also p. 63.
61. Theodor Adorno and Max Horkheimer, *Dialectic of Enlightenment,* trans. John Cumming (New York: Verso, 1979), p. xiv. On the Frankfurt School's critique of language, see also p. xii; Jay, *The Dialectical Imagination,* p. 263; and Herbert Marcuse, *One-Dimensional Man: Studies in the Ideology of Advanced Industrial Society* (Boston: Beacon Press, 1991), pp. 84–103.
62. Adorno and Horkheimer, *Dialectic of Enlightenment,* p. 81.
63. Habermas, *The Philosophical Discourse of Modernity,* p. 112.
64. Albert Speer writes in his memoirs that the "principles of utility" he adopted destroyed "all considerations and feelings of humanity." *Inside the Third Reich,* trans. Richard Winston and Clara Winston (New York: Macmillan, 1970), p. 375. Speer continually associates the sublime of technology and industry not only with destruction but also with the social machinery of totalitarianism. He blames especially communications technology for enabling the homogenization of discourse (520–521, 212, 367, 524, 69, 41).
65. See *The Essential Frankfurt School Reader,* ed. Andrew Arato and Eike Gebhardt, intro. Paul Piccone (New York: Continuum, 1982), which includes Max Horkheimer, "The End of Reason" (1941), p. 39.
66. Marcuse, *One-Dimensional Man,* pp. 12, 33, 23. See also Herbert Marcuse, "Some Social Implications of Modern Technology" (1941), in *The Essential Frankfurt School Reader,* pp. 138–162. For more on the critique of instrumentality, see Charles Taylor, *Sources of the Self: The Making of the Modern Identity* (Cambridge, Mass.: Harvard University Press, 1989), pp. 500–501.
67. Jay, *The Dialectical Imagination,* p. 254. On the rise of the Fascist movement in Italy and the ascendance to power of National Socialism in Germany, Habermas writes: "There was no theory of contemporaneity not affected to its core by the penetrating force of fascism. This holds true especially of the theories that were in their formative period in the late 1920s and early 1930s—of Heidegger's fundamental ontology, as we have seen, no less than of Bataille's heterology or Horkheimer's Critical Theory" (*The Philosophical Discourse of Modernity,* p. 216).
68. Adorno and Horkheimer, *Dialectic of Enlightenment,* pp. 105–06.

69. Joseph Libertson, "Bataille and Communication: Savoir, Non-Savoir, Glissement, Rire," in *On Bataille: Critical Essays,* ed. Leslie Anne Boldt-Irons (Albany: State University of New York Press, 1995), pp. 210, 209–232.

70. On the function of the grotesque body in Bataille, see "The Use Value of D.A.F. de Sade," in *Visions of Excess: Selected Writings, 1927–1939,* ed. Allan Stoekl (Minneapolis: University of Minnesota Press, 1985), pp. 91–104.

71. Martin Heidegger, *Being and Time,* trans. John Macquarrie and Edward Robinson (New York: Harper and Row, 1962), p. 97.

72. See Heidegger's discussion of failed tools in *Being and Time,* pp. 102–107. *Dasein* "makes use of [successful tools] without noticing them explicitly" (105).

73. "That with which our everyday dealings proximally dwell is not the tools themselves. On the contrary, that with which we concern ourselves primarily is the work—that which is to be produced at the time" (*Being and Time,* p. 99). I am indebted here and elsewhere to Elaine Scarry's work on tools and artifacts. See for instance *The Body in Pain,* pp. 278–326.

74. Magda King, *Heidegger's Philosophy: A Guide to His Basic Thought* (New York: Macmillan, 1964), p. 44.

75. Martin Heidegger, "The Question concerning Technology," in *Martin Heidegger: Basic Writings,* ed. David Farrell Krell (San Francisco: Harper and Row, 1977), pp. 307, 314. See especially pp. 297–298.

76. Martin Heidegger, "The Question concerning Technology," p. 303.

77. *The Heidegger Controversy: A Critical Reader,* ed. Richard Wolin (Cambridge, Mass.: MIT Press, 1993), Herbert Marcuse, "An Exchange of Letters," p. 157.

78. Georges Bataille, *Inner Experience,* trans. Leslie Anne Boldt (New York: State University of New York Press, 1988), p. 49. See also Michele H. Richman, *Reading Georges Bataille: Beyond the Gift* (Baltimore: Johns Hopkins University Press, 1982), pp. 3, 40.

79. Jünger quoted in Wolin, *The Heidegger Controversy,* pp. 122, 129.

80. Georges Bataille, *The Accursed Share: An Essay on General Economy,* vol. 1, *Consumption* (New York: Zone Books, 1991), pp. 56–58. He first developed his ideas on waste in "The Notion of Expenditure" (1933). For more on utility and transcendence in Bataille, see Joseph Libertson, *Proximity: Levinas, Blanchot, Bataille, and Communication* (Boston: Martinus Nijhoff, 1982); "On Bataille," spec. issue of *Yale French Studies,* ed. Allan Stoekl, 78 (1990).

81. Scarry, *The Body in Pain,* p. 275.

82. Bataille, *The Accursed Share,* pp. 40, 51.

83. On war see Bataille, *The Accursed Share, passim;* see also his *Inner Experience,* p. 45.

84. Bataille, *The Accursed Share,* p. 190.

85. Ibid., pp. 70–71, 54–55.
86. Ibid., p. 23.
87. Ernst Jünger, *The Storm of Steel,* pp. 102, 105, 132, 140, 255. In a review of Jünger's work, Walter Benjamin highlighted Jünger's "aestheticist's" appreciation of modern combat: "This new theory of war . . . is nothing other than an unrestrained transposition of the theses of *l'art pour l'art* to war" (Walter Benjamin, quoted in Wolin, *The Heidegger Controversy,* p. 122).
88. F. Scott Fitzgerald, *This Side of Paradise* (New York: Collier Books, 1920), pp. 258, 245, 163.
89. Hannah Arendt, *The Origins of Totalitarianism* (New York: Harcourt Brace, 1973), p. 328. See also Jean-Michel Besnier, "Georges Bataille in the 1930s: A Politics of the Impossible," *Yale French Studies,* 78 (1990): 169–180.
90. Arendt, *The Origins of Totalitarianism,* p. 334.
91. Ibid., pp. 328, 334, 328, 331.
92. Jean Paulhan quoted in Arendt, *The Origins of Totalitarianism,* p. 330. "In France, since 1930," Arendt writes, "the Marquis de Sade has become one of the favored authors of the literary avant-garde" (330). See also Edmund Wilson, *The Bit between My Teeth: A Literary Chronicle of 1950–1965* (New York: Farrar, Straus and Giroux, 1965), pp. 168–171. On the attraction to the "horrible" (stimulated by literature), see Jünger, *The Storm of Steel,* p. 23.
93. Susan Rubin Suleiman, *Subversive Intent: Gender, Politics, and the Avant-garde* (Cambridge, Mass.: Harvard University Press, 1998), pp. 75–76.
94. Bataille, *Inner Experience,* pp. 14–15. For Bataille on language, see Habermas, *The Philosophical Discourse of Modernity,* pp. 236–237. William Connolly argues against the Habermasian sacralization of deliberation in an article that lucidly tracks the productive role of the nonverbal ("visceral" "proto-thoughts") in intersubjectivity and public life. See Connolly, "Refashioning the Secular," in *What's Left of Theory? New Work on the Politics of Literary Theory,* ed. Judith Butler, John Guillory, and Kendall Thomas (New York: Routledge, 2000), pp. 157–191.
95. Bataille, *Inner Experience,* pp. 16, 38–39, xxxii; Steven Shaviro, *Passion and Excess: Blanchot, Bataille, and Literary Theory* (Tallahassee: Florida State University Press, 1990), pp. 77, 83–85, 4–6. See also Giorgio Agamben, *Language and Death: The Place of Negativity* (Minneapolis: University of Minnesota Press, 1991), pp. 49–53. Bataille's irrationalism is a radicalization of elements identifiable in Anglo-American modernism, which experimented with difficulty in language as a means of revitalizing (rather than repudiating) language's capacity to map experience in the world. "As I say," writes Gertrude Stein, "a thing that is very clear may easily not be clear at all, a thing that may be confused may be very clear." "Lectures in America," in *Gertrude Stein: Writings, 1932–1946,* ed. Catharine R. Stimpson and Harriet Chessman (New York: Library of America, 1998), p. 292.

96. Maurice Blanchot, *The Infinite Conversation,* trans. Susan Hanson (Minneapolis: University of Minnesota Press, 1993), p. 42. "Toute parole est violence": *L'Entretien Infini* (Paris: Gallimard, 1969), p. 60.

97. C. Wright Mills, *The Power Elite* (New York: Oxford University Press, 1956), p. 222.

98. Bataille, *Inner Experience,* pp. 14, xxxii, 36; translator's introduction, *Inner Experience,* p. x. Shaviro explains of Bataille: "One cannot oppose fascism by reasserting the civilized values of which fascism is only the final and most massive growth; but only by reaffirming the gratuitousness of catastrophe which the fascist rage for order strives to repress." And earlier: "Bataille's rhetoric has the form of an ethical imperative, but its content is a demand to dissolve all grounds and all imperative necessities, including its own" (*Passion and Excess,* p. 101). For a post–World War II tribute to the moral and political importance of silence, which at the same time laments the broad cultural retreat from expressive, precise language, see George Steiner, *Language and Silence* (New York: Atheneum, 1977), pp. vii–x, 12–54. Against the romanticization of ineffability as style, see Primo Levi, "This Above All: Be Clear," *New York Times Book Review,* 20 November 1988, pp. 1, 59–60.

5. Language, Violence, and Bureaucracy

1. Some of these estimates are taken from Paul Fussell, "Almost Beyond Human Conception," in his *The Norton Book of Modern War* (New York: W. W. Norton, 1991), p. 307. David Rieff writes: "In World War I, the proportion of military to civilian casualties was ninety to ten. In World War II, the proportions were roughly even. Today, for every ten military casualties there are on average ninety civilian deaths." "The Humanitarian Illusion," *New Republic,* 16 March 1998, p. 28.

2. For an analysis of border disruption and monstrosity in *Gravity's Rainbow,* see Terry P. Caesar, "'Beasts Vaulting among the Earthworks': Monstrosity in *Gravity's Rainbow,*" *Novel,* 17, no. 2 (1984): 158–170.

3. Joseph Heller, *Catch-22* (New York: Simon and Schuster, 1961), e.g., pp. 60, 75, 227, 297, 338, 347. Cited hereafter in the text.

4. *Hiroshima Mon Amour,* text by Marguerite Duras, for the film by Alain Resnais, trans. Richard Seaver (New York: Grove Press, 1961), p. 9.

5. Paul Fussell, *Wartime: Understanding and Behavior in the Second World War* (New York: Oxford University Press, 1989), p. 134. On silence and World War II generally, see pp. 132–137.

6. Hannah Arendt, *On Revolution* (New York: Viking Press, 1963), p. 9. See also Aleksandr Solzhenitsyn, *The Gulag Archipelago, 1918–1956,* vols. 1–2, trans. Thomas Whitney (New York: Harper and Row, 1973), p. x.

7. Claude Lanzmann, *Shoah: The Complete Text of the Acclaimed Holocaust Film* (New York: Da Capo Press, 1995), pp. 3, 4, 9, 39, 40, 45, 63, 127, 129, 136, 183. On the difficulty of representing the Holocaust, see Getrud

Koch, "The Aesthetic Transformation of the Image of the Unimaginable: Notes on Claude Lanzmann's *Shoah,*" *October,* 48 (1986): 15–24. For a related analysis of post–World War II reflections on the difficulty of representing war, particularly but not exclusively as it relates to questions of gender and authenticity, see Susan Schweik, "Writing War Poetry Like a Woman," *Critical Inquiry,* 13, no. 3 (1987): 532–556. For an analysis of how language is distorted and restricted as a matter of policy in the contemporary military-industrial complex, see Dennis Hayes, "The Cloistered Work-Place: Military Electronics Workers Obey and Ignore," in *Cyborg Worlds: The Military Information Society,* ed. Les Levidow and Kevin Robins (London: Free Association Books, 1989), pp. 82–83.

8. Lanzmann, *Shoah,* p. 61.
9. Nadine Fresco, "Remembering the Unknown," *International Review of Psychoanalysis,* 11, no. 4 (1984): 419.
10. Lanzmann, *Shoah,* e.g., 103.
11. Ibid., pp. 107–108. For more on the relationship between Holocaust trauma and witnessing, see Geoffrey Hartman, "Learning from Survivors: The Yale Testimony Project," *Holocaust and Genocide Studies,* 9, no. 2 (1995): 192–207.
12. Lanzmann, *Shoah,* p. 152. On the "will to bear witness," see Terrence Des Pres, *The Survivor: An Anatomy of Life in the Death Camps* (New York: Pocket Books, 1976), pp. 33, 29–50.
13. See David Minter, *William Faulkner: His Life and Work* (Baltimore: Johns Hopkins University Press, 1980), pp. 223–224; Richard Gray, *The Life of William Faulkner: A Critical Biography* (Oxford: Blackwell, 1994), pp. 324, 333–334. On Faulkner's ambivalent relationship to the power of language, see Judith Lockyer, *Ordered by Words: Language and Narration in the Novels of William Faulkner* (Carbondale: Southern Illinois University Press, 1991), pp. 145–146.
14. Faulkner, *Selected Letters of William Faulkner,* ed. Joseph Blotner (New York: Random House, 1977), p. 125.
15. In a letter to Robert Haas, Faulkner sums up the argument of *A Fable* thus: "In the middle of that war, Christ (some movement in mankind which wished to stop war forever) reappeared and was crucified again . . . We did this in 1918; in 1944 it not only MUST NOT happen again, it SHALL NOT HAPPEN again. i.e. ARE WE GOING TO LET IT HAPPEN AGAIN?" (*Selected Letters of William Faulkner,* p. 180; see also p. 166). See also Minter, *William Faulkner,* p. 200; and Lockyer, *Ordered by Words,* p. 135.
16. William Faulkner, *A Fable* (New York: Vintage Books, 1978). Cited hereafter in the text.
17. Faulkner repeatedly characterizes hope as a possession of the pacific civilian crowd, a possession rejected with contempt by military careerists (see pp. 19, 51, 57, 277, 292, 294, 308).
18. See Karl Zender, "Faulkner and the Power of Sound," *PMLA,* 99, no. 1 (1984): 89–108, esp. pp. 101–103.

19. Peter Drucker argued in 1946 that it was the new production demands of the war which led to the reimagination of corporate organizational forms and potentials necessary for the postwar economic transformation. *Concept of the Corporation* (New York: John Day Company, 1946), pp. 22–26, 182–199.

20. Robert Presthus, *The Organizational Society: An Analysis and a Theory* (New York: Alfred A. Knopf, 1962), p. 72.

21. Ibid., pp. 69, 79.

22. Ibid., pp. 84, 91.

23. Lynne G. Zucker, "Organizations as Institutions," *Research in the Sociology of Organizations,* ed. Samuel Bacharach, 2 (1983): 20.

24. William Faulkner, *Essays, Speeches, and Public Letters,* ed. James B. Meriwether (New York: Random House, 1965), p. 63. On Faulkner's antiorganizational attitude, see Kenzaburo Ohashi, "Behind the 'Trinity of Conscience': Individuality, 'Regimentation,' and Nature in Between," in *Faulkner: After the Nobel Prize,* ed. Michel Gresset and Kenzaburo Ohashi (Kyoto: Yamaguchi Publishing House, 1987), pp. 29–43. On bureaucracy and Faulkner, see Joseph Urgo, *Faulkner's Apocrypha* (Jackson: University Press of Mississippi, 1989), pp. 94–125.

25. "An Impolite Interview with Joseph Heller," *The Realist,* reprinted in *A "Catch-22" Casebook,* ed. Frederick Kiley and Walter McDonald (New York: Thomas Y. Crowell, 1973), p. 291. "*Catch-22,*" Heller declared in a later interview, "is concerned with physical survival against exterior forces or institutions that want to destroy life or moral self." Interview with George Plimpton, "The Art of Fiction," *Paris Review,* 60 (1974): 141, 126–147. On Heller's characterization in *Catch-22* of the absurdity of bureaucracies, see Charles B. Harris, *Contemporary American Novelists of the Absurd* (New Haven: College and University Press Services, 1971), pp. 33–50. Malcolm Cowley generalizes of World War II literature that distrust of large organizations forms one of its unifying themes. *The Literary Situation* (New York: Viking Press, 1954), pp. 32–33.

26. See for instance D. A. Miller's brilliant analysis of *Bleak House* in *The Novel and the Police* (Berkeley: University of California Press, 1988), pp. 58–106. It is no criticism of Miller to point out that his project has goals different from my own: his contribution to our understanding of representations of power is indisputable. Miller's method is Foucauldian in the best sense. Foucault writes: "I wish to suggest that one must analyze institutions from the standpoint of power relations, rather than vice versa, and that the fundamental point of anchorage of the relationships, even if they are embodied and crystallized in an institution, is to be found outside the institution." "The Subject and Power," in *Michel Foucault: Beyond Structuralism and Hermeneutics,* ed. Hubert Dreyfus and Paul Rabinow (Chicago: University of Chicago Press, 1982), p. 222.

27. Alan Liu, "Local Transcendence: Cultural Criticism, Postmodernism, and the Romanticism of Detail," *Representations,* 32 (1990): 94. See also Alan

Liu, "The Power of Formalism: The New Historicism," *ELH*, 56, no. 4 (1989): 732, 735.

28. Liu, "Local Transcendence," pp. 75–113, 93. Foucault, in the last interview he gave, "confessed that in previous books he had used 'somewhat rhetorical methods of avoiding one of the fundamental domains of experience'— namely, the domain of the subject, of the self, of the individual and his conduct. But in fact each of his books, as 'a kind of fragment of an autobiography,' could be approached as a 'field of experience to be studied, mapped out and organized,' precisely by reinserting the previously occluded dimension." James Miller, quoting Foucault, *The Passion of Michel Foucault* (New York: Simon and Schuster, 1993), p. 31. See also Lawrence Buell on the turn to the individual in Foucault's later work, which Buell points out reflects a self-oriented focus even in his earlier work emphasizing structure. "In Pursuit of Ethics," *PMLA*, 114, no. 1 (1999): 9.

29. See for instance Anthony Appiah's critique of determinism and the structure-agency dichotomy in literary criticism, "Tolerable Falsehoods: Agency and the Interests of Theory," in *Consequences of Theory*, ed. Jonathan Arac and Barbara Johnson (Baltimore: Johns Hopkins University Press, 1991), pp. 63–90. Dieter Freundlieb argues that the epistemological role played in Foucault by discourses or discursive formations is neither conceptually coherent nor capable of providing an adequate space for human agency. "Foucault's Theory of Discourse and Human Agency," in *Reassessing Foucault: Power, Medicine, and the Body*, ed. Colin Jones and Roy Porter (New York: Routledge, 1994), pp. 152–180.

30. Jean Howard, "The New Historicism in Renaissance Studies," *English Literary Renaissance*, 16, no. 1 (1986): 13–43, 39. See Liu, "Local Transcendence"; see also Liu, "The Power of Formalism," pp. 742–745. On the inability of the New Historicism to resolve the agent-structure dichotomy, see Sharon O'Dair, "Theorizing as Defeatism: A Pragmatic Defense of Agency," *Mosaic*, 26, no. 2 (1993): 111–121. On the problems of the analytic status of culture, see Mary Margaret Steedly, "What Is Culture? Does It Matter?" in *Fieldwork: Sites in Literary and Cultural Studies*, ed. Marjorie Garber, Paul B. Franklin, and Rebecca Walkowitz (New York: Routledge, 1996), pp. 18–25.

31. Charles Perrow, *Complex Organizations: A Critical Essay*, second ed. (Glenview, Ill.: Scott, Foresman and Company, 1979), pp. 146–147. The questions of organizational structure I will be analyzing could be raised, in one way or another, of all organizations, but they are made especially urgent and clear in contemporary military bureaucracies because of their geographical scope, the magnitude of their membership, and the diversity of services they are required to perform.

32. Morris Janowitz, *Sociology and the Military Establishment* (New York: Russell Sage Foundation, 1959), p. 5.

33. Responding to Terry Eagleton's suggestion that he overstresses how people

"legitimate prevailing forms of power," and thus how he leaves little room for "dissent, criticism and opposition" in human action, Bourdieu counters that "the capacity for resistance, as a capacity of consciousness," is overestimated even in the most economistic of theories. Pierre Bourdieu and Terry Eagleton, "Doxa and Common Life: An Interview," in *Mapping Ideology,* ed. Slavoj Žižek (New York: Verso, 1994), pp. 268–269, 265–277). For a discussion of the definition of structure, with a critique of the determinism built into Bourdieu's use of the concept, see William H. Sewell, Jr., "A Theory of Structure: Duality, Agency, and Transformation," *American Journal of Sociology,* 98, no. 1 (1992): 1–29, esp. p. 16. For more on determinism or the dominance of structure over agency in Bourdieu, see R. Jenkins, "Pierre Bourdieu and the Reproduction of Determinism," *Sociology,* 16, no. 2 (1982): 270–281. See also Mustafa Emirbayer and Ann Mische, "What Is Agency?" *American Journal of Sociology,* 103, no. 4 (1998): 963, 981–984, 1003–1005; Paul DiMaggio, "Review Essay: 'On Pierre Bourdieu,'" *American Journal of Sociology,* 84, no. 6 (1979): 1460–1474; Friday Morning Group, "Conclusion: Critique," *An Introduction to the Work of Pierre Bourdieu,* ed. Richard Harker, Cheleen Mahar, and Chris Wilkes (London: Macmillan, 1990), pp. 195–225, esp. p. 205; Judith Butler, *Excitable Speech* (New York: Routledge, 1997), pp. 154–159; and Jon Elster, *Sour Grapes: Studies in the Subversion of Rationality* (Cambridge: Cambridge University Press, 1983), pp. 69–71, 101–108. Bourdieu vigorously defends himself against frequent charges of determinism. See Pierre Bourdieu, *In Other Words: Essays towards a Reflexive Sociology,* trans. Matthew Adamson (Oxford: Polity Press, 1990), pp. 12–17. On the problems of agency in Foucault, see Roger Friedland and Robert R. Alford, "Bringing Society Back In: Symbols, Practices, and Institutional Contradictions," in *The New Institutionalism in Organizational Analysis,* ed. Walter W. Powell and Paul DiMaggio (Chicago: University of Chicago Press, 1991), pp. 253–254; Thomas McCarthy, *Ideals and Illusions: On Reconstruction and Deconstruction in Contemporary Critical Theory* (Cambridge, Mass.: MIT Press, 1991), pp. 56–60. On determinism in Foucault, as well as the theoretical homogenization of culture in Foucault and Bourdieu, see also Michel de Certeau, *The Practice of Everyday Life,* trans. Stephen Rendall (Berkeley: University of California Press, 1984), pp. xiv, 63.

34. Judith Butler offers an especially sophisticated post-Foucauldian theory of action. She goes to some lengths to argue for the possibility of unauthorized "resignifications" and for the adequacy of such a theoretical account for understanding agency. For a critical engagement with Butler on the question of agency, see Nancy Fraser, "False Antithesis: A Response to Seyla Benhabib and Judith Butler," *Praxis International,* 11 (1991): 172. On the "disappearance of agency" (6) in literary theory, see Meili Steele, *Theorizing Textual Subjects: Agency and Oppression* (Cambridge: Cambridge University Press, 1997), pp. 1–107.

35. See n. 25 above. See also Michel Foucault, *Power/Knowledge: Selected Interviews and Other Writings, 1972–1977*, ed. Colin Gordon, trans. Colin Gordon, Leo Marshall, John Mepham, and Kate Soper (Brighton, Sussex: Harvester Press, 1980), pp. 96–97. On culture as representations rather than action, see Liu, "The Power of Formalism," pp. 734–735.

36. Fields cover areas as broad as "the economic," "religion," and "science." And the habitus, writes Paul DiMaggio, "is a kind of theoretical deus ex machina" ("Review Essay: 'On Pierre Bourdieu,'" p. 1464). For a critique of Bourdieu's theory of social reproduction, see especially R. W. Connell, *Which Way Is Up? Essays on Sex, Class, and Culture* (Boston: George Allen and Unwin, 1983), pp. 140–153.

37. See Richard Jenkins, *Pierre Bourdieu* (New York: Routledge, 1992), p. 123.

38. Although the terms "institution," "organization," and "bureaucracy" are closely related, each has a separate function in this chapter. "Organization," the basic unit of analysis, signifies complex, coherently bounded social groups managed through explicit rules and unified by specific and limited productive functions. Thus the Board of Education of the City of New York is an organization, but families and nations are not (because as categories the latter are variable with respect to the existing array of production choices). "Bureaucracy," a more specific term, is the basic organizational form of modern society, and to that degree is interchangeable with "organization." Its characterization comes from Weber and includes such primary features as a complex division of labor, hierarchy, and explicit, impersonal, universally applied rules and standards. "Institution" is a broader category than "organization" and means, essentially, a fixed, socially reproductive form (families are thus an institution). I will use the word throughout partly interchangeably with "organization" to denote what "organization" denotes, as one might switch between "literature" and "the novel" in describing the prose of an era. However, when used it is always meant to evoke that aspect of the organization as a social fact that exceeds its most specific definitions and incarnations. Where, for instance, does the Board of Education of the City of New York end? Who are its stakeholders, and are they "members"? The board is imbricated in many other organizations and, indeed, functions sometimes as an extension of them. Is it then better described as a part of the organization "city/state/federal government"?

39. On the creation of social facts (ideas through consent achieving material force), see John R. Searle, *The Construction of Social Reality* (New York: Penguin Press, 1995).

40. Norbert Elias, *Power and Civility: The Civilizing Process*, vol. 2, trans. Edmund Jephcott (New York: Pantheon Books, 1982).

41. Ibid., pp. 258–271. For a brief history and critique of the "words-weapons" intellectual paradigm, see Carol J. Greenhouse, "Reading Violence," in *Law's Violence*, ed. Austin Sarat and Thomas R. Kearns (Ann Arbor: University of Michigan Press, 1992), pp. 105–139. Tzvetan Todorov traces the

words-weapons binary to the European Renaissance in *The Conquest of America,* trans. Richard Howard (New York: Harper and Row, 1984), p. 92. For a critical history of theories of the civilizing process that place violence outside human sociability, see Pierre Saint-Amand, *The Laws of Hostility,* trans. Jennifer Curtiss Gage (Minneapolis: University of Minnesota Press, 1996).

42. Elias, *Power and Civility,* pp. 271–291, 300–319.

43. Max Weber, *Max Weber: The Theory of Social and Economic Organization,* trans. A. M. Henderson and Talcott Parsons, ed. Talcott Parsons (New York: Free Press, 1964), p. 337.

44. Max Weber, *From Max Weber: Essays in Sociology,* ed. H. H. Gerth and C. Wright Mills (New York: Oxford University Press, 1946), p. 231.

45. Weber, *The Theory of Social and Economic Organization,* pp. 337, 339, 332. See also Weber, *Essays in Sociology,* pp. 197, 213, 230.

46. Weber, *Essays in Sociology,* p. 233.

47. Weber, *The Theory of Social and Economic Organization,* p. 337.

48. On the development of interior lexicons in a bureaucracy, see Peter M. Blau, *The Dynamics of Bureaucracy: A Study of Interpersonal Relations in Two Government Agencies,* rev. ed. (Chicago: University of Chicago Press, 1963), p. 106; Ralph Hummel, *The Bureaucratic Experience* (New York: St. Martin's Press, 1977), p. 37.

49. Relevant here is Harold Garfinkel's ethnomethodological analysis of communication, which points to the near total incompatibility of dialogue and assumptions of distrust. *Studies in Ethnomethodology* (Englewood Cliffs, N.J.: Prentice-Hall, 1967), pp. 50–53.

50. On the mobility of the corporal, see Doreen Fowler, "'In Another Country': Faulkner's *A Fable,*" *Studies in American Fiction,* 15, no. 1 (1987): 51–52.

51. On organizational memory and its consequences, see Anthony Downs, *Inside Bureaucracy* (Boston: Little, Brown, 1967), pp. 18–19.

52. Perrow, *Complex Organizations,* p. 48.

53. On the pyramid-like structure of America's military in the world wars, see Morris Janowitz, *The Professional Soldier: A Social and Political Portrait* (New York: Free Press, 1960), p. 65.

54. In Horace Benbow, Faulkner demonstrates, according to Judith Lockyer, how words can trap us "in thought-filled inaction" (*Ordered by Words,* p. 2).

55. James G. March and Herbert A. Simon write: "Rational behavior involves substituting for the complex reality a model of reality that is sufficiently simple to be handled by the problem-solving process." *Organizations* (New York: John Wiley and Sons, 1958), p. 151. Charles Perrow explains that organizations demand a variety of minimization tactics, including "specialization of activities and roles so the attention is directed to 'a particular restricted set of values'[;] rules, programs, and repertoires of action that limit choice in recurring situations and prevent an agonizing process of optimal

decision-making at each turn; a restricted range of stimuli and situations that narrow perception; [and] training and indoctrination enabling the individual to 'make decisions, by himself, as the organization would like him to decide'" (*Complex Organizations,* p. 145).

56. March and Simon, *Organizations,* p. 165.

57. Perrow, *Complex Organizations,* p. 146.

58. March and Simon, *Organizations,* p. 165.

59. See ibid., pp. 164, 153–154, for more on how information gathering produces inaccurate results because of organizationally required "frames of reference" and filtering mechanisms.

60. The phrase is from Erving Goffman, *Asylums: Essays on the Social Situation of Mental Patients and Other Inmates* (Chicago: Aldine Publishing, 1962), p. 53. Malcolm Cowley notes in a comprehensive review of World War II literature that "almost all the authors agree . . . that a gulf exists between the two military castes," and that they emphasize this in their representations with a variety of techniques (*The Literary Situation,* p. 31).

61. For an analysis of these lapses in organizational intelligence, see Harold L. Wilensky, *Organizational Intelligence* (New York: Basic Books, 1967), pp. 43–45, 48–50.

62. Perrow, *Complex Organizations,* p. 148. Janowitz points out that from 1910 to 1950 entry into "the elite nucleus" of military command was made possible in most cases only through an unconventional career pattern (*The Professional Soldier,* p. 150).

63. This notion of military premise-setting is related but not identical to Veblen's concept of "trained incapacity" and Dewey's notion of "occupational psychosis." Trained incapacity, Robert Merton summarizes, "refers to that state of affairs in which one's abilities function as inadequacies or blind spots." "A way of seeing is also way of not seeing," he writes, "a focus upon object A involves a neglect of object B." *Social Theory and Social Structure,* rev. ed. (Glencoe, Ill.: Free Press, 1957), pp. 197–198.

64. See Simone Weil, *The Iliad, or, The Poem of Force,* trans. Mary McCarthy (Wallingford, Pa.: Pendle Hill), originally published in 1940, pamphlet no. 91, p. 22.

65. I derive these categories and their subsequent characterizations from Perrow: see *Complex Organizations,* pp. 150–151.

66. On the implausibility of conceiving law in stable institutions as "threats backed by force," see H. L. A. Hart, *The Concept of Law* (Oxford: Clarendon Press, 1961), pp. 18–25. Hannah Arendt argues that control through violence is not the basic structure of institutional control but rather a sign of its disintegration. See *On Violence* (New York: Harvest, 1970), pp. 44–56.

67. On the post–World War I transformation of military control from domination and sanctions to manipulation and incentives, see Janowitz, *The Professional Soldier,* pp. 42, 21–37. While both Faulkner and Heller go to great lengths to trace the rise in military bureaucracies of domination through the

organizational structuring of cognition, they also never let us forget that these are organizations centered on the threat and use of force. The force is directed not only outward, against the enemy, but also inward, against their own members: *A Fable* revolves around several acts of disciplinary execution, and in *Catch-22* the internal violence is so pervasive that General Dreedle (with all of his subordinates) is incredulous when he discovers that he cannot kill anyone he chooses once he has invoked the justification of maintaining order (218; see also 378).

68. Division of labor does not only promote efficiency and specialization of skills. As Ralph Hummel writes, labor is divided to make workers "dependent on managerial control." He explains: "exactly because of that specialization, it is often impossible for one expert to solve an overall problem without the cooperation of other experts. But for this purpose of mobilizing cooperation we need the manager" (*The Bureaucratic Experience,* p. 30).

69. *The New Institutionalism in Organizational Analysis,* ed. Walter W. Powell and Paul DiMaggio (Chicago: University of Chicago Press, 1991), pp. 10–11. This position is not unnuanced. Friedland and Alford write: "Institutions . . . provide individuals with vocabularies of motives and with a sense of self. They generate not only that which is valued, but the rules by which it is calibrated and distributed. Institutions set the limits on the very nature of rationality and, by implication, of individuality. Nonetheless, individuals, groups, and organizations try to use institutional orders to their own advantage" ("Bringing Society Back In," p. 251). Bourdieu, analyzing at the level of "the daily class struggle" of the social world, puts it this way: "The legitimatization of the social order is not the product, as certain people believe, of a deliberately biased action of propaganda or symbolic imposition; it results from the fact that agents apply to the objective structures of the social world structures of perception and appreciation that have emerged from these objective structures and tend therefore to see the world as self-evident" (*In Other Words,* p. 135). See also Jeffrey Pfeffer, *Power in Organizations* (Boston: Pitman, 1981), pp. 5–6. Garfinkel's analysis of the background rules of communication reveals the comprehensive way in which the "objective facts" and "rational" consensual judgments of the external world are organizationally determined (*Studies in Ethnomethodology,* pp. 1–75). His study shows in particular how social evaluations are retroactively constructed, in other words, how evidence is interpreted in order to match whatever organizational expectations require (18–24).

70. On these concepts, see Perrow, *Complex Organizations,* pp. 146–147.

71. Against individual-interest theories of decisions and action, see Paul DiMaggio, "Interest and Agency in Institutional Theory," in *Institutional Patterns and Organizations: Culture and Environment,* ed. Lynne Zucker (Cambridge, Mass.: Ballinger, 1988), pp. 3–21.

72. On the corporal as Christ figure, see *Faulkner in the University,* ed. Frederick Gwynn and Joseph Blotner (Charlottesville: University of Virginia Press,

1993), pp. 27, 85–86, 117. See also Urgo, *Faulkner's Apocrypha,* pp. 94–125; and Carl Ficken, "The Christ Story in *A Fable,*" *Mississippi Quarterly,* 23, no. 3 (1970): 251–264.

73. Goffman, *Asylums,* pp. 1–124.

74. Ibid., pp. 14, 23, 44.

75. Building on Robert Merton's theory of the "role-set," Rose Laub Coser argues that contradictions between an individual's multiple roles and expectations are not the source of alienation, as is typically argued, but rather the source of greater "rationality" and "freedom." "The Complexity of Roles as a Seedbed of Individual Autonomy," in *The Idea of Social Structure: Essays in Honor of Robert Merton,* ed. Lewis Coser (New York: Harcourt Brace Jovanovich, 1975), pp. 237–263, 239, 241.

76. Sidney Tarrow, *Power in Movement: Social Movements, Collective Action, and Politics* (Cambridge: Cambridge University Press, 1994), pp. 122–123.

77. Hannah Arendt, *The Origins of Totalitarianism* (New York: Harcourt Brace, 1973), p. 323.

78. Emirbayer and Mische, "What Is Agency?" p. 1007.

79. Perrow, *Complex Organizations,* p. 142.

80. Robert Merton writes: "Adherence to the rules, originally conceived as a means, becomes transformed into an end-in-itself; there occurs the familiar process of *displacement of goals* whereby 'an instrumental value becomes a terminal value'" (*Social Theory and Social Structure,* p. 199). See also Blau, *The Dynamics of Bureaucracy,* p. 46. A similar process, though on a macroorganizational level, is behind the military-industrial complex's continual search to find enemies against whom to expend resources.

81. On subgoals, see March and Simon, *Organizations,* pp. 151–154.

82. Perrow writes: "The successful executive is judged on the basis of the growth of her or his organization, the size of the budget, the contacts with elites, the accommodations it has with other powerful organizations, and the number of programs it has. We admit that it is very hard to measure the effectiveness of the programs, or the quality of the care; but it is easy to measure size and even clout. The executive knows this also. Why should she or he not act accordingly?" "Demystifying Organizations," in *The Management of Human Services,* ed. Rosemary C. Sarri and Yeheskel Hasenfeld (New York: Columbia University Press, 1978), pp. 105–120, 113.

83. "The exercise of authority, far from diminishing through use," writes Jeffrey Pfeffer, "may actually serve to enhance the amount of authority subsequently possessed" (*Power in Organizations,* p. 4).

84. On the escape from language, see Tony Tanner, *City of Words: American Fiction, 1950–1970* (London: Jonathan Cape, 1971), pp. 16, 73–74, 77, 81–84. On language breakdown, see Michael Moore, "Pathological Communication in Heller's *Catch-22,*" *Etc: A Review of General Semantics,* 52, no. 4 (1995–96): 431–439; Carol Pearson, "*Catch-22* and the Debasement of Language," *CEA Critic,* 38, no. 4 (1976): 30–35. Absurdity as an escape

from the system in *Catch-22* (or as a fact of language's discontinuity with the world) has been analyzed in a variety of ways by many critics. See Robert Brustein, "The Logic of Survival in a Lunatic World," *New Republic,* 145, no. 20 (13 November 1961): 11–13. See also the contributions of Jesse Ritter, Douglas Day, Robert Protherough, Vance Ramsey, Nelvin Vos, and Jean Kennard to *A "Catch-22" Casebook,* ed. Frederick Kiley and Walter McDonald (New York: Thomas Y. Crowell, 1973).

85. For a theory of "selective behavior" that emphasizes the choices and control available to subordinates in a bureaucracy (e.g., they can choose to be "efficient" or "inefficient" in dealing with the requests of superiors), see Albert Breton and Ronald Wintrobe, *The Logic of Bureaucratic Conduct* (Cambridge: Cambridge University Press, 1982), pp. 30–54.

86. I have paraphrased from Emirbayer and Mische, "What Is Agency?" pp. 1008–1009.

87. I borrow the idea of types of agency and the phrase "agentic orientations" from Emirbayer and Mische, "What Is Agency?"

88. Claude Lanzmann writes: "There are many ways of being silent . . . To talk too much about the Holocaust is a way of being silent, and a bad way of being silent." "The Obscenity of Understanding," in *Trauma: Explorations in Memory,* ed. Cathy Caruth (Baltimore: Johns Hopkins University Press, 1995), p. 208.

89. Hannah Arendt, *Eichmann in Jerusalem: A Report on the Banality of Evil* (New York: Penguin Books, 1994), p. 28.

90. Ibid., pp. 49, 48. See Václav Havel's critique of the "ritualization of language": *Open Letters: Selected Writings, 1965–1990,* ed. Paul Wilson (New York: Vintage Books, 1992), p. 12.

91. Arendt, *Eichmann in Jerusalem,* p. 49.

92. On deliberation, see Amy Gutmann and Dennis Thompson, *Democracy and Disagreement* (Cambridge, Mass.: Harvard University Press, 1996), p. 42. Jean-François Lyotard writes: "The right to speak implies a duty to announce. If our speech announces nothing, it is doomed to repetition and to the conservation of existing meanings. The human community may spread, but it will remain the same, prostrated in the euphoria it feels at being on such very good terms with itself." "The Other's Rights," in *On Human Rights: The Oxford Amnesty Lectures, 1993,* ed. Stephen Shute and Susan Hurley (New York: Basic Books, 1993), p. 143. For more on the use of programmed discourse in the twentieth century, see Claudia Springer, "Military Propaganda: Defense Department Films from World War II and Vietnam," in *The Vietnam War and American Culture,* ed. John Carlos Rowe and Rick Berg (New York: Columbia University Press, 1991), pp. 95–114.

93. Martha Gellhorn, *A Stricken Field* (New York: Penguin Books, 1986), e.g., pp. 40–41.

94. Arendt, *Eichmann in Jerusalem,* pp. 87–89.

95. Hannah Arendt, "Lying in Politics," in *Crises of the Republic* (San Diego: Harcourt Brace Jovanovich, 1972), p. 20.

96. Arendt, *Eichmann in Jerusalem*, pp. 85, 105. For more on Fascism's damage to language, see George Steiner, *Language and Silence* (New York: Atheneum, 1977), pp. 95–109; and George Orwell, "Politics and the English Language," in *The Orwell Reader* (New York: Harvest, 1956), pp. 355–366. To assert that the description "extermination" is objectively accurate and therefore applicable and that "resettlement" is inapplicable is not to deny that we are engaged in interpretation when describing these events. Objectivity is composed of rules governing the fair use of evidence and requiring corrections for structurally generated motivations to seek, or tendencies to see, limited subsets of data. Interpretation governed by the regulative ideals of objectivity and sincerity are theoretically distinguishable from attempts to disable the cognition of others (e.g., concealment of evidence, lying). Attempts to impair rather than expand the comprehension of others, however, can be included *within* interpretive institutions as tools for achieving objectivity or other valued effects—for instance, in the adversarial legal system.

97. The bewilderment Garfinkel's experimental subjects display when background assumptions about communication such as sincerity and an orientation toward mutual understanding are breached reveals the extent to which even the most simple, quotidian acts of communication rely upon and therefore repetitively reinforce these assumptions (*Studies in Ethnomethodology*, pp. 1–75).

98. See Elaine Scarry, *The Body in Pain: The Making and the Unmaking of the World* (New York: Oxford University Press, 1985), pp. 133–136, 127–129, 150.

99. Faulkner writes: "To be a good soldier infers not only a capacity for being misled, but a willingness for it: an eagerness even to supply the gaps in the logic of them who persuade him to relinquish his privacy" (*Selected Letters of William Faulkner*, p. 166).

100. "The ways in which people understand their own relationship to the past, future, and present make a difference to their actions; changing conceptions of agentic possibility in relation to structural contexts profoundly influence how actors in different periods and places see their worlds as more or less responsive to human imagination, purpose, and effort" (Emirbayer and Mische, "What Is Agency?" pp. 962–1023, 973).

101. For a more thorough analysis of the discontinuous relationship between signifier and signified in *Catch-22*, see Gary Davis's compelling article "*Catch-22* and the Language of Discontinuity," *Novel*, 12, no. 1 (1978): 66–77.

102. Weil, *The Iliad, or, The Poem of Force*, p. 3.

103. Arendt, *Eichmann in Jerusalem*, p. 131.

6. *Total War, Anomie, and Human Rights Law*

1. Richard Beardsworth, *Derrida and the Political* (New York: Routledge, 1996), p. 18. Steven Shaviro writes: "Truth in language is always a consequence of this violent making-absent, of domination enforced by the threat of murder. Such a relation of power, such violence, is present in any discourse of knowledge or of truth, as in any attempt to assign identities or names." *Passion and Excess: Blanchot, Bataille, and Literary Theory* (Tallahassee: Florida State University Press, 1990), p. 18. Judith Butler writes that "the vulnerability to being named constitutes a constant condition of the speaking subject." *Excitable Speech* (New York: Routledge, 1997), p. 30. Elsewhere she writes: "If the terms by which 'existence' is formulated, sustained, and withdrawn are the active and productive vocabulary of power, then to persist in one's being means to be given over from the start to social terms that are never fully one's own . . . Vulnerable to terms that one never made, one persists always, to some degree, through categories, names, terms, and classifications that mark a primary and inaugurative alienation in sociality. If such terms institute a primary subordination or, indeed, a primary violence, then a subject emerges against itself in order, paradoxically, to be for itself." *The Psychic Life of Power: Theories in Subjection* (Stanford: Stanford University Press, 1997), p. 28. See also Harold Schweizer's introduction to Barbara Johnson's *The Wake of Deconstruction* (Oxford: Blackwell, 1994), pp. 1–10.
2. Jacques Derrida, *Of Grammatology*, trans. Gayatri Chakravorty Spivak (Baltimore: Johns Hopkins University Press, 1976), p. 112.
3. See Toril Moi's lucid statement on naming in *Sexual/Textual Politics: Feminist Literary Theory* (New York: Routledge, 1985), pp. 158–161.
4. International Covenant on Civil and Political Rights, 16 December 1966, reprinted in *Twenty-five Human Rights Documents* (New York: Columbia University Center for the Study of Human Rights, 1994), art. 16.
5. International Covenant on Civil and Political Rights, art. 24; italics mine.
6. On the power of naming as a source of dignity, see John R. Searle, *The Construction of Social Reality* (New York: Penguin Books, 1995), pp. 93–94.
7. For a synopsis of the debates over the role of deconstruction in legal interpretation, see Ian Ward, *Law and Literature: Possibilities and Perspectives* (Cambridge: Cambridge University Press, 1995), esp. pp. 43–58. For a conspectus of works concerned with the problem of identifying "theory" and establishing its relation to social practices, some of which make convincing arguments contrary to this essay, see Christopher Norris, *Reclaiming Truth* (Durham: Duke University Press, 1996); *Deconstruction and Pragmatism,* ed. Chantal Mouffe (New York: Routledge, 1996); Ernest Gellner, *Postmodernism, Reason, and Religion* (New York: Routledge, 1992); *Universal Abandon? The Politics of Postmodernism,* ed. Andrew Ross (Minneapolis:

University Minnesota Press, 1988); Barbara Johnson, *A World of Difference* (Baltimore: Johns Hopkins University Press, 1987); *After Postmodernism: Reconstructing Ideology Critique,* ed. Herbert W. Simons and Michael Billig (London: Sage Publications, 1994).

8. Criticizing antifoundationalists like Richard Rorty for drawing from the common observation that there are no "timeless, necessary, and unconditioned" structures of knowledge the conclusion that there is also no justification for a view of human reason that retains a context-transcendent, regulative, and critical force, Thomas McCarthy presents Habermas as a postmetaphysical universalist whose theory of communicative action maintains a rigorous cultural and historical self-consciousness without reducing all validity claims to context. Habermas, he writes, "offers an alternative to radical contextualism not by denying the situatedness of reason but by illuminating features of our situation that are invisible from the contextualist perspective, features that might be characterized as social-practical analogues to Kant's 'ideas of reason.' The basic move here is to relocate the tension between the real and the ideal *within* the domain of social practice by showing how communication is organized around idealizing, context-transcendent presuppositions." *Ideals and Illusions: On Reconstruction and Deconstruction in Contemporary Critical Theory* (Cambridge, Mass.: MIT Press, 1991), p. 27. As suppositions that we cannot avoid making when seeking to arrive at mutual understanding, he states elsewhere, they "are actually effective in organizing communication *and* typically counterfactual in ways that open de facto agreements to future criticism" (3).

9. See for instance Martha Nussbaum, *Sex and Social Justice* (New York: Oxford University Press, 1999).

10. Michel Chaouli writes of literary theory's notion of truth: "Rather than an idea of truth yielding only to the force of logic, it presupposes a truth inextricably linked to rhetoric, and thus to the subjective and contingent distortions of opinion, affect and taste—a notion of truth that has the natural sciences and the social sciences holding their noses. It may not feel like it most of the time, but we are the ghosts that haunt the rationalist disciplines; we are *their* worry." "What Do Literary Studies Teach?" *Times Literary Supplement,* 26 February 1999, p. 14.

11. Tzvetan Todorov, *Literature and Its Theorists,* trans. Catherine Porter (Ithaca: Cornell University Press, 1987), p. 190.

12. Terry Eagleton, "Deconstruction and Human Rights" in *Freedom and Interpretation,* ed. Barbara Johnson (New York: Basic Books, 1993), p. 123. See Johnson's introduction for important commentary on the theory-rights conflict.

13. On the ethical challenges to literary theory, and more broadly on the full range of ethical stances available to literary analysis, see Lawrence Buell, "In Pursuit of Ethics," *PMLA,* 114, no. 1 (1999): 7–19. Stephen White argues against those who would characterize postmodernism as quietistic. He

argues that in postmodernism language functions as "world-disclosing" rather than "action-coordinating"—but that both are forms of moral responsibility. *Political Theory and Postmodernism* (Cambridge: Cambridge University Press, 1991), pp. 27–28. See also Allan Stoekl, *Politics, Writing, Mutilation: The Cases of Bataille, Blanchot, Roussel, Leiris, and Ponge* (Minneapolis: University of Minnesota Press, 1985), p. xii.

14. Nancy Armstrong and Leonard Tennenhouse, Introduction, *The Violence of Representation: Literature and the History of Violence,* ed. Nancy Armstrong and Leonard Tennenhouse (New York: Routledge, 1989), p. 2 (describing rather than endorsing this view).

15. International law is relevant to internal as well as international conflict through the minimal humanitarian provisions of Common Article 3 of the 1949 Geneva Conventions. See Geneva Convention for the Amelioration of the Condition of the Wounded and Sick in Armed Forces on the Field, 12 August 1949, art. 3, 6 U.S.T. 3114, 3116, 75 U.N.T.S. 31, 32–34 (hereinafter Geneva Convention I); Geneva Convention for the Amelioration of the Condition of the Wounded, Sick and Shipwrecked Members of the Armed Forces at Sea, 12 August 1949, art. 3, 6 U.S.T. 3219, 3220–3222, 75 U.N.T.S. 85, 86–88 (hereinafter Geneva Convention II); Geneva Convention Relative to the Treatment of Prisoners of War, 12 August 1949, art. 3, 6 U.S.T. 3316, 3318–3320, 75 U.N.T.S. 135, 136–138 (hereinafter Geneva Convention III); Geneva Convention Relative to the Protection of Civilian Persons in Time of War, 12 August 1949, 6 U.S.T. 3516, 3518–3520, 75 U.N.T.S. 287, 288–290 (hereinafter Geneva Convention IV).

16. American Anthropological Association, "Statement on Human Rights," *American Anthropologist,* 49, no. 4 (1947): 542.

17. For a critical analysis of rights organizations, see *Empire* (Cambridge, Mass.: Harvard University Press, 2000), pp. 35–37, 309–314. Zygmunt Bauman criticizes both the social contract theory of self as well as the communitarian vision: "In the same way as the clarion call of 'unencumbered' self served all too often to silence the protest against the suppression of moral autonomy by the unitary nation-state, the image of 'situated' self tends to cover up the 'communitarian' practices of similar suppression." *Postmodern Ethics* (Cambridge, Mass.: Blackwell, 1993), p. 47.

18. Amartya Sen asserts that this argument against the universality of human rights is in fact an authoritarian ruse that succeeds only insofar as it ignores the basic history of Asian cultures. See *Development As Freedom* (New York: Alfred A. Knopf, 2000), pp. 231–240; see also Charles Taylor, "Conditions of an Unforced Consensus on Human Rights," in *The Politics of Human Rights,* ed. Obrad Savić (New York: Verso, 1999) pp. 101–119.

19. As Elvin Hatch writes, the anthropological relativist, when encountering violence that is "an expression of the people's values," is "placed in the morally awkward position of endorsing the infant's starvation, the rape of abducted women, the massacre of whole villages." *Culture and Morality: The*

Relativity of Values in Anthropology (New York: Columbia University Press, 1983), pp. 92–93. For more on the perceived problems of cultural relativism, see Bauman, *Postmodern Ethics,* pp. 2–3; Stanley Fish, *There's No Such Thing as Free Speech: And It's a Good Thing, Too* (New York: Oxford University Press, 1994), pp. 186–191; and Geoffrey Harpham, *Getting It Right* (Chicago: University of Chicago Press, 1992), pp. 52–54.

20. See, for instance, Sandra Harding, "The Instability of the Analytical Categories of Feminist Theory," *Signs,* 11, no. 4 (1986): 656–657.

21. See Carlo Ginzburg's discussion of Hayden White, "Just One Witness," in *Probing the Limits of Representation: Nazism and the "Final Solution,"* ed. Saul Friedlander (Cambridge, Mass.: Harvard University Press, 1992), pp. 91–95, and Saul Friedlander's Introduction, in the same volume, pp. 6–7. See also Seyla Benhabib, *Situating the Self: Gender, Community, and Postmodernism in Contemporary Ethics* (New York: Routledge, 1992), pp. 222–223; F. R. Ankersmit, "Historiography and Postmodernism," *History and Theory,* 28, no. 2 (1989): 137–153.

22. I am thankful to Amanda Grzyb for her enlightening discussion of these points. For a critical analysis of the political implications of major works in neopragmatism and poststructuralism, see Richard Wolin, *The Terms of Cultural Criticism: The Frankfurt School, Existentialism, Poststructuralism* (New York: Columbia University Press, 1992), pp. 149–217.

23. Fish, *There's No Such Thing as Free Speech,* pp. 215, 200–230. Richard Rorty argues that the continuing theoretical work of deconstruction has little or no political significance: see "Feminism, Ideology, and Deconstruction: A Pragmatist View," in *Mapping Ideology,* ed. Slavoj Žižek (New York: Verso, 1994), p. 231, and "Response to Simon Critchley" in Mouffe, *Deconstruction and Pragmatism,* p. 45. Judith Butler, by contrast, calls theory's premises "the very precondition of a politically engaged critique." "Contingent Foundations: Feminism and the Question of 'Postmodernism,'" in *Feminists Theorize the Political,* ed. Judith Butler and Joan W. Scott (New York: Routledge, 1992), pp. 6–7. See also Harpham, *Getting It Right,* pp. 46–47.

24. Gayatri Chakravorty Spivak, *In Other Worlds: Essays in Cultural Politics* (New York: Methuen, 1987), pp. 197–221. For an endorsement and development of Spivak's conception of strategic essentialism, see Diana Fuss, *Essentially Speaking: Feminism, Nature, and Difference* (New York: Routledge, 1989).

25. Chantal Mouffe, *The Return of the Political* (New York: Verso, 1993), pp. 76, 147. See also Ernesto Laclau, *Emancipation(s)* (New York: Verso, 1996), pp. 84–104. Mouffe repeatedly distinguishes her view from "other forms of 'postmodern' politics which emphasize heterogeneity, dissemination and incommensurability and for which pluralism understood as the valorization of all differences should be total." "Democratic Politics Today," in *Dimensions of Radical Democracy: Pluralism, Citizenship, Com-*

munity, ed. Chantal Mouffe (New York: Verso, 1992), p. 13; see also her *Return of the Political,* pp. 7, 131–132. "No state or political order, even a liberal one, can exist without some forms of exclusion. My point is . . . that it is very important to recognize those forms of exclusion for what they are and the violence that they signify, instead of concealing them under the veil of rationality" (*The Return of the Political,* p. 145). Laclau adds: "The universal values of the Enlightenment, for instance, do not need to be abandoned but need, instead, to be presented as pragmatic social constructions and not as expressions of a necessary requirement of reason" (*Emancipation(s),* p. 103).

26. Barbara Herrnstein Smith, *Belief and Resistance: Dynamics of Contemporary Intellectual Controversy* (Cambridge, Mass.: Harvard University Press, 1997), pp. 1–36, 61–72, 73–87, 118–123.

27. See Drucilla Cornell, *The Philosophy of the Limit* (New York: Routledge, 1992), p. 182.

28. See "Force of Law: The 'Mystical Foundation of Authority,'" in *Deconstruction and the Possibility of Justice,* ed. Drucilla Cornell, Michel Rosenfeld, and David Gray Carlson (New York: Routledge, 1992), pp. 15, 3–67; *Spectres of Marx: The State of the Debt, the Work of Mourning, and the New International,* trans. Peggy Kamuf (New York: Routledge, 1984). See especially Ernesto Laclau's sympathetic analysis and extension of *Spectres of Marx* in *Emancipation(s),* pp. 66–83. For a negative appraisal of Derrida's later work, see Thomas McCarthy, "The Politics of the Ineffable: Derrida's Deconstructionism," in *Hermeneutics and Critical Theory in Ethics and Politics,* ed. Michael Kelly (Cambridge, Mass.: MIT Press, 1990), pp. 146–168; and Mark Lilla, "The Politics of Jacques Derrida," *New York Review of Books,* 25 June 1998, pp. 36–41. See also Peter Dews, *The Limits of Disenchantment* (New York: Verso, 1995), pp. 6–7. For criticism of Fish and Smith, see Steven E. Cole, "Evading the Subject: The Poverty of Contingency Theory," in Simons and Billig, *After Postmodernism,* pp. 38–57; on Fuss, Smith, and Derrida, see Meili Steele, *Theorizing Textual Subjects: Agency and Oppression* (Cambridge: Cambridge University Press, 1997), pp. 27–43.

29. For a detailed analysis of the derealization of "cultural realities" associated with war, see Elaine Scarry, *The Body in Pain: The Making and the Unmaking of the World* (New York: Oxford University Press, 1985), pp. 127–129.

30. See *Maurice Blanchot: The Demand of Writing,* ed. Carolyn Bailey Gill (New York: Routledge, 1996); Jeffrey Mehlman, *Legacies of Anti-Semitism in France* (Minneapolis: University of Minnesota Press, 1983); Deborah M. Hess, *Politics and Literature: The Case of Maurice Blanchot* (New York: Peter Lang, 1999).

31. Maurice Blanchot, *The Writing of the Disaster,* trans. Ann Smock (Lincoln: University of Nebraska, 1995), p. 47; *L'Écriture du Désastre* (Paris:

Gallimard, 1980), p. 80. Cited hereafter in the text, English translation first, followed by the French. See also *Probing the Limits of Representation: Nazism and the "Final Solution,"* ed. Saul Friedlander (Cambridge, Mass.: Harvard University Press, 1992), Introduction, p. 5. On formulations of the Holocaust's "irrational swerve" from Western political culture, see Vincent P. Pecora, "Habermas, Enlightenment, and Antisemitism," in Friedlander, *Probing the Limits of Representation,* p. 160.

32. In language that illuminates poststructuralist argument, Thomas Weiskel writes: "Perhaps *being* and *depth* have no independent ontological status; perhaps they are reifications of the signifying power, spontaneously created by the mind at the zero degree, in the mere reflex of making absence significant." *The Romantic Sublime: Studies in the Structure and Psychology of Transcendence* (Baltimore: Johns Hopkins University Press, 1986), p. 28.

33. John Treat, *Writing Ground Zero: Japanese Literature and the Atomic Bomb* (Chicago: University of Chicago Press, 1995), p. 28. Treat writes that there are inherent "contradictions implicit in a form of writing that would give a beginning, middle, and conclusion to events defying such narrative domestication" (3). He continues: "No more words: language, its reliability already devalued by philosophy, has become almost criminally suspect in the wake of world wars. It has even collaborated in our collective victimhood" (27). For more on the Holocaust and the ethical risks of representation, see Geoffrey Hartman, "The Cinema Animal: On Spielberg's *Schindler's List,*" *Salmagundi,* 106–107 (1995): 127–145.

34. Adorno argues that absolutist tendencies in Western philosophy are linked together with political violence. For Adorno, writes Martin Jay, there was "a subterranean connection between phenomenology and fascism—both were expressions of the terminal crisis of bourgeois society." *The Dialectical Imagination: A History of the Frankfurt School and the Institute of Social Research, 1923–1950* (Berkeley: University of California Press, 1973), p. 70.

35. Against the argument that history's violence can bring about the end of rationalist philosophical/political thought by introducing into it the "unthinkable," see Alain Badiou, *Manifesto for Philosophy,* trans. Norman Madarasz (Albany: State University of New York Press, 1999), p. 31.

36. Invoking Blanchot, Ann Smock celebrates Sarah Kofman's *Rue Ordener, Rue Labat* because it is "bathed in a lucidity unclouded by insight. No sense of understanding or ultimate resolution—no relief, no consolation whatsoever—mars it. It is clear." The work preserves language from the drive "to grasp, comprehend, master." Ann Smock, Introduction, in Sarah Kofman, *Rue Ordener, Rue Labat,* trans. Ann Smock (Lincoln: University of Nebraska Press, 1996), pp. x, xii.

37. See also Treat, *Writing Ground Zero,* pp. 32–33, 59. For Bataille's rejection of the "instrumentality of words" (what Sartre called Bataille's "hatred" of

language), see Michele H. Richman, *Reading Georges Bataille: Beyond the Gift* (Baltimore: Johns Hopkins University Press, 1982), pp. 125, 112–138. For more on antifoundationalism and indescribability in Blanchot, see Shaviro, *Passion and Excess,* pp. 1–34.

38. Throughout his life, de Man kept secret his early Fascist political alignment. For arguments that cast his theory as a repudiation of these earlier views, along with arguments that cast it as an extension, see *Responses on Paul de Man's Wartime Journalism,* ed. Werner Hamacher, Neil Hertz, and Thomas Keenan (Lincoln: University of Nebraska Press, 1989).

39. Paul de Man, "The Epistemology of Metaphor," in *Aesthetic Ideology,* ed. Andrzej Warminski (Minneapolis: University of Minnesota Press, 1996), p. 48. Hereafter cited in the text.

40. On nonreferentiality and De Man, see Stanley Cavell, "Politics as Opposed to What?" *Critical Inquiry,* 9, no. 1 (1982): 157–178.

41. Elsewhere de Man asserts the salubrious quality of theory's dismantling of socially accepted interpretations and meaning. See Paul de Man, *The Resistance to Theory* (Minneapolis: University of Minnesota Press, 1986), p. 11. Against the implicit celebration of the instability of the signifier, see Terry Eagleton, *Ideology* (New York: Verso, 1991), pp. 196–197; see also pp. 106–107, 186. Against what he characterizes as the "pluralist ('language-games') approach," see Christopher Norris, *Uncritical Theory* (London: Lawrence and Wishart, 1992), pp. 79, 177. Norris specifically relates his critique to war representation by centering it on Baudrillard's postmodern evaluation of the hyperreality of the Gulf War (122). For an analysis of literary-theoretical approaches to nuclear politics, see Jane Caputi, "Nuclear Visions," *American Quarterly,* 47, no. 1 (1995): 165–175.

42. On the problem in Blanchot of embracing constructive political action with a purportedly apolitical deconstructive method, see Stoekl, *Politics, Writing, Mutilation,* pp. 22–36.

43. Commenting on de Man's work on Shelley, Claudine Torchin-Kahan writes that de Man "at once *formalizes* and *naturalizes* the inevitability of linguistic violence." She explains of de Man: "Violence precedes meaning, precedes the subject himself/herself. Meaning is then predicated on forgetting, on a forgetfulness both transitive and intransitive: it is the *reflexive forgetfulness of violence by itself* that seals the ineluctability of this narrative about language and its indifference to human subjectivity." Later she concludes: "By interpreting the inadequacy of language to facts as the silence of forgetting or the lie of figuration, de Man substitutes foreclosure for pathos, erasure for vulnerability. What is finally dismissed is the precious fragility of all witnessing." "Witnessing Figures," *Boundary 2,* 18, no. 2 (1991): 47–64, 61, 64. See alternatively Cathy Caruth, "The Claims of Reference," *Yale Journal of Criticism,* 4, no. 1 (1990): 193–205, which analyzes de Man's treatment of the concept of referentiality in literary theory.

44. For a case study of such a relation between language theory and political

praxis, see Richard Weisberg, *Vichy Law and the Holocaust in France* (New York: New York University Press, 1996), pp. 386–429. The phrase "less moveable" is from Weisberg.

45. Scarry, *The Body in Pain*, p. 127.

46. For examples, see Elaine Scarry, Introduction, *Literature and the Body: Essays on Populations and Persons* (Baltimore: Johns Hopkins University Press, 1988); *The Body in Pain*, pp. 192, 269–270. Scarry writes on the work of stabilizing language: "In this closed world [of torture] where conversation is displaced by interrogation, where human speech is broken off in confession and disintegrates into human cries . . . it is not surprising that the most powerful and healing moment is often that in which a human voice, though still severed, floating free, somehow reaches the person whose sole reality had become his own unthinkable isolation, his deep corporeal engulfment . . . In acknowledging and expressing another person's pain, or in articulating one of his nonbodily concerns while he is unable to, one human being who is well and free willingly turns himself into an image of the other's psychic or sentient claims, an image existing in the space outside the sufferer's body, projected out into the world and held there intact by that person's powers until the sufferer himself regains his own powers of self-extension" (*The Body in Pain*, 50). See also Hayden White's discussion of Berel Lang's *Act and Idea in the Nazi Genocide* in Friedlander, *Probing the Limits of Representation*, pp. 44–47.

47. Marcus Tullius Cicero, *The Speeches of Cicero: Pro T. Annio Milone*, trans. N. H. Watts (Cambridge, Mass.: Harvard University Press, 1953), p. 16.

48. Scarry, *The Body in Pain*, pp. 130, 131.

49. Blanchot emphasizes our inability to understand traumatic experiences in the moments of their occurrence, as well as our inability to integrate them into a personal history of serial "present" moments. He writes: "The disaster does not put me into question, but annuls the question, makes it disappear—as if along with the question, 'I' too disappeared in the disaster which never appears. The fact of disappearing is, precisely, not a fact, not an event; it does not happen, not only because there is no 'I' to undergo the experience, but because (and this is exactly what presupposition means), since the disaster always takes place after having taken place, there cannot possibly be any experience of it" (*The Writing of the Disaster*, p. 28). Cathy Caruth argues that post-traumatic stress disorder as a cognitive structure of return is a symptom of a history that is necessarily experienced as incomplete and incompletable. *Trauma: Explorations in Memory*, ed. Cathy Caruth (Baltimore: Johns Hopkins University Press, 1995), p. 5.

50. For more on the debates during the Civil War over what was appropriate conduct, see James McPherson, *Battle Cry of Freedom: The Civil War Era* (New York: Ballantine Books, 1989), pp. 501–502, 778, 794, 811.

51. Sherman employed this metaphor frequently. See for instance Gerald Linderman, *Embattled Courage: The Experience of Combat in the American Civil War* (New York: Free Press, 1987), p. 209.

52. Michael Walzer, *Just and Unjust Wars: A Moral Argument with Historical Illustrations* (New York: Basic Books, 1977), pp. 12–13.

53. Ibid. Moral articulation motivates in a positive manner as well, as Charles Taylor explains: "Moral sources empower. To come closer to them, to have a clearer view of them, to come to grasp what they involve, is for those who recognize them to be moved to love or respect them, and through this love/respect to be better enabled to live up to them. And articulation can bring them closer. That is why words can empower; why words can at times have tremendous moral force." *Sources of the Self: The Making of the Modern Identity* (Cambridge, Mass.: Harvard University Press, 1989), p. 96.

54. *Lieber Instructions 1863* in *The Laws of Armed Conflicts,* ed. Dietrich Schindler and Jirí Toman (The Netherlands: Sijthoff and Noordhoff, 1981) pp. 3–23.

55. Ibid., p. 7.

56. Ibid., p. 4.

57. Ibid., p. 6.

58. Argument ideally conceived is illuminated by Stanley Cavell's distinction between the moralist and the propagandist, between convincing and persuading. The former, Cavell argues, appeals to a person through reasons normatively conceived and attempts to make her see a particular position while also respecting her autonomy as a moral agent. The latter is concerned only with causing a certain set of actions or behaviors, and uses reasons as well as "appeals to his fears, your prestige, or another's money" without distinctions in legitimacy. See *The Claim of Reason* (Oxford: Oxford University Press, 1979), p. 278.

59. For an analysis of the opposing views and practices of *jus in bello* during the Civil War, see Linderman, *Embattled Courage,* pp. 181–213.

60. J. Henry Dunant, *A Memory of Solferino* (Washington, D.C.: American National Red Cross, 1939).

61. See Frits Kalshoven, *Constraints on the Waging of War* (Geneva: ICRC, 1987), to which I am indebted; see p. 8. W. B. Gallie argues that the end of the Napoleonic Wars initiated a new epoch in war making. Previously wars had been accepted as part of the unchangeable international landscape. In part it was the unprecedented atrocities of the Napoleonic Wars, Gallie argues, that forced communities to interrogate their necessity: thereafter, "Why war?" seemed an inevitable question. *Understanding War* (New York: Routledge, 1991).

62. Dunant, *A Memory of Solferino,* pp. 86–95.

63. For a history of the ICRC and the laws of war, see Kalshoven, *Constraints on the Waging of War,* pp. 8–23. See also Michael Ignatieff, *The Warrior's Honor* (New York: Henry Holt, 1997), pp. 109–163.

64. Ibid., pp. 22, 12.

65. Ibid., p. 22.

66. Carl von Clausewitz, *On War,* trans. Michael Howard and Peter Paret (Princeton: Princeton University Press, 1976), p. 75.

67. Against this view of binding transnational norms and customs is the tendency, reinforced even in the Charter of the United Nations, to view the world as morally organized and organizable only through the unit of the nation-state. See Daniel Patrick Moynihan, *On the Law of Nations* (Cambridge, Mass.: Harvard University Press, 1990), pp. 68, 103–104.

68. See R. B. J. Walker and Saul H. Mendlovitz, "Interrogating State Sovereignty," in their *Contending Sovereignties: Redefining Political Community* (Boulder: L. Rienner, 1990). Hannah Arendt, *The Origins of Totalitarianism* (New York: Harcourt Brace, 1973), pp. 290–299.

69. Martha Gellhorn, *A Stricken Field* (New York: Penguin Books, 1986), p. 69.

70. Antonio Cassese, *Human Rights in a Changing World* (Philadelphia: Temple University Press, 1990), pp. 22, 23.

71. Raymond Aron, "The Anarchical Order of Power," in *Conditions of World Order,* ed. Stanley Hoffmann (Boston: Houghton Mifflin, 1968), p. 25. As one military thinker writes: "In the last analysis the action of States is regulated by nothing but power and expediency." Quoted in Samuel P. Huntington, *The Soldier and the State* (Cambridge, Mass.: Harvard University Press, 1985), p. 66. For commentary on the limits of both the United Nations and the collective nonviolent pressure of the international community, see Adam Roberts, "The Laws of War: Problems of Implementation in Contemporary Conflicts," *Duke Journal of Comparative and International Law,* 6 (1995): 47.

72. Thomas Hobbes, *Leviathan* (Harmondsworth, Eng.: Penguin Books, 1962), p. 223. Hannah Arendt attacks this view by reformulating power as an expression of consent which both includes moral norms and excludes violence. *On Violence* (New York: Harvest, 1970), pp. 35, 41. Stanley Hoffman insists that ideas enshrined as law achieve "a constraint comparable to force in its effects." "The Study of International Law and the Theory of International Relations," *Proceedings of the American Society of International Law, Fifty-seventh Annual Meeting,* 25–27 April 1963, pp. 33–34. According to H. L. A. Hart: "To argue that international law is not binding because of a lack of organized sanctions is tacitly to accept the analysis of obligation contained in the theory that law is essentially a matter of orders backed by threats." He explains: "This theory . . . identifies 'having an obligation' or 'being bound' with 'likely to suffer the sanction or punishment threatened for disobedience.' Yet . . . this identification distorts the role played in all legal thought and discourse of the ideas of obligation and duty. Even in municipal law, where there are effective organized sanctions, we must distinguish . . . the meaning of the external predictive statement 'I (you) are likely to suffer for disobedience,' from the internal normative statement 'I (you) have an obligation to act thus' which assesses a particular person's situation from the point of view of rules accepted as guiding standards of behavior." *The Concept of Law* (Oxford: Clarendon Press, 1961),

pp. 212–213; for more on law as based on consent and not force, see Searle, *The Construction of Social Reality,* pp. 90–92. In a study that combines sociological field work with game theory, Robert Ellickson argues that in close-knit communities behavior is regulated by binding norms that arise independently of any legal framework. He critiques "legal centralism" (modeled on Hobbes), which equates lawlessness with disorder. Norms produce order, he writes, "even under conditions of anarchy." *Order without Law: How Neighbors Settle Disputes* (Cambridge, Mass.: Harvard University Press, 1991), p. 138. See also John Phillip Reid, *Law for the Elephant: Property and Social Behavior on the Overland Trail* (San Marino, Calif.: Huntington Library, 1980), pp. 339–340; Donald Black, *The Behavior of Law* (New York: Harcourt Brace Jovanovich, 1976), pp. 123–131. It is an additional argument, of course, to propose that the international community could be cultivated in such a way that it might meet certain minimal requirements for practical organizational or imaginative "close-knittedness." Kant, for one, argues not for the possibility but rather the inevitability of the development of binding international obligations. *Kant: Political Writings,* ed. Hans Reiss, trans. H. B. Nisbet (Cambridge: Cambridge University Press, 1991), pp. 102, 104. I would argue that those skeptical of the international imagination seriously underestimate both our capacity for empathy and our ability to construct social organizations that reappropriate empathy from collections of individual minds, concretize it in superpersonal institutional structures, and reflect it back to the individual in a dramatically magnified fashion. Indeed, the sedimentation over time even of noninstitutionalized argument can help transform tentative moral claims into binding international beliefs.

73. H. L. A. Hart points out: "What [international laws] require is thought and spoken of as obligatory; there is general pressure for conformity to the rules; claims and admissions are based on them and their breach is held to justify not only insistent demands for compensation, but reprisals and countermeasures. When the rules are disregarded, it is not on the footing that they are not binding; instead efforts are made to conceal the facts" (*The Concept of Law,* pp. 214–215). Relatedly on rules, see Jack Knight, *Institutions and Social Conflict* (Cambridge: Cambridge University Press, 1992), pp. 66–73.

74. Geneva Convention III, art. 2, 6 U.S.T. at 3318, 75 U.N.T.S. at 136.

75. Kalshoven, *Constraints on the Waging of War,* p. 27. For more on the attempt linguistically to camouflage war, see Searle, *The Construction of Social Reality,* p. 89.

76. Jürgen Habermas, *The Philosophical Discourse of Modernity,* trans. Frederick Lawrence (Cambridge, Mass.: MIT Press, 1987), p. 107.

77. Quoting John Adams, Hannah Arendt emphasizes that when language artifacts are instantiated through intersubjective dialogue and consent, they acquire palpable force: "A Constitution is a standard, a pillar, and a bond

when it is understood, approved and beloved. But without this intelligence and attachment, it might as well be a kite or balloon, flying in the air." *On Revolution* (New York: Viking Press, 1963), p. 145. Relatedly, see Elaine Scarry on consent and the uses of language in "The Declaration of War: Constitutional and Unconstitutional Violence," in *Law's Violence*, ed. Austin Sarat and Thomas R. Kearns (Ann Arbor: University of Michigan Press, 1992), pp. 23–76.

78. As Adam Roberts notes, the Federal Republic of Germany's 1992 military manual for all land-, sea-, and air-based forces lists thirteen primarily treaty-based means for inducing obedience to international law, most of which do not require a transcendent enforcement mechanism. They include, for instance, consideration of public opinion, fear of payment of compensation, international fact-finding, and activities of protecting powers. See "The Laws of War," p. 18. For more on the role of fact-finding commissions, see p. 33. For an analysis of various compliance and redress mechanisms, see Martha Minow, *Between Vengeance and Forgiveness: Facing History after Genocide and Mass Violence* (Boston: Beacon Press, 1998); and Mark Osiel, *Mass Atrocity, Collective Memory and the Law* (London: Transaction, 1997).

79. Geneva Convention III, art. 41, 6 U.S.T. at 3350, 75 U.N.T.S. at 168.

80. See Elaine Scarry's notion of the deliberative process as an impediment to external violence in "War and the Social Contract: Nuclear Policy, Distribution, and the Right to Bear Arms," *University of Pennsylvania Law Review*, 139, no. 5 (1991): 1257–1316; see also Hannah Arendt, *The Human Condition* (Chicago: University of Chicago Press, 1989), pp. 26–27 (discussing speech's displacement of violence); Christopher Norris, *Uncritical Theory*, p. 59 (discussing how unconstrained public debate can work against the impulse to war); John Rawls, *Political Liberalism* (New York: Columbia University Press, 1993), pp. 110–118, 223–227, and esp. pp. 340–348 (discussing how internal violence can be prevented through amplification and structuring of opportunities for discourse); and James Boyd White, *When Words Lose Their Meaning: Constitutions and Reconstitutions of Language, Character, and Community* (Chicago: University of Chicago Press, 1984) (discussing the disintegration and reconstitution of language in a context of violence).

81. See Protocol Additional to the Geneva Conventions of 12 August 1949, and Relating to the Protection of Victims of International Armed Conflicts (Protocol One), June 7, 1977, art. 59, 1125 U.N.T.S. 3, 30 (hereinafter Protocol I).

82. Geneva Convention III, art. 41, 6 U.S.T. at 3350, 75 U.N.T.S. at 168. Geneva Convention III, art. 127, 6 U.S.T. at 3418, 75 U.N.T.S. at 236. See, for instance, *Practical Guide for National Red Cross and Red Crescent Societies on Methods of Dissemination of International Humanitarian Law*

and the Principles and Ideals of the Red Cross, ed. Danuta Zys (Geneva: Henry Dunant Institute, 1983).

83. Geneva Convention I, art. 47, 6 U.S.T. at 3146, 75 U.N.T.S. at 62; Geneva Convention II, art. 48, 6 U.S.T. at 3248, 75 U.N.T.S. at 114; Geneva Convention III, art. 127, 6 U.S.T. at 3418, 75 U.N.T.S. at 236; Geneva Convention IV, art. 48, 6 U.S.T. at 3616, 75 U.N.T.S. at 386. For more on implementation through education rather than criminal prosecution, see Roberts, "The Laws of War," p. 16.

84. See Geneva Convention I, art. 38, 6 U.S.T at 3140, 75 U.N.T.S. at 56; see Protocol I, art. 56.7, 1125 U.N.T.S. at 28–29; see Protocol I, art. 66.4, 1125 U.N.T.S. at 34.

85. Protocol I, art. 47, 1125 U.N.T.S. at 25.

86. Protocol I, art. 8, 1125 U.N.T.S. at 10–11.

87. Protocol I, art. 8, 47.

88. Kalshoven, *Constraints on the Waging of War,* pp. 89–91.

89. For more on the discursive strategies in international law to establish its own foundations, see David Kennedy, *International Legal Structures* (Baden-Baden: Nomos, 1987).

90. Kalshoven, *Constraints on the Waging of War,* p. 40.

91. Protocol I, art. 37, 1125 U.N.T.S. at 10–11; Geneva Convention IV, art. 5, 6 U.S.T. at 3520–3522, 75 U.N.T.S. at 290–292. On the moral basis for the illegality of disguises in war, see Walzer, *Just and Unjust Wars,* p. 183.

92. The full question of the legitimacy of "minimal moral norms" (how these norms are produced and whether or not it might be considered a matter of uncontroversial general good or utility that they benefit from these strategies of repetition, clarity, and comprehensiveness) is, of course, a question far beyond the scope of this chapter. I would provisionally suggest, along Habermasian lines, that one can distinguish between legitimate and illegitimate moral norms by looking at how they align with the three discursive criteria I have listed, in terms of both their development and their communicative legacies.

93. See, e.g., Geneva Convention III, arts. 99–108, 6 U.S.T. at 3392–3400, 75 U.N.T.S. at 210–218 (establishing the requirements of judicial proceedings).

94. See John Keegan, *The Face of Battle* (New York: Vintage Books, 1977), p. 266.

95. David Grossman, quoting Gwinne Dyer, argues in contrast that *"Conditioning,* almost in the Pavlovian sense," is necessary to overcome our deep-rooted resistance to intraspecific violence. The laws of war can be viewed as counterconditioning to a training that makes soldiers "kill without hesitation." *On Killing: The Psychological Cost of Learning to Kill in War and Society* (Boston: Little, Brown, 1995), p. 18.

96. Simone Weil, *The Iliad, or, The Poem of Force,* trans. Mary McCarthy

(Wallingford, Pa.: Pendle Hill), originally published in 1940, pamphlet no. 91, p. 35.

97. Egregious rather than routine violations are at least in part the result of strategically cultivated and powerful counterdiscourses (government propaganda, exclusionary cultural narratives, etc.) that are equally artifactual.

98. On the formulation of war as "defense, preservation, life saving," see Jean Elshtain, *Women and War* (New York: Basic Books, 1987), p. 179.

99. For a discussion of the doctrine of discrimination and in particular noncombatant immunity, see Robert Phillips, *War and Justice* (Norman: University of Oklahoma Press, 1984), pp. 20–70.

100. G.A. Res. 2444, U.N. GAOR, 23d Sess., reprinted in *United Nations Resolutions, Series 1: Resolutions Adopted by the General Assembly, 1968–1969,* vol. 12, ed. Dusan J. Djonovich ed. (Dobbs Ferry, N.Y.: Oceana, 1975), pp. 164–165. See also Kalshoven, *Constraints on the Waging of War,* p. 22.

101. See G.A. Res. 2444, U.N. GAOR, 23d Sess.

102. Protocol I, art. 51, 1156 U.N.T.S. at 26.

103. Ibid.

104. On the doctrine of distinction and its moral basis (particularly in relation to nuclear weapons), see Walzer, *Just and Unjust Wars,* pp. 200, 203, 280; see also Thomas Nagel, *Mortal Questions* (Cambridge: Cambridge University Press, 1991), pp. 53–74.

105. One possible criticism of international law would focus upon its attempt to achieve departicularization. Consider Seyla Benhabib's critique of neo-Kantian political theory, which, she argues, elevates abstract categories of the self over personalized identities and stories. See "The Utopian Dimension in Communicative Ethics," *New German Critique,* 35 (1985): 94.

106. Special thanks to Kenneth Anderson for conversation on these topics. Samuel Huntington emphasizes the evacuation of subjectivity from military thinking: "In estimating the security threats the military man looks at the capabilities of other states rather than at their intentions. Intentions are political in nature, inherently fickle and changeable, and virtually impossible to evaluate and predict. The military man is professionally capable of estimating the fighting strength of another state" (*The Soldier and the State,* p. 66). Thomas C. Schelling writes that in the conduct of war punitive measures (i.e., threats) must be indexed against visible deeds and quantifiable actions rather than against intentions. *The Strategy of Conflict* (Cambridge, Mass.: Harvard University Press, 1980), pp. 40–41.

107. See Maurice H. Keen, *The Laws of War in the Late Middle Ages* (Hampshire, Eng.: Gregg Revivals, 1993), p. 65.

108. On Christianity's evolution to a state-oriented, war-making religion, see Phillips, *War and Justice,* pp. 5–9.

109. Origen, *Contra Celsum,* ed. and trans. Henry Chadwick (Cambridge: Cambridge University Press, 1953), p. 557, quoted in Sydney Bailey, *Prohibi-*

tions and Restraints in War (New York: Oxford University Press, 1972), p. 3.

110. Bailey, *Prohibitions and Restraints in War,* pp. 3–4. On the possible collusion between just war ethics and the perpetuation of war, see David Smock's paper "Religious Perspectives on War" (Washington, D.C.: United States Institute for Peace, 1992), p. xvii. For a feminist critique of just war theory, see Sara Ruddick, "Notes toward a Feminist Peace Politics," in *Gendering War Talk,* ed. Miriam Cooke and Angela Woollacott (Princeton: Princeton University Press, 1993), pp. 109–127. Ruddick hypothesizes that "as one learns to speak within the theory, to unravel the puzzles the theory sets for itself, to assess 'causes' and strategies by criteria the theory establishes, it becomes increasingly difficult to give *weight* to the varieties of loss and pain suffered by individual victims and conquerors, their communities, and their lands" (116).

111. For more on the legitimating function of the laws of war during the 1990–91 Gulf War, see Roberts, "The Laws of War," pp. 48–49. For a discussion of the computerization or postmodernization of war, see Chris Hables Gray, *Postmodern War: The New Politics of Conflict* (New York: Guilford Press, 1997).

112. Clausewitz, *On War,* pp. 21, 580–581.

113. I am thankful to Kenneth Anderson here, as elsewhere, for introducing me to this material.

114. Kalshoven, *Constraints on the Waging of War,* p. 2.

115. See, for instance, Eric Blumenson, "Mapping the Limits of Skepticism in Law and Morals," *Texas Law Review,* 74, no. 3 (1996): 523–576. See also Mark Lilla, "The Politics of Jacques Derrida," *New York Review of Books,* 25 June 1998. See also Jean Bethke Elshtain, "The Right Rights," *New Republic,* 15 June 1998, pp. 11–12.

116. Gellner, *Postmodernism, Reason, and Religion,* p. 86.

117. One important shortcoming of using the term "antifoundationalist" is that it necessarily implies that those who do not accept their views are foundationalist in some crude sense. Seyla Benhabib's disagreement with Jane Flax over the claims of postmodernism is emblematic. It is important, Benhabib writes, "to note right at the outset that much of the postmodernist critique of western metaphysics itself proceeds under the spell of a meta-narrative, namely, the narrative first articulated by Heidegger and then developed by Derrida that 'Western metaphysics has been under the spell of the "metaphysics of presence" at least since Plato . . .' This characterization of the philosophical tradition allows postmodernists the rhetorical advantage of presenting what they are arguing against in its least defensible versions: listen again to Flax's words: 'For postmodernists this quest for the Real conceals the philosophers' desire, which is to master the world' or 'Just as the Real is the ground of Truth, so too philosophy as the privileged representative of the Real . . .' etc. But is the philosophical tradition so monolithic

and so essentialist as postmodernists would like to claim? Would not even Thomas Hobbes shudder at the suggestion that the 'Real is the ground of Truth'? What would Kant say when confronted with the claim that 'philosophy is the privileged representative of the Real'? . . . In its strong version, the 'death of metaphysics' thesis suffers not only from a subscription to a grandiose meta-narrative, but more significantly, this grandiose meta-narrative flattens out the history of modern philosophy and the competing conceptual schemes it contains to the point of unrecognizability." Benhabib, *Situating the Self,* pp. 223–224; for a related critique of poststructuralist misprisions of Kant, see Christopher Norris, *Reclaiming Truth* (Durham: Duke University Press, 1996), pp. 33–37. Postmetaphysical universalists do not believe they have found Truth; rather, they believe they have put together a chain of moral justification, composed of widely accessible reasons developed through fair procedures of inclusive deliberation, that goes further (temporarily) than other systems into the infinite regress of skeptical interrogation; they view their claims as situation-transcendent, and therefore generalizable, as well as fallible and constructed within a historical horizon, like all forms of human knowledge. Local claims do not (in advance of scrutiny) possess a special legitimacy lacked by universal claims, but any particular claim can, of course, be more or less robust, more or less in accord with empirical evidence and agreed-upon procedures for reasoning and deliberation, or more or less generalizable because more or less free from identifiable distortions (e.g., deception, bias based upon interests not relevant to the claim's validity or lack of validity, or other like factors that in principle limit an argument's ability to be validated by others from different positions with different interests in imagined idealized circumstances of intersubjective transparency). In addition, claims can be differentiated based upon their fields of inquiry, which can be more or less internally coherent and more or less compatible with other fields of inquiry important as bases for actions and decisions.

118. Benhabib, *Situating the Self,* p. 6.
119. Slavoj Žižek's *Ticklish Subject* announces its intention to recuperate a theoretically informed Cartesian subject as a foundation for "engaged political action." *The Ticklish Subject: The Absent Centre of Political Ontology* (New York: Verso, 1999), p. 4. He resolves the paradox of a theoretical position that speaks on behalf of universal emancipation, while denying the validity of a neutral, objective argumentative position, thus: the position "can be conceived only if the [radically antagonistic character of society is also] *inherent to universality itself,* that is, if universality itself is split into the 'false' concrete universality that legitimizes the existing division of the Whole into functional parts, and the impossible/real demand of 'abstract' universality . . . The leftist political gesture *par excellence* . . . is thus to question the concrete existing universal order on behalf of its symptom, of the part which, although inherent to the existing universal order, has no 'proper

place' within it . . . One pathetically asserts (and identifies with) the point of inherent exception/exclusion, the 'abject', of the concrete positive order, as the only point of true universality" (224).

120. The contemporary scene of cultural translation, writes Judith Butler, "is one in which the meaning intended is no more determinative of a 'final' reading than the one that is received, and no final adjudication of conflicting positions can emerge. That lack of finality is precisely the interpretive dilemma to be valued, for it suspends the need for final judgment in favor of an affirmation of a certain linguistic vulnerability to reappropriation. This vulnerability marks the way that a postsovereign democratic demand makes itself felt in the contemporary scene of the utterance" (*Excitable Speech*, p. 92). In an earlier article Nancy Fraser points out that as a consequence of Butler's position, "critique"—which remains connected to the concepts of warrant and justification—is discarded in favor of the epistemically neutral "resignification." "False Antithesis: A Response to Seyla Benhabib and Judith Butler," *Praxis International*, 11 (1991): 172. Meili Steele writes: "If poststructuralism shows how cultural differences have been suppressed, it provides no way of articulating the ethical goods of alternative cultures or of deliberating about these conflicting goods" (*Theorizing Textual Subjects*, p. 62); see also Richard Rorty's supportive review of Habermas's *Philosophical Discourse of Modernity*, a book that criticizes an array of antifoundationalist positions. "Posties," *London Review of Books*, 3 September 1987, pp. 11–12.

121. It is possible to answer questions of justice and legitimacy, Mouffe argues, "but this can only be done from within a given tradition, with the help of standards that this tradition provides" (Ross, *Universal Abandon?* p. 37).

122. Mouffe writes: "Once we have abandoned the rationalist idea that a formula can be found through which men's different ends might be harmonized . . . we have to accept with [Carl] Schmitt that 'the phenomenon of the political can be understood only in the context of the ever present possibility of the friend-and-enemy grouping'" (*The Return of the Political*, p. 128). "War as the most extreme political means," Schmitt writes, "discloses the possibility which underlies every political idea, namely, the distinction of friend and enemy." *The Concept of the Political*, trans. George Schwab (New Brunswick: Rutgers University Press, 1976), p. 35. Jane Flax, in a summation of postmodernism's relation to politics, argues that truth claims are meaningful only within the rules of the local, "often incommensurable" discourses that produce them, and therefore that adjudication of truth claims across discourses is impossible. Moreover, since the unified categories built upon truth claims are inevitably the result of "domination," "philosophers and other knowledge constructors should seek instead to generate an infinite 'dissemination' of meanings." Relatedly, she asserts that because "there is no evidence" that appeals to truth or justice through frameworks of rational argument uniquely move people to change, and be-

cause such frameworks enable a 'dangerous' evasion of the postmodern conception of social reality (namely, that our claims to truth are mystifications of a contingent desire for power that often excludes others), then questions of injustice should be addressed through "persuasive speech, action, and (sometimes) violence" rather than through claims of truth or transcendental justice. "The End of Innocence," in *Feminists Theorize the Political,* ed. Judith Butler and Joan W. Scott (New York: Routledge 1992), pp. 445–463, 452, 454, 458, 459.

123. On the thinning out of the distinctions between force and violence in Foucault and Derrida, see McCarthy, *Ideals and Illusions,* pp. 110, 53–55. Insisting that persuasion and force cannot be construed as opposites, Laclau writes that social antagonism is constitutive of community, and that it leads to a perpetual "war of position." "Each pole of the conflict will have a certain power and will exercise a certain violence over the other pole. The paradoxical corollary of this conclusion is that the existence of violence and antagonisms is the very condition of a free society . . . Let us suppose that we move to the opposite hypothesis, the one contained in the classical notion of emancipation—that is a society from which violence and antagonisms have been *entirely* eliminated. In this society, we can only enjoy the Spinozian freedom of being conscious of necessity. This is a first paradox of a free community: that which constitutes its condition of impossibility (violence) constitutes at the same time its condition of possibility. Particular forms of oppression can be eliminated, but freedom only exists in so far as the achievement of a total freedom is an ever receding horizon" (*Emancipation(s),* pp. 115–116). On the blending of the multiple conceptions of force, see Stanley Fish, *Doing What Comes Naturally: Change, Rhetoric, and the Practice of Theory in Literary and Legal Studies* (Durham: Duke University Press, 1989), p. 520; and Harpham, *Getting It Right,* pp. 27–30 (on the instability of Stanley Cavell's distinction, previously discussed, between the moralist and the propagandist, between convincing and persuading).

124. Benhabib, *Situating the Self,* pp. 225–228. See also McCarthy, *Ideals and Illusions,* pp. 19–20.

125. Amy Gutmann and Dennis Thompson, "Reply to the Critics," in *Deliberative Politics: Essays on Democracy and Disagreement,* ed. Stephen Macedo (New York: Oxford University Press, 1999), pp. 258, 257–259; see also Ronald Dworkin, "Objectivity and Truth: You'd Better Believe It," *Philosophy and Public Affairs,* 25, no. 2 (1996): 87–139. On Mouffe and Laclau, see Stanley Aronowitz, "Postmodernism and Politics," in Ross, *Universal Abandon?* p. 52.

126. As Ronald Dworkin writes of antifoundationalism in law: "They say there are no right answers but only different answers to hard questions of law, that insight is finally subjective, that it is only what seems right, for better or worse, to the particular judge on the day. But this modesty in fact contradicts what they say first, for when judges finally decide one way or another

they think their arguments better than, not merely different from, arguments the other way; though they may think this with humility, wishing their confidence were greater or their time for decision longer, this is nevertheless their belief." *Law's Empire* (Cambridge, Mass.: Harvard University Press, 1986), p. 10.

127. Simon Critchley, "Deconstruction and Pragmatism—Is Derrida a Private Ironist or a Public Liberal?" in Mouffe, *Deconstruction and Pragmatism*, p. 25. Rorty defends the compatibility of irony and commitment by arguing for a stable public-private partition in intellectual action. *Truth and Progress* (Cambridge: Cambridge University Press, 1998), pp. 307–326. Nancy Fraser calls Rorty's position "seriously flawed." *Unruly Practices: Power, Discourse, and Gender in Contemporary Social Theory* (Minneapolis: University of Minnesota Press, 1989), pp. 100–105. Korsgaard suggests that theoretical-practical misalignment of subjectivism, emotivism, and the various permutations of relativism not only vitiates the effectiveness of commitment but also, because it fails to give an adequate account of the "full weight of our commitment to the moral life," establishes a binary separation between the theoretical and practical conceptions of self that diminishes the value of the latter. She goes on to argue for the imbrication of the theoretical and practical through the common principles of reason. See *The Standpoint of Practical Reason* (New York: Garland, 1990), pp. 1–33, 3. Richard Brown argues, in contrast, for the strict separability of epistemic relativism and judgmental relativism. "Reconstructing Social Theory after the Postmodern Critique," in Simons and Billig, *After Postmodernism*, pp. 27–28. On emotivism, see Alasdair MacIntyre, *After Virtue* (Notre Dame: University of Notre Dame Press, 1984), pp. 16–22. For more on beliefs about beliefs, see Gerald Cohen, "Beliefs and Roles," *Proceedings of the Aristotelian Society*, 66 (1966–67): 53–66.

128. Laclau, *Emancipation(s)*, pp. 122–123. See also Michael Bérubé's compelling contribution "The Return of Realism and the Future of Contingency," to *What's Left of Theory? New Work on the Politics of Literary Theory*, ed. Judith Butler, John Guillory, and Kendall Thomas (New York: Routledge, 2000), pp. 137–156.

129. McCarthy, *Ideals and Illusions*, pp. 33–34, 5.

130. Habermas argues that communicative ethics offers an alternative to deconstruction without reproducing Enlightenment errors. "A different, less dramatic, but step-by-step testable critique of the Western emphasis on logos," he writes, "starts from an attack on the abstractions surrounding logos itself, as free of language, as universalist, and as disembodied. It conceives of intersubjective understanding as the telos inscribed into communication in ordinary language, and of the logocentrism of Western thought, heightened by the philosophy of consciousness, as a systematic *foreshortening* and *distortion* of a potential always already operative in the communicative practice of everyday life, but only selectively exploited." He continues later:

"This communicative rationality recalls older ideas of logos, inasmuch as it brings along with it the connotations of a noncoercively unifying, consensus-building force of a discourse in which the participants overcome their at first subjectively biased views in favor of a rationally motivated agreement. Communicative reason is expressed in a decentered understanding of the world" (*Philosophical Discourse,* pp. 311, 315). Habermas argues that theorists who use argument as a means of disproving rationality or any of the other basic premises of argumentation are caught in a "performative contradiction." See for instance *The Communicative Ethics Controversy,* ed. Seyla Benhabib and Fred Dallmayr (Cambridge, Mass.: MIT Press, 1990), pp. 8–9. Against Habermas, see Butler, *Excitable Speech,* pp. 86–87, and also pp. 92–93, 161; see also Mouffe, *The Return of the Political,* pp. 8, 145–146. In his later work Derrida has begun to produce statements increasingly susceptible to reconciliation with Habermas's original stance on the idealizations built into language. See "Remarks on Deconstruction and Pragmatism," in Mouffe, *Deconstruction and Pragmatism,* p. 82.

131. Stanley Fish argues that we need to retain and reaffirm concepts such as justice, fairness, and dignity. Without them "we will have deprived ourselves of the argumentative resources those abstractions now stand for; we would no longer be able to say 'what justice requires' or 'what fairness dictates' and then fill in those phrases with the courses of action we prefer to take. That, after all, is the law's job—to give us ways of redescribing limited partisan programs so that they can be presented as the natural outcomes of abstract impersonal imperatives" (*There's No Such Thing as Free Speech,* p. 222).

Index

Aaron, Daniel, 8

Absurd, 62–67, 112

Adorno, Theodor, 101, 149–150, 286n34

Agency, 2, 22, 37, 38, 45, 123–124, 155, 165, 174, 177–179, 182–184, 187, 201, 228n72, 232n30, 273nn33,34, 280n100. *See also* Autonomy; Freedom

Alcott, Louisa May, 43–48, 49, 53–54, 55, 63, 66, 133; *Hospital Sketches,* 43–45, 133

Althusser, Louis, 19

American Anthropological Association, 195

Anderson, Sherwood, 77–78, 84–85, 224n29; *Memoirs,* 77; *Winesburg, Ohio,* 84–85, 92

Andric, Ivo, 3; *Bridge on the Drina,* 3

Antifoundationalism, 192–197, 216–217, 295n117

Apel, Karl-Otto, 21, 22

Arendt, Hannah, 2, 17, 19, 22, 87, 110, 153–154, 158, 178, 184–186, 190–191, 221n3, 290n72, 291n77; *Eichmann in Jerusalem,* 184–185

Aristotle, 113; *Nicomachean Ethics,* 113

Aron, Raymond, 205

Atlanta Campaign, 69, 200–202

Auden, W. H., 173; "The Managers," 173

Austin, J. L., 18; *How to Do Things with Words,* 18

Autonomy, 108–112, 115, 116, 117, 125, 177, 193, 218. *See also* Agency; Freedom

Bakhtin, Mikhail, 132, 135, 150

Barker, Pat, 104, 132; *The Eye in the Door,* 104; *The Ghost Road,* 132

Barnard, Chester, 180

Bataille, Georges, 17, 150–155, 160, 190

Baym, Nina, 235n62

Bellamy, Edward, 229n9

Benhabib, Seyla, 17, 217

Bérubé, Michael, 299n128

Bierce, Ambrose, 7, 227n58; "Chickamauga," 7, 227n58

Blanchot, Maurice, 17, 19, 22, 155–156, 194, 196–199, 210, 288n49

Body: as machine, 71–72; and machine, 95, 99; and natural environment, 105; as grotesque, 135, 142

Body count, 29–34, 53, 97, 101, 140, 157, 230n15; vs. naming, 30–31, 53

Borders: conceptual and physical, 107–108, 131–143, 147, 201, 209, 211–213, 215; deconstruction of, 132–143, 146–147, 150; and liminality, 136. *See also* Grotesque; Referentiality of language

Bourdieu, Pierre, 17, 18, 165–166, 225–226n51, 273n33

Bourne, Randolph, 125, 127–128